Ius Gentium: Comparative Perspectives on Law and Justice

Volume 93

Ius Gentium is a book series which discusses the central questions of law and justice from a comparative perspective. The books in this series collect the contrasting and overlapping perspectives of lawyers, judges, philosophers and scholars of law from the world's many different jurisdictions for the purposes of comparison, harmonisation, and the progressive development of law and legal institutions. Each volume makes a new comparative study of an important area of law. This book series continues the work of the well-known journal of the same name and provides the basis for a better understanding of all areas of legal science.

The *Ius Gentium* series provides a valuable resource for lawyers, judges, legislators, scholars, and both graduate students and researchers in globalisation, comparative law, legal theory and legal practice. The series has a special focus on the development of international legal standards and transnational legal cooperation.

More information about this series at http://www.springer.com/series/7888

Raúl Márquez Porras • Riccardo Mazzola •
Ignasi Terradas Saborit
Editors

Vindicatory Justice

Beyond Law and Revenge

Springer

Editors
Raúl Márquez Porras
Department of Social Anthropology
University of Barcelona
Barcelona, Spain

Riccardo Mazzola
Department of Legal Sciences
'Cesare Beccaria', Faculty of Law
University of Milan
Milan, Italy

Ignasi Terradas Saborit
Department of Social Anthropology
University of Barcelona
Barcelona, Spain

ISSN 1534-6781 ISSN 2214-9902 (electronic)
Ius Gentium: Comparative Perspectives on Law and Justice
ISBN 978-3-030-79594-8 ISBN 978-3-030-79595-5 (eBook)
https://doi.org/10.1007/978-3-030-79595-5

This Springer imprint is published by the registered company Springer Nature Switzerland AG.
The registered company address is: Gewerbestrasse 11, 6330 Cham, Switzerland

Preface

This book originates from a collaboration (started in 2011) between scholars from the Department of Legal Sciences "Cesare Beccaria" of the University of Milan and the Department of Social Anthropology of the University of Barcelona. Eventually, a number of scholars from the universities of the Basque Country, Cagliari, Crete, Helsinki, Milano-Bicocca, Pavia, and Tel Aviv University joined the initiative.

The idea behind this volume is to offer a new theoretical approach to the analysis of the law/revenge binary. The volume attempts to dismantle the common idea of revenge as lacking in any legal or moral content or rationality. In fact, the book depicts a complex system of justice—that we name "vindicatory"—wherein vendetta is performed as *authorized revenge*. However, the core of vindicatory systems does not (just) lie in vengeance but rather in settlement procedures for peace—or *compositions*. More precisely, dissociating composition and authorized revenge from a conceptual and procedural standpoint may lead to misunderstanding of the nature of vindicatory systems. Such dissociation usually occurs when vendetta is observed as not related to its legal counterpart, composition, as is usually the case with "culturalist" interpretations of historical and indigenous revenge systems that link vengeance to honor and simultaneously disregard the close interplay between revenge and composition.

In-depth studies of vindicatory systems have revealed numerous phenomena, ranging from feud and evaluations of defenselessness to ordeals, authorized vengeance, compositional procedures, and—quite crucially—*formal reconciliation*, as the ultimate aim of vindicatory justice. The social and legal "validity" and effectiveness of those phenomena depend on several factors, such as the interaction between the nature of the offense and the political and moral purposes that vindicatory procedures acquire in specific cultural settings. Thus, parties in conflict may be interested in ending a feud and establishing peace (or vice versa), for example, for political reasons or for personal motivations. But even in more extreme scenarios of violence, the vindicatory justice paradigm allows the recognition within a dispute or feud of a legal obligation to reach a final agreement and establish peace.

This volume attempts to provide a comprehensive overview of vindicatory justice in general and of the aforementioned core phenomena in particular and comprises two main parts.

Part I—"Vindicatory Justice: Conceptual Analyses and Forerunners"—aims to disclose the nature of vindicatory justice and to shed light on the structure of the so-called vindicatory systems. In the Introduction, *Ignasi Terradas Saborit*—who, in his 2008 seminal work, *Justicia Vindicatoria*, renewed interest in the fields of anthropology, legal history, and philosophy in the study of revenge and allied concepts as a legal phenomenon—identifies the constitutive elements of vindicatory systems that justify their recognition in past and present societies. The chapter also outlines the linguistic-etymological and conceptual roots of vindicatory justice, particularly emphasizing the relationships among homicide (as a prototypical offense), composition, and authorized revenge. Terradas Saborit's introductory remarks serve as a guide to those who first approach the paradigm of vindicatory justice and orient readers better within the content of the volume. *Paolo Di Lucia and Lorenzo Passerini Glazel* reconstruct Hans Kelsen's vision of vengeance as a social practice contextualized in a wider system of justice. The authors' conceptual and bibliographical effort allows a comparison between the paradigm of vindicatory justice and Kelsen's "classic" conceptualization of revenge as a social technique, the preeminence of which stood out in the evolution of law and legal systems. *Kaius Tuori* takes on a fundamental premise of Terradas Saborit's theory, which goes as follows. The Western legal culture's "civilizing narrative" has traditionally (and ambiguously) interpreted vengeance as a cycle of lawlessness and savage violence. Tuori highlights continuities and discontinuities in the history of the civilizing narrative, mainly discussing the influence of lex talionis, biblical, Roman and Greek traditions, and Christian morality. In the subsequent chapters, *Edoardo Fittipaldi* and *Riccardo Mazzola*, respectively, illustrate what vindicatory justice is by clarifying what it is *not*. Fittipaldi outlines a distinction between (striving for) revenge and (striving for) punishment, through the lens of legal psychology and psychoanalysis. The author aims at causally explaining several sociological phenomena, such as authorized revenge and composition-by-submission in vindicatory systems. Mazzola addresses the conceptual relationship between restorative justice and vindicatory justice. The author shows that despite sharing several traits, the two forms of justice, restorative and vindicatory justice, have a fundamental distinction that lies in the role of the so-called solidarity groups and the manner that they shape the compositional–vindicatory procedure. Afterwards, *Paolo Di Lucia, Giuseppe Lorini, Olimpia Giuliana Loddo*, and *Miguel Doñate Sastre* stress the role of Italian philosopher Antonio Pigliaru and French lawyer Jacques Busquet as *forerunners* of vindicatory justice theory. Di Lucia, Lorini, and Loddo analyze Pigliaru's 1959 code of the code of Barbagian vendetta (Sardinia), demonstrating how the author discovered—in a series of interviews with the local shepherd community—the existence of an established legal system wherein "regulated" vengeance denoted a tool for legal protection. Doñate Sastre illustrates Jacques Busquet's groundbreaking conception of the Corsican vendetta as a legal notion and institution closely related to the reconciliatory practice of pace. As Doñate Sastre shows, Busquet's work instantiated an early and powerful account of legal pluralism, depicting as it did the relationship between the Corsican vindicatory system and the law of the different governments that succeeded on the island.

Part II—"Mapping Vindicatory Justice"—illustrates by examples gathered from a series of sociolegal contexts the dynamic relationship between composition and authorized revenge in vindicatory systems. This part shows that a historical perspective of *longue durée* renders possible a clear identification of composition and authorized revenge as aspects of the same system. However, as is the natural course of events in the study of limited historical periods, either composition or revenge may appear predominant (or even mutually exclusive) in certain settings. *Mariona Rosés Tubau* provides insight into the limits and possibilities of legal pluralism in relation to conflict resolution processes. As Rosés Tubau shows, indigenous proceedings in Madagascar are mainly *compositional* interactive processes *endorsed by the state*. A thorough analysis of indigenous rituals emphasizes several essential features of the basic notion of "composition" at the core of vindicatory justice. *Pablo Romero Noguera* analyzes the manner in which vindicatory culture in Barbagia—originally depicted by Pigliaru—*persists* today in Sardinia although corrupted by the penetration of capitalism among traditional communities. In such a scenario, as Romero Noguera discusses, violence has taken on a new role, by shaping social relationships and overcoming the vindicatory logic of composition and reconciliation. Afterwards, *José Maria Ortuño Aix* provides an interpretation of the present-day Tiv (Nigeria) legal system as a vindicatory order. In addition, Ortuño Aix shows how the prohibition of traditional marriage by colonial authorities disrupted the basic reciprocity in Tiv society mainly arranged through matrilinearity, which is essential to promoting social peace in conflict situations. The next chapter by *Marta Alsonso Cabré* recognizes in Islamic *diya* an essential form of vindicatory composition. Alonso Cabré—through an accurate survey of how Muslim law in Mauritania regulates conflicts arising from car accidents—shows that *diya* ultimately aims at reconciliation between the parties in conflict, overcoming the simple purpose of repaying the material damage caused by the offense. *Carlotta De Menech* and *Giorgio Remotti* evaluate the survival of vindicatory rationality in Western legal culture and more specifically in the Italian civil liability system. De Menech and Remotti examine specific rules (punitive damages and damages granted in the case of violation of intellectual property rights), revealing peculiar traits influenced by the ancient function of "restorative" revenge. The chapter by *Cosimo Nicolini Coen* looks for traces of vindicatory rationality in biblical law. More precisely, Nicolini Coen highlights the "friction" among the ancient customary obligation to avenge the murdered kin's blood; the prescriptions for projecting such an obligation into an institutional framework by establishing a fair trial for the offender; and the interdiction of private vengeance, as well as the obligation of repentance for one's own past actions. The chapter also recognizes the centrality of the concept of "duty" as a key feature of Jewish normative experience. *Elena Mamoulaki* analyzes the sociolegal reaction of the Cretan community that was triggered by the decision of the University of Crete to award an honorary doctorate to German historian Heinz Richter, who willfully denied recognized war crimes committed in Crete by the German army between 1941 and 1945. Mamoulaki's analysis reveals this as a case that represents an occasion for Cretans to "avenge" German denial about Cretan history and the present-day Greek situation. *Raúl Márquez Porras* and *Sílvia Bofill-Poch* consider the issue that is the plight of domestic workers in Spain facing judicial procedures on the allegation of theft. As the authors emphasize, domestic workers represent a vulnerable community seeking justice in a situation of defenselessness and disproportionate retaliation from employers. *Lidia Montesinos* and *Margaret Bullen* describe the symbolic value of women's participation in rituals in festival contexts in Spain, stressing that a symbolic action is also an effective means of reparation. This view connects with other symbolic acts of reparation, such as sentences, commemorations, and various types of solemnization of the recognition of damage inflicted on women and forced inhibitions.

As editors, we wish to thank the International Institute for the Sociology of Law (Oñati, Spain) that, in May 2019, hosted the workshop "Vindicatory Justice: Revenge, Composition and Reconciliation in a Historical and Contemporary Sociolegal Perspective," allowing us to exchange ideas about vindicatory justice and to organize the publication of this volume. We particularly thank Noé Cornago, Vincenzo Ferrari, Malen Gordoa Mendizabal, Leire Kortabarria, Marije Mesonero, and Maite Elorza Plazaola. Moreover, we are profoundly grateful to the *Ius Gentium: Comparative Perspectives on Law and Justice* series editors, Mortimer Sellers and James Maxeiner, for hosting the volume, to Springer editors Anja Trautmann and Manuela Schwietzer, and to project coordinator Daniel Jagadisan for their assistance in the publishing process.

Barcelona, Spain — Raúl Márquez Porras
Milan, Italy — Riccardo Mazzola
Barcelona, Spain — Ignasi Terradas Saborit

Contents

Contributors

Sílvia Bofill-Poch Department of Social Anthropology, University of Barcelona, Barcelona, Spain

Margaret Bullen Faculty of Education, Philosophy and Anthropology, University of the Basque Country, Donostia-San Sebastián, Spain

Marta Alonso Cabré Department of Social Anthropology, Universitat de Barcelona, Barcelona, Spain

Carlotta De Menech Department of Law, University of Pavia, Pavia, Italy

Paolo Di Lucia Department of Legal Sciences 'Cesare Beccaria', Faculty of Law, University of Milan, Milan, Italy

Miguel Doñate Sastre Department of Social Anthropology, Universitat de Barcelona, Barcelona, Spain

Edoardo Fittipaldi Department of Legal Sciences 'Cesare Beccaria', Faculty of Law, University of Milan, Milan, Italy

Lorenzo Passerini Glazel School of Law, University of Milan-Bicocca, Milan, Italy

Olimpia Giuliana Loddo Department of Law, University of Cagliari, Cagliari, Italy

Giuseppe Lorini Department of Law, University of Cagliari, Cagliari, Italy

Elena Mamoulaki Department of Philosophy and Social Sciences, University of Crete, Rethymno, Greece

Raúl Márquez Porras Department of Social Anthropology, University of Barcelona, Barcelona, Spain

Riccardo Mazzola Department of Legal Sciences 'Cesare Beccaria', Faculty of Law, University of Milan, Milan, Italy

Lidia Montesinos Doctorate School, University of the Basque Country UPV/EHU, Donostia-San Sebastián, Spain

Cosimo Nicolini Coen Department of Jewish Thought, Bar Ilan University, Tel Aviv, Israel

José Maria Ortuño Aix Department of Social Anthropology, University of Barcelona, Barcelona, Spain

Giorgio Remotti Department of Law, University of Urbino "Carlo Bo", Urbino, Italy

Pablo Romero Noguera Department of Social Anthropology, University of Barcelona, Barcelona, Spain

Mariona Rosés Tubau Department of Social Anthropology, University of Barcelona, Barcelona, Spain

Ignasi Terradas Saborit Department of Social Anthropology, University of Barcelona, Barcelona, Spain

Kaius Tuori Faculty of Social Sciences, University of Helsinki, Helsinki, Finland

Part I
Vindicatory Justice: Conceptual Analyses and Forerunners

Introduction

Understanding Vindicatory Systems

Ignasi Terradas Saborit

Abstract The purpose of this chapter is to define what vindicatory legal systems are, emphasizing their internal consistency and external unity. The chapter specifies the elements that justify the name and recognition of vindicatory justice in history and society. Also, the chapter gives emphasis to the relationship between homicide and composition at the core of vindicatory norms and values. As will be pointed out, vindicatory systems are better explained by legal theories that embed action and process. In this sense, a case-law approach lies closer to the understanding of the vindicatory system than the legislative one. Finally, the chapter will show how the most important ethnocentric biases have impaired the recognition of vindicatory systems as consistent legal orders in different societies.

1 Introduction

I propose the formulation of the vindicatory system as a proper legal system,[1] existing in its own right. This means that several legal institutions found in some "primitive",[2] ancient, medieval and contemporary societies, constitute a system

[1]From the very beginning, I have to underline a linguistic paradox regarding the use of the terms: legal, law, right, juridical, legislation, and jurisprudence. Conventionally, the Anglo-Saxon *legal* stands for the Latin *juridical* (legal anthropology or anthropology of law equalling *antropología jurídica*), but the Anglo-Saxon tradition is rather *jurisprudential* whereas the Latin tradition is rather *legislative*. Therefore, a Latin reader could wrongly expect a legislative approach under the title of "legal", and an Anglo-Saxon reader could expect, wrongly, a rather jurisprudential approach under the title of "juridical". It could be so, but the Latin tradition is still anchored in the legislative pre-eminence as much as the Anglo-Saxon tradition is in the jurisprudential one. See Assier-Andrieu (2011).

[2]"Primitive": there is no positive word to refer to these civilisations, which are considered primitive because of their technologies, social organisations and ways of living. This, within an evolutionary

I. Terradas Saborit (✉)
Department of Social Anthropology, University of Barcelona, Barcelona, Spain
e-mail: terradas@ub.edu

R. Márquez Porras et al. (eds.), *Vindicatory Justice*, Ius Gentium: Comparative Perspectives on Law and Justice 93, https://doi.org/10.1007/978-3-030-79595-5_1

endowed with its own logic and values.[3] This view opposes that of a perfective progress of law for any society, leading necessarily to the laws, processes and values of the positive law. The perspective I stand for implies the assumption of several criteria of the realist school of law,[4] with a critique of the strict positivist legal theory. But, at the same time, we can partly conceive the vindicatory system as Kelsen[5] did for a pure legal system.

I think that the understanding of these systems assumes a basic criticism of the positivistic isolation of law, but, to criticise isolation does not involve a rejection of legal unity. This is to say, I defend the existence of a vindicatory legal system also constituting a system of values and logic.[6] This allows us to speak of the homogeneous or congruent nature of its institutions and predicates, that is, constituting a unity of interrelated meanings. However, at the same time this normative system, which can be fully appreciated as a legal system, is permeated by elements of a diverse character: they come from religion, morals, economy, politics, ecology, etc. This is what would puzzle the positivistic view of a proper legal system and a Kelsenian first glance. But once it is admitted that "primitive" societies have law, as Kelsen did,[7] and adding the realistic perspective together with ethnographic knowledge, we find no difficulty in admitting the existence of a vindicatory system, although intermingled with a lot of religious, political, economic and other elements.

I have dedicated two books[8] to the purpose of showing both empirically and theoretically the existence of the vindicatory system. This chapter tries to synthesise their major outcomes to provide a clear understanding of the principles and corollaries of the vindicatory legal system. In a way, my present contribution wishes to satisfy a demand of the philosophy of law, although I base my position on historical and anthropological data.[9] My main interest is to establish the values and logic that underpin vindicatory cultures, showing them as consistent legal systems.

Once we admit the existence of a vindicatory system in societies throughout history, we face a similar question to that encountered by anthropologists and

---

bias of progression towards some technologies and conventional accumulation and concentration of wealth.

[3]In other publications, I developed the reasons to compare these societies in legal terms. See Terradas Saborit (2008a, 2019). I totally agree with Détienne regarding comparative methods (2000). Compositions, reconciliation ceremonies, authorised vengeances, ordeals, legal duels, oaths, oracles, legal clamours, proclamations of infamy, formulae of defiance and claims for satisfaction, all appear together in ancient and medieval codes and compilations, as well as in the jurisdictional spaces of primitive Societies (and to some extent in societies that have developed a vindicatory system isolated from the state; see Terradas Saborit 2008a, b).

[4]See especially the views of Llewellyn and Hoebel (1941), Llewellyn (1962), Frank (1949), and Twining (1985).

[5]See Kelsen (2000, 2015).

[6]See also Di Lucia (2010a).

[7]See esp. Kelsen (2015).

[8] See esp. Kelsen (2015).

[9]See previous note.

economists when considering "primitive" societies. They discovered that to understand their economy (also intermingled or embedded with other cultural elements, as in Polanyi's famous statement),[10] they could not interpret facts and attitudes according to pre-market or pre-capitalist labels or simply as inferior economies.

Malinowski, Firth, Mauss, and Polanyi[11] soon discovered that they were facing another system, in which reciprocity and a gift system stood, if not in opposition, at least in clear differentiation with market and capitalist rationalities.[12] There was a need both for the acknowledgement of a different system in these societies and of a scientific paradigm[13] to understand the system. A new perspective was needed to understand a cultural and social complex of relations, attitudes and ideas. We find the same phenomenon in attempting to identify a vindicatory legal system in these cultures. It is different from the civil/criminal order we know in our societies and differs from the strict positivistic paradigm (together with that of an evolutionary perfection leading towards our own legal system). Law as it is studied nowadays—having lost the wide comparative perspective of mid-nineteenth century jurists[14]—is inadequate for understanding "other" legal systems. Only Roman law stands partially as an exception.[15] But the limits of our own legal system are asking for a broader scope of enquiry and reflection upon the human experience of normative and instituted processes.[16] It started with the realist movement in law studies. Karl Llewellyn,[17] one of its major exponents, gave a new and decisive thrust to legal anthropology.

In studying social and cultural phenomena linked to results that evoke justice and law, we find the constitution of a whole system. It is made of semantically coherent and logically consistent institutions for obtaining justice. This is contrary to the idea of archaic, rudimentary and scattered elements, which only served as precedents for our more perfect legal system.

---

[10]See Polanyi (1965).

[11]See Malinowski (1935, 1978), Firth (1959, 1965), Mauss (1950), and Polanyi (1965, 1994).

[12]An analogous opposition between rationality and irrationality occurs dealing with legal cultures that can be treated in complete accordance with the vindicatory rationality. For instance, see Colman (1974).

[13]In terms of Kuhn (1996).

[14]These jurists were the founders of social anthropology with a strong emphasis on normative phenomena: mainly Morgan (1870, 1962, 1995), Maine (1871, 1965), Bachofen (1996), and McLennan (1970). To this generation must be added the French legal historian Fustel de Coulanges (1889–1908, 1984). In his course of 1936–1937, Marcel Mauss explained to his students: "Nous entendons par droit, en ethnologie, ce que les Anglo-Saxons nomment *social anthropology*, c'est-à-dire, en fait, notre sociologie juridique et morale". See Mauss (1967).

[15]See the criticisms of Ramis Barceló (2015).

[16]There were jurists in several countries that in criticising the limits of their national legal systems discovered customary alternatives serving better the principles of realistic equity. See Costa (1908), Costa et al. (1902), Assier-Andrieu (1981, 1987, 2001), and Terradas Saborit (2010b). The seminal work of Marx has been crucial for the theoretical standing of the perspective on customary law and equity: see Xifaras (2002), Bensaïd (2007), and Di Lucia (2010b).

[17]See Llewellyn (1962) and Llewellyn and Hoebel (1941).

The other system, the vindicatory, is not something exotic and unfamiliar. On the contrary, it has been and still is universal. It still lies in the background and within the limits of our system of law. Here the philosophical standpoint turns to Wittgenstein and his remarks on Frazer's *The Golden Bough*.[18] Wittgenstein showed how rituals can be understood through parts of our own historical experiences (thus revealing these rituals to be somewhat universal) while still highlighting their apparent otherness. The idea is coincident with the epistemology of Meyer Fortes when he talks about the explicit and implicit or hidden motives in comparing different cultures.[19]

Allow me to make it very clear from the beginning, that both the vindicatory system and the civil/criminal system have their limitations and inconsistencies. In fact, we can see how, in a way, they look to each other when confronted with their own limitations. Thus, for instance, the civil/criminal system reflect on the vindicatory system when faced with the unsatisfactory treatment of victims (leading to restorative or reparative institutions[20] that try to compensate for the lack of corporate solidarity in our society). On the other hand, the vindicatory system, when vitiated by the arbitrary power of judges, made a claim to the legislative unity and equality provided by the Republic.[21] Thus, both systems are no strangers to each other. Instead, they constitute two ways of combining rights and justice. This is why we can retain the philosophy of Wittgenstein, when he argues that the exotic other, once perceived in a radical empirical way, shares with us a familiar substratum.

As I have indicated before, the Vindicatory system can be established logically in terms close to Kelsen's philosophy of law, but with an intimate relationship with morality, politics or religion, which would have created a problem for the strictness of Kelsen's legal enclosure.[22] This is why I view the vindicatory system as both a legal system with a historical existence and as a scientific paradigm.[23] It is both a *system* in itself and a *view* of this system, as well as a standpoint from which to look at other systems. In other words, since the vindicatory system includes norms and values, it is necessary to understand its logic and value-meanings to come to terms with it. Also, these same legal and moral elements—forming a system—serve to understand the limits of other systems, and vice versa.

[18]See Wittgenstein (1971). This essay has to be read in the context of at least some of his other works (1980, 1981a, b).

[19]See Fortes (1987). Also, as a philosophy of anthropology see Winch (1972) and Skorupski (1978).

[20]See Pinto (2005) and Batos et al. (2005). For a balanced criticism see Allison Morris (2002). See the chapter by Riccardo Mazzola in this volume.

[21]As it appears in the classical essay of Beccaria (1994).

[22]That is to say, the vindicatory system can be understood as a logical system within a semantic order (if we follow, for instance, Carnap's neopositivistic theory), but this is not an obstacle to finding the terms of the system imbued semantically with religious, political and moral references. For Kelsen's ideas see Kelsen (2000, 2015)

[23]I am not presenting here all the empirical ethnographic and historical background that I have discussed elsewhere; Terradas Saborit (2008a, 2019). Rather I propose to focus on the philosophical validity of the system when looked at directly.

Thus, apart from being a guide for diverse social settings throughout history, the vindicatory system helps us to understand major juridical problems in our own society, especially problems related to the social conception of justice. In our society, we attribute or expect to solve many problems by changing the forms of the judicial process or by refining laws. I venture to say that most of these problems come from individualistic conceptions and their biases, as well as from the pretence of isolating our legal system against the facts that point to its continuous embedment of morality, religion, politics, and economics,[24] a reality transcending the knowledge created in our philosophy of law under the hegemony of positive law.[25] It is not strange that the development of legal anthropology that has facilitated the acknowledgement of a vindicatory system comes from the realist movement in the philosophy of law. Karl Llewellyn[26] has been the main anthropologist-jurist evidently accepting and making clear the intermingling of law with other social and cultural fields. He has established the tasks of law and justice as the main motives for legal attention, even if the languages of law in other cultures are difficult to translate to our legal jargon. This means that if, for instance, a dance is the language used by a community for sealing a compositional covenant, dance has to be accepted as a legal language.[27]

As stated before, I am adding to the reasoning of the realistic philosophers of law some ideas from Wittgenstein on the philosophy of language and its traps. Thus, if we accept our legal fictions and make new deductive sentences from them, we have to also accept the legal fictions of other cultures. Thus, we have the fiction of the heir in assuming the personality of only one of the deceased (coming from Roman Law) to legitimise individual property. This fiction cannot be used to discredit the fiction of another culture, such as the personality of the collective heirs in assuming the personality of a host of ancestors, which is effected to legitimise common property (also with another concept for acknowledged possessions), as happens in clanship societies.[28]

Various questions have to be retained in the background when establishing the vindicatory elements in an integrated system. These are: non-independence of the legal institutions from moral, political, economic or religious motives; fusion between the legal theory of action and that of process; the intermingling of private and public law, civil and criminal law, subjective and objective law, and moral and legal legitimacy.

---

[24]The economic conditioning of law is without doubt more important today than its theological conditioning, but it is not the same for other societies and historical periods. For an anthropological sense of the effect of the law and economics school, see Moore (2001).

[25]See Bobbio (1984).

[26]See Llewellyn (1962) and Llewellyn and Hoebel (1941).

[27]As it happens in the classical example provided by Radcliffe-Brown (1964). See also Lorini (2010), who establishes a proper legal system behind what is perceived only as a general ethos. See also Schapera (1977)

[28]See Assier-Andrieu (2011) pp. 180–186; Mazzola (2018).

2 The Unity and Consistency of the Vindicatory System

I argue that the vindicatory system constitutes a set of interrelated elements or institutions forming a unity of logical-legal ideas and ethical motives.

I first consider the fusion between action and process.[29] That is, between the special active role of the plaintiff and the procedure to transform any conflict into a predicate of justice. This fusion involves three conditions: first, that each party is a collective unit with corporate rights and duties, the most important of these being the solidarity in responsibility or redistribution of accountability. This means that, for instance, in the reception and distribution of compositions for torts and crimes, corporate groups, such as clans, do appear clearly as units of responsibility (whereas they can appear more fuzzily in other matters, or even disappear).

Second, the plaintiff or litigant party has the power to enter into the trial, which in comparison to the modern civil or criminal process appears joining judicial attributes. Third, consequently, we cannot speak properly of criminals and their victims as individuals, or plaintiffs and defendants as individuals. The *principium individuationis* taken into account by Schopenhauer in building a theory of justice[30] does not apply in vindicatory societies. We have to speak instead of offended and offending parties.

The beginning of the vindicatory justice process is recognition. It is the social ("social" in the widest sense of the term) acknowledgement of offences. The offence can be primarily a subjective feeling, but its juridical relevance is given by the fact that simultaneously a group of people also acknowledges the offence.[31] It is also an intersubjective phenomenon inserted into the general principle of reciprocity. This means, even if other groups in society would not acknowledge the indictment for the offence as clearly as the accusers would, the standards of reciprocity require that perception and consequent representation. Everything that causes damage is an offence because it is primarily judged in terms of the damaged entity, not according to the harmful or harmless intention of the entity doing the damage. A reciprocal consideration (i.e., others accepting one's own sense of offence) stands for the effort to recognise mutual offences. Thus, the necessary duties of reciprocity for survival and social continuity create a relative expansion of obligatory solidarity. This solidarity in offending and being offended unifies torts and crimes. This is the basic and universal principle of vindicatory justice: the priority of repairing the damaged party; whereas the priority of criminal justice is to punish the offender. In vindicatory societies, you can get reparations even if the real culprit is not found,

[29]Cf. Terradas Saborit (2019), based mainly on Orestano (1967, 1978), and Satta (2004, 2013).

[30]I used the Spanish version of Roberto R. Aramayo (Schopenhauer 2001).

[31]It is the feeling shared by a solidarity group. It is not asking empathy or sympathy but it is created by irrevocable primordial bonds (consanguinity, blood brotherhood and similar ties).

while in criminal law societies that would be very difficult unless there is a committed public responsibility for the damage or insurance.[32]

The vindicatory treatment of offences works as if a kind of tort law accounted for all criminal offences and material and personal damages. The intention is to give a gift to establish calm and compensate for the offence. It is not a price adjusted to the calculated value of the altered or damaged goods. Neither is it a *pretium doloris*, that is, a compensation reduced to a material value to account for a moral sufferance. It is a gift: this means something the nature of which is unrelated to the quality of the subject to be appeased and without pretending to be a definitive settlement. When an object is given as a gift, there is a recognition of the state of friendship. It is not a "final" recognition, concluding the relationship, but it is effectively made to keep it alive. The gift is only a symbol. It is not of the same substance as friendship.[33] If a gift is likened to the price or to the material estimate of the value of friendship, that would essentially mean its corruption. Thus, in compositional processes, the wealth given to the offended party is a gift of acknowledgement and appeasement for the offence. It is part of a process leading to reconciliation. In vindicatory justice, we can find reconciliation without direct material compensation, but not the latter without reconciliation. We must consider the relevance of reconciliation in the context of communities in which economic cooperation, multi-layered sociability and mutual aid—including a demarcated corporate responsibility in all legal issues—are continuous and comprehend all the institutions of society.[34]

The vindicatory ethos[35] establishes the subjective duty and the objective obligation to repair any offence and damage. Damages also account as offences for passive subjects, because they cause moral and/or material suffering. It is from this experience that arises the universal right to recognition and repair. Again, the question is the decision whether to put in first place either the reparation of the offended or the punishment of the offender. I do not mean that each of these options excludes the other (we know perfectly well the coexistence of criminal punishment and civil responsibility), but the establishment of one of these priorities affects in many ways the legal system and the society it represents. They are historical choices. We know nowadays how much the priorities of criminal law are criticised due to a lack of concern for the victim's suffering and the provision of realistic rehabilitation to the culprit. On the other hand, vindicatory systems can be blamed for creating different sorts of impunity and using a system of venality.

The paradigmatic vindicatory process consists of a judgment establishing the composition and an associated ceremony to reconcile the different parties. The

[32]The quest for a responsibility, beyond strict criminal guilt, appears also in our philosophy of law. See Young (2011).

[33]The ancient Greek *symbolon* required the parallel meeting of two friends (usually involved in a hospitality relationship) with that of the two separated pieces of the same object.

[34]See Terradas Saborit (2019).

[35]Here I use *ethos*, meaning the embedment between a legal (juridical) norm and a moral duty. The term *jural* refers to the same phenomenon but emphasises the legal aspect. See Vinogradoff (1913).

relevant issue is the harm or injury sensed by the offended party. This is what creates universal accountability, which has to be found at any cost and by any means. And is also why even magical methods (divination) can help in determining this accountability. If there is no direct guilt in the causal agency of the offence, some responsibility can be attributed to a more indefinite intentionality[36] (from some carelessness in the duties of reciprocity or to an old enmity).[37] We have to keep in mind that the concept of offence has a double nature: it is perceived intersubjectively, and it is objectively treated in a social court. Thus, judgments are not primarily processes for the application of norms[38] but the moral, religious, political and legal contextualisation of cases in which norms can appear as implicit guides,[39] or rather as the results of a nuanced jurisprudence.

The compositional judgment is the legal prototype for the rest of the actions and processes of the vindicatory system. It works as the "handbook" for them all. It constitutes the moral and legal—*jural*[40]—paradigm for dispute settlement. It is the source of justice. Contrary to an extended opinion, it is always held under judicial authority.[41] This authority can be a judge or an arbitrator. It has three legal powers: that of undertaking the promoted action, that of guaranteeing the rules for the process, and that of authorising a binding resolution (although consensual or negotiated with both parties).

The interpretation that overlooks judicial authority and sides with mediation or negotiation as forms of dispute settlement[42] is due to two partial examinations. In vindicatory societies, people endowed with judicial authority try to solve disputes before they become a court issue. Thus, they visit or arrange visits to solve the dispute in informal terms. There is often a continuum between their role as judges and that of mediators.[43] They can hold informal meetings as well as court sessions. It is something similar to the traditional endeavours of many justices of the peace before the meeting in the local courtroom. Also, traditionally, several "good men" could try with their comings and goings to appease conflicts. The point is that in our local and traditional societies, these activities were clearly differentiated from those of judges when following strictly courtroom procedures. While in the case of vindicatory societies, there is a continuum between both activities. Even a high

[36]As I have stated before, this problem also appears in our society in terms of responsibilities that are not accountable as guilty acts: see Young (2011).

[37]I have treated these issues in my previous books. See the fundamentals: Malinowski (1929, 1947), Gluckman (1965a, b, 1972), Radcliffe-Brown (1964).

[38]This is a topic for African legal ethnography (Cf. Comaroff and Roberts 1977).

[39]This appeared soon to Pigliaru (1975).

[40]Again, see Vinogradoff (1913) and Fortes (1987).

[41]The criticism of the idea of compositions as mediations without judicial authorities can be traced since Fustel de Coulanges (1889–1908) and can be applied to all legal monographs that describe the details of the process. See Gluckman (1965a, 1967).

[42]Gulliver (1972, 1977) stands as the classic promoter of such a view.

[43]See Bogoras (1904), Holý (1974), Just (2001), Llewellyn and Hoebel (1941), Rosés Tubau (2013), Aljoxami (Al-Jusani) (1914), and Srinivas (1991). See Torrens (2013) for a customary figure of familiarity and judicial authority among shepherds.

judicial authority can be involved in mediation before taking the dispute to the proper court procedure. It is something similar to arranging many labour disputes (or in other civil actions)—with the suggestions of the judge—to avoid the assignment of rights following the court judgment. In these cases, a negotiation that often entails the dismissal of one's own rights can be the "good agreement" that replaces justice.

The other point of confusion comes from the observation that judicial authorities in community courts (i.e., in many *panchayats*) try to achieve their resolutions with the maximum consensus between them and the disputants.[44] They make an effort to bring all wills into harmony and to understand both sides with empathy. This helps to maintain social cohesiveness, or a given set of powers, i.e., a social order. These judges will not appear to have the same distance, formalism and adjudicatory attitude as those in Western courts, rather, they operate as mediators.

Mediation can also be—as in our society—a simple evasion of justice, or its corruption.[45] If there is an imbalance of de facto forces in a dispute ("inequality of arms"), mediation can easily serve to legitimise an injustice.

Overall, ethnographic samples tend to be prisoners of their ethnographic present, while the processes of feuding and reconciliation are historical, lasting sometimes for more than a generation.[46] Also, reconciliation can mean very different things according to time and place. There is customary reconciliation and forced reconciliation,[47] formal and felt, occurring once or re-enacted in frequent encounters and social meetings.

The compositional process (or trial) under a judicial authority is the primordial process to inform all other actions within the vindicatory order. In some sense, we can say that it appears as "civilising" the criminal process. I mean that, as in the Roman *actiones*, the compositional action and process aims to determine material compensation for damages and any kind of offence.[48] Nevertheless, we have to bear in mind that to reduce compositions to just material indemnities vitiates them. To think of compositions just like tariffs for wrongdoings—as happened during medieval times—confuses the social value of compositions. Compositions are vitiated when wealth or money as impersonal payments substitute the personal gift that

[44]See Hayden (1999), and the works of Gluckman on Barotse jurisprudence (1963, 1965a, 1967). Also Schapera (1977) and Gibbs (1973)

[45]See Louis Assier-Andrieu (1996).

[46]This is what Fletcher (2002) recollects, studying a conflict according to its longue durée. See also Miller (1990). But usually the ethnographic time recollects only a one-sided account that gives more emphasis to feuding and vendettas or to compositions. Thus, we can compare Holý (1974), talking only about compositions (*diyat*), with other authors putting more emphasis on feuding and vendettas (Gillen 1899). Or, together with mediations and banishments, like Ginat (1997). Or with suggestions of an equilibrium between both issues, in spite of the predominance of one of them in their fieldwork period, like Warner (1937), Peters (1990), Evans-Pritchard (1969), Gluckman (1963, 1964, 1965a, b), and Sacco (1985).

[47]See the criticism of Du Toit (2007).

[48]I develop this idea with more precision in Terradas Saborit (2019).

creates an everlasting nexus and the reconciliation of the two parties. It is not just an ethical issue; it is a necessary social outcome for a specific social order. An order in which trust, continuous cooperation and dependency are conditions for survival.

In vindicatory justice (this differs from the development of the Roman *actiones*) we find a great variety of matters for a single judicial process. Compositions and ordeals (which in practice are similar to compositions) serve a variety of civil and criminal matters. Thus, a dispute about hunting lands can be solved through an ordeal, a judicial combat (a duel on behalf of the two parties), a verbal hearing in court, or a judgment on the spot of the dispute, on the hunting field itself. The same is valid for a criminal accusation. The selection of procedure depends on a range of legal, moral and social circumstances. These include the consideration of vices or abuses prevailing in some of these procedures, which may suggest another choice. A clan authority, a medieval prince or a community council can decide on that question. Usually, political situations and social conflicts do account better than legal considerations for these changes. We must always remember that the mingling of law with politics, religion, morals, economic and social needs and powers is constant in vindicatory societies.[49] This does not cause perversion of the system, but is brought about by a lack of harmony between all these realms.

There is also a background in our society of seeking this harmony. However, the historical experience of Western societies has led to the doctrine of the independence of legal and, especially, of judicial power from other institutions. However, in harmony or disharmony, we cannot pretend that morality, political and economic interests, religious beliefs and even aesthetic considerations do not influence laws and judgments. Vindicatory societies accept all this intermingling as a matter of fact. They try to bring at least some harmony to the system. This is achieved in "primitive" societies by the intervention of "magical" divination[50] in relation to criminal accountability. Also, by moral condemnations not adjusted to the facts for incrimination and by consideration of the duties regarding reciprocity[51] between social roles. Thus, religious forms, economic and social obligations, and morality stand for legal pursuits.

In ancient societies, Machiavelli already paid attention to the role of oracles and oaths in military discipline and political values.[52] The legal culture of the Ancient Greek polis reveals an intermingling of religious, political, economic and psychological values with legal arguments and judgments. They also tried to build harmony between correlated meanings and values for interests, justice and political

[49]For all this section see Terradas Saborit (2008a, 2019).

[50]When ethnographically described it consists in intuitions, confident knowledge and political opportunities (for peace or conflict) brought about by the diviner in relation to local and contiguous social groupings. See Gluckman (1972).

[51]See Malinowski (1947) for the establishment of reciprocity as a general social norm guiding also legal institutions in a primitive society.

[52]See Machiavelli (1977).

dominance. Demosthenes is one example among many of this multiplicity of domains in making a legal argument.[53]

In Early Medieval societies, religion, economic interests and politics stood very close to judicial decisions and their legislative outcome. Ordeals, judiciary combats, oaths and compositions reveal an inextricable fusion between law and religion, moralities, economic interests and political endeavouring.[54]

The vindicatory process—the compositional form being its paradigm—deals with any civil suit or criminal cause.[55] Many methods have been used, including: a verbal process of conciliation, an ordeal to defy another's accusation or defence, composition, an oath to prove and to solve[56] a dispute, and finally, judicial combat or battle (which are also subject to metaphysical sanction).

3 Vengeance in the Vindicatory Order

The main epistemological bias I found in anthropological and legal literature for the establishment of vindicatory law as a system, comes from the supposed pre-eminence of vengeance and similar retaliatory practices, especially among "primitive" or traditional societies.[57] Instead, I propose a view of the system based primarily on the compositional processes and with the subsidiary validity of vengeance that actually appears, both ethnographically and historically, ruled by a judicial authority. Otherwise, it lacks legitimacy and it can be treated as an ordinary crime. Part of the epistemological bias for not seeing the whole of the vindicatory system lies in the separation between the study of vengeance and that of composition.[58] There is copious anthropological literature in which vengeance is separated from composition.[59]

Once the coupling of feud-vengeance (*faida-vendetta*) is separated from the legal order in which they are instituted, they become intimately connected with other cultural topics (mainly to those of the honour-shame complex). Indeed, there is a very important symbolic relation with these topics—an interplay of conventional

---

[53]See Vinogradoff (1922), Glotz (1904a, b, 1988), and Terradas Saborit (2019).

[54]Cf. Terradas Saborit (2008a), chapter on the Varad register (pp. 1208–1235).

[55]Of course, I use this ethnocentric distinction here in order to better understand the vindicatory proceedings.

[56]In fact, in the vindicatory order, the oath is always ordalic and generates a sentence by itself.

[57]See Waldmann (2001). For a balanced general view see Di Lucia and Mancini (2015).

[58]See the opposed trend in Fustel de Coulanges (1889–1908), Gagarin (1981), Bogoras (1904), Deacon (1934), Elwin (1939), Fison and Howitt (1991), Fletcher (2002), Hinojosa (1915), Rutter (2007), and Peters (1990). For the variations between compositions and authorised vengeances or analogous procedures in vindicatory compilations, see, for instance, Dennis (1980), Salis (1973), Rascón García and García González (1996). Ancient and medieval compilations deal with the interplay between compositions and authorised vengeances: see Terradas Saborit (2008a).

[59]The work of Black-Michaud (1975) has synthesised most of its theoretical meaning.

values—but if we want to know exactly how the feud-vengeance complex works, first it has to be linked to legal (juridical) elements.[60] We have to know first *what* and *who* decides about behaviour in feuds and vendettas.

Pigliaru[61] was the first to establish rules for vendettas that had a legal (juridical) sense: proportion, progression and caution. The feud-vengeance complex is closely linked to that of composition-reconciliation. It is a distortion to put this relationship sideways and to directly link the legal push of the feud-vengeance complex to exclusive cultural content, namely that of honour-shame. This overlooks the legal nature and logic of much of the workings of the feud-vengeance coupling.[62] In vindicatory societies, feud is given by a formal declaration of enmity. It can be further developed by the formalities of duel or challenge. In some societies (medieval), public authorities give the right for feud and vengeance under given rules (with the formula *exeat inimicus*). Thus, the feud-vengeance complex reaches a kind of statutory status. Depending on its configuration, reconciliation and composition can be reached with more or less difficulty. Between an open war of extermination and a simple skirmish, there are several choices aimed at sustaining the enmity or bringing reconciliation. The entire process is subject to many historical and local variations. For instance, Deacon[63] observed in Malekula (Vanuatu) the statutory difference between truce and peace.

In conclusion, the cultural content of feud and vengeance does not explain the procedures they take in their actions (types, degrees and limits for violence). It explains the cultural code that can motivate such actions, but not the considerations that are taken in choosing actions for their legal and political results.

Very often, the fact that ethnography emphasises the practice of feud-vendetta or that of composition-reconciliation (instead of bringing them together) is due to the lack of a historical perspective. Thus, the studies gathered by Jacob Black-Michaud stress the isolated existence of the feud-vendetta processes, whereas other ethnographies exclusively talk of composition-reconciliation[64] while others talk more about both processes.[65]

On the other hand, there is a problem for jurists. Even when data shows that a compositional process appears closely linked to the option of vengeance, it is difficult for them to accept a legal institution that is above both vindictive and compositional issues. In other words, it is very difficult for jurists to escape the commonplace topic of "private war" when vengeance is at stake. Usually, they enter into a contradictory argument, accepting both an authority to decide through a

[60] See Terradas Saborit (2019). For a well-balanced study of vindictive motives, taking into account both mediation and judgments, as well as the impact of the culture of honour, see Gómez Mestres (2005).

[61] See Pigliaru (1975).

[62] See Fletcher (2002), Rutter (2007), and Terradas Saborit (2019).

[63] See Deacon (1934).

[64] Such as that of Holý (1974, 1991)

[65] See Peters (1990) and Terradas Saborit (2019).

judicial process and the autarchy of each clan or lineage to indulge in a "private war".

Thus, in his study of a Somalian legal system, Rodolfo Sacco[66] admits, on the one hand, that the conflict is not between two physical persons, but between two lineage groups, to which the persons involved belong to. Also, he states that there is no acknowledged authority above these groups.[67] This condition leaves no other options for these two groups other than war[68] or peace, to be decided by themselves. However, he states something that begins to reveal the presence of a superior authority: in the words of Sacco, conciliation extinguishes any juridical pretension (*pretesa giuridica*)—civil or criminal—arising from the facts that had created the conflict. Moreover, very soon and very clearly, he admits that there was the constitution of a council made by the two parties in conflict, and this council had a judicial authority—among other things, to decide over the nature of those juridical pretensions. This council, affirms Sacco, had the power to impose rulings over the case, specifically regarding the group made responsible for the offence.[69] Nevertheless, this power to impose rulings soon disappears in Sacco's next paragraph, where he asserts again that the power is diffuse (*potere diffuso*), that the solution of conflicts depends only on the groups involved, and that the dispute is solved through negotiation (*componevano la disputa con un negoziato*). The lack of a permanent institution like an international court dismisses the legal validity and political effectiveness of the readymade councils, which nevertheless have the power to adjudicate binding resolutions.

Rodolfo Sacco has analysed in exquisite detail several crucial issues of comparative law. This is why I quote him. However, I understand that perhaps due to the traditional authority of the Germanic school of private law, it is very difficult to avoid its imperative idea: that primitive, ancient and medieval conflicts fall under the category of private wars, private dealings and private resolutions, as if there could not be a superior authority besides that of the state. This perspective coincides with the *negotiatory* and *payback* paradigms that pervade African and Australian anthropology, despite the detailed ethnographies where compositions, ordeals and vendettas fall under the rulings of councils.[70]

---

[66]See Sacco (1985).

[67]*Al di sopra dei due gruppi non esistevano autorità riconosciute* (1985), p. 24.

[68]Although Sacco adds that war was followed also by conciliation.

[69]*Questo comitato, o* Guddi, *aveva il potere di imporre le misure del caso al gruppo responsabile dell'offesa* (1985), p. 24.

[70]I treat this largely in Terradas Saborit (2008a, 2019).

4 Why "Vindicatory"?[71]

I use the term "vindicatory" according to etymological, historical and holistic criteria. First, when Tacitus[72] discovered the pre-eminence of composition among the Germans, he referred to it with the Latin verb *vindico*, *vindicare*. This first contextual meaning was that of claiming for damages. It was something closely related to the Roman *Sacramenti actio* or action of *vindicatio*.[73] However, it was soon realised that the German *vindicatio* included damages of any type and also those derived from criminal offences. Composition was already in existence, and has lately become very well known during the medieval period (*compositio*). The compositional process constituted precisely one of the most recognisable elements or institutions of the so-called Germanic law. Nino Tamassia[74] clearly detected the "civil" aspect of the Germanic general action for offences when Tacitus recognised the terms of the party that reclaimed composition (*is qui vindicatur*).

On the other hand, Louis Gernet[75] has treated the Roman *vindicatio* as one of the most ancient examples of the inner value of the judicial process. In this ancient process, it is clear how the conflict that is brought by the action is re-enacted in a new way (ritual) to transform the conflict into what is recognised as a work of justice. The philosophy of the *vindicatio* establishes an equilibrium between the authority of the process itself, the reason or motivation of each party, the terms of the conflict and the judicial power to judge.[76]

Fustel de Coulanges[77] has signalled the prevalence of compositions in terms of legal validity and social effectiveness in systems where feuds and vendettas also have an active role. Paul Vinogradoff[78] also studied the ancient Greek combination of damage suits and criminal prosecutions, always under judicial authorities.

Raymond Verdier[79] explicitly uses the French term *vindicatoire* to refer to the public statute and collective responsibility for an authorised vengeance. He leaves the term *vindicatif* for private vengeance. However, he does not integrate composi-

[71]For further developments of the topic here, see Terradas Saborit (2019).

[72]See Tacitus (1970) and Tamassia (1964a).

[73]Betti (1915) did relate the origins of the Roman *vindicatio* to actions of authorised vengeance or of a more strict self-help; but within the scheme of the evolutionary progress of law, establishing a legal inferiority for the first evolutionary stages.

[74]See Tamassia (1964b) and Terradas Saborit (2014).

[75]See Gernet (1982).

[76]The works of Orestano (1967, 1978) and Satta (2004, 2013) help to understand the interpenetration and holistic meaning of action and process. See Terradas Saborit (2019).

[77]See "La cultura jurídica vindicatoria y la historia después de Fustel de Coulanges" in Terradas Saborit (2008a).

[78]See Vinogradoff (1922).

[79]See Verdier (1980).

tion into the system, although he feels compelled to treat reconciliation as a necessary corollary when dealing with vengeance.[80]

Thus, vindication refers first to composition, while in societies where composition constitutes the main action and process of reference, there also appear feuds and vendettas. There is a statutory status for both vengeance and reconciliation. Civil claims can be understood as vindications since Tacitus and vengeance still work in the same system. Therefore, I think we can name the whole system vindicatory. In this way, we maintain the Latin-Roman etymology for a civil action, and we do not dismiss the presence of feuding and vengeance.

5 The Prototypic Action: Homicide

The main value and norm of the vindicatory system as such lies in the imperative for repairing any damage, a kind of universal right for reparation. It is a historical option to which I have referred earlier. It does not derive from the obligation to repair via the person who has produced the damage, but from the imperative to obtain reparation as a damaged party. For that reason, when there is no apparent accountability for the damage, it can even be attributed to witchcraft or sorcery.[81] Then, the responsibility for the damage can be attributed to doubtful attitudes, suspicions, undue behaviour, political conveniences, factional allegiances, etc. The point is that if there is damage, there must be repair. Accountability must be found in any way, because nobody can be left without a repair. There are no accidents in the vindicatory world. To understand this universal principle of accountability, that transcends individual responsibility, we must turn to the meaning of homicide in the vindicatory ethos.

In trying to find the sense of composition beyond the idea of price or tariff, which as previously stated, is precisely the idea that nullifies its legal and ethical validity, we face the notion of the gift. In any society, the gift does not equal the buying of a commodity or a service. The gift is displaced from the price to pay. It is a token of recognition, not an exchange value adjusted to the relationship between offer and demand. Certainly, a gift can prepare or induce an exchange, as well as corrupt a rightful exchange. It is less and more than the exchange itself. In being "less" it can be more from an ethical and aesthetical point of view. The point is that, contrary to price, the gift is not valid for an exchange other than an exchange of gifts. The gift is the appropriate advancement for recognising that what it compensates cannot be bought or satisfied by the gift-value it would receive in a strict market of gifts. The gift, much more than other offers, recognises the superior value of the person to whom it is addressed. The gift, by its special nature, has a humble value before the person. Otherwise, it would be blackmail.

[80]See Verdier (2004).

[81]See Gluckman (1972).

This ethical and legal inferiority of the gift is most evident when the gift tries to recognise something that is impossible to be paid for, or even more than that, something unattainable for any human power. Recovery from death is the case in point. Death cannot be bought by any wealth. The group of people that claims the loss of human life cannot be properly compensated for it. The proper blood debt for homicide cannot be paid. It is something analogous to the gift given when a group loses a woman that marries a man from another group.[82] The interpretation of the gift as a payment implies a vitiation of the common custom. Ethnographically, the spread between the two interpretations appears clear. They can succeed one another, or they can coexist. They can represent a massive social change or the attitude and values of a minority.[83] Something similar occurs with the wealth transferred after a homicide. It can be interpreted as a gift of recognition of the irreparability of the offence or as the price to discharge ones' responsibility. Thus, for instance, when the American army tried to compensate for civil deaths they caused in Islamic countries, it was not so easy.[84] There were victim's families that did not accept the American ingenuity. Anthropologists gave advice, but the values and attitudes could not be taught. Some Muslims felt that the Americans were only concerned with the discharge of responsibility. This vitiated the whole meaning of composition and reconciliation in transforming a gift into a payment.

In vindicatory societies, homicide is as an offence where only gifts can serve to recognise its real unattainable reparation. No price can compensate for the dead person. This is why we find three usual ways to deal with homicide in composition.

First, to assemble a big gift that is usually paid in instalments. This implies the assumption of shared collective responsibility by the offending group (although with distinctions between the contributions of the close kin and the more distant relatives). Reciprocally, there is the solidarity of the offended group that shares the composition (although, also, with distinctions between the close kin of the victim and the rest of the clan members or kindred).[85]

Second, the gift must create an everlasting tribute offered to the offended party, which can be in force for several generations. This shows the link or nexus that creates a blood "debt" for homicide. It can be an annual offer of a sacrificial animal, of the fruits of a field or a similar gift. Thus, it performs a commemorative function that can indeed last many generations.[86]

Third, to give a person to the offended group in replacement for the lost one. Again, it is a vicious interpretation to understand that another pays (supposedly through bad treatment or slavery) for the life taken. If it happens, it is the analogous

[82]See Rospabé (1995).

[83]See Schapera (1966).

[84]See Slyomovics (2011). For the legal and moral tasks of the *diya* see Holý (1974), and the chapter by Marta Alonso in this volume. See also Terradas Saborit (2008a, 2016, 2019).

[85]This holds true for very distant vindicatory traditions: Arab-Islamic, Icelandic, Germanic and African Islamic, and non-Islamic. See Terradas Saborit (2008a, 2019).

[86]See also Terradas Saborit (2008a), especially based on Charachidze's history and ethnography.

vice to that of turning a gift into a price. The gift of the person in its own right is made in terms of adoption or marriage. It goes from group to group, no matter who is brought to fulfil the purpose.[87]

In all vindicatory societies, there is a judgment for homicide distinguishing between manslaughter and murder. Besides, expiation can complement composition. Nevertheless, expiation is not the same as punishment,[88] although both can cause sufferance. The universality of composition and its focus on the victim's characteristics (status, gender, religious, political condition) could have suggested the lack of distinction between unintentional homicide and wilful murder. But this distinction is not supported ethnographically and historically. We always find its distinction in judgment. Although it can occur that composition for an unintentional homicide is greater than that for an intentional homicide. This is explained by the condition of the victim. Thus, for instance, the Hammurabi-Biblical *lex talionis* comes from the extraordinary consideration given to the pregnant woman when she is the victim of an unintentional homicide or abortion.[89]

Expiation involves a ritual of purification and a joint ceremony integrating the offended and the offending parties. Expiation may involve banishment or exile. Although the banishment of the whole group rather corresponds to the eventuality of an authorised vengeance. We know examples of both procedures in "primitive", ancient, medieval and traditional societies (i.e. Roma and other gipsy societies).[90] Usually, a judicial authority (that has deliberated over the case and its settlement) decrees the banishment (for an individual, a family or a group) and if the culprit is reluctant to comply with the fixed terms, then an authorised vengeance can ensue. In ancient and medieval societies, authorised vengeance was predicated as a right given to anybody to kill the culprit. This highlights the overall meaning of banishment: it is a decree affecting the whole community in relation to a person or a group (usually a kinship group). Thus, the whole community becomes endowed with the right of authorised vengeance: it has to tolerate its execution within a standard of shared responsibility. This is why the formula allocates a collective responsibility in its execution. The execution of the culprit is conceived as if any member of the community could be authorised to perform it. Here the executive power for an authorised vengeance is given directly to the community, although there is an offended party that is supposed to take charge of the duty. Legitimacy mingles that party with the rest of the community. This contrasts to the criminal order, where punishments are administered by an intermediary and not directly by the community, or the offended party. To put it more realistically, in vindicatory societies, it is the

[87]See Rospabé (1995).

[88]Actually, punishment is closer to vengeance than to expiation (or closer to an augmented power considered as authority. See Fittipaldi's chapter in this volume). Paliero (2018) shows the social genesis of punishment for penal law entering into the legal system from a purely social convention of punishment. Paliero stresses that there is no theory of punishment in the penal legal system. His proposals deserve much consideration, which I expect to display in a future study.

[89]Cf. Terradas Saborit (2008a), VI, 4, passim.

[90]All this is very well illustrated by ancient Greek samples (Terradas Saborit 2019).

offended party that receives the right for vengeance with the solidarity and shared responsibility of the whole community. Even in medieval kingdoms, we can see how kings approved this procedure.[91]

We can compare authorised vengeance in the vindicatory order with the death penalty in the criminal order:

1. Vengeance and the death penalty are not necessary in either order. Expiations, banishments and exiles can resolve the most cruel and impious offences in vindicatory orders. In the criminal order, we have long imprisonments and even life sentences.
2. It depends on historical and local political, ethical and legal changes to cause more or fewer compositions instead of authorised vengeances, as well as to cause more or fewer death penalties instead of long imprisonments.
3. The great difference between the two orders lies in the possibility of social reintegration and moral rehabilitation. Return from expiation and banishment is not the same as a return from jail. The social stigma is also different.
4. In the vindicatory order, for grave offences, expiation and banishment can be more compatible with composition. Whereas in the criminal order, imprisonment makes it difficult to comply with civil responsibility. This is due to two obvious reasons: the responsibility of the offender's group can be maintained in spite of banishment (even the gifts of the banished can diminish the period of banishment), and there are more chances to satisfy debts when indebtedness is collective and there is more freedom to solve it.

In several societies still ruled by the vindicatory order, we find extreme public punishments (*supplicia*) which are also practised in societies with the civil/criminal order. These *supplicia* and other punishments of public *vindicta*, follow the logic of authorised vengeance, but with a clear disproportion or disequilibrium for future conciliation of the parties.[92]

Kingship, state, religion or nationhood account for the dismissal of the proper vindicatory order. They dismiss an arrangement of conflicts allowing a minimum of expectation for reconciliation. Instead, when the aim of the punishing party is the complete annihilation of the other party (extermination of political or religious groups, genocide of groups or nations), then massive and cruel assassinations, as well as executions with torture of their leaders, become the current practice. In these cases, the idea of vengeance of the vindicatory order does not apply. The power wishes for the total destruction of its enemy without any chance for reconciliation. Often, this goes together with a discharge of cruelty out of the anger of having been wronged.

There is also the urge to inflict terror on other possible opponents. Here occurs a basic political change in which the equilibrium between parties (clans, kinship

[91]Documentary basis in Hinojosa (1915), Terradas Saborit (2008a), Allen (2000), and Carey (1997).

[92]See the chapter on authority by Edoardo Fittipaldi in this volume.

groups, communities) is substituted by a unique power, namely the state, for which politics is no longer an affair between several parties, but between a unique power and the rest of society. In this situation, we no longer find a reciprocity sustained between the offenders and the offended. In state societies, this will be left to the "civil parties". Otherwise, we find a unique and legitimate power with its offenders. These are termed rebels, traitors, or criminals (against the state's laws). Then, especially when its absolute power is challenged, it reacts with authority,[93] understood as an augmentation of power, which is contrary to the equilibrium for compositions. The latter will only occur internationally, between states.[94]

Whereas, the overreaction of the power exercised as this type of authority over all subjects obeys the principles of total subjugation, the annihilation of other powers and terrorising potential rebels and criminals. This engenders a political attitude that is responsible for both penal populism and state terrorism.[95] It is antithetic to the conciliatory aims of the vindicatory order. This is why when the limits of the penal order face vindicatory elements (for instance, with the approach of restorative justice), and try to introduce reforms to achieve more peaceful policies, there are overreactions favouring the contrary direction.[96]

6 Imprecations, Ordeals and Oaths

We have seen that the vindicatory system has two extremes regarding actions: composition and vengeance. However, it is more complex. It has another series of actions ranging from oaths to imprecations, with ordeals in between. These are apparently extraordinary processes to obtain justice. Nonetheless, they are linked to the key values and logic that underpin the vindicatory system. Without them, the philosophy of law underlying vindicatory justice cannot be properly understood. The compositional process establishes justice as a social construct; something produced by an instituted social action. This constitutes the prevalent idea of justice, emanating from an instituted experience in society. Composition constitutes the realistic basis of vindicatory justice. The referential idea of justice is what happens in a compositional process. Justice is what everyone learns from the processes required to obtain it: the social form of these processes gives birth to the idea of justice, not the reverse. Thus, we can say that in the vindicatory order, the sociology of justice

---

[93]Not in the Weberian sense of legitimacy (traditional, rational-legal-bureaucratic, charismatic).

[94]See Merry (2006) for a view that articulates human rights, international law and indigenous legal traditions. For an important aspect of the process of disarticulation, see Mayerfeld (2007).

[95]See Fassin (2017), Cantarella (2007), and Salas (2005, 2012). Anarchist theorists were obviously the first to notice the vindictive dimension of the state; see Kropotkine (1901).

[96]There was controversy over applying restorative justice or a more severe penal justice for juvenile offenders in the 2011 riots in London and other cities. There are several articles in the *British Journal of Criminology* and other journals on this question. See, especially, Lightowlers and Quirk (2014).

antedates, and in a communicative way precludes, its philosophy; because we deal with the justice *in* the case. This is why the experience of vindicatory justice is purely jurisprudential. The "substantial norms" have to be inferred, or they seem to be reduced to a few. Whereas in reality, there is a lot of substantial normative thinking in the handling of each case. But not in terms of applying "a law" to the case, rather of thinking the case in such a way as to produce a judgment that works as law.[97] This is also true in jurisprudential traditions where the doctrines of the precedent, the singular equity and the leading case defy the over-generalisation brought about by homogeneous legislations.

Oaths are instituted processes used to obtain justice when other means are lacking. Usually, when testimonies or clear indictments are missing. Usually, oaths are taken and given in particular places, with particular formulas and under two judicial authorities, one human and another spiritual.

In the vindicatory order, oaths are not only methods of proof but also sentences, because the spiritual authority that decides the validity of the oath is irrevocable. Oaths serve to assert, to justify, to exonerate or to promise.[98] All known oaths have an ordalic element: they are sworn by or against a sacred or metaphysical authority. To swear is to sustain a truth under the risk of perjury. The spiritual authority that reserves a proper punishment for perjury knows this. The punishment for perjury can also be human, once the falsehood of an oath is known.[99]

It is very important for oaths' validity that they are declared according to given formulae. This is a criterion of moral psychology and effective social legality (*juridicity*). It has to be manifested with a language form that prevents easy perjury. This is why there are several important circumstances surrounding an oath: a transcendent place,[100] solemnity, invocations, body position and touching, statement redundancy and parallel ceremonies for the sake of sincerity, rectitude of mind and purity of intention. Or, there can be simply the invocation of a deity to punish in case of perjury. Thus, in oaths, the physical and social elements of the process receive a symbolic emphasis before the metaphysical power that presides over the whole judgment.[101]

Ordeals are oaths joined by a supernatural indication. Like oaths, ordeals are proofs and sentences. A proof passed to assert or deny a statement of fact, and a sentence given by the proof itself. An ordeal is the sentence given by the gods (God's judgment) or ancestors' spirits. Paradigmatically, the ordeal consists of a ritual in which a person (by himself or on behalf of a group) undergoes a challenge through

[97]See Pigliaru (1975) and Comaroff and Roberts (1977).

[98]See La Preuve (1963), Verdier (1980), Di Lucia (1997), Fezas (1991), and Terradas Saborit (2008a).

[99]See Verdier (1980).

[100]From sacred places where only truth can be said in "primitive" societies (i.e., the Ti oath among the Toda) to the "Churches for oath taking" in medieval Europe. See Verdier (1980) and Terradas Saborit (2008a).

[101]See Verdier (1980) and Terradas Saborit (2008a).

enduring pain or through a painless hazard.[102] This is done to obtain the sanction of the case by a supernatural judicial authority.

In "primitive", ancient and medieval societies, the ritual has three main phases: (1) the preparation of the ordeal taker and of the ordeal's substance, usually comprising ceremonies of purification, prevention or conjuration; (2) the material execution of the ordeal, consisting in the contact of the body with a painful object or with a hazardous contingency—a prodigy, miracle or heroic endurance must happen to achieve the ordeal's purpose, so that Justice descends towards the human process, and (3) the judicial interpretation of the result of the ordeal—in spite of the possible public evidence of the success or failure of the ordeal, a judicial authority ultimately sanctions the sentence given by the spiritual agency.[103]

Oaths and ordeals stand in the vindicatory order as testimonies of the accepted difficulty in approaching justice.[104] They rely on the help of an extraordinary power. The necessary truth for justice—when evidence is weak—is asked to gods and spirits. Still, oaths and ordeals are socially instituted approaches to justice. They involve an organised social event. People are congregated and follow rules of interaction in order to achieve a manifestation of justice. Nevertheless, there is an even weaker approach to justice according to vindicatory cultures. It happens when the social congregation of people to approach justice fails. Then, the claim of justice is left to imprecations. These are accorded to states of defencelessness, deprivation of rights, and to a diverse range of injustices (slavery, captivity, incapacity, eviction, oppression, poverty).

An imprecation[105] is a formula that can be easily confused with a malediction. However, it is different in four basic characteristics:

1. It is formulated as an indictment that could have been presented in a courtroom. It briefly refers to the injustice that afflicts the claimant.
2. It is addressed as a prayer to a spiritual authority endowed with the power to judge and to punish.
3. It does not curse the offending part, but it asks for the action of supernatural justice.
4. It expects the resolution of the deity or spirit without interfering in its judgment, although from conviction it can ask for just deserts.

Thus, imprecation is formulated with all the possible legitimacy acquired in a judicial process. It is the claim that could not have been presented before a court. But it is somewhat as if it was presented and heard properly in a court. However, in lacking a human court, it is presented to a divine tribunal.[106]

---

[102]See Terradas Saborit (2008b).

[103]See Terradas Saborit (2008a).

[104]Exceptionally, ordeals have entered into modern civil law when legal pluralism obtained some possibilities. For the case of British India, see Terradas Saborit (2017).

[105]See Terradas Saborit (2008a), Pitrè (2016), and López Jimeno (2001).

[106]See Terradas Saborit (2008a, 2019), regarding the Greek *Ará*.

With imprecation, we face one of the main principles of vindicatory justice. Imprecation means the actuality of defencelessness and allied conditions. It is a real possibility for any taking of justice. It recalls a common and very old experience of human life: the rootedness of injustice in the world. Injustices pour over people in cascades. Justice is, in many situations, simply a dream. Even now, in democratic societies, for many people access to justice is completely out of reach or obstructed by many obstacles.[107] Then, it is easy to conceive justice as prodigious, a miracle.[108] One has to imagine or to expect a superhuman force to introduce justice in the world. Imprecations lie at the root of such expectations. When they are taken as valid and legitimate—as in vindicatory societies—they obey the hope of a correct judgment. The authority for this judgment must be superhuman, spiritual or divine. Omnipotence, goodness and the cleverest equity are conceived for these extraordinary judgments. Imprecations are the personal expressions of them. There are also other imaginations of utopian justice for the defenceless, such as final judgments and signs attributed to divine providence.[109]

7 The Vindicatory Background in Criminal Law

The vindicatory legal system has embraced many societies and cultures. The normative universe of "primitive", ancient, medieval and contemporary traditional societies has been structured mainly by the vindicatory system. Both vindicatory and civil/criminal systems obey the fundamental needs and wishes of societies, but they fulfil them only partially, with limited possibilities in their separated developments. This separation has been historically necessary, since both systems follow remarkably different social conditions. Nevertheless, we can also see that both systems intersect. This is precisely due to the urge of societies to settle questions of law and justice for which these systems offer partial and limited solutions. Other quests—utopian philosophies—fall outside the facts of the effective social application of law and justice.

We can trace the basic distinction between vindicatory and criminal systems comparing their normative synthesis; vindicatory codes and compilations compared to criminal codes. In the vindicatory system (ancient and medieval), the classification of offences operates in terms of personal damages and their deserved reparations (the so-called "compositional tariffs" for the medieval codes). Whereas, in the criminal system, as evident in the key work of Beccaria, they appear as offences (crimes) and their deserved punishments or penalties. These classifications are correlated with the priority given to the offended party in taking action and getting satisfaction in the vindicatory system; and with the priority in the criminal system of

[107] See Madrid (2010a, b).

[108] See Abou-Zeid (1956).

[109] See Plutarch (2010) and Grégoire de Tours (1996).

determining the type of crime defined by the law and getting the culprit punished accordingly to this type.

In the criminal system, the right to damages comes afterwards as a "civil responsibility" created by the offence. Thus, when in the penal system the offended party—the victim's side—is perceived as diminished in action and satisfaction, and when the culprit's party is correlatively perceived as diminished in moral responsibility (substituted by criminal and material responsibility), there occurs a move towards what was badly lost from vindicatory cultures. But it would be ludicrous to turn backwards in history, since society has changed in several aspects. So, a new paradigm offers reform of the penal system, namely, restorative or reparative justice.

However, reforms to the criminal system aim at a new attention or regard towards the victim's side, and to address the offender in its full moral responsibility and consequent action (without being changed or consumed as a pure penal responsibility). These are fundamental objectives of vindicatory justice. Thus, the reform of the criminal system is a return to some basic values of vindicatory justice. This is why we can claim that it was badly lost. Even restorative justice cannot imagine all that has been lost in repudiating all vindicatory values. The dogmatic dismissal by the criminal ethos of the realities of vengeance, victimisation, defencelessness and of the indirect consequences of sentencing causes misunderstandings and unnoticed wrongs.

This is further aggravated by the individualist ethos of our society.[110] A symptom of the situation is brought about by the increasing demand of many professionals to cope with the individualist disarray that characterises our society. But theirs is not a sufficient effort to compensate for the solidarities and responsibilities collectively acted out. The loss of straightforward and effective solidarities cannot be matched by an inter-individual assistance achieved by contract.

On the other hand, we know especially well through the work of Beccaria and other writings,[111] how the vindicatory system had to be historically reformed and substituted by the penal one. Excesses in the discretional power of judges, which turned into arbitrary despotism, and the lack of equality and proportion in sentences asked for by law applied equally to all citizens of a nation. The cruel and inhuman proofs (ordeals),[112] interrogations (torture) and punishments (death with torment) led to the conception of the prison regime.

However, the essential distinction between vindicatory and criminal legal systems lies in the relationship between these systems and their associated societies.

[110]See Terradas Saborit (2010a).

[111]Although the reforms of the vindicatory system go back to the classical period of Athenian democracy and to the Roman Republic, we find their clearest expression facing a new penal system in the criticisms antedating the French Revolution. The Cahiers de doléances express particularly well the vices of the vindicatory system—although mixed with those of the absolute monarchy—asking for a systematic new legal order: constitutional, civil, and penal.

[112]The contamination and different abuses in the practice of ordeals were probably as old as the institution itself. Ibn-Munqidh (1929) was scandalised by the brutality of the Frankish performance of judicial battles in the period of the Crusades.

The vindicatory order applies well to societies where the parties in conflict are collective.[113] They are arranged in terms of collective solidarity and responsibility. Whereas the civil/criminal system applies much better to individualist societies where responsibility lies with the individual.

The reform of the criminal system envisages new roles for offenders and the offended that evoke their previous roles in the vindicatory system. Besides this, there are also other remarkable influences of the vindicatory system on the penal system. These refer to a background in which the moral values linked to vindicatory practices still exist. It is a phenomenon more characteristic of the legislation and jurisprudence of the nineteenth century. Still, they somewhat have retained their influence up to the present. I am currently studying these effects in Spanish legislation and jurisprudence. In these, there appears a sort of vindicatory background to the criminal system. It appears mainly in the extenuating and aggravating circumstances of criminal responsibility:

1. The criminal code excludes any right of vengeance, but there is a mitigating circumstance for criminal responsibility: the *Vindicación próxima de ofensa grave*. It means the vindication of a grave offence executed immediately after the offence. Spanish jurisprudence greatly restricted this extenuating circumstance of criminal responsibility. When applied, the criterion was manifold: that the offence was indeed serious; that it did not contravene legal and moral norms and values; that the reaction to vindicate followed the offence closely in time. Courts used this sparingly, but lawyers and public prosecutors persistently requested it. One of its paradigmatic solicitations and applications was in favour of husbands committing crimes against their adulterous wives.
2. The duel has been termed a "privileged crime". Various extenuations of criminal responsibility were granted to duels, if performed according to duelling norms and under the authority of the duel's godfathers. This appears clearly established in the Spanish Criminal Codes of 1848 and 1870 and confirmed at subsequent jurisprudence. These norms were clearly envisaged to conduct the duel with equality of arms, regular field measures, truthful behaviour by duellists, and a supervising authority. The duel's godfathers had the power to invalidate or sentence the duel in view of the duellists' actions. Thus, the duel was treated deferentially provided it was undertaken according to its rules. In this way, the criminal responsibility of the duellists was mitigated. Criminal law, in a way, "respected" the duel, when it was performed *comme il faut*, orderly. This legitimacy has clear antecedents in vindicatory procedures. These are the judicial battle and the right to conquer or recover one's rights by fighting. The respect for the hard action of defending honour and rights in valiant combat, without deceits or inequality of arms, allowed tolerance for duelling. The main difference between vindicatory combat and a modern duel lies in the ordalic nature of the

[113]Even when historically (usually due to colonisation) the indigenous judicial authorities which stood over the parties in conflict vanish, collective responsibility and collective meetings still settle conflicts. See Spencer (1959).

former and its legal and public process. Vindicatory combat was clearly sanctioned by a judicial authority, and it could involve the honours or causes of two authorities or collective entities. Besides, it could involve a ritual for wounding the offender (as in Australian cultures) or God's judgment (as in medieval Europe).[114] Whereas the singular duel usually involved only honours or causes exclusively related to two people and no supernatural power was invoked to assist the truth in question.

3. The moral and legal standing of treason. Treason is one of the most important crimes in vindicatory societies. It goes against the solidarity and reliance necessary for the economic and political undertakings of people based on corporate groups for work and exchange. Clanship, kindred loyalties and different sorts of community allegiance exclude egoistic attitudes, which easily arise in treachery. Also, allegiance to hierarchical authorities demands a loyalty for which treason is the antithesis. From the vindicatory order, treason is transferred to the criminal one with two main meanings. First, treason—as high treason—constitutes the chief political crime. Rebellion, sedition, conspiracy, defection, mutiny, insurrection and rioting are all equivalent to some sort of treason.[115] Second, treachery is what introduces inequality in a fight, combat or duel. Assassination is the most unequal method of killing somebody. The aggravating circumstance of *alevosía* (medieval *aleve*) stands for the treacherous homicide. It has been defined in the first penal codes—and is still defined—as an attack on a person performed in a way that takes most advantage of his or her defencelessness and ensures the efficacy of the aggression and avoids being attacked by the victim. Thus, treacherous homicide, murder, is a "fight" against another carried out in the most unfair and cowardly way. The background to judging the presence of treachery—*alevosía*—is vindicatory. Also, the unfaithfulness of the wife is judged as treason, and Blackstone[116] remembered the "petite treason" applied to the killing of the husband by his wife, evoking a regicide. The infidelity of the wife has justified all sorts of violence against her and leniency towards her husband, including her murder.
4. Righteous manslaughter[117] lies behind another mitigating circumstance for criminal responsibility: when the attack of the offender comes soon after a provocation or threat effectuated by the victim. It is something like the *Vindicación próxima de ofensa grave*; it also requires proximity in time. It has to be a quick and violent response to a threat or provocation. Again, the offence that provokes the criminal response has to be accepted by the legal and moral standards sustained by the law and the judges. In practice, it is like the *Vindicación próxima* but with a wider

[114] Warner (1937), Fustel de Coulanges (1889–1908), and Terradas Saborit (2008a).

[115] The *Siete Partidas* of Alfonso X retained 14 types of treason against the king.

[116] See Blackstone (1979).

[117] See Katz (1988).

field for its application and specificity regarding threats. Again, it involves a right to fight back in response to an attack, the right to engage in just combat or fair duel. The attempt at equilibrium in the fight is what mitigates the criminal responsibility. This also applies for the exemption of self-defence and legitimate defence of other persons. The requisite is always the same: the approach to fair combat; the use of proportionate means to repel the attack and the justification of the legal and moral value of what is defended (physical integrity of the person, property values, honour, authority, sacredness).

5. The role of a *vindex*.[118] In vindicatory societies, the figure of a *vindex* or vindicatory protector for kin, friends or community members is fundamental. The figure can be exerted collectively or individually, and looks out for the personal and social security of the protected. He can support them in many ways and in any conflict. This includes fighting for them vindictively. The vindicatory protector can be a brother in arms or a sworn brother. However, the figures that primarily are transferred to the penal law are fathers, tutors and husbands in respect to their sons, daughters and wives. Vindicatory action is transformed into penal action, maintaining the legal incapability of the protected/vindicated. Women constitute the case in point with whom subordination and protection/vindictiveness are exerted with the utmost zeal. The key offences relate to sexual matters. Fathers and tutors vindicate *estupro*,[119] dishonest abuses and husbands' adultery. Legally, they have penal and civil actions in relation to both crimes.

In the last decades of the twentieth century and up to the present, there has been a power transfer from patriarchal power (father and husband) to state power. This process has taken place during women's greater access to freedom and agency. Nonetheless, even feminists discuss the contradiction between apparent liberation from the patriarchy and state intervention in their lives. For, on the one hand, there is the demand of effective judicial protection (penal recognition of offences against women) and, on the other, there is a compromise with the right of women to enjoy life in freedom. But the reality is that women still are trapped in a patriarchy of

[118]In the vindicatory order, it corresponds to the Greek *timorós*, whose duties conform to general vindicatory issues. See Terradas Saborit (2008a, 2019). There is also the complementary figure of the *xevghaltis* or companion for truce; see Xanthakou (1993) p. 119 et passim.

[119]*Estupro* was defined as sexual intercourse with a woman above 12 years of age and below 23, performed by a public authority, a priest, a servant, a menial worker, a tutor, a teacher or person responsible for education and care of the victim. The punishment was between 6 months and 3 years in prison. Incestuous intercourse was also considered *estupro* even if the woman would be more than 23 years old. In addition, any man who had intercourse with a woman of the same age range (12–23) by deceit (*engaño*) also committed *estupro*. This was the most frequent case denounced by the father of a girl against a man that did not comply with the promise to marry when the woman became pregnant. Cf. Spanish Penal Code of 1870 and Leyes de Enjuiciamiento Criminal (1908).

proximity (fathers and husbands, and brothers and other relatives, depending on the society), and the security offered by the state cannot successfully ensure their independence. Partly, the state has taken over the role of vindication held beforehand by fathers and husbands. But, in doing so, the state did not overcome the criminal power of patriarchs and its intervention has been deemed unsatisfactory.

Thus, for instance, in Mexico the state is considered criminally responsible, mainly due to its negligence—if not as an accomplice—in handling gender violence and femicide.[120] Also, the state has been blamed for victimising, even more, the victims and treating them as incapable of solving their conflicts. From a point of view of *longue durée,* it could be said that the state is unable to solve women's problems because, with the transfer of patriarchal power and responsibility, it has also taken on patriarchal prejudices. Thus, the jurisprudence still reveals—although critical opponents exist—various prejudices against women.[121] Overall, it is difficult to overcome the political impasse in which women can easily feel trapped. The patriarchal control of their lives has been partly transferred to the state, with little gain of effective personal freedom of choice in facing conflicts. This is a sign of the limits of both vindicatory and criminal legal systems

Appendix: Synoptic Table of Vindicatory Justice

Vindicatory systems: core criteria. By Silvia Chiara Congiu, based on her thesis (Congiu 2019) University of Cagliari. silvia.chiara.congiu@tiscali.it

Essential features of the vindicatory system	Substance	Is it a basic characteristic of the vindicatory system?
1. Composition	Institute of ancient derivation, which was particularly studied in relation to the ancient German legal system. This system consisted of both reconciliation and a gift for reparation, the latter being a compensation for damages. The compensation for damages that the guilty (and his lineage) gives to the victim and/or his family should be enough to satisfy them and avoid the occurrence of vengeance and/or feuds. Composition is the general rule for dispute resolution in vindicatory systems. Only if it was not possible to	The presence of the legal institution of composition is necessary in order to consider a legal system as being vindicatory. Composition can, therefore, be considered the backbone of the entire vindicatory system. The expression 'vindicatory system' refers to composition. In fact, it was the Roman historian Publius Cornelius Tacitus who first used the verb *vindico* to describe the practice of Germanic composition—and not in reference to institutional vengeance.

(continued)

[120]See Padgett and Loza (2014) and Corte Interamericana de Derechos Humanos (2009).

[121]I am studying several biases against women's credibility, responsibility, strength of will and good faith in recent sentences.

Essential features of the vindicatory system	Substance	Is it a basic characteristic of the vindicatory system?
	use the composition (e.g. in the case of offences judged too outrageous, inexpiable or when an agreement was not reached between the families of the parties) were other 'legal' solutions used such as exile or, as *extrema ratio*, vengeance.	
2. The role of clans	Deliberation of a council, mainly composed of the elders of the lineages and constituting a 'vindicatory court', was implemented by the parties' families and in particular by the clan leaders of each party, who acted as 'legal representatives'. This involved an active role for both families in managing the resolution of the conflict. Thus, this procedure prevented the triggering of an endless chain of consequential counter-offences: namely, the so-called feud. What allowed the vindicatory systems to work, and to solve concrete cases, was the awareness of the 'collective responsibility' placed on the entire clan of the guilty. Members of the culprit's clan responded to the offence of their relative with all their wealth. There was no autonomy in assets among family members, in the event of a crime committed by a member of the lineage.	In all vindicatory systems, lineages played an essential role. We can define them as a '*longa manus*' of the vindicatory judicial authority, as they were responsible for carrying out those functions usually attributed to judicial corpus in legal systems. All clan negotiations and all legal solutions that could be practised (even vengeance) had to be authorised by the court. So, these were not instances of private negotiations (typically private vengeance) but judicially authorised actions adopted or practised by the families of the parties. The collective responsibility had two important consequences: First, as a mechanism of self-control among all members of the lineage that served as a deterrent to offences. Second, the offended party and his family were confident that they could obtain satisfaction to their 'compensation claims'.
3. The vindicatory court	In all vindicatory systems (as well as in legal systems in general) there was a need for a person or more frequently a college of elders to elect a 'third-party' to resolve disputes arising between members of society. Usually, judges were elders from the lineages involved in the dispute, although in some cases an 'arbitrator' was found among foreign clans or tribes. In all cases, the judges played their role impartially. They were responsible for: (1) Ascertaining the fulfilment of a crime. (2) Ensuring that the offence had actually been provoked by the 'accused' person.	A vindicatory court and a judge (or judges) were always required in vindicatory systems. Otherwise, all negotiations carried out by the parties would have been an expression of private justice, and not expressions of a legal system. There are cases—for example, the vindicatory system of Barbagia—in which due to the incompleteness of the sources, it is difficult to reconstruct the role and the figure of the vindicatory court. However, it is unthinkable that legal solutions would apply without a judge. There is always a need for a historical reconstruction to

(continued)

Essential features of the vindicatory system	Substance	Is it a basic characteristic of the vindicatory system?
	(3) Pronouncing a judicial decision. The judges handed down the sentence only after having heard from both sides and tried to settle the conflict with composition. Often, the judicial 'vindicatory' decisions were enacted by clans. For example, if the judge ordered vengeance, this was usually perpetrated by the offended party's family.	better know the development and the erosion of vindicatory institutions.
4. The vindicatory trial	If we search for law in vindicatory systems, we should first look for the trial. Indeed, in the vindicatory system, it is not for the law to create (and regulate) trial, but vice versa. Vindicatory systems followed the test case-rule (with variations depending on the specific system). Vindicatory systems are led by unwritten and customary sources according to which judgment and resolution of the case instantiate the 'creation of law'. Starting from that judgement, a rule will be created and passed down orally from generation to generation. In vindicatory systems, there was then a fusion between 'action' and 'procedure'. To consider 'action' as something separated from 'procedure' seems more a semantic custom of Roman derivation rather than an ontological necessity. Actions are instruments through which it was possible to instruct a procedure that allowed the parties to obtain justice, through a public and standardised trial, without having to resort to private justice. In vindicatory systems, the figure of the offended party was a key one, so that the vindicatory procedure was aimed at emphasising the capacity of the action and the trial to promote the protection of the offended party.	The trial is a characteristic of all vindicatory systems, as in all legal systems. The judge complies with his role by pronouncing a *formula*, considered a new proposition of justice or *resolutio*. A key feature of the vindicatory trial is the prediction of solutions that today, through the lens of modern jurisprudence, may seem a part of the world of out-of-court settlements of disputes. In fact, vengeance and composition were solutions authorised by the trial and the judge. They were then not an alternative to judgement, but part of it.
5. Vengeance	It is appropriate to distinguish 'legal' and 'social' vengeance (vengeance as an institution) from vengeance as brute instinct (vengeance as a subjective feeling). In vindicatory systems,	Vengeance is a residual institution of vindicatory justice, which means that the presence of vengeance alone is not enough to consider a system as vindicatory. In fact, a vindicatory

(continued)

Essential features of the vindicatory system	Substance	Is it a basic characteristic of the vindicatory system?
	the existence and social importance of instinctive vengeance is not to be excluded. Vindicatory systems show less hypocrisy than state systems in admitting that even instinctive vengeance may have a role in the quest for justice. But vindicatory systems try to transform the instinct of revenge into reconciliation; or, alternatively, to admit the irreparability of offence—its enormous gravity—and to authorise a special kind of punishment that—given the centrality of the offended party in the vindicatory procedure—can be called 'vengeance'. Revenge is then an inevitable consequence of the offence, not intended as a harm to the individual, but as a harm to the community. However, in any legal system (state or vindicatory), it is always necessary to set limits to vengeance. If there were no limits, there would have been situations of inevitable drift: the endless feud. The possibility to practise vengeance is, in the vindicatory systems, subject to a judicial authorisation by the vindicatory court. Authorised vengeance is a controlled practice characterised by proportion, prudence and progression. Authorised vengeance is inspired by the principle of 'the least possible harm'.	system is always defined by the presence of composition. There is an ethnocentric prejudice that prevents lawyers and legal theorists from considering vengeance as a legal institution. Many scholars believe that vengeance is antithetical to law. This is because many of them focus on the analysis of instinctive revenge, mistakenly deeming this to be the backbone of the vindicatory system, excluding the role of composition. To think that vengeance is the fundamental institution of vindicatory justice is as flawed as arguing that the death penalty or life imprisonment is the fundamental institution of criminal law-systems.
6. The way to peace	The ultimate goal of vindicatory legal systems is to resolve conflicts and restore peace between factions. For this reason, it is important that in cases where vengeance is enacted, it is proportionate, prudent and progressive. In fact, if vengeance cannot be controlled, it is no longer possible to restore peace.	All vindicatory systems have 'a peaceful soul', because otherwise an endless feud would be triggered. Endless or massive feuds lead to genocides of clans, communities and even tribes. This has happened in history, but it deviates from the aims of vindicatory justice, as well as deviating from the aims of criminal law justice.

References

Abou-Zeid AM (1956) The great oasis: a study of the social institutions of El-Kharga. D. Phil. Thesis. Bodleian Library, Oxford
Aljoxami (Al-Jusani) (1914) Historia de los jueces de Córdoba. EAUSA, Granada
Allen DS (2000) The world of Prometheus. The politics of punishment in democratic Athens. PUP, Princeton
Aramayo R (2001) Spanish version of Schopenhauer, A. Metafísica de las costumbres, Trotta, Madrid
Assier-Andrieu L (1981) Coutume et rapports sociaux. CNRS, Paris
Assier-Andrieu L (1987) Le peuple et la loi. LGDJ, Paris
Assier-Andrieu L (1996) Le Droit dans les sociétés humaines. Nathan, Paris
Assier-Andrieu L (2001) Penser le temps culturel du droit. Le destin anthropologique du concept de coutume. L'Homme 160:67–90
Assier-Andrieu L (2011) L'autorité du passé. Essai anthropologique sur la Common Law. Dalloz, Paris
Bachofen JJ (1996) Le Droit Maternel. Recherche sur la Gynécocratie de l'Antiquité dans sa nature religieuse et juridique. L'Age d'Homme, Lausanne
Batos M et al (eds) (2005) Justiça Restaurativa. PNUD, Brasilia
Beccaria C (1994) Dei delitti e delle pene. Tascabili Economici Newton, Roma
Bensaïd D (2007) Les dépossédés. Karl Marx, les voleurs de bois et le droit des pauvres. La fabrique, Paris
Betti E (1915) Il Filangieri. Società Editrice Libraria, Milano
Black-Michaud J (1975) Feuding societies. Basil Blackwell, Oxford
Blackstone W (1979) Commentaries on the laws of England. The University of Chicago Press, Chicago
Bobbio N (1984) Giusnaturalismo e positivismo giuridico. Edizioni di Comunità, Milano
Bogoras V (1904) The Chuckchee. Brill, New York
Cantarella E (2007) Il ritorno della vendetta. Pena di morte: giustizia o assassinio? Rizzoli, Milano
Carey C (1997) Trials from classical Athens. Routledge, London
Colman RV (1974) Reason and unreason in early medieval law. J Interdiscip Hist 4:571–591
Comaroff J, Roberts S (1977) The invocation of norms in dispute settlement: the Tswana Case. In: Hamnett I (ed) Social anthropology and law. Academic Press, London
Congiu S Ch (2019) La giustizia vendicatoria ed il sistema vendicatorio in Ignasi Terradas Saborit. Tesi di Laurea. University of Cagliari, Cagliari
Corte Interamericana de Derechos Humanos (2009) Caso González y otras ('Campo algodonero') vs. México. Sentencia de 16 de Noviembre, 2009
Costa J (1908) El problema de la ignorancia del derecho y sus relaciones: el status individual, el referéndum y la costumbre. Soler, Barcelona
Costa J et al (1902) Derecho consuetudinario y economía popular de España. Soler, Barcelona
Deacon B (1934) Malekula. A vanishing people in the new hebrides. Routledge, London
Dennis A et al (1980) Laws of early Iceland. University of Manitoba Press, Winnipeg
Détienne M (2000) Comparer l'incomparable. Seuil, Paris
Di Lucia P (1997) L'universale della promessa. Giuffrè, Milano
Di Lucia P (2010a) Le due vendette. In: Piga G, Pulina G (eds) La ricerca di Antonio Pigliaru (1922–1969) sulla vendetta barbaricina. Nuova Tipografia Popolare, Pavia, pp 67–74
Di Lucia P (2010b) Cómo hacer reglas con cosas. In: Di Lucia P (ed) Derecho, lenguaje, acción. Fontamara, México, pp 25–36
Di Lucia P, Mancini L (2015) La Giustizia vendicatoria. ETS, Pisa
Du Toit L (2007) Feminism and the ethics of reconciliation. www.eurozine.com/articles/2007-03-16-dutoit-en.html. Last accessed 4 Feb 2020
Elwin V (1939) The Baiga. Murray, London

Evans-Pritchard EE (1969) The Nuer. A description of the modes of livelihood and political institutions of a Nilotic People. OUP, New York
Fassin D (2017) Punir: une passion contemporaine. Seuil, Paris
Fezas J (1991) Malédictions, Imprécations, Ordalies et Serments dans la tradition juridique indienne. In: Verdier R (ed) Le Serment. CNRS, Paris
Firth R (1959) Social change in Tikopia. Allen, London
Firth R (1965) Primitive polynesian economy. Routledge, London
Fison L, Howitt W (1991) Kamilaroi and Kurnai. Robertson & Spencer, Melbourne
Fletcher R (2002) Bloodfeud. Murder and Revenge in Anglo-Saxon England. Penguin, London
Fortes M (1987) Religion, morality and the person. CUP, Cambridge
Frank J (1949) Courts on trial. Myth and reality in American Justice. PUP, Princeton
Fustel de Coulanges DN (1889–1908) Histoire des Institutions Politiques de l'Ancienne France. Hachette, Paris
Fustel de Coulanges DN (1984) La Cité Antique. Flammarion, Paris
Gagarin M (1981) Drakon and early athenian homicide law. Yale UP, New Haven
Gernet L (1982) Droit et institutions en Grèce antique. Flammarion, Paris
Gibbs JL (1973) Two forms of dispute settlement among the Kpelle of West Africa. In: Black D, Mileski M (eds) The social organization of law. Seminar Press, New York
Gillen FJ (1899) The native tribes of Central Australia. Macmillan, London
Ginat J (1997) Blood revenge. Family honor, mediation and outcasting. SAP, Portland
Glotz G (1904a) La solidarité de la famille dans le droit criminel en Grèce. Fontemoing, Paris
Glotz G (1904b) L'ordalie dans la Grèce primitive. Fontemoing, Paris
Glotz G (1988) La cité grecque. Michel, Paris
Gluckman M (1963) The reasonable man in Barotse Law. Order and rebellion in tribal Africa. The Free Press, New York
Gluckman M (1964) Closed systems and open minds: the limits of naivety in social anthropology. Oliver & Boyd, Edinburgh
Gluckman M (1965a) Custom and conflict in Africa. Basil Blackwell, Oxford
Gluckman M (1965b) The ideas in Barotse jurisprudence. Yale UP, New Haven
Gluckman M (1967) The judicial process among the Barotse of Northern Rhodesia. MUP, Manchester
Gluckman M (ed) (1972) The allocation of responsibility. MUP, Manchester
Gómez Mestres S (2005) Ordre i conflicte en terres catalanes de frontera (1799-1850). Universitat de Lleida, Lleida
Grégoire de Tours (1996) Historiae Francorum in Patrologiae Cursus Completus. Accurante J.-P-Migne, Book VII: XLVII, etc
Gulliver PH (1972) Dispute settlement without courts: the Ndendeuli of Southern Tanzania. In: Nader L (ed) Law in culture and society. Aldine, Chicago, pp 24–68
Gulliver PH (1977) On mediators. In: Hamnett I (ed) Social anthropology and law. Academic Press, London, pp 47–78
Hayden RM (1999) Disputes and arguments among Nomads. OUP, Oxford
Hinojosa E (1915) El elemento germánico en el derecho español, Madrid
Holý L (1974) Neighbours and Kinsmen. A Study of the Berti People of Darfur. St. Martin's Press, New York
Holý L (1991) Religion and custom in a Muslim society. The Berti of Sudan. CUP, Cambridge
Ibn-Munqidh U (1929) An Arab-Syrian gentleman and warrior in the period of the crusades. Columbia University Press, New York
Just P (2001) Dou Donggo justice. Conflict and morality in an Indonesian society. Rowman & Littlefield, Oxford
Katz J (1988) Seductions of crime. Basic Books, New York
Kelsen H (2000) Lineamenti di dottrina pura del diritto. Einaudi, Torino
Kelsen H (2015) Che cos'è la giustizia? Lezioni americane. In: Di Lucia P, Passerini Glazel L (eds) Quodlibet, Macerata

Kropotkine P (1901) L'organisation de la vindicte appelée Justice. Les Temps Nouveaux, Paris
Kuhn TS (1996) The structure of scientific revolutions. Chicago UP, Chicago
Leyes de Enjuiciamiento Criminal y del Jurado (1908) El Consultor, Madrid
Lightowlers C, Quirk H (2014) The 2011 English "Riots": prosecutorial zeal and judicial abandon. Br J Criminol 55:65–85
Llewellyn K (1962) Jurisprudence. Realism in theory and practice. The University of Chicago Press, Chicago
Llewellyn K, Hoebel EA (1941) The Cheyenne Way. Conflict and case law in primitive jurisprudence. University of Oklahoma Press, Norman
López Jimeno A (2001) Textos griegos de maleficio. Akal, Madrid
Lorini G (2010) Antonio Pigliaru, filosofo della giuridicità. In: Pigaa G, Pulina G (eds) La ricerca di Antonio Pigliaru (1922-1969) sulla vendetta barbaricina. Nuova Tipografia Popolare, Pavia, pp 75–81
Machiavelli N (1977) Il Principe e Discorsi. Feltrinelli, Milano
Madrid A (2010a) El acceso a los derechos: la experiencia del Proyecto dret al Dret. Anuario de Filosofía del Derecho 2:32–56
Madrid A (2010b) La política y la justicia del sufrimiento. Trotta, Madrid
Maine HS (1871) village communities in the east and west. Murray, London
Maine HS (1965) Ancient law. Dent, London
Malinowski B (1929) The sexual life of savages in North-Western Melanesia. Eugenics, New York
Malinowski B (1935) Coral gardens and their magic. American Book Company, New York
Malinowski B (1947) Crime and custom in savage society. Kegan Paul, London
Malinowski B (1978) Argonauts of the Western Pacific. Routledge & Kegan Paul, London
Mauss M (1950) Essai sur le Don. PUF, Paris
Mauss M (1967) Manuel d'Ethnographie. Payot, Paris
Mayerfeld J (2007) Playing by our own rules: how U.S. marginalization of international human rights law led to torture. Harv Hum Rights J 20:89–140
Mazzola R (2018) Indigenous intellectual property: a conceptual analysis. Franco Angeli, Milano
McLennan JF (1970) Primitive marriage. The University of Chicago Press, Chicago
Merry SE (2006) Anthropology and international law. Annu Rev Anthropol 35:99–116
Miller WI (1990) Bloodtaking and peacemaking. Feud, law, and society in Saga Iceland. The University of Chicago Press, Chicago
Moore SF (2001) Certainties undone: fifty turbulent years of legal anthropology. J R Anthropol Inst 7:95–116
Morgan LH (1870) Systems of consanguinity and affinity of the human family. Smithsonian, Washington DC
Morgan LH (1962) League of the Iroquois. Citadel Press, New York
Morgan LH (1995) Ancient society. The University of Arizona Press, Tucson
Morris A (2002) Critiquing the critics. A brief response to critics of restorative justice. Br J Criminol 42:596–615
Orestano R (1967) I fatti di normazione nell'esperienza romana arcaica. Giappichelli, Torino
Orestano R (1978) Azione, Diritti soggettivi, Persone giuridiche. Il Mulino, Bologna
Padgett H, Loza E (2014) Las muertas del Estado. Grijalbo, México
Paliero CE (2018) Il sogno di Clitennestra: Mitologia della pena. Pensieri scettici su modernità e archeologia del punire. Rivista italiana di diritto e procedura penale 61:1121–1213
Peters E (1990) The Bedouin of Cyrenaica. Studies in personal and corporate power. CUP, Cambridge
Pigliaru A (1975) Il Banditismo in Sardegna. La vendetta barbaricina come ordinamento giuridico. Giuffrè, Milano
Pinto R (2005) en Batos, M. et al. (orgs.) Justiça Restaurativa, MJ y PNUD, Brasilia
Pitrè G (2016) Il linguaggio dei gesti in Sicilia. Antares, Palermo
Plutarch (2010) Sur les délais de la justice divine. Les Belles Lettres, Paris

Polanyi K (1965) The economy as instituted process. In: Polanyi K et al (eds) Trade and market in the early empires. The Free Press, New York, pp 1–19
Polanyi K (1994) El sustento del hombre. Mondadori, Barcelona
Polanyi K, Arensberg C, Pearson H (eds) (1965) Trade and market in the early empires, 2nd edn. The Free Press, New York
Preuve L (1963) Recueils de la Société Jean Bodin. Librairie Encyclopèdique, Brussel
Radcliffe-Brown AR (1964) The Andaman Islanders. The Free Press, New York
Ramis Barceló R (2015) En torno a la antropología jurídica romana. Revista de Antropología Social 24:201–219
Rascón García C, García González JM (1996) Ley de las XII Tablas. Tecnos, Madrid
Rosés Tubau M (2013) Responsabilitats adjudicades, compromisos heretats. PhD Thesis. Universitat de Barcelona
Rospabé P (1995) La Dette de vie. La Découverte, Paris
Rutter O (2007) The Pagans of North Borneo. Opus, Deacon
Sacco R (1985) Le grandi linee del sistema giuridico somalo. Giuffrè, Milano
Salas D (2005) La Volonté de punir, essai sur le populisme penal. Hachette, Paris
Salas D (2012) La justice dévoyée. Critique des utopies sécuritaires. Éd. Des Arènes, Paris
Salis LR (1973) Leges Burgundionum. En Monumenta Germaniae Historica. Leges, Hannover
Satta S (2004) Soliloqui e colloqui di un giurista. Ilisso Edizioni, Nuoro
Satta S (2013) Il Mistero del Processo, 2nd edn. Adelphi, Milano
Schapera I (1966) Married life in an African tribe. Faber & Faber, London
Schapera I (1977) A handbook of Tswana law and custom, 2nd edn. Frank Cass, London
Schopenhauer A (2001) Metafísica de las costumbres. Trotta, Madrid. See Aramayo
Skorupski J (1978) The meaning of another culture' beliefs. In: Hookway C, Pettit P (eds) Action and interpretation. CUP, Cambridge, pp 83–106
Slyomovics S (2011) American "Blood Money" and a question of reparations. Middle East Rep 259:44–46
Spencer R (1959) The North Alaskan Eskimo. Smithsonian, Washington DC
Srinivas MN (1991) The remembered village. OUP, New Dehli
Tacitus (1970) Germania. In: Hutton M (ed) Loeb Classical Library, Boston
Tamassia N (1964a) Scritti di Storia Giuridica. CEDAM, Padova
Tamassia N (1964b) Il diritto nell'epica francese dei secoli XII e XIII. In Scritti di Storia Giuridica. CEDAM, Padova, pp 46–97
Terradas Saborit I (2008a) Justicia Vindicatoria. De la ofensa e indefensión a la imprecación y el oráculo, la vindicta y el talión, la ordalía y el juramento, la composición y la reconciliación. CSIC, Madrid
Terradas Saborit I (2008b) La construcción primitiva de la identidad sucesoria y la génesis de la ordalía. Anuario da Facultade de Dereito da Universidade da Coruña 12:965–985
Terradas Saborit I (2010a) Limits and possibilities of restorative justice. Presented at the 6th Biennial Conference, European Forum for Restorative Justice, Bilbao
Terradas Saborit I (2010b) Antropología jurídica: costumbres y conflictos. In: Arévalo JM et al (eds) Nos-otros: miradas antropológicas sobre la diversidad. Asamblea de Extremadura, Mérida, pp 609–623
Terradas Saborit I (2014) Giovanni (Nino) Tamassia y la Jurisprudencia Vindicatoria. Sociologia del Diritto 41:57–94
Terradas Saborit I (2016) La Etnografía del Procedimiento vindicatorio. In: Mármol C (ed) Compromisos etnográficos. Un homenaje a Joan Frigolé. UB, Barcelona, pp 65–96
Terradas Saborit I (2017) Sir Wilfrid Grigson (1896-1948) Juez y Etnólogo. Casos juzgados. Justicia vindicatoria y Código penal de la India colonial. Ius Fugit 20:265–299
Terradas Saborit I (2019) La justicia más Antigua. CSIC, Madrid
Torrens M (2013) Pagesos del Post-Socialisme. Un Estudi de Comunitat a Transilvània, PhD Thesis. Universitat Autónoma de Barcelona, Bellaterra
Twining W (1985) Karl Llewellyn and the realist movement. Weidenfeld & Nicolson, London

Verdier R (1980) Introduction: le système vindicatoire. In: Verdier R (ed) La vengeance. Cujas, Paris, pp 1–21
Verdier R et al (2004) Vengeance. Le face-à-face victime/agresseur. Autrement, Paris
Vinogradoff P (1913) Common sense in law. Williams & Norgate, London
Vinogradoff P (1922) The jurisprudence of the Greek City. OUP, Oxford
Waldmann P (2001) Revenge without rules: on the renaissance of an Archaic Motif of violence. Stud Confl Terrorism 24:435–450
Warner WL (1937) A black civilization. A social study of an Australian Tribe. Harper & Brothers, New York
Winch P (1972) Ethics and action. Routledge & Kegan Paul, London
Wittgenstein L (1971) Remarks on Frazer's "Golden Bough". In: Miles AC, Rhees R (eds) The Human World, Oxford
Wittgenstein L (1980) Remarks on the philosophy of psychology. Basil Blackwell, Oxford
Wittgenstein L (1981a) Philosophical investigations. Basil Blackwell, Oxford
Wittgenstein L (1981b) Zettel. Basil Blackwell, Oxford
Xanthakou M (1993) Mémoires Grecques. Hachette, Paris
Xifaras M (2002) Marx, Justice et Jurisprudence. Une lecture des "Vols de Bois". Revue Française d'Histoire des Idées Politiques 15:63–112
Young IM (2011) Responsabilidad para la Justicia. Morata-Paideia, Madrid

Hans Kelsen's Philosophy of Revenge

Paolo Di Lucia and Lorenzo Passerini Glazel

Abstract Hans Kelsen devoted significant attention to "primitive" law, particularly to the phenomenon of blood revenge. His analysis of blood revenge bears witness to the intent to offer a general theory of law, in all its different manifestations. Such a theory, far from being restricted to the centralized legal systems of modern states, also accounts for more decentralized legal systems, including those of "primitive," stateless societies and international law. The present chapter develops both an analysis of Kelsen's sociological and anthropological works on revenge and an examination of the role that revenge played in his famous pure theory of law.

1 Primitive Law As a Completely Decentralized Legal Order Based on Blood Revenge

1.1 Blood Revenge Systems As the Earliest Form of Law

Hans Kelsen's pure theory of law is often regarded as a powerful theory for describing the highly centralized and hierarchically structured law of modern states. However, it is sometimes considered less suitable for giving an account of more "primitive" legal orders, where neither the production of legal norms nor the imposition of sanctions is of exclusive competence of specific centralized organs, such as parliaments or courts.

This article is the joint work of two authors. Paragraphs 1 and 2 were written by Paolo Di Lucia, while paragraphs 3 and 4 were authored by Lorenzo Passerini Glazel. The authors assume responsibility for the statements made.

P. Di Lucia (✉)
Department of Legal Sciences "Cesare Beccaria", Faculty of Law, University of Milan, Milan, Italy
e-mail: paolo.dilucia@unimi.it

L. Passerini Glazel
School of Law, University of Milan - Bicocca, Milan, Italy
e-mail: lorenzo.passerini@unimib.it

R. Márquez Porras et al. (eds.), *Vindicatory Justice*, Ius Gentium: Comparative Perspectives on Law and Justice 93, https://doi.org/10.1007/978-3-030-79595-5_2

Kelsen, however, devoted great attention to primitive law, notably to the phenomenon of blood revenge.[1] The analysis of blood revenge bears witness to Kelsen's specific intention to offer a theory of not only the law of modern states but also law in general, in all of its different manifestations; a theory that would be capable of accounting also for more decentralized legal systems, including those of primitive, stateless societies and international law, non secondarily.

According to Kelsen, primitive societies based on the principle of blood revenge exhibit at an early stage the essential features of a legal order. Their relatively simple normative system, relying exclusively on self-help for the application of sanctions, can be considered the earliest form of law, or a law *in statu nascendi*,[2] and interestingly enough, it constitutes for Kelsen a paradigm for construing the international law of his time.[3]

1.2 *Law As a Social Technique of Indirect Motivation Based on Coercive Sanctions*

Kelsen maintains that, "despite the vast differences that exist between the law of ancient Babylon and that of the United States of today, between the law of the Ashantis in West Africa and that of the Swiss in Europe," there is a common element that justifies the use of the word "law" with reference to all of these phenomena. This common element is "the specific social technique of a coercive order," that is, "the social technique which consists in bringing about the desired social conduct of men through the threat of a measure of coercion which is to be executed in case of contrary conduct."[4]

Such a social technique is one of *indirect* motivation of behavior: rather than directly prescribing the desired behavior, legal norms provide a sanction for the behavior that is contrary to the desired one. This indirect technique distinguishes law from other normative orders, such as morality, that rather adopt a technique of *direct* motivation, wherein the desired behavior is simply prescribed, without the provision of specific sanctions in the case of contrary behavior. To prevent theft, for instance, "morality says, thou shalt not steal. The law says, if one steals, he shall be punished."[5]

---

[1]This is testified not only by the publication of works like *L'âme et le droit* (1935–1936), *Vergeltung und Kausalität* (1941b), and *Society and Nature* (1943) but also by the fact that one of the courses he taught at the University of California, Berkeley, between 1942 and 1952, was titled "Origins of Legal Institutions." See Kelsen ([1947]2008), p. 137.

[2]Kelsen (1942), p. 51.

[3]See in particular Kelsen (1942).

[4]Kelsen (1942), pp. 7–8.

[5]Kelsen (1941a), p. 87.

Kelsen distinguishes between negative sanctions and positive sanctions. The former consist in a disadvantage threatened in case of disobedience, whereas the latter consist in an advantage (a reward) promised in case of obedience. According to Kelsen, however, positive sanctions play only a secondary role in society, and mainly in the private relations of individuals. As far as the social organization of the group is concerned, "essentially only one method of bringing about socially desired behavior is taken into account: the threat and the application of an evil in case of contrary behavior."[6]

Law is thus for Kelsen a social technique based on negative sanctions, that is, on the threat of a measure of coercion generally consisting in "a deprivation of possessions—life, health, freedom, or property."[7]

From this perspective, the "two fundamental facts of the law" are, for Kelsen, delict and sanction. One of the essential features of law is the connection established by legal norms between a delict and a sanction. Legal norms can ultimately be reduced, according to Kelsen, to the logical form: "If there is *A* (a delict), then there ought to be *B* (a sanction)."

The earliest form of legal sanction was, for Kelsen, blood revenge, a form of sanction that is applied through self-help, that is, in a completely decentralized manner. The execution of sanction is delegated to all individuals of the social group whose interests, protected by the law, have been violated. Nonetheless, Kelsen maintains,

> it is entirely justifiable to call the still decentralized coercive social order of primitive society by the name of law, in spite of its rather crude technique; for this decentralized order constitutes the first step in an evolution that ultimately leads to the law of the state, a centralized coercive order.[8]

2 Kelsen's Account of Blood Revenge from a Sociological and Anthropological Perspective: Blood Revenge As a Social Phenomenon

Kelsen investigated the phenomenon of revenge in the context of not only his pure theory of law but also his sociological and anthropological works, such as *Society and Nature* (1943), which were devoted to the analysis of "certain ideas existing in men's mind that operate as causes of their behavior."[9] Among such ideas are the principle of retribution (the idea that if you behave rightly, you ought to be rewarded;

[6]Kelsen (1945a), p. 18.
[7]Kelsen (1941a), p. 78.
[8]Kelsen (1942), p. 51.
[9]Kelsen (1945b), p. XIV.

if you behave wrongly, you ought to be punished) and one of its manifestations, the principle of vengeance and more specifically blood revenge.[10]

In *Society and Nature*, Kelsen challenges the theories of revenge that consider it the expression of a mere instinctive reflex of self-preservation that is based on a natural desire for aggression.[11]

2.1 The Subjective Aspect of the Social Character of Revenge

For Kelsen, revenge is characterized by "the intent not only to parry the evil but also to inflict an evil in turn, either on the 'author' of the evil or on someone associated with him who is thus regarded as collectively responsible."[12] Kelsen claims that the intent to inflict "an evil in turn" implies a "direction against the culprit" and thus reveals the social character of vengeance as something different from a mere instinctive reflex of self-preservation.

In what sense, however, do the intent to inflict an evil in turn and the direction against the culprit imply a social character of revenge?

Kelsen distinguishes two aspects of the social character of vengeance: a *subjective* and an *objective* one.

The *subjective* aspect concerns the relationship between the injurer and the injured party. For Kelsen, the injured party experiences a specific feeling of inferiority toward the injurer, aroused by sustained evil. Revenge is motivated by the attempt to neutralize this feeling of inferiority "by placing the injurer in the situation of the injured."[13]

Such motivation is more than a reflex of self-preservation because it implies "a sense of value" that exists between the parties, and according to Kelsen, this relationship that implies a sense of value is possible only in a society.[14]

---

[10]Kelsen famously develops his pure theory of law as a science of law exclusively devoted to the knowledge of law and based on the methodological principle of the exclusion of all extraneous elements and contamination from different sciences, such as psychology, biology, ethics, and sociology. However, Kelsen clarifies that "the pure theory of law has never claimed to be the only possible or legitimate science of law" and recognizes that the sociology of law and the history of law and other sciences "are necessary for a complete understanding of the complex phenomenon of law" (Kelsen 1948, p. 383). *Society and Nature* is ascribable to one of Kelsen's lifelong projects of research devoted to a sociological analysis of the idea of justice. Besides *Society and Nature*, Kelsen wrote a manuscript titled "Sociology of the Belief in the Soul" that remains unpublished (See Kelsen [1947]2008, p. 137; Nitsch 2009, p. LXII).

[11]Kelsen's main polemic targets in *Society and Nature* are Rudolf Steinmetz and Edward Westermarck.

[12]Kelsen (1943), p. 49.

[13]Kelsen (1943), p. 50.

[14]Kelsen (1943), p. 50.

2.2 *The Objective Aspect of the Social Character of Revenge*

In addition to the subjective aspect of the social character of revenge, Kelsen underlines an even more relevant *objective* aspect, which more directly involves the relationships between the parties and their respective social groups. This objective social character is testified by four specific features of revenge highlighted by Kelsen.

The *first* feature is related to the notion of collective responsibility.

In revenge systems, the responsibility for an unjust evil is not limited to the author of the evil; it is extended instead to the other members of their family or social group, which is linked to the collectivistic mentality that is typical of primitive societies, according to Kelsen. This mentality causes the act of revenge not to be directed necessarily against the author of the evil but against another member of their family or group as well.

The collectivistic mentality of primitive societies is linked as well to the *second* feature of revenge: revenge "is always more or less accompanied by the feeling that [...] one's own injury is indirectly an injury to the other members of the group as well."[15]

Thus, the injury is not only *subjectively* perceived as an unjust evil but also *objectively* considered an unjust evil within the social group. Indeed, on the presupposition that "the evil arousing the reaction has been unjustly inflicted" and that it then constitutes "a breach of a social norm," revenge can be applied in accordance with the social principle of retribution.[16]

This leads to the *third* feature of revenge: revenge "can be explained objectively by its preventive effect." Revenge has the objective function of preventing the iteration of the behavior that is socially considered unjust. Such a preventive function is possible, for Kelsen, "only in the relationship between individuals living together socially."[17]

It is certainly not necessary for the avenging individual to *subjectively* aim at such an effect; nonetheless, through their revenge, the individual indirectly fulfills the *objective* social function of revenge, which is to prevent the iteration of the behavior considered unjust. As Kelsen clarifies, "it is always not only an individual but also a collective interest which is satisfied by vengeance in a primitive society."[18]

It is particularly in this sense that Kelsen considers blood revenge the earliest form of the social technique of law, consisting in "bringing about the desired social conduct of men through the threat of a measure of coercion which is to be executed in case of contrary conduct."[19]

---

[15]Kelsen (1943), p. 55.

[16]Kelsen (1943), pp. 50–51.

[17]Kelsen (1943), p. 50.

[18]Kelsen (1943), p. 55.

[19]Kelsen (1942), pp. 7–8.

This finally leads to the *fourth* feature of revenge: vengeance is also "more or less accompanied by the feeling that it is approved or even demanded by the members of the group."[20] This is proved, for instance, by the fact that the avenger is not necessarily the individual who was directly injured by the evil. This is particularly clear in the case of blood revenge, which is the sanction provided for murder. The victim obviously cannot execute the revenge; therefore, it is the duty of their relatives to avenge them.

In his reconstruction of blood revenge, Kelsen in fact attributes the utmost importance to the belief in the soul, for as he highlights, originally, the soul of the victim *demands* that their relatives avenge their death. This demand is strengthened by the soul of the victim through the threat of a retaliation against their relatives in case they omit to accomplish revenge. Thus, Kelsen claims, "it is more the fear of the 'revengeful' soul of the dead than the thirst for revenge which urges the relatives to revenge."[21]

This also explains, according to Kelsen, the phenomenon of sham vengeance and that of substitutive vengeance. Notably, in sham revenge—which can hardly satisfy the thirst for revenge—the party who has the duty to revenge "by various means feigns to the superhuman authority which has urged him to vengeance against his inclinations and interests, that he has fulfilled his obligations."[22]

Blood revenge, thus, shows, on the one hand, that there is not only a social *approval* of revenge but also a specific social *duty* for the relatives of the victim to revenge. On the other hand, it consequently proves, for Kelsen, that revenge proceeding from individuals who are not directly affected by the murder "is more a conscious action, determined by social norms, than a reflex movement caused by strong feelings of pain."[23]

3 Kelsen's Account of Revenge in the Pure Theory of Law: Blood Revenge As a Normative Phenomenon

As we have seen, Kelsen's anthropological and sociological analysis of revenge shows revenge as not only a social but also a normative phenomenon, one that presupposes the violation of a social norm and is authorized (or prescribed) by social

---

[20]Kelsen (1942), p. 55.

[21]Kelsen (1943), p. 307. Kelsen devoted specific attention to the fact that, originally, the legal order of blood revenge was mixed and intertwined with the religious order. While the social norm that threatens—and thus authorizes—the execution of revenge by human beings belongs to the legal order, the norm that threatens a sanction from some supernatural being in the case of omission of revenge—and thus prescribes the obligation to revenge—belongs to the religious order. See, for instance, Kelsen (1945a), pp. 16–17; ([1949]2015), p. 90.

[22]Kelsen (1943), p. 307.

[23]Kelsen (1943), p. 307.

norms. Such normative dimension of revenge is more thoroughly investigated by Kelsen within the framework of the pure theory of law.[24]

3.1 Blood Revenge and the Principle of Imputation

A main tenet of the pure theory of law is that in every fact that is considered a legal fact, two elements should be distinguished: an *external event* perceptible to the senses that takes place in space and time and a *legal meaning* that is attached to that event by legal norms.

The killing of a human does not in itself have either the meaning of a murder or the meaning of capital punishment. Such legal meanings are ascribed to the killing of a man only by way of customary or statutory norms of law. If a legal norm provides that in the event that a man kills another man, a specific sanction ought to be applied to the killer, then the killing of a man acquires the legal meaning of a murder. If, on the contrary, a legal norm provides that, under certain circumstances, a man ought to be killed as a sanction for a specific behavior, then the killing of that man acquires the meaning of capital punishment.

This specific relation between external events and their legal meanings is explained by Kelsen through what he calls the "principle of imputation," which is a transcendental principle implied in every legal norm. As we have seen in Paragraph 1.2, legal norms are those that establish an objective connection between two facts, the delict and the sanction, according to the logical form: "If there is *A* (a delict), then there ought to be *B* (a sanction)." The relation between *A* and *B* is not a *causal* relation; instead, it is a relation of *imputation* that is *established by the legal norm*.[25] By way of a specific legal norm, the sanction *B* is imputed to the delict *A*, and it is only by virtue of this relation of imputation that the fact *A* acquires the meaning of a delict and the consequence *B* acquires the meaning of a legal sanction respectively.[26]

It is within the framework of this principle of imputation that Kelsen sees blood revenge as the earliest form of legal sanction. It is in virtue of a *legal* norm, indeed, that blood revenge is imputed as a sanction for murder. If a human unjustly kills another human, they (or another member of their group) ought to be killed by the parents of the victim.

---

[24]Kelsen developed his famous pure theory of law throughout his life and in particular in Kelsen (1934, 1945a, 1960). For a comprehensive reconstruction of the theory of vindicatory justice that also considers the perspective of Kelsen's pure theory of law, see Ignasi Terradas Saborit (forthcoming). The theory of vindicatory justice was originally formulated by Terradas Saborit in Terradas Saborit (2008, 2019).

[25]Kelsen ([1949]2015, 1950).

[26]On the principle of imputation as opposed to the principle of causality, see in particular Kelsen (1950). For an analysis of the specific meaning of "ought" (*sollen* in German) with reference to the principle of imputation, see Di Lucia (1998).

The creation of such a norm in primitive societies is obviously based on custom. In fact, the widespread opinion is that the pure theory of law is modeled only on the mainly statutory and centralized law of modern states. However, Kelsen recognizes that the creation of law is not always a "deliberate aim of people" and that custom is nothing but a decentralized way of creating norms "by collaboration of all the individuals subject to the legal order."[27]

However, in Kelsen's view, what is essential for asserting that blood revenge is the earliest form of law is not the *origin* of the norm, but rather the *content* of the norm, that is to say, the specific nature of the sanction provided.

What justifies the use of the word "law" with reference to the system of blood revenge is ultimately that the norm of blood revenge provides a coercive measure (blood revenge) as a sanction for the delict of murder. Kelsen defines law as "a coercive order providing for coercive acts as socially organized sanctions" and expressly asserts that coercion is an essential element of law.[28]

3.2 The Avenger As an Organ of the Community and the Monopoly of the Employment of Force

Kelsen underlines an apparent paradox of the system of blood revenge: the sanction threatened is of the same kind as the behavior that it aims to prevent. Kelsen remarks that "the institution of blood revenge [...] indicates that death is not only the oldest crime but also the oldest socially organized punishment."[29]

In fact, this paradox seems to be intrinsic to law in general, inasmuch as the specific instrument of law, the coercive measure, "is of exactly the same sort as the act which it seeks to prevent in the relations of individuals; the sanction against the socially hurtful act is itself a hurtful act."[30]

The paradox, however, is only apparent. As early as in primitive societies, there is a fundamental distinction "between murder as a delict, and manslaughter as a fulfillment of a duty to avenge." This "means that killing is only permitted if the killer acts as an organ of his community, if his action is undertaken in execution of the legal order. The coercive measure is reserved to the community, and is, in consequence, a monopoly of the community."[31]

[27]Kelsen expressly asserts that the method of creation of law by way of custom "during thousands upon thousands of years [. . .] was the only way of creating legal norms" (1941a, p. 93).

[28]Kelsen ([1949]2015), p. 74. Kelsen remarks that "the pure theory of law does not restrict itself to the investigation of the logical structure of the rule of law [. . .]; it tries to determine the specific content of this rule, as compared to other social laws" ([1949]2015), p. 76.

[29]Kelsen (1943), p. 54.

[30]Kelsen (1942), p. 11.

[31]Kelsen (1942), p. 50.

It is only the community that can authorize (or prescribe) the adoption of coercive measures. Indeed, the humans avenging the murder of their fathers are not regarded as murderers themselves but as organs of the community because "by [their] act [they execute] a norm of the social order constituting the community."[32] In fact, they do not act merely as individuals: self-help is a social mechanism that constitutes the earliest form of application of the law.

This is a key point in Kelsen's theory of blood revenge: it means that the system of blood revenge comprises not only the threat of a coercive measure in case of violation of social norms—which is, as we have seen, one of the essential elements of law—but also the regulation of the application of the coercive measure. This is, for Kelsen, another essential feature of law: "the law attaches certain conditions to the use of force in relations among men, authorizing the employment of force only by certain individuals and only under certain circumstances."[33] Kelsen makes this view explicit as follows:

> By determining the conditions under which, and the way in which, force shall or may be applied by an individual to another individual the legal order reserves the employment of force—that is the performance of coercive acts—to definite individuals. If we designate these individuals as organs of the community constituted by the legal order, we may characterize the essential function of the law as the establishment of a force monopoly of the legal community.[34]

In this sense, law is specifically "an organization of force."[35]

4 Blood Revenge in the Evolution of Law As a Specific Social Technique

From Kelsen's analysis of blood revenge, two correlated essential features of law as a coercive order emerge.

The *first* feature concerns the *static* dimension of law, that is, the dimension of the content of legal norms. As has been seen, law attaches to certain conditions particular coercive measures as consequences.[36]

The *second* feature concerns the *dynamic* dimension of law, that is, the dimension of the procedures of the creation and application of the law. Law determines the conditions whereunder and the manner wherein force shall, or may, be applied. The

---

[32]Kelsen (1942), p. 49.

[33]Kelsen (1941a), p. 81.

[34]Kelsen ([1949]2015), p. 77.

[35]Kelsen (1941a), p. 81.

[36]Kelsen (1941a), p. 87.

legal sanction is a *socially organized* sanction. In other words, law specifically regulates its own application.[37]

4.1 Blood Revenge As a Decentralized Legal Order

It is certainly well known that according to Kelsen, one of the peculiarities of the law in general is that "it regulates its own creation and application."[38]

This is true also for primitive law. Both the creation and the application of law are regulated by the law itself, even though, according to this regulation, they are both completely decentralized:

1. The norms of the law are created not by specific centralized legislative organs but by custom, that is, by the collaboration of all the individuals subject to the legal order.
2. The norms of the law are applied not by specific centralized organs of application but directly by the individuals whose interests have been violated by the delict.

It is important to remark that this decentralization does not contradict the idea of the monopoly of the employment of force. Even though force may be employed by all individuals subject to the legal order, they are allowed (or obliged) to do so only under specific circumstances and in the way established by the norms of the community. The employment of force is thus already a monopoly of the community.

4.2 From Blood Revenge to the Law of Modern States

Although, as we have seen, Kelsen maintains that the system of blood revenge already exhibits the essential features of law, he considers such a system a primitive form of law.

Kelsen adopts an evolutionary perspective on law and traces the main lines of an ideal history of law wherein the social technique of law gradually evolved from the completely decentralized systems of blood revenge to the almost completely centralized legal systems of modern states.

In his reconstruction of the ideal history of law,[39] Kelsen remarks on a surprising fact, that the centralization of the law-applying function precedes the centralization

[37]The distinction between the static and the dynamic dimension of law is introduced in Kelsen (1941a), and it is later developed in the *General Theory of Law* (1945) as a distinction between a *nomostatics* and a *nomodynamics* of law that will be a fundamental distinction of the pure theory of law (Kelsen 1945a).

[38]Kelsen ([1949]2015), p. 55.

[39]See Sammarco (2019).

of the law-creating function. Customary law remained the only method of creation of general legal norms during thousands upon thousands of years, and the introduction of special legislative organs is a relatively late evolution,[40] suffice to say, the centralization of the law-creating function was long preceded by the centralization of the law-applying function.

However, the evolutionary process of law not only involves the gradual *centralization* of law-applying and law-creating functions. It also involves, on the one hand, an increasing differentiation in the static dimension of legal norms, that is, the content of the norms providing the specific sanctions of law, and on the other hand, an increasing differentiation of the stages of the dynamics of law.

With regard to the static dimension of law, Kelsen marks three lines of *differentiation* concerning the determination of sanction and delict. The first one is the differentiation between criminal law and civil law sanctions, both in terms of the kind of sanction provided and of the procedures of initiation of the judicial process. The second one is the differentiation between individual responsibility and collective responsibility. The third one is the differentiation between absolute liability and culpability.[41]

With regard to the dynamic dimension of law, Kelsen outlines the only two stages involved in articulating the dynamics of primitive law as follows:[42]

1. the creation of the general norm through custom
2. the application of the general norm by the subject whose interests, protected by this norm, have been violated

Throughout the evolution of law, different stages have been introduced and continue to be introduced both in the creation of the general norm (for instance, in the articulation of the relationships between a constitution and the statutes enacted by the lawmaking body) and in its application.

4.3 *The Gradual Differentiation of the Three Stages of the Application of Law*

According to Kelsen, the full-fledged procedure of the application of general legal norms to concrete cases involves three distinct stages:[43]

1. the establishment of the facts—the facts that constitute the delict in the general norm must be established

[40] Kelsen (1941a), p. 93.
[41] Kelsen (1941a), pp. 89–93.
[42] Kelsen (1941a), p. 88.
[43] Kelsen (1941a), pp. 93–94.

2. the decreeing of the sanction—the sanction provided by the general norm must be ordered to be applied to the concrete case
3. the execution of the sanction—the sanction must be executed against the individual responsible for the delict

At the origins of law, these three stages are neither differentiated nor centralized. In blood revenge, the subject whose interests have been violated must (1) determine whether a delict has been committed, (2) determine whether they must fulfill the sanction, and (3) execute the sanction.

In the law of modern states, in contrast, these three stages are differentiated and centralized.

However, the three stages of the procedure of application of law do not necessarily become centralized at the same time. According to Kelsen, "the centralization of the first two stages has probably preceded the centralization of the third stage."[44]

The centralization of the third stage, that is, the exclusive attribution of the execution of the sanction to a special organ of the community requires, for Kelsen, the existence of a powerful administration, the development of which allows for the centralization of the stage of the execution of the sentence, whereafter self-help and blood revenge can be supplanted. It is thus possible, in Kelsen's view, to speak of a state.

However, Kelsen assigns the greatest importance to the earlier centralization of the first stage, that is, attributing to an "objective authority," such as a court, the establishment of the fact of an actual violation of the law. The importance of this step depends, for Kelsen, on the fact that "in the province of law there are no absolute, directly evident facts, no facts 'in themselves,' but only facts established by the competent authority in a procedure described by the legal order."[45] Kelsen explains:

> It is not the theft as a fact in itself to which the legal order attaches a certain punishment [. . .]. [T]he legal order attaches a certain punishment only to a theft established by the competent authority following a prescribed procedure.[46]

Without the establishment of the fact by the competent authority being instituted by the legal order, the assertion that an individual has committed a theft "can only express a subjective opinion." Only the opinion of the authority instituted by the legal order to establish the fact is decisive: "any other opinion as to the existence of a fact as determined by the legal order is irrelevant from a juristic point of view."[47]

In the most primitive form of law based on blood revenge, the legal order does not provide for specific organs for the establishment of facts. It is thus "the interested parties themselves that are called upon by the legal order to establish the existence of

[44]Kelsen (1941a), p. 94.
[45]Kelsen (1941a), p. 94.
[46]Kelsen (1941a), p. 94.
[47]Kelsen (1941a), p. 94.

the facts in the concrete case,"[48] which can be done only by agreement of the parties to the dispute.

Such an agreement on the establishment of facts is essential to give the objective meaning of the execution of a legal sanction to the act whereby blood revenge is accomplished. However, Kelsen remarks that an agreement is seldom reached.[49] In addition, if the parties do not agree on the facts, the essential legal issue concerning whether a delict has been committed remains undetermined, and it consequently remains undetermined as to whether the act of coercion executed by an individual who subjectively claims to have been injured is objectively a sanction or rather a delict.

Therefore, the differentiation and centralization of the first stage of the application of law are of the greatest importance. It is possible to apply the law in all cases, independently of the agreement of the parties, only through the institution of a court, that is, an objective special organ for the establishment of the facts and the determination of the essential legal issue.

However, the courts in this early stage of the evolution of law are not the same as the typical courts of a modern state. At their origin, the courts were hardly more than tribunals of arbitration: they only "had to decide whether or not the delict had actually been committed, as claimed by one party, and whether or not that party was authorized to execute a sanction against the other."[50]

At this point, Kelsen makes an interesting remark, such that the authorization by the court to execute the sanction of blood revenge was subordinated to the impossibility of reaching a resolution through other means. The court authorized the execution only "if the conflict could not be settled by peaceful agreement" between the parties.[51] According to Kelsen, the first task of the tribunal was probably "to bring about such a peaceful agreement, enabling the vendetta to be replaced by wergild."[52]

4.4 *The Relevance of the Procedural Dimension in Kelsen's Theory of Blood Revenge*

Kelsen's remarks concerning the differentiation and centralization of the first stage of the application of law—that of the establishment of the facts—has a threefold relevance for a thorough understanding of Kelsen's theory of blood revenge.

First, in Kelsen's perspective, there is no coincidence between the development of courts and the abolition of self-help and blood revenge. The introduction of a

[48] Kelsen (1941a), p. 94.

[49] Kelsen (1941a), p. 94.

[50] Kelsen (1941a), p. 95.

[51] Kelsen (1941a), p. 95.

[52] Kelsen (1941a), p. 95.

court that has the specific function of establishing the facts and determining whether one party is authorized to execute revenge is a fundamental step in the evolution of law that takes place already within the system of blood revenge.

Second, the system of blood revenge is from the outset a whole legal system that has substantive rules and procedural regulations of the application of law. It establishes socially organized sanctions, and it regulates its own application.

Third, the above-mentioned remark that "in the province of law there are no absolute, directly evident facts, no facts 'in themselves'" and that even in the system of blood revenge, only the facts that are agreed upon by the parties or determined by the competent authority have an objective legal meaning, explains why Kelsen insisted on the distinction between the *subjective* and the *objective* aspects of the social dimension of blood revenge in that the mere subjective dimension of revenge is not sufficient to speak of blood revenge as a legal sanction. What is necessary as well is the objective dimension introduced by social agreement or by the determination of the facts by an objective competent authority.

References

Di Lucia P (1998) Sollen between semantics and pragmatics. In: Egidi R (ed) In search of a new humanism. The philosophy of Georg Henrik von Wright. Kluwer, Dordrecht, pp 215–220

Kelsen H (1934) Reine Rechtslehre. Einleitung in die rechtswissenschaftliche Problematik. Franz Deuticke, Wien

Kelsen H (1935–1936) L'âme et le droit. In: Droit, Morale, Mœurs, IIe Annuaire de l'Institut International de Philosophie du Droit, et de Sociologie Juridique. Travaux de la seconde session. Sirey, Paris, pp 60–82

Kelsen H (1941a) The law as a specific social technique. Univ Chicago Law Rev 9:75–97

Kelsen H (1941b) Vergeltung und Kausalität. Eine soziologische Untersuchung. W. P. van Stockum, The Hague

Kelsen H (1942) Law and peace in international relations. The Oliver Wendell Holmes Lectures, 1940-41. Harvard University Press, Cambridge

Kelsen H (1943) Society and nature. A sociological inquiry. The University of Chicago Press-Kegan Paul, Chicago

Kelsen H (1945a) General theory of law and state. Harvard University Press, Cambridge

Kelsen H (1945b) Preface to the Spanish edition. In: Kelsen H, Sociedad y naturaleza. Una investigación sociológica. Depalma, Buenos Aires

Kelsen H (1948) Law, state, and justice in the pure theory of law. Yale Law J 57:377–390

Kelsen H (1950) Causality and imputation. Ethics 61:1–11

Kelsen H (1960) Reine Rechtslehre. Franz Deuticke, Wien

Kelsen H ([1947]2008) Autobiografia. In: Kelsen H, Scritti autobiografici. Diabasis, Reggio Emilia, pp 67–138

Kelsen H ([1949]2015) Elementi di teoria pura del diritto. I dattiloscritti della Bancroft Library. In: Kelsen H, Che cos'è la giustizia? Lezioni americane. Quodlibet, Macerata

Nitsch C (2009) "Holmes Lectures, 1940-41". Studio storico-critico su Hans Kelsen in America. In: Kelsen H, Diritto e pace nelle relazioni internazionali. Giuffrè, Milan, p V-LXXXI

Sammarco S (2019) Il diritto in movimento. Hans Kelsen e l'evoluzione macrostorica degli ordinamenti giuridici. PhD Thesis. University of Milan, Milan
Terradas Saborit I (2008) Justicia vindicatoria. De la ofensa e indefensión a la imprecación y el oráculo, la vindicta y el talión, la ordalia y el juramento, la composición y la reconciliación. Consejo Superior de Investigaciones Científicas, Madrid
Terradas Saborit I (2019) La justicia más antigua. Teoría y cultura del ordenamiento vindicatorio. Consejo Superior de Investigaciones Científicas, Madrid
Terradas Saborit I (forthcoming) Teoria dell'ordinamento giuridico vendicatorio

Revenge, Violence and the Civilizing Narrative

Kaius Tuori

Abstract The purpose of this chapter is to explore the uses of the past in the debates over justice and retribution, discussing the reception of ancient texts in modern discussions. One of the most persistent narratives of Western history is the civilizing narrative, the story of how the growing influence of the state gradually brought an end to the lawless violence and misery inflicted by cycles of vengeance. The problem of tradition, violence and revenge is central to the civilizing narrative. Lex talionis occupied a critical point between unrestrained revenge and the state monopoly of punishment and violence and became a key preoccupation for observers of primitive law in the nineteenth century. Issues like the purpose and morality of revenge were initially discussed using the Biblical, Roman and Greek traditions and the examples they furnished. The history of interpretations on lex talionis shows a clear trajectory from a moralizing to a cultural interpretation of law and revenge. The Early Modern authors had observed mainly ancient sources and made their interpretation based on Christian morality. The aim of the present paper is to demonstrate continuities and discontinuities in the discussions and the role that the ancient and Biblical past had, both as an example of the early savagery and as an authoritative example.

1 Introduction

The notion of vindicatory justice has sought to transform the debate that juxtaposes law and revenge and to seek new ways in which the notions of feelings of justice and giving redress to the victim would be addressed. In many ways, this discussion has foundered on rigid ideas of revenge and retribution, where concepts such as civilization, culture and society are presented in ways that have presupposed a linear notion of progress. In them, revenge has been conceptualized almost exclusively as a violent act, with destructive repercussions to both the individual and the community. Due to these cultural obstacles, it has been very difficult to even begin an analytical

K. Tuori (✉)
Centre for European Studies, University of Helsinki, Helsinki, Finland
e-mail: kaius.tuori@helsinki.fi

R. Márquez Porras et al. (eds.), *Vindicatory Justice*, Ius Gentium: Comparative Perspectives on Law and Justice 93, https://doi.org/10.1007/978-3-030-79595-5_3

debate over the merits and challenges of the alternatives to the criminal justice system.[1] I argue that the reason for the obstinate nature of these cultural challenges is that the very notion of development from revenge to law is inbuilt in the narrative of the emergence of law in the Western cultural experience. In order to overcome these obstacles, one first needs to come to grips with the origins of these notions, these narratives of progress that are inherent in some of the main foundational works of European culture.

The purpose of this paper is to explore the uses of the past in the debates over justice and retribution, discussing the reception of ancient texts in modern discussions. One of the most persistent narratives of Western history is the civilizing narrative, the story of how the growing influence of the state gradually brought an end to lawless violence and misery brought about by cycles of vengeance.[2] In this text, I will argue that through its many iterations, this civilizing narrative still conditions a certain response to new ideas in criminal justice, such as taking into account the emotive side of justice. Popular themes regarding revenge in the media may be grouped into two categories, first alarmist stories of the resurgence of barbarism and the existence of revenge as proof, second, the idea that culturally explainable forms of revenge should be seen as a sign of cultural incompatibility. Both of these have a highly racialized media coverage.

The problem of tradition, violence and revenge is central to the civilizing narrative. This chapter will explore foundational texts and historical examples to illustrate the idea of linear progress inherent in the civilizing narrative. *Lex talionis* occupied a critical point between unrestrained revenge and the state monopoly of punishment and violence and became a key preoccupation for observers of primitive law in the nineteenth century. Issues like the purpose and morality of revenge were initially discussed using the Biblical, Roman and Greek traditions and the examples they furnished. The history of interpretations on *lex talionis* shows a clear trajectory from a moralizing to a cultural interpretation of law and revenge. Early Modern authors had observed mainly ancient sources and made their interpretation based on Christian morality. The aim of the present chapter is to demonstrate continuities and discontinuities in the discussions and the role that the ancient and Biblical past had, both as an example of the early savagery and as an authoritative example.

Through the analysis of several disconnected historical examples and their treatment, this chapter seeks to lay bare the inherent background notions of these narratives and the ways in which they influence the responses to alternatives to the state-centred criminal law system. In the early studies on revenge and legal primitivism, two competing views on "early man" may be seen, Hobbes's and Rousseau's, which either demonized or idealized "pre-civilized" peoples. These two stereotypes provided two strong master narratives that were often imposed on the explanations

---

[1]On this debate, see Terradas Saborit's chapter in this volume.

[2]I have written about the civilizing narrative previously in Tuori (2015a). Similar notions of developmental narratives and law have been earlier presented by Stein (1980) and Kuper (1988). On legal primitivism, see also Wilf (2009).

of indigenous peoples by Western observers. This in turn led to the primitivization of the same indigenous peoples, often with little regard to their actual circumstances.[3]

In order to facilitate a new discussion on retribution, revenge and justice, it will hopefully become evident that a new viewpoint to these themes is vital. Otherwise these deeply rooted stereotypical narratives of civilization and justice will dominate the debate and prevent new ideas from emerging. Even a concept such as revenge is tied to cultural connotations that are often in a revealing manner contradictory to the notion of unilinear development from revenge to punishment by the state. For instance, in the Roman judicial discourse one could describe the avenger (*ultor*) as the person who would pursue culprits by raising charges in a court of law. In a similar sense, the Hebrew term of the blood avenger, *go'el ha'adam* (Numbers 35:19), has in the Rabbinical literature been repurposed to signify the state authorities responsible for apprehending and prosecuting culprits. In both cases, the underlying notion is the same, namely that the purpose of the system of justice is conducive to the idea of revenge.

2 The Civilizing Narrative

Among historians, there is a term called "Whig history" or the "Whig interpretation of history". It refers to a criticism of the nineteenth-century writing of English history as an inevitable process of advancement, where during the course of history everything gradually gets better. Living conditions improve, society becomes more democratic and equal, and the position of the individual more secure. The name Whig history comes from the liberal Whig party that was dominant in Britain during the nineteenth century, Whig interpretations of history embodying liberal notions of progress.[4]

While Whig history referred more to British early modern social, economic, political and especially constitutional development, similar historical notions of progress and advancement have been very popular. In all of these, the idea of the spread of civilization is understood as a process of becoming. One of the most famous of these is the idea of the civilizing process by German sociologist and historian Norbert Elias. While Elias's theory was a subtle panorama of the development of both internalized social norms and forms of behaviour as well as public life from the early middle ages to the modern era, it was often seen as a kind of teleology of the advance of civilization. Manners and self-restraint first adopted in high court society that spread gradually among the general populace had a constraining effect not only on violence in general but equally on what was considered acceptable and expectable behaviour.[5]

[3]On the primitivization of indigenous peoples, see Tuori (2015b) and Fitzpatrick (1992).

[4]Within historiography, the term Whig history is more often than not used as an insult.

[5]Elias (2000).

Even though this constraining of violence had a direct impact in the acceptability of revenge, the development from revenge to compensation was already imbued in much earlier foundational texts of Western culture from religion to law. As such, they had distinct moral and ethical underpinnings. While in the Old Testament, revenge and an eye for an eye had been acceptable, Jesus preached forgiveness and turning the other check. In early natural law theories by Grotius and Pufendorf, natural law was seen to be against talion and revenge. In general, early modern legal thought combined moral and legal development, seamlessly utilizing both legal and religious authorities to make their point.[6]

In these theories, the rise of the state as an actor was interpreted as a sign of society becoming more civilized. Gradually, a sequence formed where the component stages were first war as the only method of conflict resolution, then the regulation of revenge through establishing norms that limited the range of possible revenge, leading to the possibility of paying off the revenge through compensation and finally the task of the avenger was taken over by the state or king that meted out punishment. This developmental sequence was a conglomeration of ancient history, usually taken from the texts of classical authors and Biblical sources.[7]

Within the process of European expansion, the idea of the state as peacemaker was converted to a legitimating factor for European colonialism. During European colonial history, the vast levels of violence and repression that were imposed on the colonized were presented as a necessary precondition to the impending peace that was brought about by state interventions. European hegemony curbed war and violence among indigenous groups, but the price that was paid was considerable, both in terms of the violence and repression practised by the colonial powers and the loss of self-determination for indigenous peoples. What colonization meant was often also the suppression of indigenous dispute resolutions that had sought to limit violence.[8]

Within these parallel narratives of the advance of civilization, there is a uniting thread of aversion to violence. This has important repercussions for the notion of

[6]Grotius (1925), pp. 472–480 (book 2, ch. 20.8-10); Pufendorf (1934).

[7]Whitman (1995) and Tuori (2015a).

[8]On this development, see i.a. Mamdani (1996). This transfer of the monopoly of violence and equally of dispute resolution was evident in the proclamation used by Theophilus Shepstone in South Africa in 1850, where the intent was to impress upon the "child-races" that revenge and blood money were in the future prohibited: "To all Native Chiefs, Petty Chieftains, Heads of Kraals and Common Native people in the District of Natal: Hear ye and listen with both ears. Whereas from your youth up you have been thought to consider a man's life to be the property of the Supreme Chief, and that it is unlawful to destroy such life without his consent; and whereas the Supreme Chief in this District is the Lieutenant-Governor, representing the Queen of England; and whereas several lives have been destroyed without trial, and without his knowledge or consent: Know ye, therefore, all Chiefs, Petty Chieftains, Heads of Kraals and Common People, a man's life has no price: no cattle can pay for it. He who intentionally kills another, whether for Witchcraft of otherwise, shall die himself, and whether he be a Chief, Petty Chieftain, or Head of a Kraal, who kills another, he shall follow his murdered brother; his children shall be fatherless and his wives widows and his cattle and all other property shall become forfeited." Brookes (1927), pp. 52–53.

vindicatory justice, as it seeks to accommodate the same mechanisms as revenge and attempts to have a conversation about revenge. In the civilizing processes, be they legal, religious, cultural, historical or colonial, the process of advancement has been that of curbing violence. Revenge was placed in the general category of the primitive, of the pre-civilized, of the uncontrolled. This meant that because the fundamental narratives begin from the premise that revenge and the impulses behind revenge are evil, backwards and inimical to justice, any theory that would seek to rehabilitate this premise faces an uphill battle.

3 The Rationalizing Process

A second influential way of understanding the development away from revenge was to see it as a process of rationalization. The civilizing narrative involved both discipline and self-control, where instead of direct revenge one would seek a measured response in tune with the offence. This idea of moving from unbound emotion to reason as the self-imposed impulse control involves the objectification of the offence and the response, in short, rationalization.

This takes the understanding of revenge to the ambit of another great narrative of Western civilization, the advance of reason and rationalism. This rationalizing process was famously defined by Max Weber as the key component of modernity, where tradition and customs are replaced by conscious and rational decisions, a new way of thinking. Within this theory of rationalization, revenge is categorized as irrational, a remnant of impulse-driven pre-rational actions.[9]

According the theory of the rationalizing process, what contributes to this rationality and what makes it so Weberian is the link to state activity. The advance of rationality is powered by the rise of state power that limits customary actions that are deemed harmful, such as revenge. The underlying notion of revenge is that of the perceived equality between actors and the lack of authority above them that could impose a solution. This notion of equality is removed by state power, which imposes a hierarchy and appoints itself as the arbiter of all conflicts. Finally, the idea of rationality is accompanied by the pre-eminence of the rule of law. While this may also spell the notion of equality, what rule of law in this case means is that the state power imposes its own rules, the law, upon the actors and forces them to obey.[10]

What all of this signifies is that the difference between revenge and law is not approached as alternative forms of dispute resolution, but as competing ways of thinking, where the former is supplanted by latter in a process of rationalization.

---

[9]Weber (1978), pp. 656–664; Roth (1987). The idea of the spread of rationality as the driving force in Western intellectual and scientific history was taken up with enthusiasm by Weber's followers in different fields. In legal history, for example, the works of scholars such as Franz Wieacker reflected this notion.

[10]On the drastic nature of this transformation in settler societies, see Ford (2010).

It is unclear whether one should approach the notion of state sovereignty through a conceptual framework that centralizes the state. It is perhaps more fruitful to see the two key concepts through the lens of post-colonial thought to illuminate how deeply ingrained statist thought is in these concepts. For instance, the idea of the state as a rational entity and as an embodiment of reason is a typically German philosophical construct, but more importantly it has served as a justificatory mechanism for the spread of state power. Local communities, be they European or indigenous, have been presented as traditional and irrational, holding back individuals in backwards customs and unproductive organization and means of production. This meant that submission to state power and the introduction of state-provided education were in fact in the best interests of the subjected. The second notion is that of the state monopoly on violence as defined by Weber. The notion of state monopoly on violence contained the notion that while traditional systems of governance were determined by feuding, revenge and the violent abuse of power by the strong against the weak, the state would bring peace and justice. All would be judged by the law and only state authorities, specifically so authorized, could use violence and coercion against wrongdoers. This has been, since antiquity, the promise of the ruler to the people: support me and I will protect you against the local elites, the warlords and the aristocracy.[11]

This state-centred notion of the advance of rationality in the form of written rules against the rule of tradition that was ripe for abuses of power has for millennia been one of the foundational narratives of the European legal and constitutional tradition. For the notion of vindicatory justice, the deeply rooted nature of this narrative means that it is not simply the system of criminal law that is opposed to the notion of vindicatory justice, but the self-understanding of the entire system of governance was formed in opposition to the egalitarian and non-hierarchical social systems that have often been linked with vindicatory justice.

4 Theories of Revenge and Restitution

These aforementioned two notions, interpretations emphasizing the civilizing and the rationalizing process behind the disappearance of revenge, depicted it as a moral and historical development, where both the improving moral and social norms and the rise of state power would extinguish the barbaric habit of revenge, were dominant up to the nineteenth century. During the nineteenth century, two new interpretations emerged: (1) legal primitivism and evolutionary theories behind it and (2) the historical school and its glorification of authentic feeling. As often happens in the history of ideas, these competing theories emerged alongside the old moralistic theory of revenge and did not completely supplant it.

[11]No one perfected this notion of the benevolent sovereign bringing peace as well as Augustus in his public propaganda. See Yavetz (1984).

These two new theoretical frameworks took diametrically opposite viewpoints concerning the idea of revenge. Using the concepts of medieval Germanic law, they spoke of the "first anger", the emotive response of the individual and the community to the insult or injury. Supporters of both theories argued that such responses are difficult to measure but that they are culturally determined. The legal primitivists saw it as a lack of impulse control, a savage and brutal way of acting that shows that people in such societies are like children in their immediate and uncontrolled ways of operating. In contrast, Jacob Grimm and other representatives of the historical school of jurisprudence saw nobility in unrestricted revenge, involving as it did pure emotions and an avoidance the corruptions of civilization. What this meant was that people were living an honourable life where the immediacy of their response was the only way of preserving their status in society.[12]

Within the historical school, much of the theory-building operated in an implicit notion of virtue and community. The idea of a blood community meant a nuclear form of society committed to avenging each other. In time this idea became mixed with concepts and notions that found a home/a ready home/in the duelling culture of nineteenth-century Germany. This development is evident in discussions of who might be the target of revenge and whether there are substitutes of sufficient status that might suffice. With legal primitivists, they shared the idea that revenge represented the "original stage" of mankind, which was either reviled or heralded. In the early anthropological theories of Henry Sumner Maine, Henry Lewis Morgan or Albert Hermann Post, the evolutionary framework and the theories of honour were more or less interlinked.[13]

The idea of restitution, compensation in some form, as supplanting revenge was an integral part of the developmental arc from revenge to punishment. Because talionic rules existed in both archaic Roman law, Biblical law and early Germanic laws, sometimes alongside regulations for controlling revenge, scholars of legal primitivism assumed that they formed part of the linear evolutionary development from an assumed earlier phase where uncontrolled revenge was dominant to a situation where violent revenge had been curtailed. Never mind that anthropological evidence of this transition in which revenge was supplanted by compensation was seldom found, except when outside forces such as colonial powers mandated it. Even then, this compensation was usually linked with a court proceeding and that part of the compensation was taken by the state as fines. In the theory of evolutionary legal primitivism, a vast literature emerged on the supposed rules for measuring and paying out compensation, who would have oversight of payment, and so on. Quite often, as revenge was seen as an alternative to compensation, compensation was interpreted as buying off revenge. Finally, there was the question of what

[12]Grimm (1828), pp. 495–496.

[13]Maine (1986), Morgan (1985) and Post (1884). On evolutionary works and their notions of progress, see Kumar (2006).

cannot be restituted, brought back and there the issue revolved around who caused a death.[14]

Evolutionary and primitivistic models of development from revenge to restitution and punishment led gradually to the naturalization of the process. This meant that revenge was not simply a social or moral commandment, but an evolutionary step in the universal development of mankind. In these theories, revenge meant almost exclusively violence towards the culprit and his or her kin, violence that had a destructive potential.

5 *Lex Talionis* from Hammurabi to Rome

Instead of trying to trace the entirety of transitional theories from revenge to compensation, what I shall focus on next is *lex talionis*, a central part of most theories about revenge and especially evolutionary theories concerning revenge. In these theories, the *lex talionis* is the link between savagery and civilization. For the purposes of this book about vindicatory justice, *lex talionis* is interesting in another sense, as it involves the balancing of the suffering of the victim and the punishment inflicted on the culprit.

Lex talionis is found in historical examples from ancient Mesopotamia to ancient Rome. It is also present in anthropological examples from Australia to Africa and Europe. This prompted evolutionary researchers to describe it as a universal institution. Its function in the systems of revenge was interpreted to act as a way to limit blood revenge, which was seen as a violent act that would destabilize the community. In a sense, it has also been interpreted as ritualized revenge.[15]

While the basic texts of the discussion on *lex talionis* were for a very long time that of the Bible and Roman law, the discovery of the so-called Code of Hammurabi in 1901 changed matters completely. We can look at the texts below:

Law of Hammurabi § 169
If a man destroy the eye of another man, they shall destroy his eye. If one break a man's bone, they shall break his bone. If one destroy the eye of a freeman or break the bone of a freeman he shall pay one gold mina. If one destroy the eye of a man's slave or break a bone of a man's slave he shall pay one-half his price.

---

[14]On this matter, legal primitivistic literature provides innumerable examples. Many sources are German (see especially Kohler 1919 but there were also British examples, see Hartland (1924), with interesting linkages with the colonial mission).

[15]On *lex talionis*, see Tuori (2007). On the philosophical argument for *lex talionis,* see Waldron (1992).

In the Hebrew Bible, a comparable notion is found in Exodus 21:24-25: "eye for eye, tooth for tooth, hand for hand, foot for foot, burn for burn, wound for wound, bruise for bruise".[16]

XII Tables, VIII
si membrum rupit, ni cum eo pacit, talio esto.

If he has maimed a part (of a body), unless he settles with him, there is to be talion

si os fregit libero, CCC, si servo, CL poenae sunto.

If he has broken a bone of a free man, 300, if of a slave, 150 (asses) are to be the penalty.[17]

These are the most famous examples of the *lex talionis*, but they also illustrate a fatal flaw in the civilizing narrative. Hammurabi depicts a completely different, more developed society from that of the Hebrew Bible or the law of the Twelve Tables. It even describes the liability of doctors for mistreating patients.[18] This did little to dent the general enthusiasm for *lex talionis* as the developmental link between the violent state of nature and the law of the state in the civilizing narrative. This was hardly surprising, because the primitivistic legal literature such as that by Morgan and others was founded on the very notion of linear progress. For the linear theory to be discredited, a new kind of research paradigm focusing on sources, both ancient and ethnological, was needed.

The discovery of both the law of Hammurabi and the beginnings of a new kind of anthropology based on participant observation were vital in the breaking up of the narrative monopoly that had thus far been enjoyed by the civilizing narrative. This development demonstrated that notions of vindicatory justice were not incompatible with organized, complex society and that the notion of vengeance did not necessarily mean that society would be brutal and that its members would live in fear. The ideas of revenge and its different forms were not incompatible with what could be understood even in modern terms as access to justice. The law of Hammurabi was difficult to reconcile with the developmental narrative of legal primitivism and with Western notions of the civilizing process, so much so that this development showed what amounted to a backwards slide towards revenge. But this difficulty is precisely why talionic regulations are interesting when studying the theory of vindicatory justice. The like-for-like notion inherent in *lex talionis* contains criteria for valuation that begins from the victim, not the interests of the state. The gruesome notions of

---

[16]Translation from the New International Version.

[17]Bruns, *Fontes iuris Romani antiqui*, vol. I (1909) table VIII, 2–3; Crawford, *Roman Statutes*, vol. 2. (1996) table I, 13–14. English translation by Crawford.

[18]§218 in the code. Diamond (1956), pp. 151–155 early on noted that the supposed evolutionary sequence did not work at all because in the Babylonian material more lenient laws were replaced by stricter punishments.

cutting off limbs or poking out eyes, central as they were to the civilizing narrative as the savage starting point, have perhaps clouded the legal principle behind them. I would argue that they should not be primarily discussed as examples of cruel punishments, but as the principle of equality, balancing the suffering of the victim and the punishment. Because we know very little of the actual application of these laws and whether they were merely figurative indications of the value or whether actual limbs and eyes were damaged as actual punishment, it may be helpful to turn to another famous historical example of the retributive notions of justice, that of medieval Iceland.

6 Icelandic Excursus

Revenge and stories about revenge are at the heart of innumerable literary traditions, but the Icelandic saga tradition from the early middle ages is in a class of its own. For instance, in the *Saga of the Burnt Njàl*, the narrative revolves around numerous stories of vengeance and vendetta, including feuding between families and individuals. Blood money is paid and all sorts of measures to arbitrate are taken, but the conflict escalates despite the main character's sincere wish for peace. The blood money being paid is, as in Icelandic sagas in general, measured according to the status of the person, a free man being more valuable than a slave and so forth. In the end, Njàl and his family die while surrounded by their enemies when their house is burnt down, but his son survives to avenge them.[19]

In the nineteenth century, the Icelandic sagas were seen as the purest extant source for the original Germanic legal culture. The notion of Germanic originalism, of seeking the earliest and purest example of the culture, was a key theme that gripped Jacob Grimm and the historical school. While there were many other sources for the Germanic tradition from historical sources, Icelandic sagas seemed to embody the *Urrecht* ideal of uncorrupted cultural products. One of the earliest scholars of the sagas as a legal source, Konrad Maurer, considered the sagas as the original stage of Germanic law. There were also talionic rules in other Scandinavian laws, but the Icelandic material clearly predated written law.[20] In other early Germanic laws, this development from revenge to compensation appeared to confirm the principle that violent revenge was being slowly curtailed. The early Anglo-Saxon law codes, such as the early seventh-century laws of King Aethelberth of Kent, had very detailed tables of compensation for each body part and injury.[21]

In the Germanic material, the notion of *Sippe* emerged, a community of avengers that represented the oldest form of society. It consisted of free men who were tied to

[19]The saga has been translated into numerous languages, in English the commonly used edition is Magnusson and Pálsson (1968).

[20]Maurer (1860), pp. v–vii, 219–221.

[21]There are numerous publications of these laws, Miller (2006), pp. 113–115 cites them at length.

communal relations through the bond of a mutual pact of vengeance. Through this original pact other communal notions emerged, such as that of communal ownership of land.[22]

The idea of a Germanic original culture was reinforced by the notion that there were numerous near universal traits from legal customs to vocabulary. Concepts such as Vergelt or Vergilt existed in England, Scandinavia and Germanic lands. The Icelandic material has been of great interest to scholars of law, who have used it as a test case for the system of blood revenge. For example, William Ian Miller has formulated a theory of value based on the Icelandic system. According to his theory, the Vergelt or blood money used to buy off revenge is at the same time an estimate of the worth of both the victim and the accuser.[23]

In this sense, Millar returns to a similar notion as presented already by Kant, namely that revenge operates with a principle of equality. What these new studies on revenge and retribution illustrate is that once the moralistic and simplistic notions that have persisted are stripped away, one begins to see the logic behind the revenge culture and the art of balancing offence and retribution.[24] Whitman has shown how the developmental narrative was strongly influenced by Hegel's idea of a shift from a strict early formalistic thing for thing equivalence to a theory of value equivalence, both as a legal and a moral development. In contrast, legal scholars such as Rudolf von Jhering emphasized the emotive side of revenge, the subjective feeling and the very public notion of honour that fed the culture of vengeance and made it hard to repress. Behind both of these notions is the conception of worth or value, from which the ideas of honour and injury ultimately stem.[25]

What the Icelandic narratives of revenge and retribution depict, or what Millar presents them as meaning, is a theory of justice that relied on a notion of balance. Revenge was a way to gain justice, to get even. Millar's idea is that the key aim of revenge as an idea of justice was that the victim would be made whole, to redress the damage done in full and in the process to recognize the worth of the victim.

7 Conclusions

The main obstacle standing in the way of rethinking the roles of the victim and the mechanisms of justice is the persistent way in which traditional alternatives to the criminal law system are presented as barbaric and immoral. The notion of vindicatory justice has emerged to reclaim the idea of restitution, of making the victim's loss count and that the objective of criminal justice is not simply to punish but to offer retribution and reparation.

---

[22]Grimm (1828), pp. 494–495.

[23]Miller (2006), on the idea of honour cultures, see Blok (2001).

[24]Kant (1995), pp. 399–400.

[25]Whitman (1995), pp. 58–65.

What I have argued in this chapter is that in traditional scholarship on revenge, a strong notion of unilinear development persists in which the arc moves from violent revenge to composition and to punishment authorized by state officials and courts. In these notions, theories of revenge are often mixed with moral and evolutionary theories that have a very long history, deeply embedded in the Western cultural tradition. Religious and moral theories shunned the idea of revenge from an ethical standpoint, while nineteenth-century social theories sought to see revenge as a factor that belonged to an early, barbaric stage of man's development. While it is in today's standards very questionable to mix historical and anthropological data to form universalistic theories, preconceived notions have remained a strong influence in criminal policy.

Theories of revenge were used to legitimate state interventions and colonialism during the nineteenth century, but they are also utilized today in the popular discussions about indigenous cultures. Typically, the existence of revenge and retributive systems are presented as proof that the indigenous culture should be subjected to education and "civilization" in order to pass the test of modern Western criteria.

In all of these theories, it is clear that the civilizing narrative, the notion of advancement of civilization as a certain process of becoming like the Western criteria, lies behind the habitual condemnation of alternative forms of dispute resolution. The basic premise of the narrative is one of rationalization, but at its core is the juxtaposition between revenge and forgiveness presented in Christianity as the fundamental teaching of Jesus. This combination of deeply embedded religious validation and the notion of reason as the opposite of a mad passion for revenge means that for most (Western) observers who share these cultural values, perhaps unconsciously, criticism of the civilizing narrative of progress goes against very deeply held preconceptions within Western self-understanding. These preconceptions, from the ideas of rationality, order and control, to the notion of civilization as the advance of self-restraint, are by and large embedded within the cultural fabric of modern society and thus externalizing them and subjecting them to discussion is difficult.

As a consequence, it is all but impossible to initiate the kind of discussion that the proponents of the theory of vindicatory justice want to have about the ideas of revenge and retribution. Not only is the natural (culturally conditioned) reaction to such proposals one of being wrong on a deep ethical level, but also that one would in a sense reverse the progress that has been made. It would mean returning to the dark ages of the past, to a more brutal and uncivilized era.

What this means is that there are two separate ways to approach the idea of revenge historically and to bring the discussions forward. The first is to deconstruct the developmental narrative and its hierarchical notions of civilization and justice and expose its underlying notions. The second is to see revenge in a wider sense as a historical development that involved a fundamental notion of balance and following the victim's sense of justice. This would enable a discussion on the deeper notions of justice and equity.

Acknowledgements This work has received funding from the Centre of Excellence in Law, Identity and the European Narratives, funded by the Academy of Finland, funding decision number 312154.

References

Blok A (2001) Honour and violence. Polity Press, Cambridge
Brookes EH (1927) The history of native policy in South Africa from 1830 to the present day. J. L. Van Schaik, Ltd, Pretoria
Diamond AS (1956) An eye for an eye. IRAQ 18:151–155
Elias N (2000) The civilizing process: sociogenetic and psychogenetic investigations. Blackwell, Oxford
Fitzpatrick P (1992) The mythology of modern law. Routledge, London
Ford L (2010) Settler sovereignty: jurisdiction and indigenous people in America and Australia, 1788–1836. Harvard University Press, Cambridge
Grimm J (1828) Deutsche Rechts Alterthümer. Dieterichschen Buchhandlung, Göttingen
Grotius H (1925) De jure belli ac pacis, vol 1–2. Clarendon Press, Oxford
Hartland ES (1924) Primitive law. Methuen & Co. Ltd, London
Kant I (1995) Die Metaphysik der Sitten (Werke 5). Könemann, Köln
Kohler J (1919) Shakespeare vor dem Forum der Jurisprudenz. Dr. Walther Rotschild, Berlin
Kumar K (2006) Maine and the theory of progress. In: Diamond AS (ed) The Victorian achievement of Sir Henry Maine: a centennial reappraisal. Cambridge University Press, Cambridge, pp 76–82
Kuper A (1988) The invention of primitive society: transformations of an illusion. Routledge, London
Magnusson M, Pálsson H (eds) (1968) Njal's saga. Helgafell, Reykjavik
Maine HS (1986) Ancient law: its connection with the early history of society and its relation to modern ideas. Dorset Press, New York
Mamdani M (1996) Citizen and subject: contemporary Africa and the legacy of late colonialism. Princeton University Press, Princeton
Maurer K (1860) Isländische Volkssagen der Gegenwart. J.C. Hinrichs'sche Buchhanlung, Leipzig
Miller WI (2006) Eye for an eye. Cambridge University Press, Cambridge
Morgan LH (1985) Ancient society. University of Arizona Press, Tucson
Post AH (1884) Die Grundlagen des Rechts und die Grundzüge seiner Entwicklungsgeschichte. Leitgedanken für den Aufbau einer allgemeinen Rechtswissenschaft auf soziologischer Basis. Schulzeschen Hof-Buchhandlung und Hof-Buchdruckerei A. Schwartz, Oldenburg
Pufendorf S (1934) De jure naturae et gentium libri octo. Volume two. The translation of the edition of 1688. Clarendon Press, Oxford
Roth G (1987) Rationalization in Max Weber's developmental history. In: Lash S, Whimster S (eds) Max Weber, rationality and modernity. Routledge, London, pp 75–91
Stein P (1980) Legal evolution: the story of an idea. Cambrdige University Press, Cambridge
Tuori K (2007) Revenge and retribution in the twelve tables: Talio esto reconsidered. Fundamina 13:140–145
Tuori K (2015a) Lawyers and savages: ancient history and legal realism in the making of legal anthropology. Routledge, New York
Tuori K (2015b) The theory and practice of indigenous dispossession in the late nineteenth century: the Saami in the far North of Europe and the legal history of colonialism. Comp Legal History 3:152–185
Waldron J (1992) Lex Talionis. Arizona Law Rev 34:25–52

Weber M (1978) Economy and society. University of California Press, Berkeley
Whitman JQ (1995) At the origins of law and the state: supervision of violence, mutilation of bodies, or setting of prices? Chicago Kent Law Rev 71:41–71
Wilf S (2009) The invention of legal primitivism. Theoretical Inquiries Law 10:451–476
Yavetz Z (1984) The Res Gestae and Augustus' public image. In: Millar F, Segal E (eds) Caesar Augustus: seven aspects. Clarendon Press, Oxford, pp 1–36

On Revenge and Punishment

Arguments for a Crucial Distinction

Edoardo Fittipaldi

Abstract In this chapter, the author proposes a psychoanalytic distinction between revenge and punishment. Punishment is conceptualized as a form of violence exerted by an authority-holder against a subordinate due to the latter's not having complied with a command or wish of the former. Instead, revenge is conceptualized as a form of violence exerted by an individual against another outside any authority relationship. After conceptualizing punishment and revenge the author shows that: (1) the same act may be caused by both an urge for punishment and one for revenge; (2) composition is possible only in the case of an urge for revenge; (3) a form of composition can be the *establishment* of a *new* authority relationship (composition-by-submission); (4) expiation, or atonement, cannot be regarded as a form of composition; (5) guilt always involves—at least at an unconscious level—the establishment of a *new* authority relationship; (6) the term "authorized revenge" may be referred to quite heterogenous phenomena.

1 Introduction

In this chapter, I propose *stipulative* conceptualizations for "revenge" and "punishment." In doing so, I move from two assumptions:

The most original idea contained in this Chapter, namely, that revenge-takers do not jurally expect their victims to accept their violence while punishers do, is an elaboration on Kurczewski (1976). I wish to thank Ignasi Terradas Saborit and Riccardo Mazzola, who read previous versions of this Chapter, for their invaluable advice. The term "composition-by-submission" was partly suggested by Mazzola. All mistakes are mine only.

E. Fittipaldi (✉)
Department of Legal Sciences "Cesare Beccaria", Faculty of Law, University of Milan, Milan, Italy
e-mail: edoardo.fittipaldi@unimi.it

R. Márquez Porras et al. (eds.), *Vindicatory Justice*, Ius Gentium: Comparative Perspectives on Law and Justice 93, https://doi.org/10.1007/978-3-030-79595-5_4

1. There exist two different psychological phenomena that can be roughly mapped onto the phenomena referred to as "revenge" and "punishment" across and within languages;
2. The existence of these two different psychological phenomena may cause the emergence of distinct terms to refer, respectively, to the first and the second type of phenomenon.

It should be also preliminarily stressed that this chapter is of a psycho-sociological nature: Psychology is understood here as a tool for sociological and anthropological research.[1]

Sociology cannot do without psychology and notably psychoanalysis. Among other things, by using psychology and psychoanalysis, a social scientist can attempt to assess the causal role of purely sociological factors—as distinct from psychological ones—when it comes to explaining social phenomena.

This attempt here can be compared to Galileo's effort to describe how bodies fall in a vacuum. Sure, Aristotle provided a "highly nontrivial correct description" (Rovelli 2015, p. 28) of the way bodies fall *in our world*. This includes the indeed accurate hypothesis that—*in our world*—their speed of fall is directly proportional to their weight (26). However, it is the hypothesization of how bodies fall *in a vacuum* that eventually made it possible to discover the law of gravitation and to describe in an even more accurate way than Aristotle the factors that affect their fall *in our world*, like fluid resistance and buoyancy.

That is to say, in this chapter I attempt to distinguish between revenge and punishment in a sort of "psychological vacuum." Hopefully, this will make it easier to investigate the non-psychological factors that affect revenge and punishment *in our social world*.

In the next section, I conceptualize punishment and revenge.[2] In Sect. 3, I discuss some remarkable phenomena in the light of the conceptualization proposed here. In the Conclusion, I briefly sum up what a conceptualization should pursue—including this one.

---

[1]Throughout this chapter, by "sociology" I mean both "sociology in a strict sense" and "anthropology."

[2]Zaibert (2006) argues against a clear distinction between revenge and punishment. However, the arguments he discusses are quite different from the ones that will be propounded here (which are chiefly based on psychoanalysis and the tradition of Polish–Russian legal realism); therefore, there is no reason to discuss Zaibert's ideas.

2 Distinguishing Between Punishment and Revenge

To conceptualize revenge and punishment it is first necessary to introduce a few preliminary concepts, which I draw from psychoanalysis and the tradition of Polish–Russian legal realism.[3]

The first concept we need is that of a *jural relationship*. By this term, I understand a relationship where some animate being[4] (D, or jural[5] duty-holder) is jurally expected to behave in a certain way to the advantage of another animate entity, experienced as entitled to that behavior[6] (R, or right-holder).

For a jural relationship to exist, it suffices that it be experienced by at least one of the participants, namely, R, D, or T ("third party").

It exists within R (e.g., Xerxes) if R has the disposition to become angry should D (e.g., the Hellespont) *not* behave in a certain way to their (R's) advantage (e.g., not destroying Xerxes's pontoon bridge), which amounts to R's jurally expecting D to behave that way, or to put it still otherwise, to R's experiencing themselves as entitled to D's behaving that way.

It exists within D (e.g., a driver) if D has the disposition *not* to become shocked or surprised should R (e.g., a pedestrian) become angry because of D's failing to behave in a certain way to R's advantage (e.g., stopping at a crosswalk), which amounts to D's recognizing R as entitled to their (D's) behaving that way.

It exists within T (e.g., a believer) if T has the disposition to become angry should D (e.g., deity_1) not behave in a certain way to the advantage of R (e.g., deity_2), which amounts to T's jurally expecting D to behave that way to the advantage of R, or to put it still otherwise, to T's experiencing R as entitled to D's behaving that way.

Four types of jural relationship can be distinguished:

1. Relationships where D is expected to endure a certain action on the part of R (e.g., R's walking on D's field);
2. Jural relationships where D is expected to endure a certain omission on the part of R (e.g., R's—D's neighbor—not removing the snow on the sidewalk in front of her own house);
3. Jural relationships where D is expected to perform a certain action advantageous to R (e.g., D's giving some money to R); and
4. Jural relationships where D is expected to abstain from a certain action disadvantageous to R (e.g., D's abstaining from assaulting R).

---

[3]Cf. Fittipaldi (2016a).

[4]Unless otherwise stated, by "animate being," I always understand the object of a perception or representation regardless of its truth. This is necessary lest it become impossible to take seriously such beliefs as that some *deity* punished a community because of its members having violated some taboo.

[5]I use "jural" as an adjective for "right," or "entitlement."

[6]I use "behavior" as a hypernym for action and omission. This means that the expression "to perform a behavior" should be understood as also possibly meaning "to abstain from a certain action."

Elaborating on Petrażycki's ideas,[7] I conceptualize authority relationships as *compound jural relationships* between authority-holders and subordinates where the following hold true:

1. Subordinates are jurally expected to uncomplainingly endure their authority-holders' actions—with or without limitations;
2. Subordinates are jurally expected to uncomplainingly endure their authority-holders' omissions—with or without limitations;
3. Subordinates are jurally expected to do something wished or expressly commanded by their authority-holders—with or without limitations; and
4. Subordinates are jurally expected not to do something their authority-holders do not wish or expressly prohibit—with or without limitations.

The prototype of all authority is the caregiver during early child-caregiver interactions. This experience belongs to an age when we are completely helpless and rely on our caregiver for all our needs. This, in turn, results in our both loving and fearing them (at least, we fear the withdrawal of their love or else their death or illness). Elaborating on Pierre Bovet,[8] Jean Piaget calls this blend of love and fear "respect," conceptualized as "a sui generis mixture of fear and love."[9,10]

To conceptualize punishment we can reformulate what subordinates are expected to do as follows:

1. They are expected to comply with their authority-holders' commands/prohibitions; and
2. They are expected to uncomplainingly endure their authority-holders' behaviors, *which may also include unpleasant reactions for not doing (1).*

I conceptualize these unpleasant reactions as punishment. This also makes it possible to conceptualize revenge.

Punishment is imposed by an authority holder against a subordinate, while revenge is taken outside an authority relationship or, within such a relationship, by a subordinate against an authority-holder (not the other way around).[11]

[7]Petrażycki ([1909/10] and [1909-10/2011]); see also Fittipaldi (2016b).

[8]See Bovet (1925/1928).

[9]Piaget (1932/1948), p. 351.

[10]When we become adults, we may also become able to experience as authority-holders animate beings other than our caregiver (including our peers, deities/gods/God, a certain state, our partner, and so on).

[11]It should be stressed that neither revenge nor punishment are acts aimed at coercing the victim into meeting a jural expectation, when this is still possible (a phenomenon I refer to as "coercion" or, in German, as "Erzwingung"). According to the conceptualization proposed here, revenge and punishment are conceptually possible only when an expectation cannot be any longer satisfied. (However, it cannot be ruled out that in some cases revenge and punishment are *unconsciously* taken or imposed in order to coerce the victim into doing something impossible, like undoing the past, along with its possibly irreversible consequences. Due to space limitations, I cannot discuss this issue here.)

It is of paramount importance to remark that in authority relationships the subordinate is not only jurally expected to endure the punishment but also to *show respect* for their authority-holder. This implies that punished persons are jurally expected not to challenge or resist punishment, and, if incarcerated, not to try to escape. Remarkably, this does not hold for those against whom revenge is taken. Quite the opposite, they are (cognitively) expected to react against revenge.

It is in order now to introduce two distinctions that will become useful below.

The first distinction, proposed by Petrażycki, is between private and public authority-holders, which is as follows:

1. *Private* authority-holders are *not* jurally expected to exert their authority *in the interest of their subordinates* (in other words, they are experienced as entitled to exert their authority in their own interest); examples are slave owners and employers.
2. *Public* authority-holders are jurally expected to exert their authority *in the interest of their subordinates*—as individuals or as a whole;[12] examples are officials in non-patrimonial states or parents in Western societies.[13]

In addition to this distinction, I believe that we should further differentiate between *asymmetrical* and *symmetrical* public authorities:

2.1. *Asymmetrical* public authority-holders are experienced as entitled to exercise their authority in the interest of their subordinates, *but* the latter are *not* experienced as entitled to claim that the former's authority be used to that end.

2.2. *Symmetrical* public authority-holders are experienced as entitled to exercise their authority in the interest of their subordinates, *and* the latter are experienced as entitled to claim that the former's authority be exercised to that end.

That is to say, if a symmetrical public authority relationship exists within a subordinate, she jurally expects the authority-holder to exert his authority to her (the subordinate's) advantage.[14]

In the next section and subsections, I will discuss a few issues from the standpoint of the distinction proposed here.

[12]In this latter case, the authority-holder's decision to have some subordinates lose their lives in the interest of the group may not shock or surprise anybody. Obvious examples are wars.

[13]See Petrażycki (1909-10) p. 728 ff. To avoid any misunderstanding, it should be stressed that this conceptualization is completely independent of juristic or legal–dogmatic ones. For example, if in a private household a governess is ascribed an authority to be exercised in the interest of that household's children, that governess is to be conceptualized as a public authority-holder (Petrażycki 1909-10, p. 745).

[14]It seems to me that in Western countries parental authority underwent a change from (1) to (2.1) and then from (2.1) to (2.2).

3 A Few Issues from the Standpoint of the Distinction Proposed Here

I will now show that: an urge for revenge and an urge for punishment may be contemporarily present in the same act (Sect. 3.1); composition is possible only in the presence of an urge for revenge (Sect. 3.2); a form of composition may be an act of submission on the part of the possible victim (Ibid.); composition-by-an-act-of-submission is tightly related to guilt (Sect. 3.3); the term "authorized revenge" can be used to refer to heterogenous phenomena (Sect. 3.4).

3.1 On the Non-incompatibility of Revenge and Punishment

Can an urge for revenge and an urge for punishment be both traced in the same act? If we accept Sigmund Freud's hypothesis the deeper strata of the human psyche ignore the principle of non-contradiction (1933/2001, p. 73), the answer is yes.

This hypothesis, if correct, implies that Ego may at the same time:

1. Experience herself as an authority-holder with regard to Alter and
2. (α) *Not* experience herself as an authority-holder with regard to Alter or (β) *at the same time* experience herself as a subordinate with regard to Alter.

This implies that the violence that Ego may exert on Alter may be experienced by Ego as both punishment and revenge at the same time.

An example has been provided by Ignasi Terradas Saborit.

> The jealous husband behaves like a father/patriarch and like a son, affectionate and, at the same time, dependent on his wife: The man's protection, security, and control are exchanged for the woman's obedience. ... [T]he man is to receive appreciation, recognition of his unique identity, his partner's unconditional affection in exchange for very little; that is, the perpetual maternal sacrifice to be found in any woman. In adultery, treason to the father or patriarch instantiates itself along with maternal abandonment. If both aspects co-escalate, the contradictory reactions of these husbands are easily brought about: both as enraged patriarchs and as abandoned children. Thus, we have violence and regret, murders and suicides.[15]

In this case, on the one hand, the man experiences himself as an authority-holder with regard to his wife, while on the other, he experiences himself as a subordinate in a symmetrical public authority relationship (see above, Sect. 2), which includes the jural expectation not to be abandoned by his wife/mother.

The experience of the insubordination of one's partner along with the unconscious experience of maternal abandonment may result in a form of violence that instantiates both an act of punishment and an act of revenge—as conceptualized here. Because we are dealing with a *symmetrical* public authority relationship, the

[15] Terradas Saborit (2019), p. 10.

authority-holder's anger elicited by an act of insubordination compounds itself with the subordinate's anger elicited by the frustration of a jural expectation in such a relationship.

3.2 *Revenge, Composition, and Punishment*

On the basis of the conceptualization proposed here, we can draw a few corollaries on the relation between composition and, respectively, revenge and punishment.

Let us start with the relation between revenge and composition, and read what Ignasi Terradas Saborit writes in this regard:

> The main epistemological bias I found in anthropological and legal literature for the establishment of vindicatory law as a system, comes from the supposed pre-eminence of vengeance and similar retaliatory practices, especially among "primitive" or traditional societies.[16]

I believe that the approach adopted here need not be incompatible with that adopted by Terradas Saborit.

Its (in)compatibility depends on how we understand the word "preeminence." If it is understood in the sense that, historically, composition precedes revenge, my approach is definitely incompatible with Terradas Saborit's. This is so because mine implies that, psychologically, revenge is a *prius* relative to composition, which emerges—if at all—as a way to avert revenge.

But another interpretation is possible.

Terradas Saborit may be stressing that there may exist vindicatory systems wherein revenge is extremely rare and somewhat in the background. This is perfectly compatible with my conceptualization, which does not rule out a scenario where a system of composition crowds out revenge altogether.

In this connection, the following question should be asked: If composition is a possible alternative to revenge, is it so also to punishment?

In other words, is an offer of composition compatible with a situation where the offeree claims a preexisting authority over the offeror?

I believe it is not.

In the case of authority relationships, the only way Alter can appease Ego is by accepting her *preexisting* authority (or pretending to do so), which includes acknowledging her right to punish him.

To cast light on these phenomena, we must distinguish between:

a. the case where Alter experiences himself as being Ego's subordinate and Ego experiences herself as an authority-holder with regard to Alter;
b. the case where Alter experiences himself as not being Ego's subordinate but Ego experiences herself as an authority-holder with regard to Alter; and

[16] In this volume, p. 13.

c. the case where Alter experiences himself as being an authority-holder with regard to Ego and Ego experiences herself as an authority-holder with regard to Alter.[17]

Let us start with (a).

In this case there is no room for composition. Alter can only *recognize* Ego's authority and his own *preexisting* submission.

This phenomenon should not be conceptualized in terms of composition but of *expiation*, or *atonement*. To conceptualize expiation/atonement, I avail myself of Jean Piaget:

> [A]dult constraint explains the formation of the idea of expiation...
>
> ...
>
> Very early in life, even before the infant can speak, its conduct is constantly being subjected to approval or censure [on the part of adults]. According to circumstances people are pleased with the baby and smile at it, or else frown and leave it to cry, and the very inflections in the voices of those that surround it are alone sufficient to constitute an incessant retribution. During the years that follow, the child is watched over continuously, everything he does and says is controlled, gives rise to encouragement or reproof, and the vast majority of adults still look upon punishment, corporeal or otherwise, as perfectly legitimate. It is obviously these reactions on the part of the adult ... that are the psychological starting-point of the idea of expiatory punishment. If the child felt nothing but fear or mistrust, as may happen in extreme cases, this would simply lead to open war. But as the child loves his parents and feels for their actions ... *respect* ... [see, above, Sect. 2], punishment appears to him as morally [in my terminology, "jurally"] obligatory and necessarily connected with the act that provoked it. Disobedience—the principle of all "sin"—is the breach of the normal relations between parent and child; some reparation [*réparation*] is therefore necessary, and since parents display their "righteous anger" [*juste collere*] by the various reactions that take the form of punishments, *to accept these punishments* [*accepter ces punitions*] *constitutes the most natural form of reparation*. The pain inflicted thus seems to re-establish the relations that had momentarily been interrupted, and in this way the idea of expiation becomes incorporated in the values of the morality of authority. In our view, therefore, this "primitive" and materialistic conception of expiatory punishment is not imposed as such by the adult upon the child, and it was perhaps never invented by a psychologically adult mind; but it is the inevitable product of punishment as refracted in the mystically realistic mentality of the child.[18]

To expiate, or atone a "crime" is to inwardly accept being punished for it, and this amounts *to recognizing the preexisting authority of the punisher*.

The situation is more complicated in cases (b) and (c). Here Ego experiences herself as authority-holder with regard to Alter, while Alter either does not experience himself as a subordinate with regard to Ego or experiences himself as an authority-holder with regard to her.

Here there can be

---

[17]Consistently with Polish-Russian legal realism, I am assuming that for an authority relationship to exist it suffices that it exist within the mind of Ego or Alter (or else a third party), and that incompatible convictions in this regard may lead to conflicts.

[18]Piaget (1932/1978), pp. 257–258; English translation modified (1932/1948), pp. 321–322, emphases added.

1. War; or
2. Alter's *act* of submission to Ego or Ego's *act* of submission to Alter, which is tantamount to the roles of authority-holder and subordinate *being thereby instituted* within the mind of Ego, Alter, or both—a different phenomenon from the recognition of a preexisting authority relationship—; or
3. Ego's or Alter's flight from conflict without any act of submission on the part of either.

Thus, we have three possible outcomes: (1) fight, (2) act of submission, or (3) flight. In case (2), we are dealing with a composition-by-an-act-of-submission, or in brief, composition-by-submission. (Technically, this is a composition only in the mind of the participant who did not previously experience themselves as a subordinate of the other).[19] I will return to this phenomenon in the next section.

3.3 From Composition-by-Submission to Sense of Guilt

In the previous section I have discussed the situation where Alter offers his submission to Ego where Ego claims authority over Alter. But Alter may offer his submission even if Ego does not claim authority over him, and so in order to avert Ego's revenge.

This means that we can hypothesize that, in certain cases, an authority relationship (for example, slavery) may emerge out of an act that both Ego and Alter experience as an offense, or, to be more precise as the frustration of a jural expectation other than the expectations that make up an authority relationship.

In such cases, composition is effected through an act of submission.

Further light on this phenomenon can be cast by spending a few words on guilt as psychoanalytically understood.

Guilt emerges from the helpless child's fear of losing their caregiver's love because of having harmed, disappointed, or disobeyed them.[20]

That is to say, guilt emerges out of an archeotypical[21] authority relationship.

Does this imply that in adults guilt necessarily involves a form of composition-by-submission and therefore the establishment of an authority relationship?

The answer is a qualified yes.

Guilt always involves the establishment of an authority relationship, even though it may be merely a short-lived unconscious one.

[19]To avoid misunderstanding it should stressed that in this case, Ego or Alter, in order to "appease," respectively, Alter or Ego may *pretend* to be recognizing the other's preexisting authority rather than instituting it.

[20]For references to the psychological literature, see Fittipaldi (2012).

[21]I use the neologism "archeotypical"—as distinct from "archetypical"—to refer to phenomena related to child-caregiver interactions.

In other words, my hypothesis is that Ego's experience of guilt toward Alter—if truly felt—always involves a form of *regression*, along with an unconscious act of submission to Alter.[22]

3.4 On "Authorized Revenge"

This chapter would be incomplete without a discussion of "authorized revenge."

In the next subsections I will discuss some phenomena that may be referred to as "authorized revenge" and show that they are quite heterogenous.

3.4.1 Violence Between Subordinates of the Same Authority-Holder

In this case, the potential exerter of violence and the victim are subordinates of the same authority-holder, and this authority-holder either authorizes or tolerates that the potential violence-exerter act against the victim because of the victim's having frustrated a jural expectation of the potential violence-exerter.

If there is *express* authorization, I would definitely speak of *authorized revenge*. Less so, if the authority-holder simply abstains from prohibiting it. To use "authorized" in such a context would be—more often than not—nothing but sheer juristic fiction.

Phenomena of these kinds can be also observed in archeotypical situations, such as where a caregiver (α) authorizes, (β) tolerates, or (γ) rules that their $child_1$ should take a toy from their $child_2$ due to $child_2$'s having damaged a toy of $child_1$. However, (α), (β), and (γ) should be kept distinct. Only in case (α) are we dealing with a form of authorized revenge. In case (β) we have a form of tolerated revenge, while in case (γ) we have a form of indirect punishment.

3.4.2 Violence Between Members in Communities Without Authority-Holders

In this case there cannot be any punishment.

There can be only revenge.

As for authorized revenge, this phenomenon is present only if something akin to a council of elders or an assembly of the entire community *expressly* authorizes the

[22]To avoid misunderstanding, it should be stressed that by using the phrase "act of submission," I am in no way implying that this *act* must be a formal one. In Grazia Deledda's novel *Reeds in the Wind*, Efix informally submits himself to Don Zame's daughters and thus expiates his having murdered their father. In this case, expiation is made possible by Efix's becoming their servant (*servo*) (cf. Deledda 1913/1999, p. 137). (I wish to thank Terradas Saborit for calling my attention to Deledda's novel).

violence-exerter to act against the victim. To speak of authorized revenge in the absence of such an express authorization would be sheer fiction.

3.4.3 Violence Between Authority-Holder$_1$'s Subordinate$_1$ and a Freeperson or Authority-Holder$_2$'s Subordinate$_2$ Which Is Exerted to Satisfy *Authority-Holder$_1$*'s Urge for Revenge

In this case, the potential violence-exerter is a subordinate$_1$ of authority-holder$_1$ who authorizes, tolerates, or commands subordinate$_1$ to act against a freeperson or subordinate$_2$ of authority-holder$_2$ because authority-holder$_1$ experiences the potential victim or their authority-holder$_2$ as having frustrated a jural expectations of theirs (of authority-holder$_1$).

In this case, I would not speak of authorized revenge because authority-holder$_1$ avails themselves of subordinate$_1$ as a tool for satisfying their own urge for revenge. In the final analysis, we are dealing here with authority-holder$_1$'s revenge, which is not authorized by anybody above them.

3.4.4 Violence Between Authority-Holder$_1$'s Subordinate$_1$ and a Freeperson or Authority-Holder$_2$'s Subordinate$_2$ Which Is Exerted to Satisfy *Subordinate$_1$*'s Urge for Revenge

In this case, the potential violence-exerter is a subordinate$_1$ of authority-holder$_1$ who authorizes, tolerates, or commands subordinate$_1$ to act against a freeperson or subordinate$_2$ of another authority-holder$_2$ because subordinate$_1$ experiences the potential victim as having frustrated a jural expectation of theirs (of subordinate$_1$). In this case, I think we can speak of *authorized revenge* but in a different sense from those discussed above. Revenge is authorized from the standpoint of the revenge-taker but not from that of the victim, who does not experience authority-holder$_1$ as an authority-holder.

4 Conclusions

I am a social scientist concerned with the problem of the conceptualization of normative concepts.

Here I offered psychoanalytical conceptualizations for revenge and punishment. I hope that despite their "alien" (i.e., non-strictly-sociological) origin, they can prove useful for the social sciences much as, for example, biological concepts can be used to investigate and compare different social constructions of human health and illness.

I cannot rule out that different conceptualizations for revenge and punishment might turn out to be as useful (or even more so) than mine.

Further, I do not even think that there must necessarily be only one correct conceptualization for phenomena.

A conceptualization proves useful if it selects *sets* of phenomena capable of playing the role of causal antecedents in causal laws or if the *clusters* of phenomena it selects have above-average probability of co-occurrence. It follows that different conceptualizations for partly overlapping phenomena may have an equal scientific legitimation, provided that they select distinct antecedents for distinct causal laws or they select distinct statistically significant clusters of phenomena.

This holds also for the various stipulative conceptualizations that can be offered for selecting sets of phenomena that intersect with (or are subsets of) those selected by the terms "revenge" and "punishment" in the English language. The cognitive salience of some of those sets might also *help* explain the possible emergence of distinct terms for "revenge" and "punishment" in English and other languages.

These are the criteria through which the scientific legitimacy of the conceptualizations proposed here should be assessed.

References

Bovet P (1925/1928) Le sentiment religieux et la psychologie de l'enfant. English translation The Child's Religion. Dent & Sons, London

Deledda G (1913/1999) Reeds in the wind. English translation of Canne al vento. Italica Press, New York

Fittipaldi E (2012) Everyday legal ontology: a psychological and linguistic investigation within the framework of Leon Petrażycki's theory of law. LED, Milan

Fittipaldi E (2016a) Introduction: continental legal realism. In: Pattaro E, Roversi C (eds) Legal philosophy in the twentieth century: the civil law world, Volume 12, Tome 2: Main orientations and topics. Springer, Dordrecht, pp 297–318

Fittipaldi E (2016b) Leon Petrażycki's theory of law. In: Pattaro E, Roversi C (eds) Legal philosophy in the twentieth century: the civil law world, Volume 12, Tome 2: Main orientations and topics. Springer, Dordrecht, pp 443–503

Freud S (1933/2001) Neue Folge der Vorlesungen zur Einführung in die Psychoanalyse. English translation. In: Freud S (Strachey J ed) New introductory lectures on psychoanalysis and other works. Vintage Books, New York

Kurczewski J (1976) Ambiguous reciprocity. Pol Sociol Bull 34(2):5–16

Petrażycki L (1909-10) Teorija prava i gosudarstva v svjazi s teoriej nravstvennosti, 2nd edn. M. Merkuševa, Saint Petersburg

Petrażycki L (1909-10/2011) Teorija prava i gosudarstva v svjazi s teoriej nravstvennosti. Abridged English Translation of the 2nd ed. In: Petrażycki L (Timasheff N ed.) Law and morality. Routledge, Abingdon

Piaget J (1932/1948) Le jugement moral chez l'enfant. English translation the moral judgment of the child. The free press of Glencoe, Glencoe

Piaget J (1932/1978) Le jugement moral chez l'enfant. PUF, Paris

Rovelli C (2015) Aristotle's physics: a physicist's look. J Am Philos Assoc 1:23–40

Terradas Saborit I (2019) Giustizia Vendicatoria e sfondo vendicatorio nella Giustizia Penale (unpublished paper)

Zaibert L (2006) Punishment and revenge. Law Philos 25(1):81–118

“To Restore” Versus “To Vindicate”

A Comparative Analysis

Riccardo Mazzola

Abstract The present chapter develops a comparison between restorative justice and vindicatory justice. This chapter first shows how restorative justice and historical–ethnographic accounts of vindicatory justice have several traits in common, such as a focus on the victim’s experience and satisfaction, the necessity of a making-amends process, and a dialogue established between the parties and social agents. The chapter then goes on to analyze the main difference between restorative justice and vindicatory justice regarding the nature of the subjects involved in the conflict. The chapter relies more precisely on the anthropological notion of “solidarity group,” which plays a pivotal role in vindicatory justice but has no place in contemporary society.

1 Introduction

This chapter aims to concisely discuss the analogies and fundamental distinctions between restorative justice (RJ) and vindicatory justice (VJ).

A certain similarity, to all appearances, between RJ and VJ notions and procedures prompted the comparative analysis that follows. It is indeed undeniable, as Sect. 2 will analytically show, that RJ and VJ share several common features and functions, as well as their conceptual (but not necessarily operational[1]) “otherness” with respect to criminal law and procedure (CL). Such a close relationship evokes questions about the actual reason for conceiving of RJ and VJ as two separate and coexisting models of justice rather than a *sole* way of dealing with the aftermath of an offense in human societies.

Some key questions are the following: Do the two models (RJ and VJ) fully overlap? Alternatively, is one of the two types a *prototypical* form of the other,

[1]On the complementarity between RJ and criminal justice, see among others Vogt (2012).

R. Mazzola (✉)
Department of Legal Sciences ‘Cesare Beccaria’, Faculty of Law, University of Milan, Milan, Italy
e-mail: riccardo.mazzola1@unimi.it

R. Márquez Porras et al. (eds.), *Vindicatory Justice*, Ius Gentium: Comparative Perspectives on Law and Justice 93, https://doi.org/10.1007/978-3-030-79595-5_5

enduring minor historical alterations? In addition, conversely, is one procedure a *refined* and *advanced* version of the other? Alternatively, quite the opposite, does any significant difference between RJ and VJ justifying the construction of two separate notions exist? Is "restoring an offense," that is, addressing the consequence of an offense by means of RJ procedures, the same as "vindicating an offense," that is, acting through the mechanism of VJ?

This chapter ultimately argues in favor of the *non-sameness* thesis, per which RJ and VJ identify structurally different constructs. As Sect. 3 will discuss, the notion of "solidarity group"—a crucial one in VJ theory—plays a decisive role in excluding a complete overlapping between the two models of justice. More specifically, the main thesis claimed here is that, while parties involved in RJ procedures are *individual* ones and their feelings and emotions are experienced subjectively, VJ works through an interaction between *groups* that *collectively* address a wrong and refer to a *shared* sense of justice. Consequently, in VJ, feelings possess a *social* dimension independent of individuals' subjective experience: what develops into one's own consciousness or intuition acquires in VJ a *shared social meaning*. As will be argued, differences in the kind of "group"—individuals *versus* groups of solidarity—exert a significant influence on how justice and compensation are sought in RJ and VJ respectively.

The conclusion of the present chapter is that although sharing most principles and procedural segments, RJ and VJ have been conceived and instantiated within *different kinds of society*—individual and "group" social agglomerates—that have shaped the structure of the two models in distinct and possibly incompatible ways.

2 "To Restore" as "To Vindicate": Analogies

2.1 *Definitions*

2.1.1 Restorative Justice

A starting point for a comparison between RJ and VJ is to examine their definitions, which share several commonalities.

As is known, the quest for a definition of "restorative justice" is still a work in progress.[2] From the standpoint of *normative* definitions,[3] the most recent one is included in the UN *Basic Principles on the Use of Restorative Justice Programmes in Criminal Matters* (Sect. 1.2):

> "Restorative process" means any process in which the victim and the offender and, where appropriate, any other individuals or community members affected by a crime participate

[2]See Van Ness and Heetderks Strong (2015), pp. 43–44.

[3]For a survey and analytic classification of RJ definitions, see Mannozzi and Lodigiani (2017), pp. 89–106.

> together actively in the resolution of matters arising from the crime, generally with the help of a facilitator. Restorative processes may include mediation, conciliation, conferencing and sentencing circles.

As can be easily noted, this definition focuses on *operational* aspects of RJ—as a "process"—more than its core criteria[4] although the dividing line between what a certain kind of justice *is* and how the same model of justice *works* can be hard to grasp.[5] To cast light on specific characteristics of RJ and the restorative "content" of the RJ procedure, *didactic–doctrinal* definitions may be of some help. It is said that RJ "promotes healing" of the offense,[6] an action that can be further specified as the process of repairing the damage either materially or symbolically.[7] Among didactic–doctrinal definitions, *community-oriented* definitions refer to RJ as a process aimed at the comprehension and restoration of social relationships between individuals.[8] In addition, *holistic* definitions of RJ mostly emphasize the collective nature of restorative procedures, such as a collective identification of harms, needs, and obligations to render things "as right as possible"[9] and a collectively addressed resolution on how to deal with the aftermath of an offense and its implications for the future.[10] The nature of such a "collective" dimension of RJ will be analyzed in Sect. 3.

2.1.2 Vindicatory Justice

As can be imagined, there is no wide discussion yet on Terradas Saborit's definition of VJ, as VJ theory, at least in the version addressed by this volume,[11] is quite a new paradigm in the social and legal sciences. Thus, today, "classic" definitions of VJ are found only in Terradas Saborit's works.[12] A basic definition refers to VJ as follows:

> [VJ is] a procedure that mixes features of Western civil and criminal law in a system prioritizing a composition [namely, a peaceful resolution] in favor of the offended party, without excluding the possibility for her of a violent revenge once authorized by a third and neutral party.[13]

---

[4]This is quite a common trait of normative definitions of RJ. See Mannozzi and Lodigiani (2017), pp. 99–102.

[5]Most scholars think that RJ does not represent a paradigm of justice per se but needs rather to work in accordance with other systems (such as CL). See Mannozzi and Lodigiani (2017), p. 362, for a recap and a bibliography on this point.

[6] Van Ness and Heetderks Strong (2015), p. 32.

[7]See Wright (1996), p. iv.

[8]See Richardson and Preston (1999), p. 1.

[9]See Zehr (1990), p. 181

[10]See Marshall (1999), p. 5.

[11]Terradas Saborit's definition of VJ is much more complex and multifaceted than the *vindicatoire* model discussed in Verdier (1980).

[12]But see also Ramis Barceló (2010), p. 519, and Márquez Porras and Mazzola (2019), pp. 73–74. However, both definitions heavily rely on Terradas Saborit's.

[13]Terradas Saborit (2014), p. 59. My translation from Spanish.

The "core criteria" or "features" of VJ can be summarized as follows:[14]

1. Ineludible *obligation to compensate/repair the offense*;
2. Priority given to a *nonviolent resolution of the conflict*;
3. Necessary *"judicial" authorization of a violent revenge* should the compositional process fail;
4. Quest for *reconciliation* between the conflicting parties;
5. *Flexible* procedures;
6. *Interweaving of "law," "ethics," and "religion"* in the vindicatory procedure;
7. Prominent role given to *factual equity* in the vindicatory judgment;
8. *Collective* and "social" nature of responsibility.

2.2 Four Common Features

Four common features can be identified as denoting a certain similarity between RJ and VJ.

First, both RJ and VJ imply a conceptual shift—with respect to CL—from a *crime/punishment* narrative to a *conflict/reparation* one. Both models of justice are supposed to "correct" indeed the "inability" of CL to repair the social tissue torn by conflict by giving the offended party some means of (re)empowerment.[15] This issue is prominently addressed in RJ literature, particularly by the most radical authors,[16] but is also a crucial feature of VJ. It is significant that both VJ and RJ maintain among their principles that the offender must *recognize* the offense, violation, or injustice (must recognize having committed an offensive action against someone). This is a duty entailed by the VJ principle establishing the "ineludible obligation" to repair the offense (Sect. 2.1). Both models of justice also maintain that "justice" must be reestablished,[17] without including any reference to the offender's "punishment" per se. It is to be noted that in vindicatory systems and the RJ normative apparatus, the wrongdoer may actually be submitted to forms of public humiliation,[18] and regarding VJ, even to wounding or injuring—such as thigh spearing in the Yolngu (Australia) ritual of *makarrata*.[19] However, those "penalties" are better interpreted as forms of reestablishment of the original status-relationship between the

[14]See Márquez Porras and Mazzola (2019), pp. 73–74. For a wider discussion on each feature, see in general Terradas Saborit (2008, 2019, 2021).

[15]On this "inability" of CL, see the pioneering work of Gil (1983), pp. 94–95.

[16]See Zedner (1994), p. 228, for an extensive (early) bibliography.

[17]Regarding VJ: Terradas Saborit (2008), p. 65; regarding RJ: Classen (2004), p. 34.

[18][18] See regarding VJ, for instance, Terradas Saborit (2008), p. 281, discussing several norms of *lex talionis* as public humiliation procedures; regarding RJ, see the conception of shame penalties as forms of "reintegrative shaming" in Braithwaite (1989).

[19]For an interpretation of *makarrata* as a form of vindicatory procedure, see Márquez Porras and Mazzola (2019), pp. 78–82, mostly relying on Hiatt's account (1987).

conflicting parties rather than as actual "punishments."[20] Alternatively, at least, punishment is not the be all and end all of the abovementioned procedures but rather the *medium* to ultimately obtain (or facilitate) reconciliation.

Second, both RJ and VJ work through flexible procedures. As seen (Sect. 2.1), the flexibility of procedural steps leading to the reparation of the offense and the parties' reconciliation is one of the key concepts upon which VJ is founded. This flexibility determines that fundamental segments in the vindicatory procedure—particularly, taking action against the offender, reporting the facts to a "third party" (judge), surrendering material or "moral" composition to the offended party, and avenging—may assume different forms with no (not always) fixed formalities. This does not mean that the VJ procedure is not formal but rather that the subjects involved in VJ may *select*—although such a selection may be influenced by the offender or the offended party's cultural framework—from a vast range of formal ways to address the conflict. VJ procedural steps are, then, according to Amedeo G. Conte's lexicon, *diapraxic* acts,[21] because they can be performed in different and equivalent ways. For instance, the victim may take action against the offender either by referring to a largely formal "judging assembly" or "court"[22] or through an imprecation (referring to a god or sacred ancestor to legitimize the counteroffense).[23] In addition, the act of revenge that follows a failed composition may take different forms, such as a proper violent action—a killing-for-a-killing—or conduct aimed at putting the offender in jail by means of perjury, the so-called judicial vengeance.[24] Similarly, RJ procedures may vary from informal figures—such as the simple expression of emotions—to a highly formal mediation or conferencing group (a victim–offender mediation or a family conferencing group), through to "immediate" restorative dialogues (semiformal), restorative dialogues (guided and formal), and peacemaking circles.[25] Both RJ and VJ informality or "selective" formality seems consistent with the function of restoring social relations by addressing the parties' feelings and emotions and adapting to each case in no preconceived manner.

Third, a parallel may be established between two key concepts for RJ and VJ, respectively: *empowerment* (RJ) and attribution of *vindicatory capacity* following recognition *of defenselessness* (VJ). "Empowerment" is a complex notion dealing with the ability to raise self-esteem and self-confidence after an offense,[26] through a renewed attitude toward self-determination. Such a personal and "internal" process entails a *recognition of the offense by the offender*, as well as the *active role of the victim* in the quest for restoring justice, producing a shift from "disempowerment"

---

[20]Regarding RJ, see: Mannozzi and Lodigiani (2017), p. 183.

[21]See Conte (2011), p. 71.

[22]Such as the Germanic "*thing*." See Terradas Saborit (2008), p. 480.

[23]On the role of imprecation in VJ, see Terradas Saborit (2008), pp. 105–164.

[24]References to "judicial vengeance" can be found in Busquet (1994), p. 122 (Corsica), and Pigliaru (1993), p. 125 (Barbagia, Sardinia).

[25]See Wachtel and Wachtel (2012), ch. 2.

[26]Cf. Bolitho (2015), p. 268. On empowerment, see (among others) Simon (1994).

(after the offense) to (re)empowerment. The VJ core trait of "recognition of defenselessness" seems very close to the RJ empowerment process because it implies a significant change in the offended party's status from being *defenseless* (from a state of *indefensión*, as Terradas Saborit calls it[27]) to being able to repair and overcome the offense. This "ability" is the main outcome of the attribution of "vindicatory capacity" to the victim, corresponding to RJ empowerment *strictu sensu*. Although enacted in radically different manners—with VJ "re-empowering" procedures being usually coarser than those of RJ are—empowerment and attribution of vindicatory capacity share at least two key features:

1. They both maintain an impact on the *future* relationship between the parties by rebalancing the "gap" between the parties' statuses that were disrupted by the offense and renewing the victim's attitude toward the offender (and vice versa);
2. They both imply the *direct* and *active involvement of the victim* as a fundamental character of the procedure in the restorative/vindicatory process; that is to say, the victim acquires the function of not only *triggering* the procedure but also *materially handling* it by *interacting* with the offender.

Point 2 is also a significant, self-evident difference between VJ/RJ and CL.

Last, both VJ and RJ rely on the *reparation* of torts and injuries. As Garapon points out, it is possible to distinguish between two kinds of reparation in RJ (but the same distinction holds for VJ): "symbolic" and "material" reparation.[28] "Symbolic" reparation seemingly deals more effectively with the kind of insults and injuries VJ and RJ usually aim to repair because they—as Terradas Saborit illustrates[29]—inhere in honorific (rather than material) torts. However, "material" reparation—through money or material goods—is in RJ and VJ more complex than mere *pretium doloris*, or the simple repayment of what the offense damaged or disrupted.[30] Ideally, pace Georg Simmel's contention that "the sole quality of money is its quantity,"[31] modern reconstructions of the use of money in RJ also attribute a *symbolic* meaning to payment. This is because it results from the *recognition* of the offense by the offender,[32] may produce *empowerment* of the victim,[33] and usually entails a wider *narrative of justice*[34] that is more inherent to the *relational* aspect of the offense (how the offense affected the relationship between the parties) than it is to a strict proportion between offense and reparation. The same logic is found in VJ "composition" as Terradas Saborit notes. In VJ as well, the reparation (composition) of the offense is primarily symbolic even when performed through payment in money or

[27]See Terradas Saborit (2008), p. 167.

[28]See Garapon (2009), p. 166.

[29]See Terradas Saborit (2008), p. 204.

[30]See Terradas Saborit (2021).

[31]See Simmel (1984), p. 47.

[32]See Sharpe (2007), pp. 29–32.

[33]See Mannozzi and Lodigiani (2017), p. 227.

[34]See Garapon (2009), p. 192.

goods. Terradas Saborit took this idea from the French historian Fustel de Coulange's analysis of the Franks' vindicatory system,[35] enlightening us that the action of surrendering money or cattle also implied a public humiliation for the offender, who was mostly forced to admit their wrong and accept the "vindication" of the victim.

To sum up, the present section identified four features shared by VJ and RJ:

1. a *conceptual shift*, with respect to CL, *from a crime/punishment narrative to a conflict/reparation one*;
2. the *flexibility* of procedural steps leading to the reparation of the offense and the parties' reconciliation;
3. the parallel between *empowerment* (RJ) and *attribution of vindicatory capacity* following a *recognition of the defenselessness* of the victim (VJ); and
4. the *symbolic function of reparation* even if such reparation consists of money and material goods.

3 "To Restore" and "To Vindicate": Individuals and Groups

3.1 Revenge and Violence: An Obvious Distinction?

The present chapter asked (Sect. 1) whether RJ and VJ may be said to identify two models of justice that fully overlap; whether they are just different names referring to the same social and legal phenomenon; or on the contrary, whether there exists any significant difference between RJ and VJ that justifies the construction of two separate notions.

The previous section presented four commonalities between RJ and VJ. However, a seemingly obvious way of disentangling the issue and answering the foundational question of the present research study is to acknowledge that RJ and VJ maintain at least one, and a fundamental, difference in their approach to dealing with offenses and conflicts. That is to say, VJ admits the possibility for the offended party to *avenge*, that is, *to use violence against the offender*, as a key feature of its structure. As Terradas Saborit points out, once the "compositional" procedure—the symbolic reparation of the offense—has failed, vindicatory "judges" may authorize indeed violent acts of vengeance. In contrast, revenge and violence have no place in RJ. It may occur, of course, that RJ facilitates an outburst of violent revenge feelings and actions.[36] However, such occurrences represent a *distortion* of RJ procedures and its significance, whereas violence is a *necessary*—although residual—segment of vindicatory orders.

[35]See Terradas Saborit (2008), pp. 199 ff.; and (2021), mainly quoting Fustel de Coulange (1905).

[36]See Kaufmann (2013), p. 188.

Nevertheless, this "obvious" answer presents a problematic aspect. Specifically, it seems to underestimate the "residuality" of revenge and violence in VJ. In fact, to say that RJ and VJ are fundamentally different systems of justice because the latter admits the use of violence is to *disregard the VJ "core" by emphasizing an* extrema ratio *measure* (violence only occurs *if the compositional procedure failed*). The same line of reasoning, that is, overlapping the essence of some kind of justice with its marginal procedural aspects, would make it possible to identify RJ with its "extrema ratio," namely, *CL*.[37]

In other words, it may be argued that because revenge is to VJ what CL is to RJ, a residual procedure to be applied once the main and preferred one has failed, then RJ also includes aspects of "violence" (such as the limitation of the offender's freedom by life imprisonment, death penalty, and so on).

Thus, the comparison between RJ and VJ presented here does not consider the residual segment of those procedures (punishment and revenge, respectively), rather focusing on the actual "core" of the two models of justice: the *reparation/composition* at the heart of RJ and VJ. As seen, reparation (RJ) and composition (VJ) possess several features in common: they allow the offender to repair the social tissue torn by the conflict by force of their symbolic (nonmaterial) significance and by promoting the acknowledgment of the offense and giving the offended party some means of (re-)empowerment (such as the ascription of a vindicatory capacity). However, the next sections will concisely discuss a specific distinction between RJ and VJ justices enlightened by the notion of "solidarity group."

3.2 *Offender and Victim: The Solidarity Group*

An inquiry into the conceptual relationship between RJ reparation and VJ composition must unavoidably consider the social frameworks wherein those models of justice are (or were originally) found.

This section will argue that RJ and VJ differ in the nature of the social agents involved in the two procedures, respectively: the "offender" (Of) and the "offended" (Od) parties. More precisely, according to the VJ model, Of and Od are two (or more) *solidarity groups* that incorporate individuals. According to RJ, Of and Od are instead two (or more) *individuals* or *groups of individuals*. As will be shown, this subtle difference in the nature of Of and Od has an impact on the structure of VJ and RJ.

What is a "solidarity group"? As Terradas Saborit states:

> In societies where we find [. . .] vindicatory justice, there are entire groups of people aligned under a mandatory law of solidarity. Usually, a whole group of kinship recognizes itself as

[37]On CL as RJ *extrema ratio*, see Abel and Marsh (1984), p. 124. An example of the distortions that may derive from this relationship is the "John Carvin case" reported in Gavin and Sabbagh (2019).

> such thanks to this solidarity. Besides, the individual alone, being the offended or the offender, cannot ask for [. . .] a legal [trial].[38]

The "mandatory law of solidarity," in Terradas Saborit's words, at the foundation, for example, of the Germanic *Sippe*,[39] was an inextricable conjunction between a certain number of people forming a nucleus wherein the group represented a "body" and each individual a "limb" of that body.[40] No individual actions or offenses were possible within such a strict "interconnected" entity, created by "irrevocable primordial bonds (consanguinity, blood brotherhood, and similar ties)."[41] French lawyer and anthropologist Jacques Busquet compared conflictual relationships between solidarity groups with conflicts between armies, wherein, for instance, killing someone in a war is hardly the killing of an individual but rather harm inflicted on the adverse nation-party.[42]

The collective and interconnected dimension of subjects in vindicatory civilizations is relevant to how VJ takes shape, possessing both an *institutional* and a *social* character that interferes with VJ procedure.

From an *institutional* standpoint, the thickness and dimension of the solidarity group constitute a *parameter* based on which the vindicatory "court" or "judge" evaluates Od's level of *defenselessness*: as Terradas Saborit writes, "vindicatory justice seeks to acknowledge the capacity of the victim for a defense obtained through the incorporation into a group of solidarity."[43] Defenselessness in VJ—largely corresponding, as seen (Sect. 2.2), to disempowerment in RJ—is then measured as *the level of incorporation of Od into their solidarity group*. In other words, defenselessness is strictly connected to the *effectiveness of the protection the solidarity group can grant to Od against Of*. In addition, the bond linking the members of a solidarity group translates into a *collective responsibility for the offense* imposed on Of's group, corresponding to a *collective right to exact satisfaction* attributed to Od's group.[44]

From the standpoint of *social relationships*, each solidarity group may exercise *social pressure* on Of and Od, for them to take part in the compositional procedure or to accept composition, respectively. As Terradas Saborit points out, referring to Of, social pressure is always on, even before the offense: "since all the members of the solidarity group have to contribute [to potential compositions], the group puts pressure on the offenders to refrain from offending." When an offense occurs, "they show to the offender the trouble that [she] has created to the whole group,

[38]Terradas Saborit (2010).

[39]See Grimm (1828), pp. 494–495; and Tuori (2014, 2021).

[40]See Pigliaru (1993), pp. 138–139.

[41]See Terradas Saborit (2021).

[42]See Busquet (1994), p. 27.

[43] Terradas Saborit (2010).

[44]To draw a line between this kind of in solido responsibility and the Western model of collective responsibility, see Spencer (1959), p. 86, and in general Santiapichi (1963). For an example of a VJ procedure enacted by groups of solidarity, see Alonso Cabré (2021).

and they declare publicly all of themselves responsible towards the offended party."[45] A clear example of social pressure put on Of and Od is the mechanism triggered by an offense in Yolngu society (Australia). Among the Yolngu, Of was often forced to take part in a *makarrata* (a reconciliatory ritual, concluded by inflicting a wound on Of, which instantiates the compositional procedure typical of vindicatory systems) *by their own community*, not, as one may think, by their adversaries. Conversely, Od's relatives usually accepted the proposal of a *makarrata* because of pressure from their allies.[46] Moreover, *makarrata* is frequently (and paradoxically) organized *by and within Of's group*, without asking for permission or notifying Od, who does not participate in the ritual. In those cases, after the *makarrata*, Of's group eventually communicated that to Od, who usually accepted the settlement (once again pressured by their solidarity group).[47]

3.3 "Collective" Versus "Individual" Justice: Answering Two Objections

Based on the existence—in VJ—of a solidarity group, it is possible to establish one fundamental difference between VJ and RJ: while the VJ procedure is carried out and completed by *collective subjects* (solidarity groups), RJ usually concerns *individuals*.

A *first* objection may be intuitively raised against this statement: it is not true that groups do not possess relevance to RJ; on the contrary, they usually take part in RJ procedures, such as *family group conferencings* (FGC). As is known, FGC—as learned from Maori and Indigenous Australian conflict-resolution processes—involve an *enlarged circle of participants* in the RJ procedure, including Od's and Of's families and social networks (acquaintances). This way of dealing with reparation seems akin to that of VJ because the subjects involved are in fact "groups" relating to Od and Of. In FGC, however and quite crucially, Od's and Of's families and social networks *are not "absorbed" into the notions of "Od" and "Of"* and *do not constitute a solidarity group*. They are not the main actors in the RJ process but rather groups of people taking part in the problem-solving procedure as *spectators*.[48] More precisely, their function is *to passively or actively influence Od's and Of's attitude* toward the restorative process[49] or *to represent Od and Of* in the procedure. Nevertheless, they *do not share Of's responsibility for the offense or Od's right to*

---

[45] Terradas Saborit (2010).

[46] See Warner (1937), p. 58.

[47] See Hiatt (1987), p. 141.

[48] See Nader and Grande (2002), especially investigating the differences between FGC and the Maori–Indigenous models from which FGC originates.

[49] See Raye and Warner Roberts (2007), p. 214; Zinsstag (2012); Mannozzi and Lodigiani (2017), p. 278.

reparation and satisfaction. Their function is to sustain Of and Od in the RJ process, but they are not Of and Od *stricto sensu*. That fundamental difference makes it possible to distinguish easily the roles of family and social network in FGC from those of solidarity groups in VJ.

A *second* objection is that groups may be involved in the RJ process in the case of *offenses to classes of people*, such as cases of hate speech against a specific gender or race. At similar instances, it may seem quite certain that Od are actually groups and not individuals because the specific "quality" subject to the offense is shared among numerous people. However, a closer look at the essence of such a "large number of people" is the key to eliminating this objection. VJ and RJ (the latter in the case of offense to a group) entail indeed *different conceptions of what a "group" is*. VJ groups, or solidarity groups, are "local, non-anonymous, moral, social and legal persons, who can [take action] against private persons and public institutions."[50] The bonds linking the members of a solidarity group *preexist with respect to the VJ procedure and persist after its conclusion*, and then, solidarity groups act *as such* throughout the procedure. RJ groups represent, instead, *social and cultural identifications*, imaginary communities[51] of people sharing the same religion, race, gender, and so on. They are *multiple individuals*[52] possessing the same "quality" or having suffered the same tort. The bonds linking members of this kind of community *may or may not* preexist and persist after the RJ process because their relevance manifests itself only *throughout* the procedure. In RJ, Od are still individuals, although they *regroup in the event of the procedure*. The following lines will clarify this statement.

The different sorts of "groups" involved in RJ and VJ shape in significant ways what these models of justice are and how they deal with conflicts.

The meaning of "restoring" justice has to do mainly with *individual* "values of psychological and moral self-help, the victim's self-respect, dignity and sense of control."[53] What follows is that "some victims will be forgiving, others will be vindictive; some will be interested in new forms of sentence, others will not."[54] The pattern of the RJ procedure, in other words, is highly influenced by *individual will* and attitude (of Od toward Of and vice versa). RJ parties are individuals, and their feelings and emotions are experienced *subjectively*. Where groups are involved in the RJ procedure, they are either *spectators* influencing Od's and Of's conduct or *multiple Ods and Ofs* regrouping precisely on the occasion of the procedure. What is lacking in RJ, even in the case of offenses to groups, is some sort of *social solidarity* that forces individuals to respect conventional procedural steps, *even unwillingly*.[55]

---

[50] Terradas Saborit (2010).

[51] On the "imaginary" nature of this kind of community, see in general Appiah (2018).

[52] See Zehr (1990), p. 12.

[53] Morris (2002), p. 598.

[54] Ashworth (2002), p. 586.

[55] See Mannozzi and Lodigiani (2017), p. 362.

Regarding VJ, the situation is different. A "sense of justice" is ultimately shared through a confrontation between *groups*, and it is determined and modified *collectively*. Feelings involved in the VJ procedure possess a social dimension *independent of the subjective experience*: what develops into one's consciousness acquires *a shared social meaning*. As Terradas Saborit's VJ theory implies,[56] an originally individual "sense of offense" has to be translated into a social statement about a breach in the social tissue. Eventually, the conclusion of the procedure with a composition or an act of vengeance *does not depend on Od's will to forgive Of or on Of's repentance* but rather on *groups' evaluations* related to *defenselessness*, *empowerment*, the *recognition of the offense*, and the *opportunity for reconciliation*. A significant (and extreme) example of the irrelevance of individual will in VJ is a well-known episode of *Njál's Saga*,[57] wherein Njál and his friend Gunnar—both married to women with a hot temper—exchange the same 12 ounces of silver as composition an uncountable number of times, while their wives perpetrate revengeful actions against each other. Over the course of the saga, the link between vengeance (of the wives) and composition is carried out regardless of Njál's, Gunnar's, and the wives' feelings (a very good relationship between the husbands and a very bad one between the wives), with reconciliation being the only interest of the two families (solidarity groups).

4 Concluding Remarks

The present chapter investigated the analogies and fundamental distinctions between RJ and VJ. The main research question was as follows: Do RJ and VJ fully overlap? The same question was then (Sect. 3.1) reformulated as follows: Do the *reparation* and *composition* procedures at the heart of RJ and VJ, respectively, fully overlap?

Section 2 discussed four analogies between RJ and VJ in general:

(a) a conceptual shift from a crime/punishment narrative to a conflict (offense)/ reparation;
(b) the flexibility of procedural steps leading to the reparation of the offense and the parties' reconciliation;
(c) the parallel between empowerment (RJ) and attribution of vindicatory capacity following a recognition of defenselessness of the victim (VJ); and
(d) the symbolic function of reparation, even if such reparation consists of money and material goods.

Section 3 highlighted then a fundamental difference between RJ and VJ inherent to the nature of subjects involved in the reparation/composition procedure. According to the VJ model, those subjects are solidarity groups that incorporate

[56] See Terradas Saborit (2021).

[57] See Tuori (2014), pp. 32–33.

individuals. According to the RJ model, those subjects are instead individuals (even multiple individuals regrouping together on the occasion of certain offensive events). From an institutional standpoint, an evaluation of the thickness of the solidarity group constitutes a parameter for discussing the offended party's level of defenselessness. In addition, a "solidarity group" conception entails an assumption of collective responsibility by the offender party and the attribution of a collective right to the offended party to exact satisfaction. From the standpoint of social relationships, each solidarity group may exercise social pressure on the offended and the offender parties to take part in the compositional procedure or to accept composition. As seen, the distinction between the VJ and RJ subjects can be furthered to identify two different notions of "groups": in VJ, groups are local, non-anonymous, moral, social, and legal persons, who can take action against private persons and public institutions. The bonds linking the members of a solidarity group preexist with respect to the VJ procedure and persist after its conclusion. In contrast, in RJ, groups are social and cultural identifications, imaginary communities of people sharing the same religion, race, gender, and so on. They are multiple individuals who possess the same "quality" or have suffered the same tort. The bonds linking members of this kind of community may or may not preexist and persist after the RJ process. The difference in how "groups" are conceived ultimately reflects on the nature of claims and conflicts in VJ and RJ. The pattern of the RJ procedure is highly influenced by individual will and attitude (the parties' feelings and emotions are experienced subjectively). However, the end goal of the VJ procedure is achieved through a confrontation between groups, and it is determined and modified collectively: feelings possess a social dimension that is independent of the subjective experience, and what develops into one's consciousness acquires a shared social meaning.

If anything can be (preliminarily) learned from this concise comparative analysis, it is that RJ and VJ, juxtaposed with a vast range of analogies, are fundamentally different models of justice as they rely on distinct subjects: individuals and solidarity groups (as seen, something more than simple aggregates of people). From this conclusion, a specular set of limits and strengths can be summarized.

On the one hand, VJ *enables the solidarity group to force individuals into the procedure* regardless of their (the individuals') feelings. In other words, *VJ grants to the parties that the procedure will be concluded* in one way or the other (peacefully or with an authorized vengeance). In RJ, in contrast, the beginning and the procedural steps of the reparation process heavily depend on individuals' attitude and desires. Thus, *RJ procedures do not always reach a conclusion* but just when the parties are able (rationally, emotionally, and so on) to implement it. In other words, *the offended and the offender parties cannot be forced into the procedure*, but they have rather to make a choice as to whether they prefer it with respect to other possible conflict-resolution disposals (as CL where available).

On the other hand, *VJ does not grant an actual reparation of the offense but just a formal/official one*. Because VJ procedure does not account for individuals' feelings, there is *no guarantee for the individual who personally and materially suffered the offense to obtain actual satisfaction*. As should now be clear, the satisfaction of the solidarity group is something different with respect to the satisfaction of the (offended) individual who participates in the group. It is not by chance that VJ systems usually establish very harsh punishments for those who violate the state of reconciliation following a composition.[58] This is perfectly consistent with the fact that the dissatisfaction of individuals could sometimes prevail over the satisfaction of groups. In this sense, RJ seems more effective in reaching an actually satisfactory agreement or reconciliation between the parties directly involved, by addressing individual feelings and emotions.

References

Abel CF, Marsh FH (1984) Punishment and restitution. A restitutionary approach to crime and the criminal. Greenwood Publishing Group, Westport

Alonso Cabré M (2021). In: Márquez Porras R, Mazzola R, Terradas Saborit I (eds) Vindicatory justice: beyond law and revenge. Springer, Dordrecht

Appiah KA (2018) The lies that bind: rethinking identity. Profile Books, London

Ashworth A (2002) Responsibilities, rights and restorative justice. Br J Criminol 42:578–595

Bolitho J (2015) Putting justice needs first: a case study of best practice in restorative justice. Restorative Justice 3:256–281

Braithwaite J (1989) Crime, shame, reintegration. CUP, Cambridge

Busquet J (1994) Le droit de la vendetta et les paci corses. CTHS, Paris

Classen R (2004) Two useful models for implementing restorative justice. ACResolution 3:34–36

Conte AG (2011) Pragmatica negativa. In: Di Lucia P (ed) Assiomatica del normativo. Filosofia critica del diritto in Luigi Ferrajoli. LED, Milano, pp 67–78

Doñate Sastre M (2021) "Une Question de Droit": Jacques Busquet and the Corsican vindicatory legal system. In: Márquez Porras R, Mazzola R, Terradas Saborit I (eds) Vindicatory justice: beyond law and revenge. Springer, Dordrecht

Fustel De Coulange ND (1905) La monarchie franque. Histoire des Institutions Politiques de l'ancienne France. Hachette, Paris

Garapon A (2009) Chiudere i conti con la storia. Colonizzazione, schiavitù, Shoah. Cortina, Milano

Gavin P, Sabbagh M (2019) Developing community courts with restorative justice in Ireland. Br J Community Justice 15:19–40

Gil J (1983) Un'antropologia delle forze. Dalle società senza Stato alle società statuali. Einaudi, Torino

Grimm J (1828) Deutsche rechts Alterthümer. Dieterichschen Buchhandlung, Göttingen

Hiatt LR (1987) Treaty, compact, Makarrata. . .? Oceania 58:140–144

Kaufmann WRP (2013) Honor and revenge: a theory of punishment. Springer, Dordrecht

Mannozzi G, Lodigiani GA (2017) La giustizia riparativa: Formanti, parole e metodi. Giappichelli, Torino

Márquez Porras R, Mazzola R (2019) Vindicatory justice and the state: accounts from Shuar and Yolngu ethnographies. Sociologia del Diritto 47:71–95

Marshall T (1999) Restorative justice: an overview. A Report by Home Office Research Development and Statistic Directorate. http://www.antoniocasella.eu/restorative/Marshall_1999-b.pdf. Last accessed 7 Feb 2020

Morris A (2002) Critiquing the critics: a brief response to critics of restorative justice. Br J Criminol 42:596–615

[58]For an example, see Doñate Sastre (2021).

Nader L, Grande E (2002) Current illusions and delusions about conflict management—in Africa and elsewhere. Law Soc Inq 27:573–591
Pigliaru A (1993) Il banditismo in Sardegna. La vendetta barbaricina come ordinamento giuridico. Giuffrè, Milano
Ramis Barceló R (2010) La Justicia Vindicatoria y el Status de la Antropología Jurídica. Revista de estudios histórico-jurídicos 32:515–529
Raye B, Warner Roberts A (2007) Restorative processes. In: Johnson GJ, Van Ness DW (eds) Handbook of restorative justice. Willan Publishing, Cullompton, pp 211–228
Richardson G, Preston B (1999) Indigenous justice. In: The Full Circle Newsletter of the Restorative Justice Institute
Santiapichi S (1963) Il prezzo del sangue e l'omicidio nel diritto somalo. Giuffrè, Milano
Sharpe S (2007) The idea of reparation. In: Johnson GJ, Van Ness DW (eds) Handbook of restorative justice. Willan Publishing, Cullompton, pp 27–43
Simmel G (1984) Filosofia del denaro. UTET, Torino
Simon B (1994) The empowerment tradition in American social work. Columbia University Press, New York
Spencer R (1959) The North Alaskan Eskimo. Smithsonian, Washington DC
Terradas Saborit I (2008) Justicia vindicatoria. De la ofensa e indefensión a la impreca-ción y el oráculo, la vindicta y el talión, la ordalía y el juramento, la composición y la reconci-liación. Consejo Superior de Investigaciones Científicas, Madrid
Terradas Saborit I (2010) Limits and possibilities of restorative justice. Presented at the 6th Biennial Conference, European Forum for Restorative Justice, Bilbao
Terradas Saborit I (2014) Giovanni Nino Tamassia y la jurisprudencia vindicatoria. Sociologia del Diritto 41:57–92
Terradas Saborit I (2019) La justicia más antigua. Consejo Superior de Investigaciones Científicas, Madrid
Terradas Saborit I (2021) Introduction: understanding vindicatory system. In: Márquez Porras R, Mazzola R, Terradas Saborit I (eds) Vindicatory justice: beyond law and revenge. Springer, Dordrecht
Tuori K (2014) Lawyers and savages: ancient history and legal realism in the making of legal anthropology. Routledge, London
Tuori K (2021) Revenge, violence and the civilizing narrative. In: Márquez Porras R, Mazzola R, Terradas Saborit I (eds) Vindicatory justice: beyond law and revenge. Springer, Dordrecht
Van Ness DW, Heetderks Strong K (2015) Restoring justice: an introduction to restorative justice. Elsevier, Waltham
Verdier R (1980) Le Système Vindicatoire: Esquisse Theorique. In: Verdier R (ed) La vengeance. Études d'ethnologie, d'histoire et de philosophie, vol I. Cujas, Paris, pp 11–42
Vogt DC (2012) The aims of restorative justice: some philosophical remarks on the challenges of integrating restorative justice into the criminal justice system. Reconciling the irreconcilable? In: Gröning L, Jacobsen J (eds) Restorative justice and criminal justice. Santérus Academic Press, Stockholm, pp 21–40
Wachtel J, Wachtel T (2012) Building campus community. International Institute for Restorative Practices, Bethlehem
Warner WL (1937) A black civilization. A social study of an Australian tribe. Harper & Brothers, New York
Wright M (1996) Justice for victims and offender. Waterside Press, Philadelphia
Zedner L (1994) Reparation and retribution: are they reconcilable? Mod Law Rev 57:228–250
Zehr H (1990) Changing lenses: a new focus on crime and justice. Herald Press, Scottsdale
Zinsstag E (2012) Conferencing. A developing practice of restorative justice. In: Zinsstag E, Vanfraechem I (eds) Conferencing and restorative justice. International practices and perspectives. OUP, Oxford, pp 12–37

Antonio Pigliaru

Barbagian Vendetta as a Legal System

Paolo Di Lucia, Giuseppe Lorini, and Olimpia Giuliana Loddo

Abstract This chapter focuses on the most famous book by the Italian legal philosopher Antonio Pigliaru, *La vendetta barbaricina come ordinamento giuridico*, first published in 1959. The book collects Pigliaru's investigations on the Barbagian code and describes the social dynamics of an ancestral folk law that emerged in the territory of Barbagia, located in a central area of Sardinia, on the Gennargentu chain. Pigliaru observes a persistent and widespread practice of vendetta in Barbagia and places it within the set of legal systems that virtually coexist with the state. An empirical analysis of the behavior of Sardinian shepherds, conducted through interviews, confirms the original hypothesis that, in that community, revenge is not an instinct but an institution. Pigliaru proposed a technical legal codification, where he formalized the unwritten Barbagian folk law. The work of Pigliaru is inspiring for studies on the interaction between state law and folk law and the philosophical analysis of vendetta.

1 Antonio Pigliaru: Legal Philosopher and Anthropologist

Antonio Pigliaru was born in Orune (Nuoro, Italy) on August 17, 1922. The works of the Italian philosophers Giovanni Gentile and Giuseppe Capograssi had a dramatic impact on the development of his scientific methodology and his philosophical background. In 1947, he graduated in philosophy from the University of Cagliari and became an assistant professor. In Cagliari, from 1955 to 1956, he was a

This article is the joint work of three authors. Sections 1 and 3, 4 were written by Paolo Di Lucia, while Sections 2, 5, 6.2 and 6.1, 7 were authored by Giuseppe Lorini and Olimpia G. Loddo respectively. The authors assume responsibility for the statements made.

P. Di Lucia (✉)
Department of Legal Sciences "Cesare Beccaria", University of Milan, Milan, Italy
e-mail: paolo.dilucia@unimi.it

G. Lorini · O. G. Loddo
Department of Law, University of Cagliari, Cagliari, Italy
e-mail: lorini@unica.it

R. Márquez Porras et al. (eds.), *Vindicatory Justice*, Ius Gentium: Comparative Perspectives on Law and Justice 93, https://doi.org/10.1007/978-3-030-79595-5_6

professor of psychology, and from 1956 to 1958, he taught theory of the state. His early scientific investigations focused on the philosophy of criminal law and the theory of the legal system.

This chapter focuses on his most famous book, *La vendetta barbaricina come ordinamento giuridico* (The Barbagian vendetta as a legal system). This book was first published in 1959 and republished in a new edition in 1970 under the title *Il Banditismo in Sardegna* (Sardinian banditry). In 1967, he was appointed professor of theory of the state at the University of Sassari. He died in Sassari on March 27, 1969.

La vendetta barbaricina come ordinamento giuridico is part of a debate (very lively in the 1950s) on legal pluralism, that is, on the coexistence of multiple legal systems, one of which is the state.

In the central area of Sardinia, on the Gennargentu chain, Pigliaru observes the persistent and widespread practice of the vendetta and places it within the set of legal systems that virtually coexist with the state legal system. An empirical analysis of the behavior of Sardinian shepherds, conducted through interviews, confirms the original hypothesis that revenge is, in that community, not an *instinct*, but an *institution*. The originality of Pigliaru's work is both philosophical and methodological. The Italian philosopher Benedetto Croce had already included in the category of legal system not only the state (the *Magna Carta*) but also other types of organizations. According to Croce, some of these organizations, such as the rules of the Sicilian mafia and the rules of the Camorra in Naples, have a criminal (*contra legem*) nature, but despite this they can be labeled "law."[1]

Pigliaru, as well as Croce, recognizes the existence of *contra legem* organizations but maintains that the legal system of vendetta is not comparable to the regulations of a criminal organization (*societas sceleris*). Legal systems, such as the one he studied in Barbagia, as well as in criminal organizations, are different in kind, with different goals and different characteristics. For instance, legal systems always aim at the survival of a community, whereas criminal organizations aim at performing criminal actions to achieve criminal economic and social advantages.[2]

Pigliaru does not start from concepts but from reality. More specifically, he does not start from the concept of "law" but from a particular regulatory system: the system that regulates and constitutes the practice of vendetta in Barbagia. His research results comprise an entirely unedited codification.[3] The output of this work of codification are the 23 articles of Barbagia's folk law.[4] This practice represents the "transcription" of Sardinian folk law "in terms of code" following

[1]Croce ([1909]1996). Cf. Di Lucia ([2002]2013), p. 321.

[2]Cf. Di Lucia (2015).

[3]Pigliaru's code is an example of nomographic codification, i.e., a codification by declarative deontic sentences. A declarative deontic sentence is one that ascertains the subsistence of an already existing norm, a "subsistent norm." See Conte ([1990]2019), p. 27.

[4]http://web.tiscali.it/Banditismo/Codice%20barbaricino.htm (last accessed 22.02.2020).

the schemes of contemporary criminal law. Pigliaru created a technical legal codification, where he formalized an unwritten folk law.

2 Vendetta as Instinct vs Vendetta as Institution

As mentioned previously, there are two different dimensions of vendetta: the instinctive individual reaction to an offense motivated by personal feelings and emotions and the social institution deeply rooted in folk law and characterized by precise rituals and norms.

It is difficult to say whether the behavior of avengers is a product of their own instinct or whether external institutional factors influence their actions. A superficial audience can observe the behaviors of an avenger without being able to decode them.

However, anger is not the only reason for carrying out vendetta. Indeed, there can be desire-independent reasons for vendetta.[5] As the Austrian legal philosopher Hans Kelsen argues, blood revenge is "the earliest socially organized sanction."[6] Moreover, a famous scientific antagonist of Kelsen, the Bukovinian jurist and sociologist Eugen Ehrlich, also analyzed the role played by revenge in ancient societies when he proposed the following image of the prehistory of law: "In the so-called pre-history of the law, there are as yet no courts. Quarrels are either peacefully settled through compromise or dragged out in bloody feuds. Generally, they are based on murder, personal injury, kidnapping, rape, enslavement, theft, abduction. Courts will appear later."[7]

The ancestral law mentioned is not only an unwritten law but also a law without legal sentences, a nonverbal law. Pigliaru's investigations on the Barbagian Code[8] and the Sardinian vendetta focus on the social dynamics of an ancestral mute law[9] that emerges in the territory of Barbagia.[10] According to Pigliaru, the avenger who operates following that code is performing a social duty. In fact, according to Pigliaru's code (Art. 1), "The offence must be avenged. Those who neglect the duty of revenge are not honorable."

Thus, the behaviors and choices of the Barbagian avenger do not derive only from their instinctive attitudes. Indeed, the Barbagian avenger reacts to an offense also

---

[5]On "desire-independent reason for action," see Searle (2001), pp. 167–213.

[6]Kelsen (1941), p. 77. See §3.

[7]Ehrlich (1922), pp. 99–100.

[8]Pigliaru ([1959]1970).

[9]Sacco (1995).

[10]Antonio Pigliaru's book *La vendetta barbaricina come ordinamento giuridico* was relevant for the anthropology of law as evidenced by the inclusion of this work in the first major bibliography of anthropology of law by Nader et al. (1966).

because of desire-independent reasons for action under the influence of folk law prescriptions.

Therefore, it is necessary to distinguish a sudden instinctive reaction against an offender from an institutionalized vendetta. In other words, it is essential to distinguish the *instinct of revenge* from the *institution of vendetta*.[11]

The legal sentences that codify the unwritten rules of Barbagian folk law, for example, the first statement of Pigliaru's code, Art. 1, "The offence shall be avenged," make the invisible structure of the relative institution visible.

This structure acquires a particular morphology because it is inscribed in a specific social context.

While the instinctive reaction to an outrage does not change, the rules governing revenge vary under the influence of the institutional and meta-institutional[12] contexts within which they are inscribed. An attitude tolerated or considered harmless in one society can be, in another social context, an offense that generates a duty of revenge for the victim.

It is no coincidence that Pigliaru dedicates the second section of the code entirely to the codification of the concept of offense in Barbagian folk law. In fact, in the second section of his code, Pigliaru accurately sets out the conditions that transform a simple harmful behavior into an offensive action and, in particular, he lists in Artt. 15 and 16 typically offensive behaviors (such as, for instance, the theft of the dairy goat intended for feeding the family, an enemy crossing your fenced land, the breach of a marriage promise).

Several cultural elements can affect the structure of the institution of vendetta. In this sense, the concept of honor is crucial for the understanding of vendetta. The concept of honor appears in Pigliaru's code, accordingly "the man that evades the duty of revenge . . . is not honourable."

According to the phenomenologist Hans Reiner, the term "honor" is part of the definition of vendetta. If the revenge is, for instance, a reaction to adultery, "[revenge] is a means to ward off the attack on the marital (human) dignity. This defence—especially in the vengeance—does not apply to the attack that has just taken place but has fundamental and therefore general meaning."[13] Injury to honor is a necessary condition for determining the revenge duty. Therefore, it is an integral part of the notion of offense. "A determined action is offensive when the event on which the existence of it depends is foreseen and desired in order to harm the honourability and dignity of others."

According to Italian jurist Jacopo Gelli, who codified the Italian code of chivalry, the honor of an individual is the result of the consideration that the other members of

[11] Lorini and Masia (2015), pp. x–xi.

[12] The meta-institutional concepts are concepts that go beyond (Greek: *metá*) the institutions whereof they are conditions of possibility. An example of a meta-institutional concept is that of game. In a culture that does not have the concept of game, we could move chessmen according to the rules of chess, and we could also perform a castling, but it would be impossible to play chess. On meta-institutional concepts, see Lorini (2014) and Miller (1981).

[13] Reiner (1956).

the society have of him. If the individual lives in conformity with the law, then he is an honorable person. Italian code of chivalry was rooted in the fact that state law sometimes offered insufficient protection for the honor of a gentleman. According to Scheler "vendetta restores his damaged feeling of personal value 'satisfaction' for the wrongs he has endured."[14] Honor is restored (in other words, dishonor is cleaned away) with revenge.

3 The Rules of the Barbagian Vendetta

It is possible to distinguish at least two ways of conceiving the legal rules governing revenge. To clarify these two conceptions of the phenomenon of revenge, we will use, developing an intuition of Amedeo Giovanni Conte, the analogy between the rules of revenge and the rules of a game.[15]

- *The first way of conceiving the "rules of the game of revenge" consists in considering these rules as coinciding with the rules of the game called "sanction."*

The author who, in the context of the philosophy of law, came closest to this conception of the legal rules of revenge was Kelsen in his research on the law of primitive societies.[16] In particular, according to Kelsen, revenge is the earliest form of legal sanction. Blood revenge, in particular, is a form of sanction that is applied through self-help, that is, in a completely decentralized manner. The execution of sanction is delegated to all individuals of the social group whose interests, protected by the law, have been violated. Kelsen writes:

> Originally the realisation of the coercive act, the punishment and the execution, is conferred by the legal system precisely to those whose interests are violated. It is the son who, for the killing of his father, must make the blood revenge (*Blutrache*) on the murderer; it is the creditor who must put his hand on the defaulting debtor to repay himself with the pledge. These are the primitive forms of punishment and execution, and these too are implemented by 'organs.' The son imposes the punishment provided for by the legal system on the father's murderer; the creditor exercises the compulsion provided for by the legal system on the debtor only because they are organs of the legal system [. . .], and only in this way these coercive acts do not constitute a new offence.[17]

---

[14]Scheler ([1912] 1994), p. 140.

[15]Cf. Conte (2011). The analogy formulated by Conte has been developed by Di Lucia and Mazzola (2020).

[16]Cf. Kelsen (1941). On Kelsen's theory of revenge, see the chapter by Di Lucia and Passerini Glazel in this volume.

[17]Kelsen (1926).

In Kelsen's perspective, the blood revenge performed by the offended person and the punishment carried out by the state are both legal sanctions, and the difference between the two is only a "technical and degree difference."

> Only in the course of the subsequent evolution the execution of these coercive acts is emancipated from offences and transformed into the exclusive function of human beings qualified in a determined way and defined as organs of the state in the strict sense. This evolution is the result of the social division of labor. There is nothing to object if we want to use the word 'state' only if there is this compulsory system that establishes organs operating according to the division of labor. However, it is necessary to be clear: between this legal and primitive system, there is only a technical distinction and not at all an essential distinction.[18]

- *The second way of conceiving the "rules of the game of revenge" consists in considering these rules not identifiable with the rules of the game called "sanction" but belonging to a different game, that is, the game of reconciliation or reparation.*[19]

In Pigliaru's view, for example, the meaning of the game called "Barbagian vendetta" does not seem to coincide with the meaning of the game called "sanction"[20] but with that of another "game" called "reconciliation" or "reparation." The hypothesis that the rules of the "Barbagian vendetta" belong to a game called "reconciliation" or "reparation" is testified by the fact that the system of the Barbagian vendetta contemplates the possibility that the offense is repaired in a way that is an alternative to the revenge: the way of peace [*de sas paches*]. Pigliaru writes, "this way is the direct way of pacification between the parties taken in the iron grip of the offence-revenge relationship, the way of peace [*de sas paches*], the way of an initiative—also institutionalised and strictly disciplined—through which the community tries to arrive with a new protocol of intervention for that settlement of the conflict, to which, moreover, this code already invites the party in question, although not suppressing, indeed perhaps for better and more peremptorily justifying [...] the duty of revenge. [...]. Therefore, finally, a peaceful composition of conflicts and offences, which in its solemn forms has its particular rite, that pacification procedure that the communities concerned by this code have prepared within their

[18]Kelsen (1926). On the continuity between punishment and revenge, cf. Paliero (2018). For an in-depth analysis of Kelsen's thought on the macrohistorical evolution of the legal systems, see Sammarco (2019).

[19]Pigliaru ([1959]1970). On the work of Pigliaru, cf. the essays dedicated to him in the following two syllogues: Piga and Pulina (2010) and Lorini and Masia (2015).

[20]On the non-assimilability of the rules of the Barbagian vendetta into the rules of the game of sanction, Amedeo Giovanni Conte speaks of "incommensurability." See also Terradas Saborit (2019). Although the "Barbagian vendetta game" is not comparable with the "sanction game," the Barbagian vendetta code is written by Pigliaru in 23 articles in the form, and with the literal tenor, of a penal code.

legal organisation."[21] In other words, the rules of the game called "Barbagian vendetta" correspond, according to Pigliaru, to the rules that determine the meaning of the game called "reconciliation" or "reparation."

4 The Barbagian Vendetta as an Instrument of Legal Protection

Pigliaru is aware of an existing divergence between state law on the one hand and folk law on the other. This contrast does not emerge unless the vendetta is interpreted from the perspectives of both state law and folk law.

Barbagian avengers explicitly reject state authority and solve their conflicts without state support.

According to state law, the avenger shall be sanctioned as a murderer because his behavior is interpreted according to the categories of state law. According to Barbagian justice, he is, instead, an avenger who restores the existing order. The avenger fulfills his duty; the murders he commits are perceived as an unavoidable consequence of his deviant behavior.[22]

The theory of vindicatory justice of Ignasi Terradas Saborit, because of the relevance attributed to the practice of composition, comes very close to Pigliaru's conception of vendetta as a legal system. Indeed, the Sardinian philosopher of law profoundly influenced the Catalan anthropologist,[23] with the latter leading the primitive, ancient, medieval, traditional vindicatory systems (such as that of the Barbargian vendetta) to a type of human society that, from a historical and ethnographic point of view, is characterized by "the absence of a distinction between civil justice and criminal justice."

The most surprising feature of vindicatory systems consists, in fact, in the prevalence of reparation for an offense, reparation that is only secondary in systems wherein there is instead a distinction between civil justice and criminal justice. Vindicatory systems, Terradas Saborit writes, "cannot be separated from the author of the damage or crime with his sanction and, secondarily, from his obligation to compensate or repair. It is based on the social recognition (cultural if desired) of the damage or injury caused to the victim and, consequently, the obligation of reparation is established or according to the seriousness of the offense, the authorization of

[21]Pigliaru ([1959]1970), pp. 162–163. On reconciliation in vindicatory systems, see Terradas Saborit (2008, 2019).

[22]Gaillard (1992), p. 186.

[23]Terradas Saborit (2008, 2019).

For an overview of the research on vindicatory justice, cf. Terradas Saborit (2021).

revenge or the punishment of the *talion*."[24] The explicit reference to the "social recognition of the offense" also explains Terradas Saborit's choice to call *vindicatory* a form of justice that is implemented through a procedure, which, to use Raymond Verdier's lexicon, is "collective, consensual and legal," and which, as such, is the opposite of a *vindictive*, "individual and semi-instinctive" act.[25]

5 The Barbagian Vendetta System as a Legal System

The critical question Pigliaru asks is, "Are those rules that regulate the practice of vendetta in the Barbagian community 'law'?"

Pigliaru answers positively to this question. He maintains that the regulatory system that controls and constitutes the institution of vendetta in Barbagia is law. That is to say (as it already says in the title of his work), it is a real legal system.[26]

Rodolfo Sacco urges us to overcome the prejudices that blind us in pursuing scientific and philosophical research on law: "the scholar also calls the law the norm whose contents do not correspond to his preferences, or which—in the limit—arouse his repulsion. Roman slavery, the Stalinist purges, the laws of Nuremberg are also called straight."[27]

As Sacco points out, the operation of "calling things by their name" when speaking of the word "law" is complicated by the fact that "law (*ius, droit, Recht, law, pravo*) is a notion that has no precise correspondent in all cultures. Islamic *šarī'a*, the faction of the Chinese tradition, the *Indian dharma* do not fully match the 'law.' We must, therefore, know of the non-universal presence of the Western category 'law.'"

Also, a forced identification between the concept of "law" and the concept of "state legal system" can be extremely problematic.

Some scholars offer the hypothesis that the opposition between the state legal system and customary systems cannot be understood too rigidly. For these scholars, the conception of state law is shaken to its foundations by "the irruption of 'culture' on the legal horizon."[28] Indeed, the work of Pigliaru can be inspiring for the most modern debate on the subject of cultural defense.[29] No legal system recognizes the

---

[24]"*No se parte del autor del daño o delito con su pena y, secundariamente, con su obligación de resarcir o reparar. Se parte del reconocimiento social (cultural si se quiere) del daño o perjuicio ocasionado en la víctima y, consecuentemente, se establece la obligación de su reparación o, alternativamente, según la gravedad de la ofensa, la autorización de la venganza o el castigo del talión.*" Terradas Saborit (2019), p. 36. According to Terradas Saborit, in vindicatory systems, vendetta is always authorized by a judicial authority. Cf. Terradas Saborit (2008, 2019).

[25]Cf. Verdier (1980).

[26]See Sacco (2007).

[27]Sacco (2007), p. 18.

[28]Ruggiu (2019), p. 200.

[29]Ruggiu (2019), p. 77. On the subject of the cultural defense, see Dundes Renteln (2005).

cultural defense. However, it is sometimes included in legal argumentation to mitigate punishment when the action qualified as a crime by the state legal system is perpetrated under the influence of specific folk law that is binding for a person who operates in a specific cultural context. According to Dundes Renteln, "the core idea behind this defence is that individuals who act under cultural imperatives should be considered less culpable under the law than those who act in the absence of such an imperative. In order for judges to evaluate the extent to which a defendant's cultural background affected his or her behaviour, they must consider cultural evidence relating to the offence."[30] Inevitably, the adoption of this sort of argument requires specific anthropological expertise because the risk of taking this kind of approach is that, on the one hand, there may be a misunderstanding of the community's code and, on the other hand, the jurist could neglect elements that can affect the behavior of the perpetrator dramatically. In this sense, the investigation conducted by Pigliaru is still groundbreaking as the anthropological skills that characterized his scientific production will become increasingly relevant for future generations of jurists who will operate in a multicultural society.

6 Two Hermeneutic Hypotheses on the Barbagian Vendetta

6.1 The Barbagian Vendetta as a Social Act

Art. 19 of Pigliaru's code is particularly significant from a social-ontological perspective. In fact, according to this article: "Normal actions of revenge are all actions foreseen as offensive if they are conducted in such a way as to make manifest their specific nature."

It is essential to point out that the "sense of revenge" of the offensive act shall be loyally manifested.[31] This is an important characteristic that allows the considering of revenge as a social act, where a social act is one that needs to be perceived by another person.[32]

However, killing a man is not, even in this case, in itself a social act. Its social profile derives from the fact that it manifests what in the Barbargian system is the legal institution of revenge.

A murderer usually does not want his actions to generate specific reactions. We only hope for a series of indirect and mechanical consequences, which would occur even if the victim had died of natural causes. These consequences are not dependent on the act of murder but on the event of the victim's death.

A murder can become a manifestation of a social act, in which case, the murder acquires the role of a signal, referring to something different from itself. It is no

[30] Dundes Renteln (2015), p. 492.

[31] Pigliaru ([1959]1970), p. 125.

[32] Reinach (1989).

longer merely the taking away of the life of another man but is aimed at communicating something to someone. For example, it can represent a warning addressed to a rival family. In the framework of the vendetta, a murder can stand for a symbolic act, in precisely the same manner as the signature on a contract can. According to Émile Bréhier,[33] symbolic acts are "signs of other acts." They are characterized by a big gap between the material side of the act and its symbolic meaning. However, the symbolic act is not the institutional act.[34] *Symbolic acts* are a tool to perform the institutional act, and at the same time, they are signs of that institutional act.[35]

6.2 Barbagian Vendetta as a Diapraxic Act

Analysis of Pigliaru's code, in particular, the third part of the code, entitled "On the measure of vendetta" (*La misura della vendetta*) (Artt. 18–23), which can be considered the procedural part of the code, reveals a philosophically exciting aspect of the act of vendetta: revenge can only be accomplished through another act. More specifically, to perform a vendetta, it is necessary to carry out an offensive act. Indeed, not every harmful act is an offense. The offensive act is a harmful act with an institutional status (clearly codified in the second part of Pigliaru's code called "On the offenses" (*Le offese*), Artt. 11–17).

In particular, for example, in Art. 18, Pigliaru writes, "By proportionate revenge is meant an offense that can cause damage greater or similar to the one suffered by the victim." Still in the third part of the code, according to Art. 19, "All actions provided for offensive (*tutte le azioni prevedute come offensive*) are normal tools of revenge (*mezzi normali di vendetta*)." Moreover, in Art. 23 Pigliaru talks about "offensive action taken by way of revenge" (*Azione offensiva posta in essere a titolo di vendetta*). It is possible to take revenge in different ways: by seducing, by stealing, by spying, or by killing. This apparent naive empirical observation leads us to point out a vital characteristic of a very peculiar kind of act. It is impossible to perform a vendetta directly. To take revenge, it is necessary to perform an offensive act (that can vary in kind and) that only in a specific context can count as a *vendetta*. In other words, I cannot perform an act of vendetta *per se*. The vendetta is a *mediated act* that is performable only through another act.[36]

This is a peculiarity that vendetta shares with other acts. Philosophers of different methodological traditions noticed this phenomenon. In this sense, for instance, philosophers Kambartel and Schneider point out: "There are acts which we perform

[33]Bréhier (1917), p. 357.

[34]Lorini (2000), p. 184.

[35]Lorini and Loddo (2018), pp. 217–218.

[36]On vendetta as a diapraxic act, see Lorini and Loddo (2018), pp. 216–218.

(actualise) by performing (actualising) other acts, like putting on the light by operating a switch."[37]

The Italian philosopher Conte calls these acts "*diapraxic acts*." Conte defines diapraxic as every act that can be performed only through the performance of another act. The performance of this second act is a *condicio sine qua non* of the diapraxic act, but that second act is not a *condicio per quam* of the *diapraxic act*. To commit a crime, to sin, to insinuate are all examples of *diapraxic acts*.[38]

These other acts can be material (turning on a light by operating a switch) or *symbolic* (offending a person by *refusing* a gift).

According to Pigliaru's words, actions foreseen as offensive are the means of vendetta.

If you consider the norms of the Barbagian vendetta code as an "epistemological key" for understanding the act of vendetta,[39] in order to understand whether a particular conduct is a vendetta, you must first be able to determine whether it is an offensive action. Subsequently, you must be able to establish whether this action has additional characteristics that allow you to consider it not merely an act of offense but also a vendetta. In this sense, the concept of "vendetta" presupposes the concept of "offense."

Offense already has an institutional qualification and a symbolic character in itself. The concept of "offense" cannot be reduced to the mere concept of "harmful action." A harmful action is not in itself an offense, and at the same time, an offense is not necessarily considered as such on the basis of the extent of material injury caused by the offender. In other words, the act of vendetta can be described both as a materially damaging act, as an offense, and ultimately, as a vendetta. However, this does not mean that the concept of "vendetta" is reducible to the concept of "offense" or to the concept of "harmful act." We can hypothesize that the concept of "offense" is a meta-institutional concept concerning the institution of vendetta (for example, in the context of Barbagian law as described by Pigliaru, the concept of "offense" is a necessary condition toward understanding the concept of vengeance).

7 The Paradox of the Barbagian Vendetta

Vendetta seems to have a paradoxical character. In fact, the institution of vendetta aims at maintaining social order, but it can lead to a feud that can represent a threat to the survival of the social group. In fact, according to Pigliaru's code (Art. 21), "[i]n the practice of revenge, no offense should preclude the use of worse forms of reaction up to blood vengeance." Vendetta is characterized by reciprocity. Thus, each vendetta can lead to a reaction by the victim, that is, each vendetta could be the

[37]Kambartel and Schneider (1981), p. 164. Cf. Lorini (2000), pp. 181–185.

[38]Conte (2011), pp. 71–72.

[39]Conte ([1990]2019).

presupposition of another (more severe) vendetta. Pigliaru's code (Art. 21) indicates reconciliation as a form of conflict resolution. However, the adoption of this solution by the families involved in a feud is not mandatory.

The paradox of vendetta can be solved by drawing a distinction between the epistemic level and the ontological level of this institution. The epistemic level presents the fact that every member of the community is aware that the code of vendetta is in force in the community. This epistemic awareness can prevent a potential perpetrator from committing an offensive act that can lead to a concrete vendetta. At this epistemic level, the vendetta can be an effective instrument for maintaining social peace.

The ontological level presents the active practice of revenge that can lead to an uncontrolled chain of murders. This chain of murders is the product of the reciprocity of the act of revenge and not of the reciprocity of a bare (epistemic) expectation that the offensive behavior could lead the victim to a vindicatory reaction.

In this sense, on the one hand, epistemic reciprocity in vendetta can be the presupposition of social balance, and on the other hand, the ontological reciprocity of vendetta can be the presupposition of potentially irreconcilable conflict, of a chain of vendetta. Vendetta seems to be an institution suitable for the preservation of social peace because it represents a deterrent to those who intend to perform offensive actions.

In other, more precise words, from an epistemic perspective, the reciprocal awareness that from an offense shall follow a vendetta can dissuade the offensive intention of a potential perpetrator.

However, once a chain of vendettas concretely starts, it could evolve into a series of status exchanges. The one who initially has the status of avenger, when he suffers the revenge of his victim and become victim himself, is authorized to assume (again) the status of avenger. This endless chain is a consequence of the fact that the vendetta is an act characterized by reciprocity.[40]

The thesis according to which the institution of vendetta is aimed at guaranteeing the protection of the social system (that is, the "homeostasis" (balance) of the system) was supported by Pigliaru, who writes, "the revenge code represents only one part of a whole legal system that does not end in this code and that, if ever, in the code has the legal and systematic organization of its protection."[41] However, as the French anthropologist Norbert Rouland points out, "The exchange on which the avenging system roots can fail. In this case, revenge produces perverse effects: it leads to a crescendo of violence which, instead of protecting them, endangers the avenging groups."[42]

If indeed the homeostasis (balance) of the system was "the goal" of the institution of revenge, then the system of revenge could work (in the sense that it could allow the maintenance of "social peace") as long as mutual expectations of revenge prevent

[40]Loddo (2015).

[41]Pigliaru ([1959]1970), p. 17.

[42]Rouland (1988), p. 278.

the perpetration of offenses. It follows that the moment characterized by reciprocal revenge expectations is compatible with what Pigliaru considers the purpose of revenge (that is, the defense and conservation of a social system). However, the expectations of the reciprocity of revenge characterize the "pathological" phenomenon highlighted by Rouland, which we also find in the Albanian (blood) revenge [*gjakmarrje*], where each act of revenge is the presupposition of a new, more cruel revenge. The reciprocity of revenge leads to a potentially infinite chain of revenge—of endless vendetta.

References

Bréhier É (1917) L'acte symbolique. Revue philosophique de la France et de l'étranger 84:345–361

Conte AG (2011) Pragmatica negativa. In: Di Lucia P (ed) Assiomatica del normativo. Filosofia critica del diritto in Luigi Ferrajoli. LED, Milano

Conte AG ([1990]2019) Athetic validity. Phenomenology and Mind 17:20–30

Croce B ([1909]1996) Filosofia della pratica: economica ed etica. Bibliopolis, Napoli

Di Lucia P ([2002]2013) Antonio Pigliaru. In: Conte AG, Di Lucia P, Ferrajoli L, Jori M. Edited by P Di Lucia. Filosofia del diritto. Cortina, Milano

Di Lucia P (2015) La vendetta in Sardegna: un'ipotesi ermeneutica. In: Lorini G, Masia M (eds) Antropologia della vendetta. ESI, Napoli

Di Lucia P, Mazzola R (2020) Diritto e vendetta. In: Di Lucia P, Mazzola R (eds) Vindicta. Studi e testi sulla giustizia vendicatoria. LED, Milano

Dundes Renteln A (2005) The cultural defense. OUP, Oxford

Dundes Renteln A (2015) Cultural rights and culture defense: cultural concerns. International encyclopedia of the social & behavioral science, 2nd ed, pp 491–497

Ehrlich E (1922) The sociology of law (trans: Isaacs N). Harv Law Rev 36:130–145

Gaillard J (1992) Cavalleria rusticana: Novella, Dramma, Melodramma. Mod Lang Notes (MLN) 107:178–195

Kambartel F, Schneider HJ (1981) Constructing a pragmatic foundation for semantics. In: Fløistad G (ed) Contemporary philosophy. A new survey. Nijoff, The Hague

Kelsen H (1926) Grundriß einer allgemeinen Theorie der Staates. Roher, Wien

Kelsen H (1941) The law as specific social technique. Univ Chic Law Rev 9:75–97

Loddo (2015) Reciprocità di aspettative e aspettative di reciprocità nella vendetta. In: Lorini G, Masia M (eds) Antropologia della vendetta. ESI, Napoli

Lorini G (2000) Dimensioni giuridiche dell'istituzionale. CEDAM, Padova

Lorini G (2014) Meta-institutional concepts: a new category for social ontology. Rivista di Estetica 56:127–139

Lorini G, Loddo OG (2018) Revenge between legal and social norms in Cavalleria rusticana. In: Annunziata F, Colombo GF (eds) Law and opera. Springer, Berlin

Lorini G, Masia M (2015) Vendetta: istinto o istituzione? In: Lorini G, Masia M (eds) Antropologia della vendetta. ESI, Napoli

Miller D (1981) Constitutive rules and essential rules. Philos Stud 39:183–197

Nader L, Koch KF, Cox B (1966) The ethnography of law: a bibliographical survey. Curr Anthropol 7:267–294

Paliero C (2018) Il sogno di Clitennestra: mitologie della pena. Pensieri scettici su modernità e archeologia del punire. Rivista italiana di diritto e procedura penale 61:447–520

Piga G, Pulina P (2010) La ricerca di Antonio Pigliaru (1922–1969) sulla vendetta barbaricina. Convegno in memoria del grande filosofo sardo a 40 anni dalla morte. Pavia (24 ottobre 2009) Nuova Tipografia Popolare

Pigliaru A ([1959]1970) Il banditismo in Sardegna. La vendetta barbaricina come ordinamento giuridico. Giuffrè, Milano
Reinach A ([1913]1989) Die apriorischen Grundlagen des bürgerlichen Rechts. In: Schuhmann K, Smith B (eds) Adolf Reinach, Sämtliche Werke. Philosophia Verlag, München, pp 141–278
Reiner H (1956) Die Ehre. Mittler & Sohn, Dortmund
Rouland N (1988) Anthropologie juridique. Presses Universitaires de France, Paris
Ruggiu I (2019) Culture and the judiciary. Routledge, London
Sacco R (1995) Mute law. Am J Comp Law 43:455–467
Sacco R (2007) Antropologia giuridica. Contributo ad una macrostoria del diritto. Il Mulino, Bologna
Sammarco S (2019) Il diritto in movimento. Hans Kelsen e l'evoluzione macrostorica degli ordinamenti giuridici. PhD Thesis, University of Milan
Scheler M ([1912]1994) Resentiment. MUP, Milwaukee
Searle JR (2001) Rationality in action. MIT Press, Cambridge, MA
Terradas Saborit I (2008) Justicia vindicatoria. De la ofensa e indefensión a la imprecación y el oráculo, la vindicta y el talión, la ordalia y el juramento, la composición y la reconciliación, Consejo Superior de Investigaciones Científicas, Madrid
Terradas Saborit I (2019) La justicia más antigua. Teoría y cultura del ordenamiento vindicatorio. Consejo Superior de Investigaciones Científicas, Madrid
Terradas Saborit I (2021) Introduction: understanding vindicatory systems. In: Márquez Porras R, Mazzola R, Terradas Saborit I (eds) Vindicatory justice. Beyond law and revenge. Springer, Dordrecht, in this volume
Verdier R (1980) Introduction: Le système vindicatoire. In: Verdier R (ed) La vengeance. Études d'ethnologie, d'histoire et de philosophie, I. Cujas, Paris, pp 1–24

‘Une Question De Droit’

Jacques Busquet and the Corsican Vindicatory Legal System

Miguel Doñate Sastre

Abstract The chapter offers an invitation to bring those who are interested in vindicatory studies closer to Corsican vindicatory justice, taking *Le droit de la vendetta et les ‘paci’ corses* (1920), by French jurist Jacques Busquet, as the starting point. What follows will explore some new avenues, as well as the characteristic closeness of Corsican vindicatory justice to the basic institutions of *vendetta* and *pace*. For example, the prevalence of one process or another within vindicatory justice as a whole, or their complex relationships within the legal sphere of Corsican society and the successive occupying states.

1 Introduction

These pages offer an invitation to bring those who are interested in vindicatory studies closer to Corsican vindicatory justice, taking *Le droit de la vendetta et les ‘paci’ corses* (1920), by French jurist Jacques Busquet, as the starting point. Although this is not a new path for me,[1] on this occasion I will explore some new avenues, as well as the characteristic closeness of Corsican vindicatory justice to the basic institutions of *vendetta* and *pace*. For example, the prevalence of one process or another within vindicatory justice as a whole, or their complex relationships within the legal sphere of Corsican society and the successive occupying states. But before moving on to develop these and other questions, I believe it is necessary to pinpoint some of the reasons for choosing the work of Busquet as the backbone for this text.

Firstly, I should highlight the pioneering and even revolutionary character of Busquet’s proposal, having been the first to take on the study of the Corsican *vendetta* phenomenon from a legal perspective due to considering it to be “*au premier chef une question de droit*” because “*l’ensemble des préceptes et des usages*

[1]See Doñate Sastre (2010a).

M. Doñate Sastre (✉)
Department of Social Anthropology, Universitat de Barcelona, Barcelona, Spain

R. Márquez Porras et al. (eds.), *Vindicatory Justice*, Ius Gentium: Comparative Perspectives on Law and Justice 93, https://doi.org/10.1007/978-3-030-79595-5_7

constitue ici des règles impératives quoique non écrites, véritables lois qui s'imposaient aux hommes".[2] In this manner, he breaks with the hegemonic tendency that, generally speaking, creates a romanticised image of the honour-based system and, at the same time, portrays a system of visceral revenge divested of any legal element and, due to this, all rationality.[3]

But he does not stop at the adoption of a legal perspective. He becomes aware that to understand the Corsican vindicatory sphere[4] in all its complexity, it is also necessary to have a diachronic perspective through the history and the profoundness that, as Ravis-Giordani[5] notes, comes from the application of ethnographic fieldwork.[6]

The success of the formula is such that *Le droit de la vendetta et les 'paci' corses* brings Busquet right up to the present time due to being the first and, to date, the only person to systematise Corsican vindicatory justice.[7] We find a similar endeavour years later, on the neighbouring island of Sardinia carried out by the Sardinian legal expert and philosopher Antonio Pigliaru with *La vendetta barbaricina come ordinamento giuridico* (1959), which, as Ignasi Terradas Saborit[8] points out, is a "prodigious endeavour for the intellectual restoration of the whole vindicatory

---

[2]Busquet (1994), p. 23.

[3]This vision can be traced back to the eighteenth and nineteenth centuries and to the fascination for certain Corsican customs—among which the most important is the *vendetta* and the figure of the bandit—emerging from literary accounts such as those of Mérimée and Maupassant, or from acculturated travellers such as R. Bonaparte (1891) or Bergerat (1998). Such a vision fed the prejudicial interpretation of *vendetta* supported by historians, administrators and "scientific" studies in the attempt to generate ideological and political positions related to national politics. The negative connotation of *vendetta* added to its supposed non-legal and irrational character other elements such as the tendency to delinquency of the inhabitants of the island. For more details see Busquet (1994), p. 21, Doñate Sastre (2010a), p. 91, Mazzola (2017), p. 108. A similar effort is not unknown in the field of legal anthropology since, as Terradas Saborit (2008), p. 68, acknowledges, "passional vengeance [...] proceeding from literary imagination" imposed "over vengeance observed in ethnographic fieldworks" and then "the dominant tendency is to ignore vengeance as administered by judicial power following a judicial procedure, and to replace it with vengeance intended as an individual emotion". For more details see Busquet (1994), p. 21, Doñate Sastre (2010a), p. 91, Mazzola (2017), p. 108.

[4]Although Busquet does not use the term vindicatory to refer to the part of customary law in charge of instituting the procedures to deal with offences, this idea must be implied in all his work on the two main institutions that make up the Corsican vindicatory legal system: *vendetta* and *pace*. See Doñate Sastre (2010a), and Mazzola (2017). But as Terradas Saborit (2008) says, it is to Verdier and his group (1980a) that we must attribute this denomination, although as Terradas Saborit (2019) completes, Verdier does not pay special attention to composition.

[5]Ravis-Giordani (1994), p. 13.

[6]Today we know a little more about the life of Busquet and the context within which he developed his investigation thanks to Mazzola (2017), p. 108, for example, that he ended up in Corsica in 1917 as a naval officer during WWII.

[7]Although Stephen Wilson (1995) deeply studied the phenomenon of *vendetta*, his efforts do not seem to possess the analytic character of Busquet's work due to the absence of a legal perspective. However, Wilson analyses the sociocultural dimension of *vendetta* (in that historical period) in much more detail than Busquet.

[8]See Terradas Saborit (2008), p. 76.

justice culture". In this way, while his excellent classification of the *vendetta* is highlighted in Pigliaru's "*Il codice della vendetta barbaricina*",[9] in Busquet this is specifically achieved by the institutional analysis of the *pace*,[10] which is at least the main instrument of Corsican vindicatory justice for putting a stop to the *nimicizia* (hostility)[11] between two or more families.[12] Consequently, the path chosen by Busquet departs from the acknowledgement of *vendetta* and *pace* as a legal system, or part of a legal system, an idea which although may seem obvious for current legal anthropology,[13] was a real departure from the hegemonic approaches in the field of law studies[14] and was similar to that undertaken by anthropologists with a greater interest in the legal sphere.[15]

1.1 A Brief Note on Legal Pluralism Since Busquet

When Busquet set himself the principal objective of "*tracer l'histoire des règles coutumières de la Vendetta et de dire les institutions qui furent employées à la*

[9]See Pigliaru (2000), pp. 137–153.

[10]The word *pace* is used to refer to both a procedure and to the result of such a procedure: mainly a peace treaty. Similar treaties encoded customary oral law into written form and have become important sources for ethnographic research.

[11]This is used to refer to a situation of declared enmity between two or more families.

[12]A study on the relationship between Pigliaru and Busquet has been to my knowledge only outlined to date—Doñate (2010a, b), Mazzola (2017), Romero Noguera (2018)—and is pending major development.

[13]A self-evidence that not all anthropologists share, as Verdier mentions (1980b). Still, there indeed exist those interpreting vengeance as a system of repression of pre-social and pre-legal states, such as Girard (1983); or as a passional reaction to the offence suffered (see fn 2).

[14]As stated, the common and dominant tendency among legal historians was to present *vendetta* as a pre-legal practice deprived of any rationality. However, it is not possible to avoid mentioning the existence of important exceptions such as Fustel de Coulanges (1905). Also, comparative law—a field in which Busquet seems to collocate his work (1994), pp. 33–40—seemed to be much more receptive since they mostly only recognise formalised customary rights, which helps to understand even more the relevance, beyond a strictly scientific level, of their contribution. Busquet was not totally unaware of such a dominant orientation and he, at least occasionally, refers to *vendetta* as a "war between families" or "private law", a terminology used by those authors who negated the legal nature of *vendetta*.

[15]As Terradas Saborit indicates (2008), pp. 191–199, although it is from Verdier that legal anthropology formulated the concept of the vindicatory order or system, also before that the "realist fidelity of several ethnographers handed precious data that could easily be interpreted as organic (. . .) to the vindicatory orders' logic and praxis" (2008), p. 91, such as Bogoras (1904), Malinowski (1969), Warner (1969), Llewellyn and Hoebel (1999), Firth (1961) and Gluckman (1967) among others. It is interesting that a similar reflection is applied to the anthropologic studies of Mediterranean societies and vindicatory cultures. Before Verdier, and beside the magnificent Pigliaru's work, there were some authors that offered interesting data on the vindicatory rationality of those societies through their ethnographies, such as Pitt-Rivers (1968, 1989), Campbell (1964) and Peristiany (1966, 1968).

réduire",[16] although it may not have been his initial intention, he places himself within the sphere of legal pluralism by analysing the interactions between Corsican vindicatory justice and the justice of the successive occupying states, between Corsican society and the institutions of these states during the period encompassing the fifteenth to the nineteenth centuries.[17] The range and complexity of the historical period[18] under analysis encompasses many different situations of legal pluralism[19] but, despite the differences found, it is evident that at least until the early decades of the nineteenth century, the analysis of these situations should not "succumb to a false legal pluralism or a sharing out of jurisdictions", as Terradas Saborit[20] emphasises, because, just as Pigliaru (2000) points out for the Barbagian legal system, it is the Corsican legal system that is truly *effective* and *universal* for this society. With this in mind, during this long period of time, the laws of the successive occupying states are not just hegemonic,[21] but they can even be considered to be marginal. This is because they are rejected by society due to both their foreign characteristics and their imposed status, as well as for being viewed as ineffective in the resolution of conflicts.[22] A dissatisfaction that increases because of the persistent aspirations of these states to substitute Corsican law through prohibition and persecution—principally of *vendetta*—but also because of appropriation and imitation, particularly

[16]Busquet (1994), p. 21.

[17]In this way, he covers most of the Genovese and French occupation of Corsica. Genovese domination lasted from the eleventh century, but only from 1347 did this translate into actual control of the island with relative continuity until 1768. The modality of Genovese management varied substantially throughout history: it was exercised sometimes by "commercial groups" such as the *Maona* and so-called *Ufficio* or *Banco di San Giorgio*; some other times directly by *Serenissima*. Frequently such groups and political entities coexisted, each one controlling cities regulated by specific statutes, territory inhabited by freemen, etc. French administration was instead continuous from 1769, with the exception of the brief dominance of the Anglo-Corsican reign (1794–1796) and the years of the Italo-German occupation (1942–1943).

[18]See, among others, Antonetti (1990), Braudel (2001), Busquet (1994), Doñate Sastre (2011), Doñate Sastre and Romero Noguera (2008), Ratzel (1899), Ravis Giordani (1983).

[19]A difference that unavoidably increases once we learn about the complete history of the island (Doñate 2011), and that is documented with a degree of accuracy since the twelfth century.

[20]Terradas Saborit (2008), p. 79.

[21]Until the late nineteenth century (under French occupation), it is not accurate to consider occupant states as actual sovereign states along with Corsica, since they are so involved in internal and external conflicts for hegemony and the exercise of power that it is more precise to speak about virtual sovereignty.

[22]Ineffectiveness that, as we will see, states implicitly acknowledge. For example, when they incapsulate within their legal orders the figure of *pacere*. It is interesting to consider that a similar perception of ineffectiveness can also be explained by referring to states' obsession with punishing the violation of the law rather than repairing the consequences of the offence. This does not mean that the Corsican vindicatory system is a perfect one, but simply that its main objective is a quest for justice, and then it produces its main effort in the search to address each case in particular.

notable with the establishment of the *pace*.[23] However, from the nineteenth century, there is a progressive loss of the hegemony of Corsican vindicatory justice and culture and a consolidation of the modern French *rule of law*. This generates new scenarios of interaction between both justice systems as well as between the different legal cultures that support them.

1.2 Vendetta, Pace*? Or* Pace, Vendetta*? The Ambiguity of the Sources*

The question of the precedence of *vendetta* over *pace* or *pace* over *vendetta*[24] within the Corsican legal system is ambiguously addressed by Busquet in *Le droit de la vendetta et les 'paci' corses* and requires a certain amount of clarification,[25] among other reasons, to place it in relation to the majority viewpoint in preference to the settlement of the vindicatory legislation as developed by Terradas Saborit in his prodigious *Justicia Vindicatoria* (2008).

I begin by noting that Busquet does not present *vendetta* and *pace* as institutions of different status within the Corsican legal system.[26] But it is during the description that he gives of these institutions through the analysis of documents and citations from other authors where a preference of Corsican society for the *vendetta*[27] process rather than *pace* is illustrated. This, as will be seen, appears mainly as the process that takes place when the former fails, or its application is rejected.[28]

However, the explanation of a *de facto* preference for *vendetta* cannot disassociate itself from factors such as the island's political potential for conflict and instability during this period, the inability to extend the laws of the states, the relative fragility of its own justice when faced with constant attacks by these states, or the

[23]We also observe several encapsulations and/or adaptations in Corsican vindicatory justice as the transcription of *paci* or the use of state trials as a form of aggression in a context of *vendetta*, something that Busquet (1994), p. 121 calls "*vendetta judiciaire*".

[24]An issue that seems to be faced by Verdier's theoretical efforts (1980a) in distinguishing a vindicatory legal system—in which vengeance is authorized by a public authority and composition precedes vengeance—and vindictive legal system—in which vengeance precedes composition.

[25]Mazzola's critical reading (2017) of my earlier works (2010b; 2011) in his analysis of Busquet's investigation emphasised the necessity of a detailed study of the issue to avoid ambiguity.

[26]As Terradas Saborit notes (2008, p. 166), "to the vindicatory order, after an offence there can be only two possible solutions: to act in vengeance or to start a composition". Such an idea of the two institutions maintaining the same importance characterises Busquet's work starting from the title until the detailed analysis of the institution of *pace*.

[27]We again refer to regulated vengeance, as a part of a legal system, and not to a personal, passionate vengeance.

[28]As we will see further in the essay, Busquet (1994, pp. 216–220) thinks it is more accurate to place *vendetta* first when considering compensation as a fundamental principle of the Corsican vindicatory legal culture against composition, which even seems, from the existing documentation, to insinuate it would be a foreign import.

transformations which are the product of modernity, among other things, since along this same vein, Terradas Saborit[29] frequently explains this preference for vengeance as a product of the vice, abuse and degeneracy of the vindicatory systems.[30]

Likewise, one needs to remember that we are dealing with a basic spoken right, that the transcribed *paci* would be part of an extraordinary process (with these, they attempted to influence the legal procedures initiated by the states for dealing with violent crimes within the context of *vendetta*). Both *vendetta* and *pace* are built upon homicide as a prototypical case, but they encompass the compensation of any type of offence. Therefore, it is not speculative to consider that *vendetta*, as the first mechanism viewed in the work of Busquet, and others, could respond to a partial vision of reality, as other situations exist where the preference may be for *pace* and, apparently, the simple possibility that *vendetta* already acts as a preventive and dissuasive mechanism.

2 *Vendetta*

> Dans la vendetta, l'idée fondamentale est celle de *compensation* du meurtre par le meurtre, de l'offense par l'offense. C'est encore celle de dette, d'obligation du sang, de revendication de l'honneur perdu à la suite d'un outrage ayant privé l'offensé de ce qui lui appartient. Compensation, obligation, revendication; il n'y a pas à s'y tromper: la vendetta repose sur des idées de droit.[31]

Vendetta appears as a "*système complexe de règlement des conflits*"[32] built on the idea of compensation for the offence caused by an offence. As homicide is the prototypical offence on which the Corsican vindicatory system is built, accepting the irreparability of a human life within all vindicatory systems, as Fustel de Coulanges (1905) and Terradas Saborit (2008) illuminate, one can understand why this compensation was obtained through the counter-offence, as this is "*fondamentalement hostile à toute réparation en argent d'un crime de sang*" as Leca points out.[33]

---

[29]Terradas Saborit (2008), p. 166.

[30]The vacuum of power, social transformations, etc. are factors also explaining the increase in the occurrences of *vendetta*, as well as of their intensity in certain periods, as Busquet (1994) and Wilson (1995) note for the mid-nineteenth century.

[31]Busquet (1994), pp. 26–27.

[32]Lari and Salini (2004), p. 1254.

[33]Leca (1989), p. 51. Sayings such as *u sangue chere u sangue* (blood wants blood) or *u sangue ùn si vende micca à baiocche sunanti* (blood cannot be sold for money) are clear reflections of this idea. With the current documentation, it is not possible to confirm the pre-eminence of *vendetta* in Corsican vindicatory order in the Middle Ages as Busquet argues (1994), pp. 216–220, but only to point out the possibility that such customary law originally included composition as its main mechanism to obtain justice, as we observed in the majority of historical and ethnographic case-studies; Terradas Saborit (2008). Examples that show this evolution as a consequence of the disappearance – in periods of high socio-political conflicts—of (permanent) customary authorities in charge of surveiling the application of compositional systems.

However, as Rospabé (1995) writes, the fact that, in general, the punishment for taking a life cannot be compensated with a simple equivalence, it does not necessarily mean an incompatibility within this arrangement. But compensation and arrangement refer to different actions, although they are sometimes mixed up in their use. The former centres on material compensation, while in the latter the material compensation is an additional element[34] in restoring coexistence and reconciliation.

While the counter-offence seeks to obtain justice and re-establish the lost equilibrium at the same time, it will be influenced by the principle of reciprocity manifested in the essential and difficult proportionality that needs to be achieved between the offence and the counter-offence. It is an extraordinarily complex equilibrium because, as a "*système – ou sous-système – à la fois d'échange et contrôle social de la violence*",[35] *vendetta* owes its effectiveness to its capacity to satisfy the offended party without then offending the prior offender and, by doing so, degenerating into a spiral of offences and counter-offences. A particularly difficult mission due to the complexity of determining the proportionality of the counter-offence when, in evaluating the offence it is found that the material dimension is not the only, or necessarily the most important issue.[36] The moral dimension stands out because, in the end, the whole offence will also be measured in relation to the affront caused to the offended family.[37] Values such as *onore*, *disunore*, *vergogna* serve to explain why very dissimilar offences can have an identical response, as well as helping to understand the chain of events leading to revenge. This is, without a doubt, one of the main flaws of establishing *vendetta* within the vindicatory systems.

Vendetta does not only rest on the legal principle of compensation, but as Busquet (1994) points out, vindication and obligation are also fundamental. The vindication of justice, the need to acknowledge the suffering caused by the offence,[38] of "*rivendicare il propio*" which, Rossi[39] says, prompts the mechanism of *vendetta* because *vendetta* is neither an authority nor a right, "*c'est une obligation régie par toute une série de prescriptions*" as Vincentelli points out.[40] Thus, the obligation of *vendetta* is principally built on its social dimension—since it is not a personal

[34]See Terradas Saborit (2008), p. 201.

[35]See Verdier (1980b), p. 16.

[36]The position—defended by Busquet (1994), Leca (1989), Wilson (1995) and me—in no case undermines the material dimension of offense, nor ignores the importance of a concept as complex as "honour". It simply points out how this and other values come into play along with material values to explain the feeling of being offended. An issue, as Terradas Saborit (2008), p. 14 notes, is that "the offence unifies and synthetises its material and moral components".

[37]A saying that perfectly sums up this idea is "*pà u padrone si rispetta u ghjacaru*". Mutilation or killing of animals was a huge offence, acknowledged in the first statutes, that normally ended with a blood vengeance.

[38]See Terradas Saborit (2008), p. 50.

[39]Rossi (1906), p. 311.

[40]Vincentelli (1933), p. 11.

matter—and the *dèbitu di sangue* which denies the offended family the ability to renounce the vindication.

A fourth fundamental legal principle exists within the *vendetta* system: solidarity.[41] Within the sphere of Corsican vindicatory culture, solidarity transfers the perspective of rights and obligations to the nature of the family as a basic societal unit, and the subordination of the individual to this rationality. In this manner, the principle of solidarity establishes that all offences to an individual are also an offence to the family group as a whole and, similarly, it considers that the offender does not act individually but as a representative of the family. This means that the counter-offence can be exercised by any family member and can be directed towards any family member. For this reason, the *vendetta transversal* is often referred to. In any event, the acknowledgement of collective responsibility does not deny the preference to return the offence to the individual offender although, frequently, this may be a complex matter.[42]

In theory, the limits of solidarity within *vendetta* are those of the family,[43] and include all family members up to the third degree of kinship in the responsibility of offering solidarity during inter-family conflicts. The inclusion of the whole group is figurative, as the execution of *vendetta* (as well as its receipt) is reserved for adult males. Elderly males, women and children are excluded. Beyond these exceptions, there are narratives in which a woman has executed a *vendetta*. The exclusion of children is relative, since they are frequently required to execute it as soon as they are no longer children.[44] The family is a timeless institution encompassing the living, the dead and even those that have yet to be born, and the obligation can be transferred

[41]Solidarity maintains a fundamental role in Busquet's analysis. However, as Doñate (2010a) and Vincentelli (1933) emphasise, the author did not include solidarity among the three legal principles here quoted.

[42]Among the most prominent would be the fact that those who offended (especially in the case of homicide) frequently escaped into the bush to avoid the retaliation of the offended family and/or, even more frequently to avoid the consequence of the official legal system. In any case, from the late-eighteenth century, a progressive change towards an individual responsibility characterising the practice of *vendetta* can be grasped.

[43]There exists a certain discussion on the limits of family in Corsica. For details, see Graziani (1997), Leca (1991) and Ravis-Giordani (1983, 1994). But their establishment at the third grade is the most accepted to explain family in Corsica in the last three to four centuries. This includes the *famiglia stretta*—people living under the same roof independently from the affiliation between them—and the *parenti*—the other relatives, that today tendentially regroups with the family core. See Ravis-Giordani (1994).

[44]According to the verses by Giammatteu's sister and his cousin before his death, as Ortoli notes (1992), we can read: "*Nun pienghjite più, surella,/ Fate un cor' di Faraone:/Ingrandatemi à Carlucciu,/ Ch'ellu sgotti à Mascarone,/ Chi tumbò prima à Matteu; / Poi ferì Francesc'Antone.*" Accordingly, also the popular saying, "*un' tumbà babbu ch'appi figliolil*" (do not kill a father with little children) gives an account of the fact that to put forward such a killing would mean to be harmed by vengeance, sooner or later. The same saying also expresses the feeling that it is a moral necessity to avoid innocent people being affected by vengeance. In this sense, the father's death would leave children with no support. The same idea is in Pigliaru (2000) regarding Barbagian society.

from one generation to another, giving rise to what has become known as the *hereditary vendetta*. In this way, every *vendetta* will also be an action to satisfy the dead, as the obligations to these are even greater. The exclusion also includes those located around the vague peripheries of the family, such as friends,[45] regular religious persons and, at the limits of otherness, foreigners. The possibility may arise (very infrequently) for a family member to refrain from participating, making this known through a series of rites, or even a whole family when faced with the seriousness of the action (from a moral viewpoint). Even so, with a certain amount of frequency, one can observe conflicts between groups which transcend these limits, such as the *stèrpi* or the *cèppi*[46] or unions like the *legi*,[47] which will demobilise once the conflict is over[48] where their responsibilities, and obligations, may follow another order. But these would not just be a response to the ideal type of *vendetta,* having also observed other motivations, apart from a hypothetical redress of the offence, which may have political or economic outcomes. It is precisely this solidarity, or rather, its progressive abandonment during the nineteenth century, that allows us to retrace the decline of the practice of *vendetta* as a consequence of, among other factors, the progressive penetration of individualism into Corsican society, the social exhaustion caused by the virulent consequences of this practice, or an increasingly effective official law for implementing individual criminal responsibility and the repressive measures placed on families.

3 The Laws of the Occupying States and *Vendetta*: Scenarios of Legal Pluralism

3.1 Genoese Law and Vendetta

In its multiple forms,[49] the Genoese administration in Corsica maintained an ambivalent relationship to traditional Corsican law. Although in quite a few aspects it was kept up to date,[50] within the specific sphere of vindicatory justice, it was revoked. A prohibition which should not cause surprise, despite not being very different to that

[45]Corsican society considers friendship as a tie that can be equated to blood. For example, the establishment of wedding alliances is called "*fà amicizia*".

[46]Family groups with a common ancestor to which individuals linked by clientele relationships could be added.

[47]They can regard two families as all the population of a *paesolu*, *paese* or *pieve*—different kinds of territorial fragmentation in Corsica.

[48]The *albergho*, of Genovese origin, would have been an exception and consisted of the ultimate union of two families that abandoned their respective surnames for a common one.

[49]Cities with specific statutes such as Bunifaziu and Calvi; manors such as Nonza, Brando et Canari and San Colombano; companies such as Maona and Ufficio di San Giorgio, and the government of Serenissima. For more details see Letteron (1884), Mazolaccio (1883-1884).

[50]See Coppolani and Serpentini (1998).

applied in the mother country[51] as it responded to the logic of power relationships, occupation and domination, the monopoly of violence and the continued fight to secure themselves throughout the island. This ambivalence allows us to talk about a formal legal pluralism—within the different statutes and bodies of laws—through which it was incorporated in civil law, as well as through the practices that appear classified as crimes in the penal or criminal sphere, such as *rimbeccu*,[52] *rumpitori*[53] or *attacar*,[54] being aware of the importance that they had in the development of *vendetta*. But we can also talk of the legal pluralism experienced by the continuity of the traditional laws as a whole, and specifically the vindicatory law, in the daily life of the native population due to this being the effective and universal practice.

Faced with the difficulties of applying its penal law, particularly for violent crimes that were devastating the island—as Serpentini (2003) points out—and putting their political, legal and even moral authority into question, the Genoese legal system adopted a series of measures to repress *vendetta* drawn from the logic of the Corsican vindicatory legal culture and whose formal objective was to combat social support for crimes. Beyond the perpetrator's individual responsibility, and that of his accomplices, a collective responsibility was applied that would impute persons without any real participation in the crimes or that, at least from the viewpoint of the Genoese culture and statutes, could not be proven as such. These extraordinary measures were particularly applied to relatives, but also to neighbours of the *paesolu*, the *paese*, and even the *capella*[55] and the *pieve*.

There are measures directed towards those family members and those close to them who were considered to be instigators of the *vendetta*. Along with the previously mentioned *rimbeccu*—public reprobation—which is pursued in the different

[51]Paradox that responds to the vindicatory component of Genoese law both in Corsica and in Genoa itself. It is to be noted once again that we are talking about a submerged law in a process of transition from a vindicatory legal culture towards official law—as can be seen through a comparative reading, for example, of the San Colombano statute (1348) and of the Corsican statute (1571).

[52]*Rimbeccu* consisted of a usually public reprobation upon the person that did not comply with the duty of vengeance—*u dèbitu di sangue*—or that simply is delaying their vengeance. As Busquet notes (1920), "*le déshonneur définitif*" is then to be added to the dishonour of receiving an offence and giving no response. The same institute is mentioned in legal documents such as the *Statuts criminels de Nonza, Brando et Canari* (there are references until 1119, but we refer now to that of 1517): in chapter 31, "De non ricordare nimicitie"; or the *Statuts criminels de la Corse* (1571) in chapter 19, "Sur ceux qui font des reproches à autri et sont coupables de rimbecco".

[53]*Rumpitori* in Corsican vindicatory law was a person that "broke" *pace* through their actions. Genovese governments considered this as an aggravating factor to commit a crime, in a context of *vendetta* as well as in a context of peace.

[54]The word *attacar* was used from the early-eighteenth century to denote a series of actions such as to kiss, to touch the face or the hands, to remove the kerchief from a head or to follow a woman without her permission in a public place. Such actions were considered, according to Corsican culture, as offences to honour, to the individual and to the family. The majority of the statutes severely persecuted these actions, since they acknowledged them as frequent causes of *vendetta*, as in chapter 42, "De ceux qui enlacent ou embrassent les femmes contre leur volonté" of the *Statuts criminels de la Corse* (1571).

[55]The *capella* (chapel) was an intermediate administrative entity.

statutes, in 1665 another step was taken when the women of the family were fined for the crime of "bad intention". This was fundamentally applied to the women of the offended family. This was an ambiguous and arbitrary law, because unlike *rimbeccu*, which was public, it would be particularly difficult to determine if there was or was not any participation or inducement, and its determination would be at the hands of the legal system, a thing which normally took place under *ex informata conscientia*.[56]

Other laws were used for making family members responsible to gain their collaboration in the arrest of a fugitive (bandit) so that he would turn himself in, such as decree 10-05-1658 of the *Libro Rosso de Corsica,* which sets out penalties of up to three years in exile for wives, offspring and close relatives of the fugitive condemned in absentia for committing or attempting to commit an act of *vendetta* which he would otherwise not have carried out. In a similar vein, there are other measures, such as those gathered in the criminal Statutes of 1571 (chapter 58) in which the judge has the power to sentence lineal relatives to pay a fine or go to prison if the cases of exile do not include the convicted person.

This assumption of responsibility often takes on an economic dimension through obligations such as paying the costs for the prosecution and upkeep of the convicted offender in the galleys, or a large number of indirect penalties on the family. Formally, they were punishments for the guilty party, but in practice, they were a punishment for the whole group and another means of forcing them to collaborate with the official legal system. For example, chapter 32 of the Statutes of 1571 documents the confiscation of all goods belonging to a convicted fugitive in exile. In the New Legislation of 1635, the confiscation is changed to the complete destruction of his possessions, normally respecting those of his wife, daughter-in-law and creditors. This does not imply a great change from the way the property system operated on the island. It is precisely this same assumption of (collective) economic responsibility that is also applied to neighbours and/or local administrations, a logic that transcends the vindicatory system's own logic by considering the solidarity of those outside the family. Basically, they are interpreted as forcing them to bear the economic costs for the damages caused when the individual cannot pay for them himself, or their capture (Statutes of 1571, chapter 45), or their obligation under penalty of fines to inform against, or even hand over, a criminal who may be found in the territory of the local entity (Statutes of 1571, chapter 62).

After this, there is a series of repressive measures associated with maintaining the peace. This is a responsibility for the family members present throughout *pace*, the difference is that the state will go so far as to contemplate actions such as the kidnapping of family members from both sides in order to avoid *vendetta*. Other practices, such as salting the fields, pulling up the vines, etc., when the crime was

[56]To act *ex informata conscientia* was basically the opportunity for the judge to decide a case due to the absence of evidence, according to his insight. Such a mechanism was an alternative to the—practically non-existent—collaboration between judges and the Corsican population. However, it became an instrument open to abuse, and was largely refused on the island, and by members of the administration of justice.

committed *sotto pace* carried an additional element of shame (Statutes of 1571, chapter 28). This severity is even more surprising if one keeps in mind that, as we will see, the Genoese state wanted to promote *paci*, and that it combined it with the granting of pardons, and even economic rewards, to criminals who were willing to kill other criminals (Statutes of 1571, chap, 58 and 80), and the granting of letters of safe passage or the opportunity to enlist in the army.

Measures like these show that the Genoese state was aware of the importance of family and community in Corsican society. Nevertheless, their political usefulness remains open to question in light of the results, as the state does not obtain the required direct results and it also generates a greater rejection of the state and its legal system.

3.2 Corsican Governments and the Law

In general, the state promoted strong and severe justice as a counterpoint to the leniency practised by Genoa in Corsica (in the metropolis it gave harsher sentences, and it also abused the granting of pardons, reprieves etc.), but also due to their desire to create a strong and united nation in the eyes of the world, as Emmanuelli (1969) points out. At the same time, the pacifying element of the Corsican vindicatory justice system was advanced by promoting it, semi-officialising or officialising it; a step towards the tolerance that had been demonstrated by the Genoese.

The different *cunsulti* and the reign of Teodoro, which took place before Paoli came to power (1755–1769), were only differentiated by the severity of the measures taken by the Genoese to repress *vendetta*. That is, they maintained individual and collective responsibility in *vendetta* crimes.

During Paoli's first government, firm actions were taken along with a clear desire to discredit *vendetta*, to present it as a shameful and dishonourable act. To do this, apart from the punishments, infamy was used—often extending to the family—and in the case of a *sotto pace* or *vendetta transversale*, commanded a death sentence, the shame of the execution (the display of the body with the *cartello*), the erection of a pillar with an explanation of the crime committed, and the exile of all immediate family members, applied up to the third generation. Independently of the evaluation made of these measures, it is worth pointing out that this was the first government on the island to understand that the eradication of *vendetta* would also require changes in societal values.

The final thing to mention is the brief period of Anglo-Corsican reign (1794–1796), an interlude in the French domination which has persisted to the present time. Paoli was once again the visible leader of this government (although the greatest power lay in British hands), but this time they chose not to address *vendetta* in any specific way in criminal law and to exclusively apply individual responsibility. Perhaps the only measure that we can relate to the violence associated with the vindicatory system is the sentence of exile for adultery, which may have been a strategy for avoiding the violent conflicts that this might have unleashed.

3.3 *French Positive Law and* Vendetta

From 1769, except for the brief period of Anglo-Corsican reign, Corsica has been under French sovereignty. For 250 years, the interactions between French positive law and vindicatory legal system have varied significantly. The deep social transformations within Corsican society and the nature of the French state are among the most important factors in this. Even so, it is necessary to consider the different forms adopted by the French state, principally during the first 50 years of occupation, since these brought about the differences in their reaction to the vindicatory system.

During the reign of the Old Regime, some of the vindicatory institutions, such as *paci,* were respected and were even adopted,[57] even though *vendetta* was considered to be another crime and the focus was on revoking Genoese penal law.[58] But the recognition of *pace* was an implicit acceptance of the existence of *vendetta,* as can also be observed in other preventative regulations such as the ban on carrying weapons or restrictive legislation against shepherds,[59] as they were considered to be part of many conflicts. But there was still more, as the collective responsibility that was initially derogated[60] soon returned to normal to put a stop to *vendetta* by applying measures such as prison or family fines in certain circumstances.

With the Revolution of 1789, individual accountability was imposed and, therefore, individual responsibility denied any possibility of collective responsibility, even in an indirect manner. The family should not suffer the consequences of a crime committed by a family member, leading to the practice of confiscating goods, the destruction of the home, etc., that had ended up being adopted.

However, between the Consulship (1800) and the end of the Empire (1814), during the governments of Miot de Melito, Morand and Berthier, the principles of penal collective solidarity were reinstated to repress *vendetta*, although these were not applied on the Continent under any circumstances. This reinstatement was carried out through different laws, orders, etc., which were exclusively enforced on the island. As had occurred during Genoese rule, these laws applied collective responsibility to the municipalities and their representatives or to family members and, as an innovation, to the testimonies relating to acts of *vendetta*. The responsibility of the municipalities was interpreted as the obligation of the mayors—under

---

[57]*Paci* are thought to be effective customs to resolve conflicts affecting entire communities in which respective official procedures do not present a solution. However, the official *paci* would not receive great acceptance and would need to punitively oblige persons to participate.

[58]France took the place of another state—the Genovese Republic—and the kind of law that it had to substitute was an official one. The French perspective was in fact to deny recognition of vindicatory law, or to consider it as a customary system to be or not be maintained.

[59]For example, in 1772 it was established that those who did not register their stay in a *pieve* after 6 months had to be imprisoned for 3 years, their money had to be confiscated and their children had to be deported to a work camp.

[60]Informally collective responsibility did not disappear. For example, a judicial decision adverse to someone who committed a vendetta usually condemned the avenger to the death penalty, to have his house destroyed and their descendants to be banished from the exercise of public functions.

penalty of fines—to advise of the existence of *nimicizia* within their municipalities and to report and detain those responsible, to anticipate their appearance, as well as to maintain the garrisons.

The pressure on families became even greater, with draconian measures imposed on family members, friends and neighbours, such as arbitrary detention until a fugitive was captured, the detention of family members of those who had left the town (automatically considering that the fugitive had gone underground), imprisonment on the Continent, the burning down of houses, fines for all the neighbours, and so on, in the pursuit of putting an end to revenge crimes within the municipalities.[61] Making those who witnessed acts of *vendetta* take on responsibility originated from an extreme interpretation of the French laws relating to no impediment crime (article 475 of the penal code), which allows the imprisonment of a large number of persons—without classifiable penal responsibility—and even the imprisonment of families and friends as a preventive measure by considering that, as they had not prevented the crime, it was equivalent to complicity. This was based on the supposition that their proximity would make them aware of the intention to commit a crime.

During the rest of the nineteenth century, there was a continued observation of measures and regulations that went beyond the strictest individual accountability, and which assumed the logic of collective responsibility as a strategy for eradicating *vendetta* at a time when it was escalating,[62] for example, by ruling in favour of preventive prison for family members and for those alleged to have been complicit in a crime.[63] In the same way, the French authorities continued to recognise this collective and social dimension through the acknowledgement of *paci,* at least until the beginning of the twentieth century.[64] It was not a legal but rather a social acknowledgement of it, as a traditional institution with a private scope that may help in the resolution of *vendetta* conflicts. The twentieth century was a time of more subtle interactions, as I have noted previously,[65] which, in particular, manifested on a moral plane in which the culture of vindicatory justice continued to rival the justice culture of the *rule of law* in certain contexts.

---

[61]For example, the Miot resolutions (1801) for Pila-Canale, Carchetto and Piediportino.

[62]The significant increase and the intensification of *vendetta* in the mid-nineteenth century can be explained by the impact of the social and cultural transformations of modernity, such as the incorporation of a modern state into Corsican society and its legal culture. See Wilson (1995), p. 54, and Doñate (2011), p. 540.

[63]The commission of police authority of 1852 noted that this practice was a frequent one in courts, as stated in article 248 of the criminal law code.

[64]See Busquet (1994).

[65]See Doñate Sastre (2011).

4 *Pace*: State Appropriation as an Acknowledgement of Its Effectiveness

Infallibility is not an intrinsic characteristic of Corsican vindicatory justice, nor is it within any other justice. However, for centuries, Corsican society has considered it to be the most effective means of seeking justice. The compensation received for damages, the re-establishment of the lost equilibrium, the solution to the conflict caused is obtained through the institution of *vendetta* and/or *pace*. Additionally, successive state laws have reacted in an ambivalent manner towards this efficiency for resolving conflicts, because when faced with the institution of *vendetta,* the response has been repression;[66] while with the institution of *pace,* it has moved between tolerance and its adaptation and incorporation.

Before looking more deeply into the institution of *pace*, into its logic and operation, its interaction with official legislation and vice versa, it is worth pointing out once again that, for a large period of history, for Busquet (1994), *vendetta* seemed like the first option of Corsican vindicatory legal system for resolving conflicts. However, as has also been noted, the complexity of determining the compensation equivalent to the offence and thereby redressing the damage and restoring the lost social equilibrium quite often causes a process of escalation that aggravates the initial conflict. The failure of the compensation makes way for the arrangement of *pace*. Established on the same principles as *vendetta*, *pace* must find "*a la compensation directe du sang par le sang, de l'offense par l'offense, il faudra trouver un substitut, un équivalent juridique*", as Busquet emphasises, that satisfies all parties within the conflict.[67] Some independent parties have demonstrated that they are unable to do this, and because of this it is essential to include a third party, an authority:[68] el *pacere*.

It is precisely in this form where one can best observe the recognition of the legal effectiveness of *paci* by the Genoese and French governments, as Jean and Coppolani (2004) emphasise. The Genoese government committed itself to creating some official *paceri,* such as the *magistrati delli pacificatori* of the seventeenth century, who were quickly replaced by the *pacificatori*—which were chosen along with the rest of the *pieve* authorities. In contrast, the formula used by French legislation consisted of encouraging members of the government to exercise the

[66]It is not possible to imagine a different kind of answer from any modern state when one of its essential characters is directly affected: the monopoly in the use of strength. See Weber (2012).

[67]Busquet (1994), p. 199. It is a complex issue, since moving from the non-reparability of a lost life and the refusal to equate blood and money, the reparation-process should develop in a way in which both parties' honour is always respected. Such a reparation should at the same time be an honourable act in which the offended party renounces vengeance and make it seem as if the offender's previous attitude was not a dishonour and that the restitution to the offended party is not a dishonour.

[68]See, among others, Fustel de Coulanges (1905), Terradas Saborit (2008).

role of the traditional *pacere*[69] without recognising their legality because of them being considered private agreements. Even so, these official changes had little success, as they did not provide an accurate response to the traditional model (the official mechanism rarely relied upon approval from the parties, who often had different legal cultures) and because the occupying governments promoted them. A rejection that was also clearly reflected when the courts, acting ex officio, summoned them, and the parties' response was silence, deceit and absence in order to make the process of the trial as difficult as possible.[70] In addition to contempt, the use of the previously noted transcription of the *paci* attempted to stall the legal process, reduce the sentence, obtain a pardon, or what was called the judicial *vendetta* described by Busquet, to refer to the self-interested use of justice to deal a blow to their foes.

While these official *paceri* intervened, driven forwards by their position as named representatives of the official government, the—traditional—*paceri* was conducted when summoned by one of the parties (if the other party accepted) or through their own initiative, as was often the case.[71] To be a *pacere* required the status of an honourable man, who was impartial and independent as, based on these values, the parties would put their trust in him. It also required a prominent and/or well-to-do person with many relatives and whose bravery was acknowledged so that, if required, he could enforce compliance with the *pace*. That is to say, the *pacere* took on the responsibility for the trial and for enforcing compliance with the agreement made.[72] The roles of the *pacere* could vary depending on the stage of *pace* and could even have different names, such as *parolanti* in the initial stage when the availability of the parties was being verified and the initial objective was to obtain the *promessa di non offendersi*. In later stages, other names appear with the *pacere*, such as the *arbitratori*, *amichevoli compositori* or *giudici eletti*, with greater powers always contained in the *compromesso di pace* and the *sentenzia*.

It is precisely through these formal documents that we can follow a complex trial like one of *pace*. The *compromesso* describes the actual trial for peace and includes, among other things: (1) the description of the events; (2) the members of both parties—everyone who had an obligation to seek revenge—and their desire to make peace, and (3) two fundamental clauses such as the pardon—in which each party acknowledges the offences committed—and the peace, which is often accompanied by gestures such as kissing each other on the mouth or embracing each other,

---

[69]Occasionally, members of the French administration that also acted as *paceri*, participating with families as such, exercised a certain effectiveness due to their prestige and their knowledge of Corsican vindicatory culture.

[70]As we noted previously, before that the Genovese state gave to judges the power to act *ex informata conscientia*, allowing them to condemn avengers based on their intuition.

[71]As to the self-initiative of *paceri*, we can mention missions promoted by the Corsican church (Busquet, 1994). For a long time, friars, monks and priests reached the whole island, especially the most detached areas, with the purpose of pacifying the whole Corsican population.

[72]*Rumpitori* are then considered the main preoccupation for all the actors, and crimes committed *sotto pace* were punished severely, also by official law.

and which includes the promise to not offend each other in the future, the renunciation of any existing or future judicial process relating to the facts gathered—with a request to the authorities—and the promise to respect the sentence and the consequences that any breach of this might entail.

The *sentenzia* itself is the execution of the *compromesso* and contains all the actions for compensation that allow for a true reconciliation. These compensations cannot appear as the cornerstone of the redress, as even when this concept does appear, it will be rejected due to the dishonour that accepting money in recompense for an offence would entail. Even though pecuniary compensation has often been observed, this has always been in relation to civil matters such as the creation of dowries or fines. One of the clauses contained is that of exile, an honourable way out for both parties, as those offended view the guilty party as having been punished and the offenders who are anxious for peace do not have to formally cut off contact with one of their members. Other clauses relate to marriage and the dowry. The former entails marrying a member of each family, which simultaneously establishes family links between families that were previously enemies, and as a logical response to compensation is the giving of a man to a family that has lost one—in practically all cases studied by Busquet (1994) the offending group gives a man to the offended group. In contrast, the dowry may or may not accompany a marriage alliance, as in those cases where a marriage cannot take place, a dowry is given so that, at the least, the woman would not be economically impoverished.

In summary, from the remaining *paci*, we can observe that *pace* is activated when *vendetta* enters an undefined process of offence and counter-offence which is unable to be drawn to a satisfactory conclusion for either party. At this moment, the *paci* offers an alternative compensation to the blood rationale through "positive" compensations such as marriage and/or, less frequently, "negative" compensations such as exile. This is all without undervaluing the importance that the act of pardon and reconciliation has throughout this process, and which is the cornerstone of any process for reconciliation. The *paci* contains the explicit acknowledgement of the actions committed by both parties, which is the most precise mechanism for establishing the lost equilibrium. Here, the pardon is understood as an act of responsibility which is indispensable and, apparently, sufficient for the moral compensation of the parties involved. The acceptance of this acknowledgement (the pardon) does not only suppose the formal rejection of the law of *vendetta* for the offences suffered, but it also establishes the basis for a true reconciliation based on new social relationships between the groups.

References

Antonetti P (1990) Histoire de la Corse. Robert Laffont, Paris

Bergerat E (1998) La chasse au Mouflon ou petit voyage philosophique en Corse. DCL Editions, Ajaccio

Bogoras V (1904) The Chuckchee. Stechert & Leiden, New York

Bonaparte R (1891) Une excursion en Corse. R. Bonaparte, Paris
Braudel F (2001) El Mediterráneo y el mundo mediterráneo en la época de Felipe II. FCE, Madrid
Busquet J (1920) Le 'rimbecco' en Corse. Revue de la Corse 4:81–84
Busquet J (1994) Le droit de la vendetta et les pacis corses. CTHS, Paris
Campbell JK (1964) Honour, family and patronage: a study of institutions and moral values in a Greek. Clarendon Press, Oxford
Coppolani JI, Serpentini AL (1998) Les statuts civils et criminels de la Corse. Albiana, Ajaccio
Doñate Sastre M (2010a) Una aproximación al derecho vindicatorio en Córcega. Reivindicando la obra de Jacques Busquet. In: Arévalo MJ, Rodríguez Becerra S, Luque Baena E (eds) Nos-otros: Miradas antropológicas sobre la diversidad. Asamblea de Extremadura, Extremadura, pp 673–690
Doñate Sastre M (2010b) Una aproximación al derecho vindicatorio corso. Le droit de la vendetta et les paci corses. (Con)textos. Revista d'antropologia i investigació social 4:90–96
Doñate Sastre M (2011) Derecho vindicatorio corso y derecho positivo continental: formas diferentes de concebir la responsabilidad. In: Terradas Saborit I (ed) Antropología jurídica de la responsabilidad. Andavira, Santiago de Compostela, pp 509–547
Doñate Sastre M, Romero Noguera P (2008) El mar, una frontera infranquejable? L'experiència de corsos i sards, dues poblacions històricament d'esquena al mar. Drassana 16:85–96
Emmanuelli R (1969) Note sur le droit pénal corse au XVIIIe siècle. Bulletin de la Société des Sciences Historiques et Naturelles de la Corse 591–592:89–106
Firth R (1961) History and traditions of Tikopia. The Polinesyan Society, Wellington
Fustel de Coulanges ND (1905) La Monarchie Franque. En Histoire des Institutions Politiques de l'Ancienne France. Hachette, Paris
Girard R (1983) La violencia y lo sagrado. Anagrama, Barcelona
Gluckman M (1967) The judicial process among the Barotse of Northern Rhodesia. Manchester University Press, Manchester
Graziani AM (1997) La Corse genoise. Economie, société, culture. Période moderne 1453-1768. Alain Piazzola, Genova
Jean F, Coppolani JY (2004) Droit. Histoire du droit corse (de la fin du 13e au 20e siècle). In: Encyclopédie Corscicae. Dumane, Bastia, pp 1–82
Lari V, Salini D (2004) Vindetta (a). In: Encyclopédie Corscicae. Dumane, Bastia, pp 1254–1260
Leca A (1989) L'esprit du droit corse d'après le plus ancien code insulaire: les status de San Colombano de 1348. Cahors, La Marge
Leca A (1991) 'Quelli dello ceppo e casale' dans les statuts corses jusqu'en 1571. Études Corses 36:7–34
Letteron LA (1884) Status civils et criminels de Nonza, Brando, et Canari. Bulletin de la Société des Sciences Historiques et Naturelles de la Corse 48:28–124
Llewellyn KN, Hoebel EA (1999) La voie Cheyenne. Conflict et jurisprudence dans la science primitive du droit. Bruylant/L.G.D.J., Paris
Malinowski BK (1969) Crimen y costumbre en la sociedad salvaje. Ariel, Barcelona
Mazolaccio B (1883-1884) Statuti civili e criminali del Comune di Bonifacio. Bulletin de la Société des Sciences Historiques et Naturelles de la Corse 2–3(71–107):13–98
Mazzola R (2017) Vendetta e paci nell'etnografia storico-giuridica di Jacques Busquet. Sociologia del diritto 3:107–126
Ortoli F (1992) Les voceri de l'ile de Corse. Cismonte è Pumonti, Petricaghju
Peristiany J (ed) (1966) Honour and Shame: The values of Mediterranean Society. Weidenfeld and Nicolson, London
Peristiany J (ed) (1968) Contributions to Mediterranean Sociology. Mouton, Paris
Pigliaru A (2000) Il Banditismo in Sardegna. La vendetta barbaricina. Il Maestrale, Nuoro
Pitt-Rivers J (1968) The stranger, the guest and the hostile host: introduction to the study of the laws of hospitality. In: Peristiany J (ed) Contributions to mediterranean sociology. Mouton, Paris, pp 94–132
Pitt-Rivers J (1989) Un pueblo de la sierra: Grazalema. Alianza, Madrid

Ratzel F (1899) La Corse, étude anthropogéographique. Annales de Geográphie 40:304–329
Ravis-Giordani G (1983) Bergers Corses. Les communautés villageoises du Niolu. EDISUD, Aix-en-Provence
Ravis-Giordani G (1994) Préface. In: Busquet J (ed) Le droit de la vendetta et les pacis corses. CTHS, Paris, pp 13–16
Romero Noguera P (2018) La persistencia de una cultura jurídica vindicatoria. El caso de los pastores de Barbagia, Cerdeña. PhD Thesis, University of Barcelona
Rossi A (1906) Osservazioni storiche sopra la Corsica. Bulletin de la Société des Sciences Historiques et Naturelles de la Corse 4:303–307
Serpentini AL (2003) La criminalité de sang en Corse sous la domination génoise (fin XVIIe-debut XVIIIe siècles). Crime, Histoire et Sociétés 7:57–78
Terradas Saborit I (2008) Justicia Vindicatoria. De la ofensa e indefensión a la imprecación y el oráculo, la vindicta y el talión, la ordalía y el juramento, la composición y la reconciliación. CSIC, Madrid
Terradas Saborit I (2019) La justicia más antigua. Teoría y cultura del ordenamiento vindicatorio. CSIC, Madrid
Vincentelli M (1933) La Vendetta. Revue de droit penal et de criminologie 7:1–20
Verdier R (ed) (1980a) La Vengeance. Études d'ethnologie, d'histoire et de philosophie. Cujas, Paris
Verdier R (1980b) Le système vindicatoire. Esquisse théorique. In: Verdier R (ed) La Vengeance. Études d'ethnologie, d'histoire et de philosophie. Cujas, Paris, pp 13–42
Warner Ll (1969) A black civilization: a social study of an Australian tribe. Peter Smith Pub, Gloucester
Weber M (2012) La política como vocación. In: Weber M (ed) El político y el científico. Alianza Editorial, Madrid
Wilson S (1995) Vendetta et banditisme en Corse au dix-neuvième siècle. A Messagera-Albiana, Ajaccio

Part II
Mapping Vindicatory Justice

Vindicatory Justice in Madagascar

The Compositional Process Among Betsileos

Mariona Rosés Tubau

Abstract This chapter presents composition as a prototypic action for vindicatory justice. In order to illustrate this point, the chapter focuses on conflicts caused by petty theft and minor disputes in rural communities of Madagascar. More specifically, the essay takes on an ethnographic case-study that allows to analyse the different and progressive stages of the composition procedure, underlying its importance as an act of reconciliation and as a social tool to re-establish the harmony prior to the conflict.

1 Introduction

Raymond Verdier (1980) uses the term 'vindicatory system' to refer to the procedures followed in the resolution of conflicts caused by offences. More specifically, one of the main differences between vindicatory law and civil and criminal law is the characterisation of the person who is harmed. While in civil and criminal law this party is the victim, vindicatory law refers to the 'offended party'. In this way, in legal proceedings for vindicatory justice,[1] restitution for the offence and an act of reconciliation take precedence, although compensation for the offended party constitutes a significant part of the proceedings.

When vindicatory justice is called upon to deal with a specific offence, the composition, or reconciliation procedure, is started. The term itself indicates that the intended objective is re-establish the situation prior to the offence. This means that for the parties involved in the conflict to reconcile, the offending party must

[1]In accordance with Terradas Saborit (2008), pp. 192–193, there is a need to differentiate between vindicatory law and vindicatory justice, keeping in mind that the concept of 'vindicatory justice' refers to the characteristic procedure, being a system that is much more jurisprudential than legislative.

M. Rosés Tubau (✉)
Department of Social Anthropology, University of Barcelona, Barcelona, Spain
e-mail: marionarosestubau@ub.edu

R. Márquez Porras et al. (eds.), *Vindicatory Justice*, Ius Gentium: Comparative Perspectives on Law and Justice 93, https://doi.org/10.1007/978-3-030-79595-5_8

acknowledge that they committed an error and ask for forgiveness and, on the other hand, the offended party has to accept to forgive. Once the forgiveness has been received, an agreement is reached on the terms to re-establish the previous situation, and the next step is material compensation for the offended party, where applicable. However, given that the goal is to create a link of personal responsibility between the offending and the offended parties, material compensation should not be interpreted as a payout for the offended party, but as a resource to alleviate the damage caused.

In any case, it is important to understand the reconciliation procedures for vindicatory justice as a social tool to heal the damage caused by a socially anomalous situation. Given this, when an offence is reported, this is an expression of a complaint for damage suffered. In this sense, the offended party is not incapacitated to obtain justice, and on the contrary, unlike in the case of a victim, a defenceless person can make a claim because they are active.[2] Accordingly, the offended party wants justice more than the application of the law.

Starting out from these initial premises, the aim of this paper is to show 'composition' as a prototype action for vindicatory justice through an ethnographic case study that takes us to Madagascar and allows us to analyse the stages of the composition process.[3]

When analysing vindicatory legal practices in African societies, it should be kept in mind that, on the one hand, as noted by Supiot,[4] social structures are the living place for the African values transmission, which means we need to have an understanding of these structures to comprehend the different legal orders present in society.[5] On the other hand, vindicatory justice societies apply a collective responsibility, normally across the entire group, as the result of alliances and blood bonds that evoke a pact of cooperation and general support, far removed from the contractual responsibility typical of civil and criminal culture.[6]

---

[2]See Terradas Saborit (2008), p. 168.

[3]In Madagascar I will focus on the Betsileo, the name for the ethnic group who live in the central region of the country. The Betsileo region borders the north with the Mania River, which separates it from the Merina. To the east lies the Tanala forest, to the west the land belonging to the Sakalava and to the south the Andringitra Massif, which divides the Betsileo from the Tanala.

[4]Supiot (2005, p. 303).

[5]Llewellyn (1941) was one of the pioneering works in delving ethnographically into the fusion between law and morals, characteristic of the vindicatory system. In terms of the relationship between political and legal aspects in vindicatory procedures, it is worth highlighting Max Gluckman's work for an African context.

[6]See Terradas Saborit (2008), p. 193.

2 *Fihavanana*: Ideology and Law

2.1 The *Fihavanana*

Betsileo society builds its social relations around an identity moral value: *fihavanana*.[7] Although there are many descriptive terms that try to demarcate or translate the idea of *fihavanana*, for example relationship,[8] friendship, solidarity, good relations or mutual aid,[9] the Malagasy accept it as a natural fact that is transformed into cultural through the integration and practical application of *fihavanana* itself.[10]

Fihavanana should not only be understood as a biological relationship, but as a form of integration that has its roots in the idea of a shared condition, one that comes from ancestry and also extends to neighbours.[11] This means that the individual shares the feeling of being part of a whole, of being part of a community through blood and shared land. This is what Dubois categorised as "*fihavanana* through genealogy" and "*fihavanana* through residency".[12]

In social relations, *fihavanana* governs the mechanisms for mutual support and exchange[13] so that, when a need arises, the network of solidarity and support is activated in response. Even so, it is not a purely sentimental concept,[14] but rather comes in obedience to a series of rules for life through which the support provided always asks for balance in turn. This means that the Malagasy learn to conduct their social relations by differentiating between the those who belong to their *fihavanana* network, and those who do not. Those who share a *fihavanana* bond must comply with certain obligations and can demand for given rights through rules and practices that each community takes on to reach the desired levels of social cohesion and solidarity, and to avoid social exclusion.[15] In this way, respect for *fihavanana* creates mechanisms and drives decisions that allow conflict to be managed. Family links and

---

[7]The name *fihavanana* is used in particular in the central area of the country as well as on the south east coast. See Raharilalao (1991), p.154; Ottino (1998), p.631 and Dubois (1978). Other terms like *filongoa* are used in the south, west and north west to similarly refer to the moral identity of the group. For more details see Randriamarolaza (1995), p. 378; Ottino (1998), p.639; Kneitz (2014).

[8] Rasamoelina (2012), pp. 4–5 specifies that the literal meaning of the word *fihavanana* relates to blood relations and family, as the root *havana* is translated first and foremost as "sharing the same blood".

[9]See Raharilalao (1991) and Kneitz (2014).

[10]For details see Dubois (1978).

[11] Ottino (1998), p. 590.

[12] Dubois (2002, p. 87).

[13]For more details see Sandron (2008).

[14]See Condominas (1991), p. 151.

[15]In this article we will focus on *fihavanana* in relation to conflict resolution and as part of the vindicatory composition procedure in the Malagasy case. It should also be mentioned that there is also a national and political use of *fihavanana* in Madagascar. For more on this perspective, see for example Rosés Tubau (2009); Rasamoelina (2012); Kneitz (2014).

power relations form the basis of the coercion needed so that *fihavanana* is respected as the law and correct procedure. Violating *fihavanana* is considered a shameful act, both towards family members and towards the "expected model" of social behaviour. For this reason, when *fihavanana* is disregarded it should be repaired by showing remorse through conciliation and composition.

Composition is the reconciliation procedure that aims to bring the situation back to the harmony prior to the conflict. In the words of Dahl, in certain conflicts, it seems like the ultimate goal is not to find the factual and objective root of the crisis or conflict, but rather to re-establish *fihavanana*, even if the consequence is to bury the underlying tensions.[16] In order to re-establish the *fihavanana* bond during composition, one has to be able to forgive, as reconciliation basically consists of publicly accepting the conflict and showing your willingness to bring it to an end. That's why the entire community needs to take part in the composition, although some members exercise the role of mediators.[17]

2.2 Considerations About Composition According to the Type of Conflict Being Judged

Although the aim of this paper is to illustrate the composition as a prototype action for vindicatory justice through an ethnographic case study, before advancing any further it is important to highlight a few key issues in order to understand the procedure and the composition itself within a Malagasy context.

First of all, it is fundamentally important to determine the nature of the conflict. In relation to composition law, the procedure is structured in different stages where first the case is presented and analysed, then a verdict is issued and finally there is an act of reconciliation. However, the structure of the procedure may vary depending on the nature of the conflict.[18] Along similar lines, the nature of the conflict indicates the type of possible regulation in accordance with Law 2001–04.[19] This means that the type of conflict determines the possibility for vindicatory justice procedures to be

[16] Dahl (2008, p. 192).

[17] It should be kept in mind that in the vindicatory process, "the figure of the third judiciary" is especially significant, as it is considered as a judge and, according to Terradas Saborit (2008), p. 51, the recognition of justice lies in him/her and this is what allows reconciliation to be validated.

[18] For example, in the case of theft the procedure has to involve a stage in which the stolen item is returned. If an area of land has been occupied, then the procedure has to include a stage that explains the history of the land, confirming its physical borders.

[19] Law 2001-004 of 25 October 2001 on the general regulation of the *dina* in terms of public security. JORM No. 2746 du 19 novembre 2001, p. 3047. In the case of the Haute Matsiatra region (Betsileo region), the aforementioned law is complemented by Decree 09/REG/HM on the application of the text on regional *dina* of the Haute Matsiatra (Dinan'i Matsiatra Ambony, 20 mars 2007. Gouvernement Malgache), and Circular 112 MIRA/SG/DGRA/DELED on territorial administration.

applied, or the obligation to apply *dina*.[20] This means we can distinguish between three categories depending on the nature of the conflict, although they should be understood as a guideline to know the applicable jurisdiction in accordance with the law:[21]

1. Conflicts that refer to one of the matters covered by the regional *dina* for Haute Matsiatra,[22] which should be resolved by applying the *dina* rulings and the corresponding fines. It should be noted that the regional *dina* cover practically all of the issues related to social organisation in communities, which means that there would be no need for local justice to be applied. Despite this, the state itself allows, without explicitly saying so, for the application of local legal customs in certain cases,[23] such as for example those related to the organisation of the *fokontany*, petty theft, water management, land disputes or education.
2. Conflicts related to regional *dina* issues considered as serious infractions or crimes, particularly homicide and zebu theft. In such cases, it is imperative to apply the rules of regional *dina* and there are high fines for communities that fail to comply. Even so, and despite not having the approval of the State, vindicatory justice procedures are either applied in parallel to state provisions, or unilaterally.[24]
3. Conflicts, infractions or crimes that are considered minor can be resolved at a local level in communities, especially in rural areas, by applying the procedures of vindicatory justice.

[20]Originally, *dina* was an agreement between the members of one or several communities, formalised through an oath in which they declare the imprecations and sanctions in case the adopted rules were not respected. However, its initial meaning has been modified throughout the political history of Madagascar, and several aspects have been redressed depending on the period, until they were eventually assimilated in a law imposed by the central power on a determined community (a Commune, Region or nationwide). For details see Condominas (1991); Njara (2000) and Rosés Tubau (2009). Pellerin (2017), p. 20 specifies that since Law 2001-004 was implemented, the *dina* have to go through a homologation process, which consists in the backing of the commune and state authorities, as well as official approval from a judge, in order to be implemented. This means that in the homologated *dina,* the original content has disappeared, giving rise to a newly created convention, although the name 'dina' is still upheld.

[21]It should be kept in mind that what is established by law does not necessarily correspond with community practices, especially in rural areas. For examples of this imbalance, see Kull (2000) and Andriamalala and Gardner (2010).

[22]State convention that regulates the *fokontany* (administrative geographical state groups for the communities that make up a region) in the Haute Matsiatra region, under the framework of government policies on decentralisation and commune management. Although the main objective is to ensure security in the region and prevent the theft of zebus while involving communities in this action, in the text, which is laid out over 11 chapters, there are details of the rules to apply in terms of disobedience or conflict in the following areas: 1. Organisation of the *fokontany* and record of the people, 2. Zebus, 3. Petty theft, 4. Forest burning, 5. Water management, 6. Assault and murder, 7. Drugs, 8. Land disputes, and 9. Education. Chapters 10 and 11 detail the means of punishment and fines.

[23]See Rosés Tubau (2011).

[24]For details see Rasamoelina (2007); Rakoto (2011) and Pellerin (2017).

Minor conflicts can be divided into three categories: The first relates to petty theft of farm products, small animals or personal belongings. The second involves disputes between relatives or neighbours for a number of reasons, the most frequent being fights between parents and children, altercations due to alcohol, and disagreements over the use of common spaces and resources. Finally, there are land disputes, in particular relating to the right to occupy and use land.

In the case of petty thefts and minor disputes, vindicatory justice is usually the first option to resolve conflicts, although this does not mean that civil and criminal justice cannot be resorted to. In the case of land disputes there are some more nuanced situations, as these issues can be judged at a local level through vindicatory justice procedures, as long as they do not involve aspects covered in the regional *dina*. This means that, within the framework of the law, hardly any land disputes can be governed through vindicatory justice, although in practice it is the most frequently used option.[25]

In order to illustrate composition procedure, I will focus on what are considered to be minor conflicts, infractions or crimes, taking into account the legal framework I presented above. More specifically, I will focus my attention on conflicts caused by petty theft and minor disputes, based on an ethnographic case study that took place in a rural *fokontany* in the Haute Matsiatra region.[26]

3 Composition in a Betsileo Context

3.1 Rules for Conflict Resolution

To resolve a conflict, the offended party should contact the president of the *fokontany* to ask to convene a meeting to present the facts and to decide when the composition will be started. In this first meeting "each party presents evidence and justifications to the *ray aman-dreny* (elders acting as judges[27]) to assess the scale of the offence and to try and reach an agreement between the parties. Problems are solved as if they were family problems".[28] This means that, as stated by Gluckman (1967), those who take on the role of mediators or judges must know the history of

[25]Law 2001-004 and the *dina* for the Haute Matsiatra region establish that in the case of land disputes, violent crimes and large-scale zebu theft, just witnesses and material evidence can be gathered, where necessary, to be presented in a state court. This means they cannot be judged at a local community level, although what actually happens indicates otherwise.

[26]The Haute Matsiatra region coincides in terms of territory with part of the region historically called Betsileo.

[27]Article 3 of Law 2001-004 states that for minor infractions, the parties in the conflict may resort to arbitration, conducted by one or more persons chosen by them, although the law does not specify who may act as mediators. However, in the Malagasy case, it is usually the *ray aman-dreny* that embody this role at a local level.

[28]A., *ray aman-dreny* acting as a judge in the proceedings, in an interview recorded in June 2009.

the relationship between the litigants in order to establish social norms and roles that reflect the relationship between the parties. To achieve this, they must take into account everything they have learned about the matter, combining their roles as judge and mediator.

Conflict resolution is considered a public act[29] in which all the *fokontany* may take part, although participation is mandatory for the parties in conflict, the elders of each family, and the president of the *fokontany*. In some cases, participants may act as witnesses to the events, including the offending and the offended parties. The composition is carried out in a place agreed by the parties, either in the village where the conflict took place, or in the office of the *fokontany*. In any case, the place is decided at the first meeting.

The *ray aman-dreny* acting as judges must follow the rules for the procedure to be carried out properly. These rules essentially consist in being impartial, listening to both parties in the conflict, and analysing the case before making a decision, ensuring the *fihavanana* is restored and verbalising this during the procedure, finding a way to compensate the offended party and applying a just ruling to the offending party, all while endeavouring to enforce the agreements reached.[30] A conflict is considered resolved if the parties accept the rulings, and as a thank you they must offer *toaka gasy* (a locally made alcoholic beverage) at the end of the composition.

3.2 Composition for Conflicts Caused by Petty Theft and Minor Disputes Between Members of a *Fokontany*

To explain the case of petty thefts and minor disputes, I will reference an ethnographic case study that will allow me to detail the different stages of the composition and indicate how the conflict in question manifests at each stage.[31]

The conflict refers to the use and management of a source located between villages A. and S. of the *fokontany*. The majority of its inhabitants share some kind of kinship, either because they are members of the same clan, or because members of different clans got married. The villages are separated by just a few metres and the water source, located at the entrance to village S., is within reach of both of them. The water arrives at the fountain via a well located a few metres north of A. and S. The conflict began as a result of mutual accusations of improper water

[29]The fact that it is a public act allows staging the priority of the composition procedure, which is none other than to make amends to the offended party.

[30]As judicial authorities, the *ray aman-dreny* must offer guarantees for the composition procedure. These verbal rules, which in some ways are implicit in their role as judges, are one way of doing so.

[31]This case study is part of the ethnographic material documented during fieldwork in the Haute Matsiatra region between 2007 and 2009. The fieldwork was mainly carried out in a *fokontany* in the Talata Ampano Commune. In order to protect the anonymity of the locals, the names of the villages will be cited by their initial. The names of the informants have been replaced with pseudonyms.

use, and the most frequent complaints revolve around three issues: People washing their feet in the water fountain, people who, in the opinion of others, use too much water, and people who wash their clothes in the fountain. The conflict took a more serious turn when Razambo from A. and Jean Pierre from S., maternal cousins, exchanged insults in public and stopped talking to each other. After this happened, the elders from both families held a meeting to start a composition. Given that the first to start the insults was Razambo from A., the family of Jean Pierre from S. took the first step, as the offended party, towards holding the composition, a request that was accepted by Razambo's family. Family members had been offended, the *fihavanana* was broken, and was important to look for responsibility, which is why the composition needed to be started as soon as possible.[32] Although the dispute is between two individuals, the continuous complaints and fights between neighbours have resulted in a conflict over who has more rights. The members of S. argue that the fountain is within the limits of their village and, therefore, they have more rights. On the other hand, the members of A. argue that S. is their place of origin so they have the same rights over water, and argue that it is a resource for the *fokontany* in general. Once the will to resolve the conflict has been expressed, it is agreed that the reconciliation procedure will begin a week later in the office of the *fokontany* in village A. It is a public act that, in this case, brings together almost all the inhabitants of S. and A. as well as other villages in the *fokontany*. Apart from Razambo and Jean Pierre, the offending and offended parties, elders from both families attend as well as five *ray aman-dreny* from other villages, who will act as judges and mediate in the composition.[33]

Below, I break down the stages of the composition, showing what happens in relation to the case study at hand.

[32]This situation reflects Dahl's idea (2006), pp. 220–221 on "traditional social norms in the Hautes-Terres of Madagascar for avoiding frank and direct confrontation". According to Dahl, hurtful behaviour leads to dishonour, so everyone strives to redirect the situation and maintain the norm of non-confrontation. On the other hand, the *ray aman-dreny*, a family authority, normally intercede in the conflict before and during the judicial procedure itself.

[33]The fact that in this case five *ray aman-dreny* from other towns were chosen to mediate the conflict can be explained for a number of reasons. In the first place, the authority of the *ray aman-dreny* at a local level, especially in a rural area, puts them in the best social position to establish themselves as judges. Second, the *ray aman-dreny*, as a judicial authority, must be able to reach the highest possible consensus between the parties in conflict, as well as with their suggestions for resolution. Given that the conflict was the responsibility of both villages, it was considered appropriate to go to use *ray aman-dreny* from neighbouring villages to emphasize impartiality and maintain legitimate authority, as there are also kinship relations and *fihavanana* ties by neighbourhood. For more information about judicial authority see Gluckman (1967).

4 Stages of the Procedure[34]

4.1 Initial Stages

Stage 1. Initial *kabary*:[35] The procedure begins with the initial *kabary*. In this case, it is led by the eldest *ray aman-dreny* present at the event. This initial *kabary* aims to present what will be done during the composition, as well as to show respect for the *ray aman-dreny* in attendance and, by extension, all the participants.

Stage 2. Uncovering the history of the events: Each party presents their version of the events that led to the conflict, then there are contributions from witnesses, where applicable, and questions from the *ray aman-dreny*. All of those present listen in silence as the speeches are given. In the case in question, Jean Pierre explains that, while at the foot of the fountain, his cousin Razambo came over shouting and insulting him publicly, saying that the village of S. was wasting the little water there was on washing feet. In response, he told him to go and find another fountain if he could, saying that he wasn't welcome at S.'s fountain if he wanted to act in that way. Razambo confirms that he insulted his cousin, calling him a bad brother, and he defends his stance, saying that S.'s village was making it increasingly difficult for the residents of A. to use the fountain. He also explains that women from S. wash their clothes systematically in the fountain, making the children from A. wait for their water.[36]

Three witnesses from each village back up the arguments presented by each litigant, explaining small daily disputes that had arisen as a result of using the fountain. When their turn come, the *ray aman-dreny* ask to clarify some of the responses. The first meeting come to a close, and the *ray aman-dreny* announce that they will study the case and convene a further meeting.

Stage 3. Study of the case and discussion between the *ray aman-dreny*: Once the explanations are given, the *ray aman-dreny* have to find the reasons for the offence. Each elder gives an opinion and considers the most important comments. In this case, the reflection time took a week, during which the *ray aman-dreny* met twice.

---

[34]These stages coincide with the justice universal procedure that is characteristic of vindicatory justice. In some stages of the procedure, the Betsileo term has been maintained, giving an explanation of the meaning of the term. In other stages, a decision was taken to translate the original expression, in order to allow the reader to understand better.

[35]Traditional speech given by the *ray aman-dreny*. Historically, the *kabary* was the speech given in public by kings to announce a law or encourage people to work. According to R.R., *kabary* reciter, "the *ray aman-dreny* have learned the rhetoric for speeches and have enriched themselves with them. In Malagasy society, elders contribute their words. They have to know the art of wordplay, have a physical presence to be seen in the field, and have a strong voice to impose themselves verbally, with strength" (personal communication, April 2009). Today, these speeches practically do not exist in the big cities, and if they are given, they are very short. In contrast, in rural areas they are upheld, mainly in ritual ceremonies and group meetings. For more about Malagasy *kabary* see Jackson (2008).

[36]The account of the arguments put forward is a translation of the Malagasy expressions used during the proceedings.

4.2 Central Stages

Stage 4. Verdict:[37] Once the *ray aman-dreny* have studied and discussed the case, they summon both parties again, along with the elders from the families and any other person who wish to attend. At this point in time the objective is not to decide who is guilty, but rather to announce the conclusions that have been reached and share the suggestions to resolve the conflict and bring the situation back to normal. The *ray aman-dreny* must be impartial in their judgement, but they should also be capable of establishing a certain level of empathy with both parties, as the ultimate goal is to uphold social cohesion. In terms of the case relating to the fountain, the spokesperson for the *ray aman-dreny* says: "This case involves resolving two conflicts at the same time. The first is to return the *fihavanana* between Razambo and Jean-Pierre, as family cannot break the *fihavanana*. Razambo was wrong and must ask for forgiveness. Jean-Pierre should help this to be so". In addition, he adds that it is necessary to bring an end to disputes related to water management, so that a similar conflict does not arise in the future. The mediating action carried out by the *ray aman-dreny* in this stage reflects, as noted by Bloch,[38] how social control is exercised in an almost invisible way, so that relationships are situated in the arbitrary domain in a natural way and, as a result, *fihavanana* is regulated.

Stage 5. *Vola tsy vaky*:[39] *Vola tsy vaky* is normally shared out at two different moments during the composition. A small part is shared after the initial *kabary* to thank the *ray aman-dreny* for their participation, and a second part is shared after the verdict is issued as a show of gratitude for having contributed to resolving the conflict. This term refers to a small amount of money, freely contributed in accordance with the financial resources of each individual. Razambo and Jean-Pierre contribute 50 *ariary* each.[40]

Stage 6. *Toro-hevitra*:[41] Once the verdict has been given, the *ray aman-dreny* should warn of the consequences of the crime committed. They address the

[37]To describe this stage in the proceedings, the Betsileo use a number of different terms. *Fitsarana* or *didim-pitsarana*, from the root *didy* meaning law or regulation, and can be translated as trial or tribunal. *Fanapahana* (authority) or *fanapahan-kevitra* (ruling), which translates as a decision taken by an authority. There is also *misafidy*, a choice that does not depend on your will. I translate the name of this stage as the verdict emphasizing the authority of the *ray aman-dreny* who, as judges, can announce a decision that is, in fact, a law.

[38] Bloch (1975), p. 4.

[39]*Vola tsy vaky* can be translated as "uncut coin", referring to the undivided coins of 5 francs that were offered in several rituals dedicated to sovereign Malagasy as a recognition of their position and status. For more details see de Veyrières and de Méritens (1967).

[40]1 euro is worth approximately 4000 *ariary*. The worth of the *vola tsy vaky* contributed is around 0.01 euros.

[41]*Toro-hevitra* can be translated as advice or recommendation.

offending party, but also everyone present, as the sermon[42] is understood as a 're-education' in the values of *fihavanana*. More specifically, given that the aim of the composition is the reconciliation of the parties and the return of *fihavanana*, the words of the *ray aman-dreny* should not be interpreted as a punishment, but as a learning experience. There are no guidelines for these sermons, because the intention is to make the offence committed understood so that mistakes are not repeated, to preserve relationships, to reach the point that "it is necessary for one of the parties concede and accept they have committed an offence. Then it shows that there is no longer any guilt".[43] For example, in our case the *ray aman-dreny* J. B. R. expressed himself in the following terms: "It is important to talk and not mess around like this, because we are all from the same family. Serious incidents like this must not happen again. These mistakes must not be repeated. If there is a need, *fihavanana* provides, and we should not forget the bond that unites us all, *fihavanana*".[44]

Stage 7. *Fifonana-Fifamelana*:[45] The act of reconciliation begins when the *ray aman-dreny* ask the parties in conflict to restore *fihavanana*. In this case, there is also no standard way to verbalise the request, and it is expressed in spontaneous terms. Continuing with our example: "This situation should not be repeated, and if you agree then you need to show *fihavanana*".[46] At this point, the offending party must hold the *fifonana* (request for forgiveness) and the offended party must offer *fifamelana* (granting forgiveness). *Famelana*, the act of "making peace", "is vitally important for the proper functioning of society,[47] therefore, in general, the offended party accepts *fifonana* and offers *fifamelana*" argues F. R.[48] In our case study, the *ray aman-dreny* require Razambo, the offending party, to apologize to Jean-Pierre, the offended party, and the *fifonana* begins when Razambo expresses his regret and

[42]The term 'sermon' is used in the sense of reprimand or extended rebuke. Although the Malagasy term can literally be translated as advice or recommendation, in the context of a composition, *toro-hevitra* also implies a well-argued and insistent warning.

[43]F. R., president of the *fokontany*, in an interview recorded in June 2009.

[44]According to Dahl (2006), p. 182 when *fihavanana* is in danger, the only solution is to find an intermediary, often a *ray aman-dreny*, to restore honour and give each participant the chance to get out of the conflict with their head held high. For this to happen, the *toro-hevitra* needs to be formulated with clarity and forcefulness because, if *fihavanana* relations are threatened or compromised, there is conflict.

[45]*Fifonana* means asking for forgiveness and *fifamelana* means giving forgiveness. It can be translated as the act of "making peace".

[46]Intervention made by *ray aman-dreny* J. B. R. during the composition.

[47]Regarding the expression used by the president of the *fokontany*, it is important to consider this statement by Terradas Saborit (2008), p. 480 regarding the efficacy of the composition. The author argues that the reconciliation is part of the judicial procedure, with several acts included so that the composition is effective, not only in legal terms but also in social terms. This reveals the composition as a social right. The *fifonana-fifamelana* stage is paradigmatic in this regard, as when asking for forgiveness the offence is explicitly acknowledged and allows *fihavanana* to be restored and social cohesion to be re-established.

[48]See note 44.

agrees not to repeat the offence.[49] The verbalisation of this commitment does not follow an established formula, and in our case study was, for example: "I will not repeat what I did, I'm regretful".[50] Even if remorse towards the offended party is expressed, the request for forgiveness is extended to the entire community. To make this happen, the offending party must contribute a small amount of money and *toaka gasy*. Similarly, the request for forgiveness falls entirely on the offending party's universe, which means that he or she should also offer *toaka gasy* to receive a blessing from the elders of his or her family, symbolising forgiveness from the ancestors. This is what Razambo does in our case. Once the *fifonana* has been carried out, the *ray aman-dreny* ask Jean-Pierre to accept forgiveness and the *fifamelana* begins. First and foremost, *fifamelana* represents the acceptance of *fifonana* by the offended party. In our case, the fact that there is a link between the parties in conflict, as maternal cousins, means *fihavanana* is easier to restore. D.R. expresses this in the following terms: "If they are relatives, and we are all relatives, things will work out. If someone has done good but commits an offence, we should help, but someone who has not contributed to community life will not be given anything. A serious offence must be forgiven, but an offence committed for the second or third time will no longer be forgiven. You will be taken to the (state) court".[51] Secondly, the burden of accepting forgiveness lies on everyone present, even though the offending party is the one who materialises it during the ritual—in this case, Jean-Pierre. In this sense, *fifamelana* represents the penance of the offending party as well as gratitude to others, particularly the offended party, for being able to forgive. Finally, to highlight the reconciliation, the *ray aman-dreny* remind those present that the offence should not be repeated and their words must be well accepted.

4.3 Final Stages

Stage 8. *Tandra*:[52] The *tandra* specifically restores *fihavanana* between the two parties in conflict, and acts as the material side of the reconciliation.[53] The *ray aman-*

[49] Accepting without remorse that the offence was committed is interpreted as the act that sets the stage for the restoration of *fihavanana* and the preservation of social relations.

[50] In case of theft, it is also possible to add "I did it because I was hungry" or "because I had no money".

[51] Interview recorded in November 2009. Own translation.

[52] According to Rajaonarimanana (1995), p. 279 *tandra* literally translates as freckle, a physical feature you cannot get rid of. In this sense, and in the context of the legal proceedings for the composition, *tandra* is translated as material compensation for the offended party, understanding this compensation as an obligation that the offending party can not avoid.

[53] It should be kept in mind that material compensation, or *tandra* in the Malagasy case, is part of the composition. This means that in the composition, as we have mentioned several times, the main objective is to avoid social fracture. Accordingly, when dealing with a conflict that might destabilise the social cohesion of the group, compensation is established as the resource to remedy an

dreny ask Razambo how much money he can give to Jean-Pierre as compensation, and he suggests 60 *ariary*.[54] They then ask Jean-Pierre if he accepts it, which he does. The offending party can give the money during the procedure or agree on a time to make the payment. When the offending party receives the money, he gives a share to the *ray aman-dreny* who have mediated the composition, as a form of thanks. Razambo gives 60 *ariary,* and Jean-Pierre gives 20 of this to the *ray aman-dreny*. Although *tandra* is considered as material compensation for the offended party, it may also include, where applicable, some kind of work that benefits the community. This is a reparation for all the members of the *fokontany*, with the aim of compensating for the offence committed towards the entire group. This is what Terradas Saborit[55] describes as creating a sense to the social ties following the offence. In this case, no work is requested.

On the other hand, despite not taking place in this case, it should be pointed out that if a dispute causes injuries, then *tandra fery* or *manasa-fery* must be applied in addition to the *tandra.*[56] Putting the *tandra fery* into effect, the specific *tandra* for injuries and blows, means giving money to the victim to buy medicine or cover the expenses caused by injuries.

Another variant of the procedure that deserves our attention refers to theft that is considered an act of desperation. When the *ray aman-dreny* consider that a theft was through necessity, in the part of the composition that corresponds to the *tandra*, a procedure known as *travail companie* is applied. This consists in offering the defendant a job for the benefit of the group, which will allow him or her to live without having to steal. In these cases, it is considered unfair to apply *tandra* because "someone with nothing has nothing to give".[57] In addition, the *travail companie* is interpreted as reconciliation between the person who committed the theft, because he or she had no other option, and the rest of the group, which has not acted in solidarity and has pushed one of its members to commit a reprehensible act. In this sense, the *travail companie* acts in some way to invert the roles of offending and offended party, since the person who receives the moral damage, being abandoned by the group, is also the one who committed the theft. With the intervention of the *travail*

---

anomalous situation. In this sense, Terradas Saborit (2008), p. 193 reminds us that compensation does not intend to buy an irresponsible act, but rather remedy, to some extent, the damage caused by a responsibility that involves the entire person (in moral, legal, religious and economic terms, etc.).

[54]In this case, material compensation has a clearly symbolic function. Since no material goods were stolen or damaged, the amount expected is not too high. If it is considered insufficient, the *ray aman-dreny* can suggest increasing the amount. The amounts are normally reasonable in relation to the act committed, and the financial means of each one are taken into account as well as, in the case of robberies, the value of the item stolen. In any case, what usually happens in the case of theft of small animals, is that compensation follows a ratio of two to one. In the case of larger animals, such as zebu, compensation follows a ratio of four to one, although it may also be two to one, depending on the stolen animals and how much it is deemed the theft has affected the offended party.

[55] Terradas Saborit (2008), p. 193.

[56]*Tandra fery* is translated as compensation for the wound, while *manasa-fery* is translated as washing the wound.

[57]D.R., personal communication, May 2009.

companie, *fihavanana* is channelled once more and the mutual support is recomposed.

Stage 9. Final *kabary*: When the *tandra* comes to an end, the final *kabary* takes place, a speech of thanks to the *ray aman-dreny* and other participants in the composition. Both parties convey their gratitude, offer *toaka gasy* to those present, and give a small amount of money to the *ray aman-dreny*.

Stage10. *Tso-drano*:[58] The *tso-drano* is carried out by the older *ray aman-dreny* in attendance at the event, and is carried out with *rano manara* (cold drinking water), which is sprinkled on the litigants, symbolising agreement with the final decision. In this way, the intervention of a spiritual agent is part of the process taking effect.

5 Conclusions

In this paper, my intention has been to explain the stages of a composition as a prototypical act of law and vindicatory justice, based on an ethnographic case.

As a conclusion, it is worth recalling the idea of the risk of the conflict being repeated, which was announced at the beginning of the case. With this in mind, the *ray aman-dreny* felt that the conflict could occur again if they did not solve the problem of water management. Therefore, at the end of the composition, they decided to appeal to *fiaraha-monina*, a term that refers to being a good neighbour and the obligation of solidarity between the families of different clans who live in and share the same space,[59] for example a village or *fokontany*. Therefore, it is a form of expressing and materialising *fihavanana*. As such, *fiaraha-monina* manifests itself in the relations between family and neighbours, although at a more discursive level it extends to broader geographical areas such as a region or the entire country. These are mandatory rules in place to maintain the union of a group, and they manifest in the obligations that need to be taken on by its members. With this gesture, the appeal to *fiaraha-monina*, there was a move to encourage the recovery of good relations, as well as *fihavanana* between neighbours. The agreement reached between the neighbours of S. and A., mediated by the *ray aman-dreny*, was brought to a close with the decision to organise regulated access to drinking water. The terms refer to opening the fountain at a restricted time (from 6 to 8 in the morning and from 4 to 7 in the afternoon), banning washing feet and clothes in the fountain, and a commitment to only taking the amount of water that is strictly necessary, respecting

[58]Literally, blessing.

[59]Members who do not reside in the community of origin are obliged to participate in village solidarity or local identity solidarity. Ottino (1998), p. 298 illustrates this idea with an example of the obligations for members who do not reside in the community, in terms of maintenance of the *tata-belona* (irrigation canals). The maintenance of these canals for rice irrigation is seen as a community issue, that is, one for both residents and non-residents. In this way, the bond of *fiaraha-monina* is understood as an obligation resulting from the identity solidarity between members of the same community.

the access of all the members of the villages. This final part of the process, a corollary of the composition between the two litigants, allows us to take some of the approaches discussed in the text as a conclusion. The *ray aman-dreny*'s decision to resolve the conflict between the two parties covers some aspects that have been highlighted in the analysis of the composition.

In their role as judges and mediators, the *ray aman-dreny* make use of their judicial authority and their arbitrary power to impose the obligation of complying with *fiaraha-monina*, a resource that allows them to maintain group cohesion and strengthen *fihavanana* through relationship obligations. As if a composition involved everyone agreeing to be the offending and offended party, while abiding by the shared responsibility to make amends to each other, accepting the commitment they have taken on as relatives and neighbours under *fihavanana*.

References

Andriamalala G, Gardner CJ (2010) L'utilisation du dina comme outil de gouvernance des ressources naturelles: leçons tirés de Velondriake, sud-ouest de Madagascar. Tropical Conservation Science 3(4):447–472

Bloch M (1975) Introduction. In: Bloch M (ed) Political language and oratory in traditional society. Academic Press, London, pp 1–28

Condominas G (1991) Fokon'olona et collectivités rurales en Imerina, 2nd edn. Orstom, Paris

Dahl O (2006) Signes et significations à Madagascar. Des cas de communication interculturelle. Présence Africaine, Paris

de Veyrières P, de Méritens G (1967) Le livre de la sagesse malgache. Proverbes, dictons, sentences, expressions figurés et curieuses. Éditions Maritimes et d'Outre-Mer, Paris

Dubois R (1978) Olombelona. Essai sur l'existence personnelle et collective à Madagascar. L'Harmattan, Paris

Dubois R (2002) L'identité malgache: la tradition des Ancêtres. Karthala, Paris

Gluckman M (1967) The Judicial process among the Barotse of Northern Rhodesia, 2nd edn. Manchester University Press, Manchester

Jackson JL (2008) Building publics, shaping public opinion: Interanimating registers in Malagasy *Kabary* oratory and political cartooning. Journal of Linguistic Anthropology 18(2):214–235

Kneitz P (dir) (2016) *Fihavanana*: La vision d'une société paisible à Madagascar. Perspectives anthropologiques, historiques et socio-économiques, 2nd edn. Universitäsverlag Halle-Wittenberg, Halle an der Saale

Kull CA (2000) Deforestation, Erosion, and Fire: Degradation Myths in the Environmental History of Madagascar. Environment and History 6(4):423–450. https://doi.org/10.3197/096734000129342361

Llewellyn K (1941) The Cheyenne way. Conflict and case law in primitive Jurisprudence. University of Oklahoma Press, Norman

Njara E (2000) Les dinan'ny fandriampahalemana ou chartes de la sécurité publique. Droits et Cultures 26:221–234

Ottino P (1998) Les champs de l'ancestralité à Madagascar: parenté, alliance et patrimoine. Karthala, Paris

Pellerin M (2017) Madagascar Dealing with Multi-faceted Crime. Notes de l'Ifri March 2017. https://www.ifri.org/sites/default/files/atoms/files/pellerin_madagascar_multi_faceted_crime_2017.pdf

Raharilalao HAM (1991) Église et fihavanana à Madagascar. Une herméneutique malgache de la réconciliation chrétienne selon Saint Paul 2 Co 5, 17-21. Ambozontany Editions, Fianarantsoa
Rajaonarimanana N (1995) Dictionnaire du malgache contemporain. Karthala, Paris
Rakoto I (2011) L'insécurité rurale liée au vol de boeufs: quelques propositions de solution. Taloha 19:213-232
Randriamarolaza LP (1995) Respecter le droit sans oublier la justice. Les fourches caudines de la transition démocratique à Madagascar. In: Esoavelomandroso M, Feltz G (dir) Démocratie et développement. Mirage ou espoir raisonnable? Karthala, Paris, pp 369–382
Rasamoelina H (2007) Madagascar. État, communautés villageoises et banditisme rural. L'Harmattan, Paris
Rasamoelina H (2012) Croyances et instrumentalisation à Madagascar. Friedrich-Ebert-Stiftung. http://library.fes.de/pdf-files/bueros/madagaskar/15128.pdf
Rosés Tubau M (2009) Le fihavanana: Du symbolisme d'un concept à un concept symbolique. Revue du MCI (Madagascar Conseil International) 48:23–35
Rosés Tubau M (2011) La responsabilidad de la justicia consuetudinaria en Madagascar: el ejemplo de la regulación de los robos de cebúes en la Región de la Haute Matsiatra. In: Terradas Saborit I (coord) Antropología jurídica de la responsabilidad. Andavira Editora, Santiago de Compostela, pp 547–579
Sandron F (2008) Le fihavanana à Madagascar: Lien social et économique des communautés rurales. Revue Tiers Monde 3(195):507–522. https://doi.org/10.3917/rtm.195.0507
Supiot A (2005) Homo Juridicus. Essai sur la fonction anthropologique du droit. Éditions du Seuil, Paris
Terradas Saborit I (2008) Justicia Vindicatoria. CSIC, Madrid
Verdier R (1980) La Vengeance: Études d'Ethnologie, d'Histoire et de Philosophie. Cujas, Paris

Vindicatory Persistence in Barbagia

Capitalist Enterprise, Agnatic Reduction of Solidarity and Vindictive Agonism

Pablo Romero Noguera

Abstract This chapter shows how the persistence of vindicatory customary law in Barbagia seems to be associated with the displacement and reduction of community life. Accordingly, it ultimately confirms the reduction of the extent of solidarity, reciprocity and hospitality and, consequently, of the mechanisms to resolve and compose conflicts and offenses. The successful contemporary adaptation to the grazing economy, which expanded to the detriment of agriculture, required the establishment of sedentary livestock enterprises and consequently a strengthening of the bond between male brothers. The success of the livestock "business", increasingly based on the private property of land and adapted to the rhythms and forms of the capitalist economy, demanded results that led to its reinforcement, since it is the male brothers who inherit and grow the cattle. A shift took place from the solidarity of a wider kinship sphere towards an agnatic reduction relegating women (historically the main keepers of reciprocity and the custodians of hospitality among houses), reducing the broader scope of kinship solidarity, and hindering the activation of prevention, composition and reconciliation mechanisms. As a result, the economy and culture of grazing persisted although without these mechanisms, and consequently tipped the scales toward bloody vengeance, explaining the most virulent and unbridled outbreak of revenge in recent decades.

This article is based on my fieldwork and doctoral thesis, which addresses the vindicatory customary legal system of the shepherds of Barbagia, a mountainous region in the centre of the island of Sardinia, from the perspective of historical and legal anthropology (Romero Noguera 2018).

P. Romero Noguera (✉)
Department of Social Anthropology, University of Barcelona, Barcelona, Spain

R. Márquez Porras et al. (eds.), *Vindicatory Justice*, Ius Gentium: Comparative Perspectives on Law and Justice 93, https://doi.org/10.1007/978-3-030-79595-5_9

1 Persistence and Involution: The Paradox of "Progress"

Antonio Pigliaru must be considered a pioneer in the recognition (and establishment) of Barbagian *vendetta* as a legal order and, more generally, a fundamental link in the genealogy of studies which consolidates vindicatory justice as a paradigm.[1] At the same time, we should take note of the paradox which involves his own consideration of the Sardinian shepherds' code of *vendetta* as the result of *progress*. As a son of legal evolutionism, he considered the code—as he "found it"[2]—a civilist evolution of the customary legal system, a result of the effort of Barbagian communities to separate themselves from the "old law of the jungle", that "savage idea of vendetta" supposedly typical of primitive societies.[3] I say paradox, because if we stick to the paradigm of vindicatory justice,[4] Pigliaru's work should argue about a priority for the compositional process, which does not seem to exist in the Barbagian order, at least in the "present edition". And also because such an absence seems rather to be the result of an *involution*: indeed, my starting point is that the Barbagian vindicatory legal order would have diminished its compositional dimension and sharpened the bloody vindictive one, that is to say, that it would have persisted until the present time by mutating in a "non-civilist" sense, reducing the scope and weight of peaceful pactism which we usually associate with civil law.[5] Pigliaru was right when he claimed that the Barbagian legal order was *itself* an objectification of law, a code which guaranteed legal certainty [*certezza giuridica*] when establishing degrees of offence and the requirement of proportionality, progressivity and prudence before it.[6] But that does not mean that this kind of procedural warranty [*garantismo*] was the result of a recent evolution, nor does it exclude the degradation or setback I suggest.

The paradox is not minor, since Pigliaru's evolutionary speculation and primitivist prejudice are part of a long and extended tradition, which recursively (historically) affirms that the "wild customs" of the Barbagian shepherds—

[1]Pigliaru (1975). For a reference to Pigliaru's work as a fundamental step in the study of vindicatory justice, Terradas Saborit (2008).

[2]Pigliaru spoke about the "present edition" of the Barbagian code referring to what we can call the "ethnographic present" of the Barbagian legal order of the time he studied it.

[3]Pigliaru (1975), pp. 167 and 168. Social anthropology as a contemporary field of study has been built largely against this kind of prejudice, so it is not the place to delve into this issue. However, it seems to have difficulty in overcoming it when it comes to the practice of revenge—in this case savagism prejudice still persists. For a basic criticism see Terradas Saborit (2008). For a criticism specifically referred to the Sardinian case see Romero Noguera (2018). For a general criticism of legal evolutionism and ethnocentrism see Rouland (1992).

[4]I refer to its historical and ethnographic analysis in a realistic perspective. See Terradas Saborit (2021).

[5]This combination of vindicatory persistence and compositional regression in the Sardinian case is one of the key ideas of my doctoral thesis (Romero Noguera, 2018).

[6]See title 3 of Pigliaru's code, entitled *La misura della vendetta* (1975). For the issue of *certezza giuridica* see Romero Noguera (2011).

paradigmatically *vendetta*—are a residue of the past to disappear, to be swept away by progress. In this work I postulate the opposite: it is precisely "progress", the capitalist development, which has led to vindictive agonism, to the persistence of the vindicatory but in its worst version, the exasperation of conflict when it no longer has any restriction, when customary counterweights, ways to prevent it, compose it or rescue it, disappear. I believe that this agonistic exasperation of *vendetta* has to do with the adaptation of pastoralism to the capitalist economy, that is to say, it is a *consequence* of it, not the simple remora of a past which does not disappear. This adaptation has also gone through an agnatic reduction of kinship groups, which would have required a strengthening of the bond between male brothers (and the relegation of the traditional role of women) to achieve success in the livestock business, increasingly based on sedentarization and private ownership of the land.

I propose a vision of *longue durée* mainly based on clues and difficult to be confirmed with certainty, but suggestive to understand a series of transformations of great depth, some of which take us to very backward times.[7] They relate, on the one hand, to the historical processes of the establishment and strengthening of private property—associated with the enclosure acts (the so-called *editto delle chiudende*), the disentailment and liquidation of communal properties—and the decay of community institutions and ethics, which began at the end of the eighteenth century.[8] And on the other hand, with something less visible, slower and with more historical depth, but related to the above and also of profound depth: the consolidation of the patrilineal forms of filiation and patrimonial transmission, which mutate in this way more or less at the same time, after having followed for centuries a seemingly anomalous (or at least not attested) pattern in Western Europe. Historians and jurists, and above all some anthropologists investigating Sardinian kinship in the contemporary era,[9] have discovered and investigated forms of residence, filiation and transmission of heritage in medieval and modern Sardinia, which suggest parallel lines of descent and transmission, precedence of matrilineage, and even the constitution of corporate groups, all of which—as we shall see—related to matrilocality, cohabitation between sisters, a greater extension of kinship and community solidarity, and collective forms of ownership.[10]

There is a reformism of a physiocratic nature that for more than two hundred years has aimed (wished) to diminish the weight of pastoralism in favour of agriculture,[11] and which now, when pastoralism has defeated agriculture and has even expanded, seeks to modify its culture, to the point of making out *as if* it had already been transformed. Following this long tradition, for decades there has been an insistence, from a perspective of "civil progress", on the disappearance of the

[7]Unfortunately, in this short essay I can only hint at some of the most significant hypotheses.

[8]Del Piano (1979), Mura (2014), Birocchi (1982).

[9]Legal historians such as Enrico Besta, Arrigo Solmi and others. As to the anthropologists, see, among others, Da Re (1993, 2003a, b), and Murru Corriga (1993, 1997, 2000).

[10]See Murru Corriga (1997), and Da Re (1993).

[11]See the introduction in Murru Corriga (1990).

vindicatory culture of shepherds, of blood vengeance, and of banditry. Cyclically, the same tropes of completion, marginality and residuality reappear, denoting the clear desire for pacification which the long-suffering mountain communities—and by extension the whole island—have. However, revenge killings do not cease and the so-called *criminalità agro-pastorale* continues to leave its mark, even if it mutates in its forms.[12] It often happens, then, that this "criminality" is attributed to the "anomie", which is characteristic of urban modernity, while homicides are denied the status of vindicatory,[13] so that both phenomena are dissociated from the customary-ethical sphere, as if they no longer participate in the customary legal system to which they have historically belonged.[14] In both cases, there is talk of futility, of individualism, of private interests, of venality. It is significant, in this sense, that there exist in parallel an insistence on the "mafioso" drift of rural crimes: for decades such a conversion has been inferred into centralised, hierarchical and sustained organisational forms over time; a mutation which, however, never ends up being verified.[15]

In the end, *vendetta* and banditry not only do not disappear, but are exacerbated. And they do so—I argue—as a result of "progress". We could almost talk about a kind of a *U-turn*, logical and diachronic: seen through the lens of vindicatory justice, we are faced with a historical *involution*. The lack of continuity in the study of the vindicatory system of Barbagia since Pigliaru has undoubtedly contributed to this misunderstanding. Despite the centrality of his figure and the recognition of his achievements, Pigliaru's work has not been updated nor has the persistence of the vindicatory order—as he described and conceived it—been seriously verified (with honourable exceptions).[16] Perhaps we should try to answer a simple question: what happened to the legal system that Pigliaru described in so much detail? We can argue that—perhaps because of the lack of real historical perspective (mainly due to the impossibility of apprehending a longer period of time)—Pigliaru himself excessively emphasized the purely bloody element of the execution of revenge;

[12]Pigliaru said that kidnapping was structurally analogous to cattle theft and contradicted the widespread opinion about the transformation that would have taken place, already in those years, in the culture of shepherds, of which the kidnappings were supposed to be the reliable proof (1975). Today, as in the time of Pigliaru, there is still talk of a "recrudescence" of criminality, but now in relation to attacks on public administrators or the assault on banks or armoured vans. See, for example, from 2016 and 2018, respectively: http://www.lanuovasardegna.it/sassari/cronaca/2016/02/02/news/la-mentalita-barbaricina-e-i-luoghi-comuni-duri-a-morire-1.12884994 and http://www.lanuovasardegna.it/regione/2018/01/20/news/visita-minniti-pigliaru-soddisfatto-1.16378193.

[13]Solvent Sardinian authors made this mistake: for the first case, Masia (1997); for the second, Angioni (2016).

[14]It should be remembered that Pigliaru (1975) organically linked revenge with banditry, placing the former organically and phenomenologically at the heart of the latter.

[15]Arlacchi (2008), one of the main analysts of mafia organizations in Italy, for example, denies the existence of such a transformation.

[16]Several authors investigated the issue, however in a partial way with respect to Pigliaru's *magnus opus*. The most self-evident example is Michelangelo Pira's work (1978). For a survey on this issue see the third chapter of Romero Noguera (2018).

institutions and mechanisms of avoidance, composition, and pacification of conflicts remain in the shadows,[17] appearing only occasionally and with little or no centrality. I wonder if his classic study can be seen as a "radiography" of a specific historical moment, a time when the bloody resolution of offences is settling down (or is already clearly established), erasing other possibilities. Seen this way, the code drafted by Pigliaru would be more the socio-legal representation of a particular historical formation (Barbagian society, the *noi pastori* ["we the shepherds"]) declined towards bloody revenge, than the pure and simple written translation of a customary legal system which lasts for centuries without significant changes. That is why I propose a vision of *longue durée*—precisely relative to the mountains of one of the most central islands of the Mediterranean[18]—which does justice to Pigliaru and, at the same time, allows us to capture the changes in Barbagian legal culture and understand the reasons for the regression in composition and for the vindictive shift.[19]

Until now I was wondering if Pigliaru, in some way, "did not want" to see the importance of the different non-bloody vindicatory mechanisms and institutions: the customary arbitration of *sos omines*, reconciliation procedures, cross-marriages between feuding families, the circulation of gifts with a pacifying function (*s'imbiatu*), etc.[20] But rather, I may have to ask if he *could not* see it because it was veiled, diminished, since those mechanisms and institutions were then in clear decline. In fact, Pigliaru's "obsession" with blood revenge responded to a historical and social reality, which was clearly expressed in the *malessere* [*social malaise*][21] and in the permanent social alarm for the numerous homicides, the intensification of cattle theft, the increase in kidnappings, etc. At the height of the "Italian economic miracle", which had lasted from the end of World War II, the Sardinian inland was being emptied (through emigration) and was bleeding to death. I even suggest that the reformist vocation of the time—which clearly assumed that changing the situation required transformations in the culture of the *zone interne* [hinterland] and, consequently, in the economic structure of pastoralism—would have made it difficult for Pigliaru, like many others, to shift the gaze from the more strictly vindictive pole and broaden the vision towards other repertoires of Sardinian customary law.[22]

---

[17]I call "avoidance" all those social structures aimed at preventing the escalade of conflicts and offenses, direct or indirect mechanisms to temper the parties' attitude, sustain dialogue, etc.

[18]According to Braudel (2001), Barbagia was an island within an island, a space affected by a long-lasting immutability.

[19]In his text in this book, Terradas Saborit (2021) shows how the difficulties that ethnographic (present) time imposes on the historical monitoring of conflicts, vendettas and reconciliation processes, which often go beyond generations, have been attempted to be solved by paying attention to the *longue durée*. Obviously, in our case we are referring to a much greater historical depth.

[20]Romero Noguera (2018). On *sos omines* see, for example, Masia (2012); for *s'imbiatu*, Zene (2005).

[21]*Società del malessere* is the name of a well-known Giuseppe Fiori essay on Barbagia (2001).

[22]Anthropologist Maria Gabriella Da Re adds Luca Pinna, a theorist of Barbagian "familism" (1971), to the list of Sardinian authors that contributed to such a reformistic orientation. According

A famous *Piano di Rinascita* and a no less famous *Comissione Parlamentare d'Inchiesta sul fenomeno del banditismo in Sardegna*[23] proposed a series of interventions to improve the basic social and economic condition and transform the agropastoral culture.[24] They were implemented, among other things, in the creation of two petrochemical sites in Porto Torres and Sarroch, and another industrial site in Ottana, Barbagia, which were aimed at attracting shepherds and, consequently, moving them away from the criminogenic environment. What is significant is that this was already the third parliamentary commission on this issue since Italian unification, which was followed by one of the Sardinian regional parliament, established in 1987,[25] and that the parliamentary commissions on the mafia (*e sulle altre associazioni criminali*), instituted in Italy at the beginning of each legislature since 1962, usually have a special section on Sardinia.[26] In fact, not long ago (2019), after the Sardinian political elections and a strong and colourful mobilisation of shepherds from the whole island for fair milk prices,[27] a Barbagian lawyer, a newly elected regional advisor, sent a letter to the new Sardinian president suggesting the creation of a new *piano di rinascita*.[28] The counselor made himself the spokesperson and talked of Barbagia as "one of the most tormented areas of the island [...] with anthropological peculiarities, an economy with serious difficulties to grow, an agro-pastoral environment and a society cyclically shaken by social malaise and violence".[29]

I insist, I believe that there has been a lack of detachment and historical perspective; a detachment and perspective which were obviously very difficult to keep at that time, but no less true. Summing up (and anticipating some things), we can say that the "obsession" of Pigliaru (and the atmosphere of the time) on vindictive violence, corresponding to its real sharpening, would have responded to a series of interwoven factors: (1) a real setback in the compositional dimension of Barbagian vindicatory justice; (2) a reformist vision which was common at the time (and beyond),[30] and which required obliterating the "positive" aspects of the culture of

---

to Da Re (2003a), the reformist imperative impeded them from valuing the forms of relationship, alliance and cooperation beyond the family group.

[23]Regione Autonoma della Sardegna (1967).

[24]For a criticism in the Sardinian literature of lectures interpreting this issue in terms of the tradition/modernity dichotomy, largely influential in the public policy of that age, see Tiragallo (1995).

[25]Regione Autonoma della Sardegna (1987).

[26]The 1996 provision, for example, informed about kidnappings and specifically Sardinian kidnappings (Parlamento Italiano 1996).

[27]See *Dinamo Press*: https://bit.ly/2JfUZSj or *Il Manifesto Sardo*: https://bit.ly/2PO8jOX.

[28]http://www.lanuovasardegna.it/nuoro/cronaca/2019/03/28/news/piano-di-rinascita-per-le-zone-interne-1.17792119.

[29][The translation is mine: "[...] una delle aree più tormentate dell'isola [...] con peculiarità antropologiche, un'economia che tarda a crescere, un ambiente agro-pastorale e una società scossa ciclicamente da fenomeni di malessere e di violenza"].

[30]In fact, it seems a persistent characteristic in Sardinian history, that can be encompassed in what has been called *questione sarda* (Ortu 2005).

the shepherds of Barbagia; (3) the strengthening of the bond between male brothers, necessary for the consolidation of livestock enterprises, increasingly based on private property, and (4) the real decline not only of the vindicatory non-bloody repertoire, but of the more extensive and general scope of sociability and community relations, that is, where hospitality and the circulation of gifts occur, and where social ties, alliances, the exchange of favours and mutual support are woven, even beyond kin solidarity.

2 Barbagian *Vendetta* in the *Longue Durée*

The idea of persistence frequently emerges when it comes to Sardinian customs, its social reality, and even more so when talking about the mountainous region of Barbagia and the economic structure and culture of the shepherds.[31] But it is not a fashionable idea: it is not exactly appreciated by apostles of progress, does not belong to the spirit of our age, a positive reading of it cannot be made from faith in development, so common today.[32] In fact, we have seen that in Sardinia this faith takes the form of the hope that "progress" will sweep away those "backward" economic structures and customs. Nor is it a well-received idea in Anthropology, from the criticism of evolutionism and its notion of survival, to the more ahistorical drifts of functionalism and structuralism, or to the isolationism of community studies, to which Wolf gave the last blow.[33] However, it does not seem to be so much to the dislike of historians or of long-lasting looks. The paradigmatic case is that of Arno J. Mayer, who applies the idea of persistence to the European *Ancien Régime* to criticise the partiality of the overly unilateral and teleological views of progress and modernisation, which would have neglected or removed "importance and value to the resistance of the forces and of the old ideas".[34] For him, the Old Regime was a pan-European phenomenon which dominated the society, politics, economy and culture of all countries until well into the twentieth century, caused the Great War of 1914 and then sponsored fascism and contributed to the Second World War.[35]

[31]As mentioned, this is another of the strong ideas in my thesis. See Romero Noguera (2018). It is a recurrent idea in Sardinian anthropological studies. Also see later in the text, by way of example, the quotation by Murru Corriga on "the persistence of family regimes" in Barbagia.

[32]See Rist (2002) for an elaborated criticism on the Western belief on development.

[33]Wolf (1982).

[34]"Scholars of all ideological trends have diminished the importance of pre-industrial economic interests, pre-bourgeois elites, pre-democratic authority systems, pre-modernist artistic languages and 'archaic' mentalities", Mayer (1984), p. 15 *et seq.* [The translation is ours].

[35]According to Mayer, between the end of the nineteenth and the beginning of the twentieth century, the Old Regime would have become an enormous reactionary force against the push of industrial capitalism, the rise of the bourgeois class and the transformations that were taking place at

Its approach interests us, above all, because it considers that European societies are essentially rural and have peasant economies, quasi-feudal, until 1914 and the collapse of the great Russian, Austro-Hungarian and Ottoman empires. Although his vision is "from above" and emphasises the moral, political and economic strength of aristocracies, great nobles and royal houses,[36] he speaks of a transversal state of things, about mentalities, social structures, legal traditions, and conservative customs characteristic to all estates and classes. In this sense, the Old Regime, especially in its last phase, can be seen as an extension, a graft, of feudalism, in a society which had already planted the seeds of a profound change.[37] But here, obviously, I do not focus so much on the reactionary element of elites and oligarchies, to which Mayer gives a purely active and political ("activist") sense, as much as on the long-standing historical inertia of local grassroots, cantonal, and peasant cultures linked to the land and based on direct personal ties, because they allow us to understand what we are talking about: about the conservation to this day—especially in the highlands—of Sardinian customary law, especially vindicatory legal customs, which seem to resist the onslaughts of modernity and adapt to new conditions.

It is surely no coincidence that the great French medievalist Jacques Le Goff speaks of the "long Middle Ages"—dismissing the supposed novelty, rupture and centrality of the Renaissance—making it last from late Antiquity (between the third and seventh centuries) until the middle of the eighteenth century.[38] Without denying the internal changes in long historical periods, such as this long Middle Ages, Le Goff considers that the great transformation, which allows us to speak of a change of era, does not occur in the fifteenth or sixteenth centuries, but in the eighteenth, corresponding, among other things, to "the progress of the rural economy warned of and theorised by physiocrats".[39] According to Braudel, Le Goff speaks of long periods "marked by phases of important, but not major, changes";[40] internal changes to the long period which allow us to talk about subperiods.[41] In this light, I believe that the persistence of legal culture (with its compositional structures and within the

all levels, until it caused the enormous cataclysm of the twentieth century, which he unifies and calls "the Great Thirty Years' War of the General Crisis of the 20th century" [The translation is mine].

[36]Mayer qualifies his investigation on "Marxist history seen from above [. . .] focused on the upper classes rather than the lower" (Mayer 1984), p. 12 [The translation is ours].

[37]That is why, says Mayer, in some regions—especially Russia, Prussia, Hungary and southern Italy—the decay of the Old Regime meant the intensification of corvée labour and legal servitude, before gradually disappearing (*id.* p. 19).

[38]Le Goff (2016).

[39]At that time, in addition to agriculture (with the physiocratic improvements), important changes took place in the economy (the application of the steam engine and industrialization), in philosophy and religion (atheism, scientific rationality and the Encyclopedia), and in politics (the French Revolution), profoundly marking a change of era (*id.*, p. 91). It is significant that Reinhard Koselleck points to this same historical moment as that of the birth of the idea of progress, which would have replaced the cyclical vision of history (cit. in Traverso 2019, p. 23).

[40]Le Goff (2016), p. 97 [The translation is mine].

[41]Braudel (2001).

extensive and intricate community customs) and Barbagian kinship structures (perhaps matrilineages, in any case with parallel forms of filiation and transmission or with precedence through the maternal line) can be understood as belonging to a movement of long duration, while the mutation of the former in a vindictive way or the second in its patrilineal consolidation can be seen as phenomena associated with cycles of shorter duration (subperiods), coinciding with the "reconquest" of pastoralism to the detriment of agriculture, an "important but not major" change, characteristic of the secular cyclical sway between both facets of Sardinian economy.[42] These last changes coincide with the profound social and economic transformations of the late eighteenth century promoted by the physiocratic reformers, but in marginal mountain areas such as Barbagia they were postponed or their effects are delayed, so that, for example, their recipes for sedentary and farmland-binding become a reality until well into the second half of the twentieth century.[43] Significantly, the Sardinian anthropologist Giannetta Murru Corriga seems to follow this scheme when she says that behind the permanence of the traditional productive relations of the world of shepherds, one can notice "the support provided by the persistence of family regimes, subject to multiple forms of manipulation and adaptation".[44]

Another of the long-lasting structural elements of the Sardinian world are grazing contracts, the so-called *soccida*. Like kinship and customary legal culture, *soccida* would also have been affected by significant changes between the end of the seventeenth century and the beginning of the twentieth century, although their basic contractual form, very malleable and adaptable to different historical contexts, would not have varied much.[45] It is a type of partnership contract existing at least since the Late Middle Ages, which continues through the formal abolition of feudalism and the privatisation of land, and whose egalitarian appearance would hide its background inequality, its servile character, and the progressive proletarianisation of the shepherd.[46] One of these mutations (perhaps a "manipulation" or "adaptation" in the sense of Murru Corriga) is the *società a compàngius* ["mates society"], a form of egalitarian cooperation between landless and

---

[42]Marrocu (1977), p. 17.

[43]Murru Corriga (1990) studies a case that we can consider paradigmatic: shepherds of Barbagia that buy land in the plain, settle down and adopt capitalist economic rationality with their cattle farm.

[44]*Id.*, p. 13 [The translation is mine].

[45]Ortu (1981).

[46]Once again, it should be noted that in the mountains, things seem to be somewhat different, since there, *soccida* has been maintained as a more egalitarian type of contract. Numerous authors highlight the highlands as a freer space than the plain, away from its bureaucratic and taxing constraints or work benefits (this is the case of Braudel himself [2001] and Hobsbawm [1976]), even as the place to which people flee and in which as a result different people converge and enormous historical processes of ethnogenesis take place (Scott 2009). For the specific Sardinian case and the imagery of the "nobility" and freedom of the "shepherd kings" and "shepherd knights" of the mountains, see Lussu (2004).

low-livestock shepherds based more on friendship than on kinship, a relationship of production halfway between the most strict adscription of kinship and the individual pure contract. Based on trust, it linked shepherds without going through kinship obligations and was an expression of a further expansion of their personal and elective freedom.[47] Carlo Maxia says that this form of agreement can be seen as a response and adaptation of Sardinian society to the slow but inexorable changes that had been affecting it for a long time, a kind of deal characteristic of a temporarily imprecise phase of transition between the "subsistence family economy and the market capitalist economy".[48] Overwhelmed by the lack of land and investment capacity and without large herds, the shepherds would have resorted to an alliance with friends in the same condition, in a historical context of weakening kinship ties but persistence of mutual support, community morality and collective responsibilities and bonds. Citing Mauss and Keith Hart, Maxia talks about the practices and logic of the gift and reciprocity which would have emerged—more free from the "total prestations" of kinship—in this long transition to the market economy, but which would now be in clear decline, just as the *società a compàngius* itself, making a reality of that economic, social and legal de-responsibility of communities that we know so well; also in Barbagia, customary forms of mutual assistance and support would have been "privatised", gradually replaced by policies, commercial guarantees and access to credit.[49] Significantly, Maxia points out that the *società a compàngius* was not necessarily linked to kinship, even that it shunned this, but that in some cases it was, almost always in relation to a certain land ownership regime. The cases he cites are from the second half of the twentieth century and correspond to situations of self-sufficiency in pasture land or of shortage of communal pastures and property fragmentation,[50] in which the strategy followed was to retain the male siblings on the family farm, in charge of the father's cattle, in order to delay the process of land division by at least one generation. I say that it is significant because something similar has been found for several villages in Barbagia from the second half of the nineteenth century: cohabitation between male siblings associated with patrilocality and in relation to economic expansion and land privatization.[51]

[47]Maxia (2010).

[48]*Id.* Here too, it would be a long process of change. Although Maxia dates it from the end of the seventeenth century, he cites references by Gian Giacomo Ortu—the leading scholar of Sardinian grazing contracts (1981)—on the existence of *compàngius* associations as early as the sixteenth century.

[49]*Id.*: pp. 85–86.

[50]*Id.*: pp. 96–97.

[51]Murru Corriga (1997), p. 273, and (1990).

3 Agnatic (Un)solidarity and Capitalism: The Drift of Bloody Revenge

When I did my fieldwork in Sardinia, in the mid-2000s, I could observe that two ways of sheep shearing [*su tussorju*] coexisted among the shepherds: a more traditional one which, as with other types of heavy or difficult work (the grape harvest, the collection of firewood for the winter, the arrangement of a roof, etc.), required the assistance of relatives, friends and neighbours and included an aspect of meeting and celebration; and another apparently more adapted to the contemporary era, implying non-stop work, no assistance, and the avoidance of festive procrastination, as this was considered to make the task less efficient. In the first case, the shepherd who received assistance invited attendees to eat and drink throughout the day—as usually happens in collective work—and defended that generosity, mutual support and exchange of favours (today for you, tomorrow for me),[52] while in the second, economic rationality was invoked to reject that more communitarian dimension. In both cases the local ideology was used to justify one's own actions: the first person said that the second was stingy and didn't ask for help to avoid having to invite people, and that therefore was breaking with the usual hospitality of the place; the second said that the first was unable to exercise the highly valued virtue of *arrangiarsi* (managing, fending for himself)—he was not sufficiently *abile*[53]—and so he asked for help.

What is significant here is that in the second way of carrying out the shearing, the one which shunned collective celebration and claimed efficiency in the task, there were two male siblings who did it, two brothers who had partnered to carry out their "livestock entreprise" in accordance with capitalist economic rationality, that is, without the disturbance of those other ways of conceiving time and work which have

[52]As in Valencian *a tornallom*, Latin American *minga*, Basque *auzolan* or the very *s'aggiudu torrau* of southern Sardinia (to give some examples), in the shearing of sheep and other neighbourhood or community work of this type, it is about labour prestations and counterprestations: one day one is asked for help, the next is the last to ask for it. In the *tusólzu* (shorn) voice of the dictionary *Vocabolario Sardo logudorese-Italiano* of the priest Pietro Casu, it is said that "the shorn sheep were once joyful pastoral celebrations" (Casu 2011).

[53]See Romero Noguera (2018). This is a very important "emic" category in Barbagia, referring to the shepherds' ability to carry on, to grow the flock and protect it, to provide for the family, to face adversities, etc. Together with the category of *balente*, very close semantically and perhaps even more important in Barbagia, it is central to the work of Pigliaru (1975). See also the interesting ethnographic research of Caltagirone (2005) on "different local identities" within Sardinia, where we can see the contrast and feedback between different ways of understanding these and other "emic" categories in different areas of the island. A whole other thing is the brabucous exaggeration of youth, which would have led to the violent decanting of the *balente*, even "forcing" (manipulating?, adapting?) the custom, and perhaps it would be reflecting a generational conflict of ignoring or rejection of adult authority (Romero Noguera 2018, p. 167 *et seq.*). But, certainly, this would merit another article.

worthily withstood in Sardinia until today.[54] As in the cases of *società a compàngius* between siblings detected by Masia in the second half of the twentieth century or in the indications of Murru Corriga about patrilocal cohabitation between male brothers since the second half of the nineteenth century, shearers are brothers who associate, have land in property, do not divide the father's inheritance and adopt a "modern" productive regime. And this is where I wanted to go, because these trends seem to point to this process of strengthening the bond between male brothers and the waning of the field of extensive kinship solidarity, which would have led, at the same time, to the persistence of the Barbagian customary legal order and the sharpening of its bloody revenge pole. In contrast, the first way of acting, the one which continues to be "a joyful pastoral celebration", refers us to the *longue durée* of the possible matrilineal corporate groups suggested, above all, by Giannetta Murru Corriga, a Sardinian kinship student who has followed the trail of parallel transmission of surname discovered by the jurist historian Enrico Besta in the famous *Quinque Libri* de Locoj, a parochial registry of a small town of Barbagia unpopulated in the late seventeenth century.[55] Groups where the consistency of the feminine principle—to put it somewhat coarsely—was a guarantee or expression of hospitality, of reciprocity, in short, of an extended solidarity beyond parental groups.[56]

From that discovery of the transmission of surnames from father to son and mother to daughter, sometimes for generations,[57] Murru Corriga's research suggests the existence of a system, unique in Western Europe, of formation of regular and consistent lines of descent in parallel, a system of bilateral or cognatic kinship associated with the differentiated or parallel transmission of heritage (cattle and pasture rights to men, orchards and farm animals [as a bridal dowry], trousseau and household items to women)[58] and with the sexual division of work and of the spaces of social life, and also with the "parallel descent" of kinship groups.[59] These are strong clues of corporated groups or lineages which would be reinforced by the logic which underlies the "relatives feasts" [*feste di parenti*], so widespread in Sardinia.[60] Maria Gabriella Da Re, for example, infers the possible existence of "pseudoparental or spiritual cognates lineages" by the peculiarities of the patron feast "of the relatives of Saint Lucia" in the town of Baunei, which brings together consanguineous groups of unrelated relatives and links them with a common ancestry which reaches the "bosses" of the *eredades* (bilateral *ego*-based filiation groups which, when it comes

[54]Naturally, I think of the contrast between the discipline of work and the conception of time of peasants and capitalists; see Thompson's classic (1995).

[55]Murru Corriga (1993, 1997, 2000). The following discussion is based on these articles.

[56]This is what Zene (2005) says about *s'imbiatu*, a particular circulation of gifts conceived almost as a "total social fact", which falls on women, as opposed to the vendetta, which falls more on men.

[57]Murru Corriga (1993).

[58]Murru Corriga (1990, 1993), Da Re (1993, 2003a).

[59]Murru Corriga (1997).

[60]Da Re (1993, 2003a), Murru Corriga (2005), and Tiragallo (2007).

to inheritance rights, are defined by ancestry), the *erederi*, who originally bought the statue of the saint which is celebrated. It is a form of adhesion or membership which recalls the 'corporated' groups but without the relevance of the rights which they distribute in other contexts. Significantly, for Da Re, the existence of these forms of aggregation in groups, which do not necessarily go through kinship, give us traces about the solidarity which, in the practice of *vendetta*, exceeds kinship and which common sense calls "clanic".[61]

However, an apparent greater consistency of the maternal surname and the probability that the house and even the scarce cereal land, which was of indifferent transmission, more anciently passed through the feminine line—as the matrilocality suggests[62]—hints at a historical tendency to matrilineage which would have changed in the last two centuries, regressing in the face of the irruption of the patrilineal system, which is now prevalent.[63] A testimony to the old model is the current persistence of parallel ascription, from father to son and from mother to daughter, as a form of identification which provides social identity to the offspring. In several villages of Barbagia and other areas, even today, if someone asks a child who are their parents, the sons give the father's name and the daughters the mother's. Church and state bureaucracies would have relegated this type of custom to orality, but it is increasingly present in documents the further back we go in history.[64]

In a study on the formation of property and inheritance groups in a town in southern Sardinia, Gian Giacomo Ortu says that during the first half of the nineteenth century the expansion of possessive individualism dynamited internal equilibrium and hit the social life with blood and fire, with outbreaks of violence of all kinds, robberies and homicides.[65] It is a phenomenon which is reproduced throughout Sardinia, but which in the central mountains manifests itself in a stubborn resistance of egalitarian equilibria and collective lands and uses, and at the same time in a reaffirmation of the grazing economy, where, as we know, land would be gained at the expense of agriculture.[66] While the political economy of grazing (soil characteristics, nomadism, production relations, community balances, etc.) would have determined certain forms of heritage transmission and the fragmentation of property, the mutation in the forms of land ownership (with the acquisition by families of shepherds of land lots abandoned by farmers) and the productivist pressure of the cheese industry would have led both to the conservation of the family economy of the shepherds and their mutation in an agnatic affirmation of the association between brothers, to the detriment of women and of wider family and community balances.[67] Murru Corriga wonders if this successful adaptation of the economy and culture of

[61]Da Re (1993), p. 50.

[62]Murru Corriga (1993), pp. 69 y 72.

[63]Murru Corriga (1993, 1997).

[64]Murru Corriga (1993), p. 53.

[65]Ortu (2000), pp. 82–83.

[66]Murru Corriga (1990), p. 13 *et seq.*

[67]*Id.*

pastoralism has had something to do with the diverse customs which regulate the hereditary transmission of its main means of production: the cattle by an exclusively male line; the land by a male and female line; unilinear return and therefore less subject to fragmentation the former; divergent return and more subject to dispersion the latter.[68]

Murru Corriga points out that legal historians already warned about the crisis of "domestic communion" (strong conjugal structure and solidarity of all *siblings*, brothers and sisters), which in the past would have guaranteed the anchoring of free grazing and the precarious existence of nomadic shepherds to the sedentary community of the mountain and its female agricultural unit. The opening of the land market since the second half of the nineteenth century would have also made the property accessible to the families of shepherds who, in order to properly exploit the acquired lands, would have had to reinforce the internal agnatic links of the "domestic community", keeping together mainly the men, who are the direct producers of merchandise and revenues, to the detriment of women, who are the reproducers of men and guarantors of subsistence.[69] I conclude, then, that these transformations would have meant the fall of the broader social consensus in the regulation of conflicts and in the management of communal lands and resources,[70] a clue which leads us towards the very persistence of the vindicatory legal culture and to the most virulent unleashing of revenge over the last decades, or even the last two centuries, since the facts seem to demonstrate a generalised sharpening of conflict and violence since the late eighteenth and early nineteenth centuries.[71]

References

Angioni G (2016) I fatti di Orune-Nule, il codice della vendetta e l'educazione dei giovani. Il Manifesto sardo. Available at https://www.manifestosardo.org/contorni-fatti-orune-nule-codice-della-vendetta-leducazione-dei-giovani/ (last accessed February 26, 2020)

Arlacchi P (2008) Perché non c'è la mafia in Sardegna. Le radici di una anarchia ordinata. AM&D, Cagliari

Biondi E (2011) Criminalità e sentimenti di vendetta in Sardegna. Narrare i Gruppi 6(1):73–89

Birocchi I (1982) Per la storia della proprietà perfetta in Sardegna. Università di Cagliari/Giuffrè, Milan

Braudel F (2001) El Mediterráneo y el mundo mediterráneo en la época de Felipe II. FCE, Madrid

Caltagirone B (2005) Identità sarde. Un'inchiesta etnografica. CUEC, Cagliari

Casu P (2011) Vocabolario sardo logudorese-italiano. ISRE, Nuoro

Da Re MG (1993) Gli eredi della Santa. Una festa di parenti a Baunei (Sardegna). La ricerca floklorica 27:43–51

[68]*Id.*, p. 14.

[69]Murru Corriga (1990), p. 15.

[70]Tiragallo (1995).

[71]Biondi (2011).

Da Re MG (2003a) Essere parenti in Sardegna. In: Angioni G, Da Re MG (eds) Pratiche e saperi. Saggi di antropologia. CUEC, Cagliari

Da Re MG (2003b) I parenti dei santi. In: Angioni G, Da Re MG (eds) Pratiche e saperi. Saggi di antropologia. CUEC, Cagliari, pp 54–78

Del Piano L (1979) Proprietà collettiva e proprietà privata della terra in Sardegna: il caso di Orune (1874-1940). Edizioni della Torre, Cagliari

Fiori G (2001) Baroni in laguna. La società del malessere. Laterza, Rome-Bari

Hobsbawm E (1976) Bandidos. Ariel, Barcelona

Le Goff J (2016) ¿Realmente es necesario cortar la historia en rebanadas? FCE, México DF

Lussu E (2004) Il cinghiale del Diavolo. Illisso, Nuoro

Marrocu L (1977) Note su agricoltura e pastorizia in Sardegna ta età giolittiana e fascismo (1900-1936). Italia Contemporanea 129:7–26

Masia M (1997) A proposito della nota di Treves su Antonio Pigliaru e la ricerca empirica: spunti per una riflessioni. In: Ferrari V et al (eds) Atti del convegno in memoria di Renato Treves (1994). Giuffrè, Milan, pp 137–148

Masia M (2012) Sistemas alternativos de resolución de conflictos en el derecho consuetudinario sardo. Revista Internacional de Pensamiento Político 8:311–324

Maxia C (2010) L'economicità delle emozioni: l'amizicia e la fiducia tra i pastori in Sardegna. In: Lai F (ed) Competizione, cooperazione, invidia. CISU, Rome, pp 16–34

Mayer AJ (1984) La persistencia del Antiguo Régimen. Alianza, Madrid

Mura S (2014) Il dibattito sulla proprietà fondiaria in Sardegna nel Parlamento del Regno d'Italia (1861–1865). In: Atzeni F, Mattone A (eds) La Sardegna nel Risorgimento (Atti del Convegno di Studi – Cagliari, December 1-3st 2011). Carocci, Rome, pp 609–633

Murru Corriga G (1990) Dalla montagna ai campidani. Familgia e mutamento in una comunità di pastori. EDES, Sassari

Murru Corriga G (1993) Di madre in figlia, di padre in figlio. Un caso di 'discendenza parallela' in Sardegna. La ricerca folklorica 27(2):53–72

Murru Corriga G (1997) Discendenza e residenza nella Sardegna moderna. In: Meloni B (ed) Famiglia meridionale senza familismo. Strategia economiche, reti di relazioni e parentela. Donzelli, Rome, pp 248–277

Murru Corriga G (2000) The Patronymic and the Matronymic in Sardinia: a long-standing competition. The history of the family. Int Quart 5:161–180

Murru Corriga G (2005) La festa come dono. Antenati, cibo e memoria culturale a Dorgali. Lares 71 (3):669–682

Ortu GG (1981) L'economia pastorale della Sardegna moderna. Saggio di antropologia storica sulla "soccida". Edizioni della torre, Cagliari

Ortu GG (2000) Il paese sul crinale. Gruppi di eredità e formazione della proprietà (Burcei 1655-1865). CUEC, Cagliari

Ortu L (2005) La questione sarda tra Ottocento e Novecento. Aspetti e problemi. CUEC, Cagliari

Parlamento Italiano (1996) Commissione Parlamentare d'inchiesta sul fenomeno della mafia e delle altre associazioni criminali similari. Rome

Pigliaru A (1975) Il banditismo in Sardegna. La vendetta barbaricina come ordinamento giuridico. Giuffrè, Milan

Pinna L (1971) La famiglia esclusiva. Parentela e clientelismo in Sardegna. Laterza, Rome

Pira M (1978) La rivolta dell'oggetto. Antropologia della Sardegna. Giuffrè, Milan

Regione Autonoma della Sardegna (1967) Comissione Parlamentare d'Inchiesta sul fenomeno del banditismo in Sardegna in relazione alle condizioni economico-sociali dell'Isola. Cagliari

Regione Autonoma della Sardegna (1987) Commissione speciale per una indagine conoscitiva sulla condizione economica e sociale delle zone della Sardegna interessate da particolari fenomeni di criminalità e di violenza. Cagliari

Rist G (2002) El desarrollo: historia de una creencia occidental. Catarata, Madrid

Romero Noguera P (2011) 'Certezza' jurídica, certeza vital: la cultura jurídica sardo-barbaricina entre la responsabilidad individual y la responsabilidad colectiva. In: Terradas I (ed) Antropología jurídica de la responsabilidad. Andavira, Santiago de Compostela, pp 475–508

Romero Noguera P (2018) La persistencia de una cultura jurídica vindicatoria. El caso de los pastores de Barbagia, Cerdeña. PhD Thesis. Universitat de Barcelona, Barcelona

Rouland N (1992) Antropologia giuridica. Giuffrè, Milan

Scott J (2009) The art of not being governed: an anarchist history of Upland Southeast Asia. Yale University Press, New Haven

Terradas Saborit I (2008) Justicia vindicatoria. CSIC, Madrid

Terradas Saborit I (2021) Understanding the Vindicatory system. In: Terradas Saborit I, Mazzola R, Márquez Porras R (eds) Vindicatory justice: beyond law and revenge. Springer, Dordrecht

Thompson EP (1995) Tiempo, disciplina de trabajo y capitalismo industrial. In: Costumbres en común. Crítica, Barcelona, pp 395–452

Tiragallo F (1995) Vendetta e competizione sociale in Sardegna: sviluppi recenti e interpretazioni. Etudes Corses 40–41:103–113

Tiragallo F (2007) Il dono della festa e la sua memoria visiva. Solidarietà, circolazione di cibo e di immagini in una festa religiosa della Sardegna centrale. Religioni e società 58:31–44

Traverso E (2019) Melancolía de izquierda. Después de las utopías. Galaxia Gutenberg, Barcelona

Wolf ER (1982) Europa y la gente sin historia. FCE, México DF

Zene C (2005) Dono e vendetta nella Sardegna centrale. Lares 71(3):683–716

Vindicatory Justice and the Colonial Encounter

The Reparation of the Tar and Its Impossibility

José Maria Ortuño Aix

Abstract The aim of this Chapter is to show that the legal system of the present-day Nigeria Tiv, belongs clearly to the type of 'vindicatory justice'. Such a legal system did not act independent from other cultural elements of society, especially of the political-ritual sphere; according to its norms, individuals participate as members of collective groups; and its main purpose is to get reparation for the damages inflicted, arbitrate conflicts and restore the social harmony between the parties with equitable judgements. As the author will show, in Tiv society the council of elders represents a fundamental tool to repair the damage done to social relations, acting often as mediator and judge, in a continuum between both roles. Also, the Chapter how the prohibition of the traditional marriage by colonial authorities disrupted the basic reciprocity in Tiv society mainly arranged through matrilinearity, essential to promote social peace in conflicts.

1 Introduction

Before the arrival of the Europeans, the Tiv of present-day Nigeria lived in a society based on segmentary lineages characterised, like other societies with this type of organisation, by the absence of any form of government or central political system. That this lack of central authority in segmentary societies did not imply a tendency towards anarchy, as the Tiv makes evident,[1] is what led Evans-Pritchard to coin the expression "ordered anarchy" to refer to that kind of social order which coexists with the absence of centralised authority.[2] It was precisely this fragmentary organisation that allowed the Tiv to resist more effectively, in contrast with other more powerful centralised societies, the British forces' attempts at penetration. The knowledge of

[1]Bohannan (1957), p. 9; Bohannan and Bohannan (1962), p. 29.
[2]Evans-Pritchard (1940), p. 6.

J. M. Ortuño Aix (✉)
Department of Social Anthropology, University of Barcelona, Barcelona, Spain

R. Márquez Porras et al. (eds.), *Vindicatory Justice*, Ius Gentium: Comparative Perspectives on Law and Justice 93, https://doi.org/10.1007/978-3-030-79595-5_10

some of the peculiarities of the Tiv kinship system was what finally allowed colonial forces to gain political control of Tivland.

The knowledge concerning the kinship relations existing in Tiv society is important because they were at the basis of the entire social building and, particularly, of the legal system, object of this article. This system was characterised by having many of the vindicatory elements that Ignasi Terradas Saborit describes in the introduction to this volume: it was a legal system that did not act independently of the other cultural elements of society, especially of the political-ritual sphere; it was a legal system where individuals participated as members of collective groups; and it was one which had the purpose of getting reparation for the damages inflicted, arbitrating conflicts and restoring social harmony between the parties instead of applying norms or laws.

From the ethnographies of Paul and Laura Bohannan, we can clearly distinguish that orientation to reparation and to reconciliation just mentioned. We will see that the councils (*jir*) of elders of the groups involved in the disputes were fundamental to "repair the *tar* (country, land)"; acting as mediators and as judges, in a continuum similar to that mentioned in the introduction, was considered to be their main job. It is striking, however, that the Bohannans did not perceive the same vindicatory mechanism in dealing with the conflicts and disputes between lineages in the pre-colonial era. Not seeing any regulatory mechanism, according to them, the Bohannans said that in important conflicts when homicides occurred between different lineages, the lineages went to "war". However, once the principles of the vindicatory system have been identified, we can deduct from the ethnographies and with the help of documents of the colonial administration evident signs that the same conflict-inhibiting mechanisms acted in that area as well.

The traditional marriage system was at the base of the Tiv society and provided the people empowered to participate in the most important ritual offices and also to act as mediators and judges in conflicts. However, a series of circumstances led colonial authorities to ban the traditional marriage system and to confiscate the ritual objects used by the elders in their ritual offices of "reparation" of society and land, an important aspect at the ending phase of the council's work.

In our study we will not address an issue that was essential in the field of power relations among the Tiv—a power considered from a transcendental perspective, which was at the basis of what they considered witchcraft. Although it is beyond the scope of our study, it is convenient to know that it was the same force (*tsav*), both the one used by the elders to repair society and land when in councils and the one used by sorcerers when perverting social order by attacking people at night.[3]

[3]Bohannan (1958b).

2 The "Peaceful Penetration" in Tivland

When the British took over the administration of Nigeria from 1 January 1900, the most difficult territories to be controlled effectively were those occupied by decentralised and socially fragmented tribes. The case of the Tiv is paradigmatic, because the high commissioner of the then Protectorate of Northern Nigeria, Sir (later Lord) Frederick Lugard, who referred to the Tiv in his first annual report as "a constant source of trouble",[4] like his successor in office, Sir William Wallace, failed in the attempt to militarily subjugate this society. Both failed because they met not with a large number of combatants but with small groups which, by means of *guerrilla* tactics, attacked British forces before immediately retreating into the bush. It was not until 1907 that Captain Charles Forbes Gordon, acting Resident of Muri Province since July of the previous year, obtained authorisation to patrol the Tiv east territory of Katsina. After the Mahdist uprising of 1905–1906 in British Northern Nigeria, which sought the overthrow of all established authorities, and whose repression ended in a true massacre in Satiru early in 1906,[5] it was not easy to obtain permission from the new Liberal government of Sir Henry Campbell-Bannerman to patrol a territory which Lugard had declared an "unsettled district". The risk of a new tragedy was too great. However, Gordon used a method which David Dorward refers to as "peaceful penetration", by taking advantage of the knowledge of Tiv customs which Gordon gained from natives living near Wukari. Following their suggestions, before sending a detachment to a Tiv territory, "friendly Tiv intermediaries were asked to intercede with their matrilineal kinsmen or *igba*, calm their fears as to the intentions of the approaching patrol, and persuade the patriarchs to consult with Gordon before he entered the territory of their lineage".[6]

The society which Gordon found, as he observed in his *Notes on the Munshi Tribe* (1907), lacked political unity, had a segmented structure and, therefore, "limitations of consensus leadership" which would only allow "a modicum power" to be built.[7] In the terminology used by American anthropologists Paul Bohannan and his wife Laura Bohannan (1962), who worked in that territory four decades later, the Tiv society was organised in patrilineages with patrilocal residence and with segments which were formed under the principle which, in the ethnographic literature of the time, was called "complementary opposition".[8] The name used by the Tiv to refer to groups of relatives was *ityo*, which literally means "agnate" and was used as a reference and treatment term. The father's brother was *ityo*, while the mother's brother was *igba*, a term which was also used to refer to all his patrilineage.

[4]Dorward (1974), p. 459.

[5]Lovejoy and Hogendorn (1990).

[6]Dorward (1971), p. 143; see also Dorward (1969), p. 319.

[7]Dorward (1974), p. 462.

[8]Evans-Pritchard (1940), p. 282.

The lineage segments were called *uipaven* (sing. *ipaven*), and the territory where the *uipaven* settled was called *tar*. Since 83% of the *tar* population belonged to the same *ipaven*, sometimes both terms were used colloquially as synonyms. In the interior of the *tar*, harmonious relations were to be maintained and conflicts avoided as much as possible both in the *tar* of the small *uipaven* and throughout the whole of the territory, the Tiv *tar*. If harmony was broken, as we will see, the Tiv said that the *tar* had been spoiled, and they took the necessary measures to re-establish harmony which, in many cases, consisted of bringing the case before the councils of elders.

3 A Legal System to "Repair the *Tar*"

An aspect that characterised the Tiv society and that should be taken into account when analysing its legal system is that they considered that any act that affected social peace (war, theft, witchcraft, quarrels) could have negative and even tragic consequences on the people who live in the *tar* since those acts spoilt the *tar,* and when that happened, not only the coexistence but also the health of the people, the success of the crops, the hunting, and even the reproductive capacity of the people were menaced.[9] If those involved in the dispute belonged to the same domestic group, the intervention of an elder (*ortaregh,* pl. *mbaterev*) would be enough to restore peace; but if they belonged to different lineage segments, the conflict was to be brought to the *jir,* the councils composed of the *mbatarev* of each of the groups involved.[10] As happened in other vindicatory societies, there was continuum between the role of elders as judges and as mediators, to which Terradas Saborit refers in his introduction.

Repairing the *tar* consisted of listening to the parties involved, finding a solution accepted by all, and finally, performing the reconciliation ceremonies between the parties and the reparation of the *akombo*, objects that represented the forces that affected the health of people and society which had been damaged by the conflict.[11] In the words of the Bohannans, "To 'repair the *tar*' is to ensure that all the activities —political, social, economic, and mystical— of the people of the *tar* are in good running order".[12] Furthermore, "it is the task of the elders of the community to smooth social relationships by resolving difficulties, and they do so by means of the moot".[13] Bohannan insists, again and again, that the purpose of the *jir* was not "to apply laws" but "to determine a *modus vivendi*",[14] "to make suggestions for

[9]Bohannan and Bohannan (1962), pp. 85–92.

[10]Bohannan and Bohannan (1962), p. 43.

[11]Bohannan (1957), pp. 3, 213.

[12]Bohannan and Bohannan (1962), p. 22; (1968), pp. 41–42.

[13]Bohannan (1957), p. 187.

[14]Bohannan (1957), pp. 19, 65.

settlement" and expect the parties "concur in judgment".[15] The community as a whole is important because as Bohannan says, "it is the opinion of the community which forces concurrence".[16]

As the purpose of the *jir* was to achieve reconciliation of the parties, the latter were not allowed to take justice by their own hands. Revenge and retaliation, carried out individually, apart from the *jir* of the *mbaterev*, are "always a matter of 'spoiling the *tar'*—even when it is recognised as a legitimised means of counteraction," "Tiv are unequivocal on this point" insisted Paul Bohannan.[17] Repairing the *tar* demanded that conflicts be brought before the *jir*.

The most serious cases dealt with in the *jir* before the arrival of the British were cases of homicide, incest and adultery. The reaction to a homicide depended on who the victim and the killer were. "As in many other African societies", says Paul Bohannan, "fratricide was never punished, but merely ritually repaired"; on the contrary, when the dead belonged to another lineage, Bohanan says that "a general war resulted", because, according to him, "institutionalized feud did not exist in Tivland".[18] The use of the term "war" for this case is not right because it removes an important part of the homicides from the scope of Tiv law and takes it to the field of war where absolute enmity predominates. Incomprehensibly, it did not occur to Bohannan that here too, as in the *jir*, there was the need to reach agreements that allowed coexistence between lineages that, by the rules of exogamy, most probably were related to each other. But now that we know the principles of the vindicatory system, we can see that in conflicts between lineages there should also be mechanisms that lead to reconciliation.

War meant the maximum possible hostility, as illustrated by the fact that among the Tiv the removal of the fallen combatants' heads when fighting foreign enemies was allowed. The heads obtained during fighting were a source of pride and prestige, and the feats of their owners were sung at their funerals.[19] But such an action was not allowed in clashes between Tiv lineages. As pointed by Middleton and Tait "the hostility between segments among the Tiv called warfare by Dr. Bohannan could rather be called feud", because unlike what happens in wars, "the relationships between the feuding parties is such that hostility between them [...] must be inhibited in those situations in which they become allies in military, economic, ritual or other collaboration".[20]

We must keep in mind that when the Bohannans carried out their field work in Tivland, between 1949 and 1952, the Tiv had been subject to colonial authorities for decades; their legal institutions had been replaced by others at the convenience of the new administrators; their *akombo u tamen* (the most important and prestigious

[15]Bohannan (1957), p. 64.

[16]Bohannan (1957), p. 65.

[17]Bohannan (1957), pp. 141–142.

[18]Bohannan (1957), p. 148.

[19]Bohannan and Bohannan (1962), p. 79.

[20]Middleton and Tait (1958), p. 21.

akombo necessaries for the repairing of the *tar*) had been banned and requisitioned. The same fate befell the traditional marriage institution, which had been prohibited, therefore preventing it from fulfilling its function of extending reciprocity networks based on kinship throughout the territory. Unable to witness the way lineages acted when they were sovereign, much of the Bohannan analysis is limited by that fact, that is Terradas Saborit's warning when he points out that many anthropologists "have studied societies which have already lost much of their jurisdictional autonomy, being under colonial regimes or new states".[21] That situation is what prevented Paul and Laura Bohannan from seeing the vindicatory system in action when lineages were in conflict.

Notwithstanding this criticism, the Bohannans left us with enough elements in their ethnographies to see that in the field of relations between lineages, the principles which characterise the vindicatory order predominated as well. And that is why we don't find the term "feud" proposed by Middleton and Tait to be satisfactory either because that term places more emphasis on hostilities and violence than on other legal institutions aimed at reparation and conciliation,[22] and also because, as Terradas Saborit points out in the introduction to this volume, the feuding and reconciliation process could last sometimes much longer than the time of anthropologists' fieldwork.

We have seen that the legal system in the colonial era was still oriented towards reconciliation and the restoration of coexistence, what the Tiv called "repair the tar", although it was unable to deal with the most serious cases such as homicide. But now we will see that in the pre-colonial era, when the Tiv lineages entered into 'wars' among each other, there were the same principles in action. Bohannan's own texts point in that direction: "It is said today," he admits "that attempts were often made to avert such wars by employing as an intermediary a man related to both lineages", and he adds "he was usually successful, it would seem, if the killing was accidental". Along the same lines, he goes on to say that "Tiv elders say that there were instances in which the murderer's lineage avoided war by deciding to give him [the offender] to the lineage of his victim, to do as they liked with him", or even "on other occasions, he [the offender] could be made to hang himself in retribution for his deed".[23] Actions such as those mentioned by Bohannan, characteristic of vindicatory systems because they implied recognition of the offence and the intention of curbing hostilities to facilitate reconciliation, were also collected by British officials in the first years of occupation: captain RM Downes pointed out that "in certain cases, offenders were handed over to individuals to wreak their vengeance upon, after the rites have been performed, the evil expelled, and the spirits appeased".[24]

When lineages were at "war" with each other, "they fought until peace could be restored by the normal means" admits Bohannan. But these "normal means" could

[21] Terradas Saborit (2019).

[22] Terradas Saborit (2019).

[23] Bohannan (1957), p. 148.

[24] Downes (1933), pp. 71–72.

not be anything other than the intervention of the *mbaterev* of the lineages with the cooperation of the *igba* related by kinship to the lineages involved in the clashes. Clearly, the testimonies given to Bohannan pointed in that direction: "a war spoils the *tar* more than anything else", and they followed that by explaining that both "peace-making [and] 'repairing the *tar*' [...] [meant] to sit and listen quietly and dispassionately to all sides... repairing *tar* is a matter of arbitration".[25]

The *igba* were the most suitable for that mediating function since "in time of war a man does not fight his *igba* nor should they harm him; he thus becomes a valued messenger".[26] This capacity of marriage alliances to avoid violence is what E. B. Tylor referred to with his oft-quoted maxim: "Again and again in the world's history, savage tribes must have had plainly before them the simple practical alternative between marrying-out and being killed out".[27] The marriage alliance was so important for the Tiv that they imitated it in other political-ritual alliances, as in the case with the *ikul* treaties. This type of treaty between two lineages made the members of each of them similar to political relatives, mutually applying the most typical considerations and behaviours of the *igba*: "first, the prohibition of any act which involves or might involve bloodshed [...] secondly, the prohibition of sexual relationships; thirdly, general rules of almost exaggerated hospitality..."[28] The logic of *ikul* treaties is reminiscent of Tylor's dilemmas, as Bohannan was told: "we make *ikul* treaties with those who might kill us but amongst whom we often travel".[29]

Everything changed shortly after the colonial administration was implemented in Tivland. Most importantly, as noted before, Tiv lineages lost their sovereignty, an essential attribute for the existence of a vindicatory system. The native legal system was eliminated as of January 1918, when the Munshi (Tiv) Province was created in order to promote political centralisation and to apply the doctrine of indirect rule. The *jir* were replaced by Government Grade D Courts, with authority to only judge cases involving a maximum fine of £25 and three months in prison.[30] In addition, most of the important institutions were banned or modified until they lost their character. In the ritual and religious field, the great *akombo* necessary to "repair the *tar*", essential in the rituals of reconciliation, were banned and requisitioned in 1929, with the British authorities mistakenly believing, according to their own testimonies, that they had been used by the elders to perform cannibalistic rituals.[31] Finally, British authorities banned the traditional marriage system which supported the rest of the institutions and which, paradoxically, had been skilfully used in the 'opening up' of Tivland by Captain Gordon.

---

[25]Bohannan (1957), p. 2.

[26]Bohannan and Bohannan (1962), p. 24.

[27]Tylor (1889), p. 267.

[28]Bohannan and Bohannan (1962), p. 30.

[29]Bohannan (1958), p. 62.

[30]Bohannan and Bohannan (1962), p. 44.

[31]Abraham (1933), p. 105.

4 Marriage by Exchange and the Figure of the *Igba*

The vindicatory legal system, as Terradas Saborit points out in the introduction, is intermingled or embedded with other cultural elements. Among the Tiv, one of the most important cultural elements was the marriage system based on the exchange of sisters since it built the entire social fabric and contributed to weaving kinship relations into society and providing the figure of the *igba* who, as we saw, was essential to keeping the social peace. The Bohannans report that "exchange marriage was not only the basic form of marriage but the standard". It comprised the following: "every man takes his immediately younger sister as his marriage ward, gives her to another man, who in return gives him his ward as wife".[32] Marriage by exchange was of such importance that it also provided identity criteria, as shown in the clashes of lineages: when a lineage went to "war" against another Tiv lineage which, despite being considered "Tiv", did not participate in the exchange marriage system, as was the case of the Iharev and Masev lineages (none of them exchanged sisters with the other Tiv lineages), it was allowed to sever the heads of combatants, as if they were foreign enemies.[33]

Any other form of marriage involving payments (*kwase* or *sha uika*, which means "woman in exchange for property") was considered temporary, only postponing the marriage by exchange; the children belonged to the maternal group until that time and therefore lacked *igba*.[34] Akiga explained the importance of exchange marriage by detailing its relationship with political and religious institutions and, in particular, with the most important *akombo* which were essential for repairing the *tar*: "The children born by exchange marriage were the right full heirs [. . .]. It was the son by an exchange marriage who built the *Poor* and [. . .] performed the rites of the *Biamegh* and other big *akombo*. [. . .] And when the idea of chieftainship arose, it was a son of an exchange marriage who was made chief".[35] The relationship between marriage and the ritual, legal and political order was clear from Akiga's testimony.

The *igba* (mother's brother and all the people belonging to his lineage) were also important in another aspect considered of vital importance for the health and safety of individuals. When a person was attacked by *tsav*, a supernatural power related to witchcraft which was considered to be the cause of all diseases and accidental deaths,

[32]Bohannan and Bohannan (1962), p. 69.

[33]Bohannan and Bohannan (1962), pp. 25–26; (1969), p. 488. Rupert East, colonial officer and translator of Akiga, wrote: "[W]ith the Tiv the exchange system cannot be considered merely as a better or worse way of getting a wife. It is, or has been, an institution of paramount importance, and lies at the base of the whole present tribal organization. Moreover, it is bound up with the strongest of supernatural sanctions; for although the spiritual life of the tribe has been severely shaken by events of recent years, the orthodox belief, still held by the old men, is that the fertility of the crops and of the women—in fact, the very existence of the tribe—is dependent on exchange marriage and the rites which are associated with it" (Akiga 1939, 99–100).

[34]Akiga (1939), pp. 158–159.

[35]Akiga (1939), pp. 118–119.

and when it was believed that the protection of the elders of his own lineage (*ityo*) had failed, he would try to escape and to seek the protection of their *igba*'s lineage. The *mbatarev* of his *igba* lineage would go to his own *ityo* and demand respect for the life of their daughter's son.[36] That reason was enough to wish to have a strong and powerful maternal lineage since they said, "it is their duty to defend me against my *ityo*".[37] Laura Bohannan insisted on this when she said that "the larger the lineages of a man's *igba* and *ityo*, the more important the affairs in which he is called upon to act as go-between, and the more likely he is to receive full protection against his agnates.[38] We can say that the marriage alliance corrected that maxim of Tylor in the sense that exogamic marriage not only prevented the Tiv from "being killed out," but also from "being killed in".

The dimension of both groups, *ityo* and *igba*, depended on the marriage of the parents since a person's *ityo* was "the group with which his father identified himself when marrying his mother" so that in the words of Rupert East, "if the two groups are closely related to each other, both will be small, for they are mutually exclusive." On the contrary, if "the marriage was a more distant one, the child will enjoy membership of larger and stronger paternal and maternal groups".[39] The Tiv kinship system complicates the search for a spouse with each new generation since it is forbidden to marry in the same lineage into which the father married, the paternal and maternal grandparents married, and the paternal great-grandfather married. In addition, as we said, the lineages with which an *ikul* treaty was made were also forbidden matrimonially. Such a set of prohibitions is what characterises the systems which Claude Lévi-Strauss called "Crow-Omaha". Instead of proposing groups of relatives as preferential spouses as other marriage systems do (the conversion of "blood relatives" into "relatives by marriage", as Lévi-Strauss said), the "Crow-Omaha" system prohibits marrying within the lineages into which previous generations were married because the system converts the "relatives by marriage" lineages into "blood relatives" lineages and therefore excludes new alliances.[40]

French anthropologist Françoise Héritier proposed that semi-complex alliance systems (as she called the Crow-Omaha systems), in addition to retaining previous alliances, allow fresh ones to be established as the prohibitions ceased to be active.[41] Héritier's proposal coincides fully with our investigation of the Tiv marriage system[42] in which we have shown that after taking marriage prohibitions into account, in addition to other factors not mentioned here, the result is a system that encouraged marriage between certain lineages so that they remained part of a network of kinship relationships thorough Tivland which allowed reciprocity

[36]Bohannan and Bohannan (1962), p. 48.
[37]Bohannan and Bohannan (1962), p. 24.
[38]Bohannan (1958a), p. 39.
[39]Akiga (1939), p. 136.
[40]Lévi-Strauss (1969), p. xxxix.
[41]Héritier (1981), p. 113.
[42]Ortuño Aix (2004, 2006).

relationships to be established that were not only useful for mediation and protection, as we have seen, but also at critical moments for survival. "In southern Tivland," the Bohannans noted, "food moves across the country during the lean season among kinsmen who 'send hunger' to one another," taking advantage of the fact that the yam collection time varies in each region. "This movement of food" they said, "takes place on a kinship or friendship basis and is morally important to the Tiv".[43]

However, the Tiv marriage system, essential for the working of the rest of the political and ritual institutions, and which provided the legal system with the mechanism by which it could intervene in conflicts to reconcile parties and "repair the *tar*", was declared illegal by colonial authorities.

5 The Prohibition of Marriage by Exchange and the Spoiling of the *Tar* as a Result

What opened the door to the prohibition of the marriage system was a dispute over the custody of some fatherless children in 1925. The missionaries of the Dutch Reformed Church (DRCM) claimed custody for the mother, resident in the mission, because in that way the children could attend school and church, which would not happen if they continued with the paternal group. The missionary authorities took the opportunity to attack traditional marriage because they said it prevented marrying off children who were Christianised. The DRCM chairman, W. A. Malherbe, regretted that "two confessing Christian boys... have come to us and said: we must choose between baptism and marriage, because it is impossible to have both under existing circumstances".[44] Captain Feasey, district officer of the Munshi Division, understood the missionaries' situation well and explained to the residents of the province: "the position of the elders is logical, they have lost a young man from their village, and if they give him a girl to make an exchange marriage with, they lose a girl as well, and no benefit can accrue to them as a result of the transaction".[45] It was also true, on the other hand, as Kenneth Dewar explained, that if the young man treated his elders with respect and fulfilled his traditional obligations, he would surely be able to marry at a reasonable age, even if he did not have a sister to exchange, as his lineage group would yield one.[46] But certainly, if the young man attended the missionaries' school, if he converted to Christianity and abandoned his family obligations, then the situation would be different. The heads of the household would refuse to assign him an *ingol* with which to marry by exchange. For that reason, the missionaries presented themselves before the British colonial authorities as champions of the liberation of women and youth. This is what missionary J. Geo.

[43] Bohannan and Bohannan (1962), p. 143.
[44] Malherbe (1925), p. 8.
[45] Feasey (1926), p. 17.
[46] Dewar (1932), pp. 68–69.

Botha did to the Benue Province Resident to get his sympathies, telling him that "the woman and her rights seem to us to be fundamental—her development, her sphere of influence and work, her emancipation [. . .] the rights of the child come second on the list".[47]

After several discussions with British officers familiar with the subject and interviews with DRCM representatives, it was agreed to ban marriage by exchange and replace it with another type called by everyone "marriage by purchase".[48] As would become evident shortly afterwards, if the issue was to improve the situation of women, that they were "bought" in the new marriage system would not be of any help. Following the logic of the *indirect rule*, which demanded that the laws be approved by the native authorities, the colonial authorities could not legislate on it directly. But the native authorities were in favour of the traditional system, so everyone was aware that some coercion would be necessary. "The best plan", explained H. E. Palmer, Lieutenant Governor of the Northern Provinces, to W. A. Malherbe, "would be for the District Officer Munshi to call a meeting of all chiefs" and make it clear that "continuing on the old way they were cutting their own throats".[49]

The district officer chosen to summon the native chiefs was Captain Feasey, an old acquaintance, who in the previous year had given exemplary punishment to some chiefs who had refused to follow his instructions. Combining suggestions and threats, Feasey got the Tiv Central Council to make the "right" decision for the Tiv Central Council,[50] which was promptly communicated by the Resident of Benue Province, W. Morgan, to the secretary of the northern provinces: "I have to report that the assembled District Heads of the Munshi Districts have unanimously decided to replace exchange marriage by marriage by purchase".[51] Soon congratulations arrived from Governor Thomson and even from the Colonial Secretary, Leo Amery who received with "great satisfaction the successful issue of the measures taken by His Honour's direction in the unanimous decision of the Munshi chiefs [. . .]".[52]

Soon it was seen, however, that this unanimity had been forced. In the Provincial Annual Report of 1929, Captain Emberton warned that "the abolition of exchange marriages continues to be very unpopular generally [. . .]" and added, "I am firmly convinced that it never had the genuine support of the Munshi Chiefs themselves".[53] In the following years, discontent among Tiv chiefs became increasingly apparent.

[47]Botha (1930), p. 51.

[48]The officer most in favour of the prohibition and who participated decisively in it was Feasey (1926, 1927a).

[49]Monk (1926), p. 2.

[50]Information about this incident is found in Akiga (1939, pp. 398–399) and in Dorward (1971, p. 276).

[51]Morgan (1927), p. 48.

[52]Baddeley (1928), p. 78. See also the different reactions to the decision in Feasey (1927b), pp. 46–47 and also Morgan (1927), p. 48.

[53]Provincial Annual Report (1929), p. 58.

They did not miss the opportunity in the Tiv Central Council, the highest Tiv authority, to protest that decision. This is reflected in the minutes of the council held in Gboko in 1932, where we read: "The Tiv Chiefs wished to ask the Governor for permission to resume the practice of exchange. . ."[54] the same occurred in 1934[55] and in 1937.[56]

Kenneth Dewar, one of the officers who knew the Tiv culture best, and was therefore aware of the importance of the marriage institution for rituals and the native legal and political system, listed the *akombo* which could only be inherited by children of a marriage by "true sister" exchange and which were necessary to be "eligible for the highest religious office".[57] Dewar concluded that "it follows in theory at least that the abolition of all forms of exchange will give rise to a generation none of whom are eligible to hold high religious office". Similarly, the district officer, D. F. H. Bride, wrote to the Resident of Benue Province reminding him "that the Central Council at Ihug last year informed His Honour that the abolition of exchange marriage had removed one of the corner stones of the Tiv social edifice".[58]

The criticism went in two directions. On the one hand, the ban had turned the marriage institution "into a mere commercial contract",[59] distorting the alliance and without improving the situation of women. On the other hand, the measure increased intergenerational tension since "it naturally gave rise to the feeling that the 'white man' was the young man's friend". According to Dewar, that sentiment caused the elders to move away from politics, "to decline office of any sort under the Native Administration and to leave the control of 'white men's matters' or 'kwagh u uke' entirely in the hands of young men". That increase in intergenerational tension led the elders—or led young people to believe that the elders—"resorted to an abnormal use of Black magic, or threats of it, against the younger generation", culminating "in the anti-Mbatsav outcry of 1929 which was epitomised (by Mr Middleton I believe) as a war between the young and the old".[60]

Social reciprocity disappeared with the conversion of marriage alliances into a "commercial trade contract" which could no longer support the alliance system, given the impossibility of erecting the great *akombo* necessary to repair the *tar* due to

[54]Tiv Central Council (1932), p. 8.

[55]Tiv Central Council (1934), p. 26.

[56]Tiv Central Council (1937), p. 84.

[57]Dewar (1932), pp. 71–72.

[58]MacBride (1940), p. 90.

[59]Dewar (1934, 75); Malherbe had already complained in 1928 in such terms despite having been the promoter of the initiative: "The Munshi woman is now in the position of a slave or a trading article – Although we are prepared to admit that this statement is probably only a temporary phase in the evolution of the New Regulations, yet we cannot help to notice with regret that one of the results of the introduction of the new marriage regulations is that the position of the woman has generally become more definitely that of a slave, –she is not considered to have the least, say or choice in her own marriage palaver, and is often 'sold' against her wish, and even whilst she is kept in ignorance of the transaction until everything has been settled" (Malherbe 1928, pp. 40–41).

[60]Dewar (1932), p. 68.

the absence of eligible people and the hostility of the colonial administration towards them. The sovereignty of the lineages had been lost, and the native councils of a vindicatory character were substituted by other courts created by the British which were more adapted to the power structure of indirect rule. Women had been converted into a simple transactional object and had lost their traditional status with the implementation of measures which, paradoxically, had been aimed at improving their situation. Given the increase in intergenerational tension to the point of making elders think that the British authorities were there to favour young people, and young people to think that the elders, as *mbatsav*, were taking revenge for the grievance received. All this could only indicate one thing: that the *tar* had been spoiled, and Captain Downes knew how to sum it up perfectly in a book published posthumously:

> Some old men and household-heads used the expression to me on various occasions 'ubutar vihi tar yo' (the white man has spoiled the land). By this I discovered they meant the abolition of exchange-marriage, which had taken place two years before, was considered by many to be an irreparable break up of Tiv family life and struck at the very foundations of the Tiv social and religious structure. (. . .) As I became more familiar with the language and the people, the elders become more out-spoken, and they would say, "the white man forbade kor (the sasswood ordeal), he prevents hoyo (communal activity against witches) . . . and now he has forbidden yamen u kwase (exchange-marriage), and you say you want us to follow our own customs. tar vihi yo (the land is ruined).[61]

References

Abraham RC (1933) The Tiv People. Government Printer, Lagos

Akiga S (1939) Akiga's story. International Institute of African Language and Cultures, London

Baddeley FM (1928) Tiv Marriage Customs, (19/1/1928), GBODIV 509. NAK, Kaduna

Bohannan L (1958a) Political aspects of Tiv social organization. In: Middleton J, Tait D (eds) Tribes without rulers: studies in African segmentary systems. Routledge and Kegan Paul, London, pp 33–66

Bohannan P (1957) Justice and Judgement among the Tiv. Oxford University Press, London

Bohannan P (1958b) Extra-processual events in Tiv political institutions. Am Anthr 60(1):1–12

Bohannan P, Bohannan L (1962) (1953) The Tiv of Central Nigeria. International African Institute, London

Bohannan P, Bohannan L (1968) Tiv economy. Longmans, London

Bohannan P, Bohannan L (1969) A source notebook on Tiv religion; vol IV. The Great Akombo. HRAF, New Haven

Botha JG (1930) Munshi marriages, MAKPROF 337. NAK, Kaduna

Dewar K (1932) Abolition of Tiv exchange marriage (24/11/1932), GBODIV 509. NAK, Kaduna

Dewar K (1934) Tiv exchange marriage (28/6/1934), CSO-26/3-26207. NAI, Ibadan

Dorward D (1969) The development of the British colonial administration among the Tiv, 1900–1949. Afr Aff 68:316–333

Dorward D (1971) A political and social history of the Tiv people of Northern Nigeria, 1900–1939. Ph.D. diss., University of London

[61]Downes (1971), pp. 13–14.

Dorward D (1974) Ethnography and administration: a study of Anglo-Tiv 'Working Misunderstanding'. J Afr Hist 15(3):457–577

Downes RM (1933) Tiv Tribe. The Government Printer, Kaduna

Downes RM (1971) Tiv religion. Ibadan University Press, Ibadan

Emberton JJ (n.d.) History of the Controversy Which Led to the Prohibition in 1927 of Exchange Marriage in the Tiv Tribe. MAKPROF 337, NAK, Kaduna

Evans-Pritchard E (1940) The Nuer of the Southern Sudan. In: Fortes M, Evans-Pritchard E (eds) African political systems. Oxford University Press, London, pp 272–296

Feasey GG (1926) From the District Officer i/c Munshi Division To The Senior Resident, Munshi Province, Makurdi (6/7/1926). MAKPROF 337, NAK, Kaduna

Feasey GG (1927a) Tiv Marriage Customs, (29/5/1927), MAKPROF 337. NAK, Kaduna

Feasey GG (1927b) Tiv Marriage Customs, (21/7/1927), SNP-17-19416. NAK, Kaduna

Héritier F (1981) L'exercice de la parenté. Gallimard, Paris

Lévi-Strauss C (1969) (1949) The elementary structures of Kinship, Beacon Press, Boston

Lovejoy PE, Hogendorn JS (1990) Revolutionary Mahdism and Resistance to Colonial Rule in the Sokoto Caliphate, 1905–6. J Afr Hist 31(2):217–244

MacBride DFH (1940) Tiv marriage rules, (18/6/1940). MAKPROF 337, NAK, Kaduna

Malherbe WA (1925) Munshi marriage customs. MAKPROF 337, NAK, Kaduna

Malherbe WA (1928) Munshi marriage question. MAKPROF 337, NAK, Kaduna

Middleton J, Tait D (1958) Tribes without rulers. Routledge, Kegan

Monk GL (1926) Notes of an Interview Between His Honour the Lieutenant-Governor, Northern Provinces, Mr. H.R. Palmer, C.M.G., C.B.E. and W.A. Malherbe, chairman, Dutch Reformed Church Mission at Makurdi on 14th July, 1926", CSO-26-3-26207/2, NAI, Ibadan; available in MAKPROF-337/18, NAK, Kaduna

Morgan W (1927) Marriage by Exchange, (28/7/1927), SNP-174916. NAK, Kaduna

Ortuño Aix JM (2004) Tar Vihi Yo: La tierra está arruinada. El desmoronamiento de la reciprocidad en la sociedad Tiv, Ph. D. diss., University of Barcelona (UB)

Ortuño Aix JM (2006) Derechos y deberes: el ideal de la reciprocidad en una sociedad africana. Studia Africana 17:53–64

Provincial Annual Report (1929) "Exchange Marriage" among the Munshi. MAKPROF-337 NAK, Kaduna

Terradas Saborit I (2019) La justicia más antigua. CSIC, Madrid

Tiv Central Council (1932) Tiv Council Meeting held at Gboko from 10th December–18th December 1932. CSO-26-3-28416, NAI, Ibadan

Tiv Central Council (1934) Tiv Central Council Meeting held at Gboko from 16th May–18th May 1934. CSO-26-3-28416, NAI, Ibadan

Tiv Central Council (1937) Minutes, 22nd February 1937. CSO-26-3-28416, NAI, Ibadan

Tylor EB (1889) On a method of investigating the development of institutions; applied laws of marriage and descent. J Royal Anth Inst 18:245–274

Law, Ethics and Religion

The Importance of Forgiveness in Contemporary Mauritania Diya

Marta Alonso Cabré

Abstract Like any composition, the diya, beyond being a simple payment, is the device that allows the reparation of the honor of the offended party in a homicide. Mandatory in case of involuntary manslaughter, it is at the mercy of the wish of the beneficiaries of the victim of a voluntary homicide. Indeed, the penalty provided in such a case is the talion, but the offended party may forgive the guilty party; In this case, the talion is automatically replaced by diya. Muslim law advises the victim's rights to forgive the voluntary homicide. We see, then, a first expression of the weight of forgiveness in the resolution of homicides in Muslim law. The second is intrinsic to the composition of the diya, which by definition is characterized by its two aspects: economic transfer between the parties and reconciliation after forgiveness. Although the official Mauritanian law includes diya, especially for not taking into account the ritual of forgiveness, the justiciable who have been the object of our study, the Mauritanian bīḍān, opt for an overlapping circuit in which the official law validates the acts customary.

1 Introduction

Moulay is originally from Rosso, is around 50 years old and works in one of the newspapers in Nouakchott. He is from the Idawalhaj (*zawāyā*) tribe on his father's side and the Wlād Beñuk (*ḥaṣān*) tribe on his mother's side.[1] When I ask him to introduce himself, he explains that he used to be from his mother's tribe and that now

[1]A common denominator among Mauritanian *bīḍān* (Arabic-speaking population) is the use of an Arabic dialectal variant called *ḥaṣāniya*. *Bīḍān* are traditionally split in three orders: (1) *ḥaṣān* or *arab*; (2) *zawāyā* or *tolba*; (3) *znaga*, *lahma* or *tlamid*, which correspond to slaves, freed people and artisans respectively. The first two groups, *ḥaṣān* and *zawāyā*, maintain the greatest degree of power in Mauritan Arab society. The name *znaga* is today in disuse, and slavery was officially abolished in 1981. Freed people and artisans are usually excluded from the exercise of power. All *bīḍān* individuals belong to a tribe, being part of the *ḥaṣān* or *zawāyā* orders.

M. Alonso Cabré (✉)
Department of Social Anthropology, University of Barcelona, Barcelona, Spain

R. Márquez Porras et al. (eds.), *Vindicatory Justice*, Ius Gentium: Comparative Perspectives on Law and Justice 93, https://doi.org/10.1007/978-3-030-79595-5_11

he is from his father's. Both have representation in Rosso. Moulay has been married twice, both times to women from the Idawalhaj tribe.

He has never caused a death, so he has not had to impose on the subjects of his tribe to collect any *diya*. However, he has participated in *diyāt* (singular: *diya*) caused by others. At the organizational meetings of their tribe, the elders distribute an annotated list in a notebook and each assistant writes the amount of money they can contribute.

Moulay says that all the *diyāt* that he remembers in which his tribe was involved were due to deaths caused by traffic accidents, accidents in which, it is explicitly stated, it is assumed that the perpetrator of the acts did not cause deliberately.

Moulay reiterates that his tribe does not usually accept the amount of the *diya*. A member of the Wlād Būsba killed a woman in a traffic accident. The victim was on the side of the road. A delegation from the offending party went to ask for forgiveness and to begin the negotiation to determine the *diya*. The rightful claimants of the woman, who had descendants in her charge, said that the accident was the result of divine will and did not accept any economic transaction.[2]

The reflections which I present are the result of field work carried out in Mauritania between 2009 and 2013, which gave rise to my doctoral thesis in social anthropology, *Shared Responsibility. The role of the diya arrangement in the legal resolution of traffic accidents in contemporary Mauritania* (2016).[3] My purpose in this chapter is to focus on the role of forgiveness in the *diya*. The argument which I will present comes from traffic accidents in contemporary Mauritania in which at least one party belongs to the *bīḍān* society, that is, to the Arabic-speaking population.

2 Generalities of the *Diya*

Let us begin by laying down the foundations of the definition of the *diya*. It is an arrangement based on two pillars: *reconciliation* between the parties and the *transaction* of a certain amount of property which is eventually delivered to the victim or their representatives due to homicide or damage to physical integrity. It is mandatory in cases of involuntary manslaughter and is subject to the decision of the victim or their rightful claimants in cases of voluntary aggression.

Etymologically, *diya* means 'that which is given as payment' and must be understood within the pre-Islamic context in which it originated, in an Arabia characterized by tribal organization, the lack of a political authority and a private

[2]See PNUD (2015).

[3]I took part in the fieldwork as a researcher for the project Estudio comparado sobre apropiaciones sociales y competencias de uso en centros urbanos de tres ciudades africanas (2011, Ref. CSO2009-12470).

justice system.[4] Even then, the *diya* was considered an alternative pacifying mechanism to revenge.

After the introduction of Islam in Arabia, the *lex talionis* or *qiṣāṣ* was applied, in which retaliation only concerned the life of the perpetrator of the crime.[5] The *diya* does not respond to an individual payment system or conciliation, but rather that of a *group*; prior to its institutionalization, the aggressor's entire tribe was required to participate in the payment. This system was not altered with the arrival of Islam; in fact, it was adopted and approved. So, in Muslim law, *fiqh*, the responsibility in cases of involuntary homicide is borne by the group. This is the only case in which the responsibility does not fall exclusively on the perpetrator of the act;[6] it is the exception to the norm of responsibility as an individual charge, which appears in the Koran (Sura 6, verse 164). This responsibility borne by an individual takes place in case the penalty of talion applies, for example, and coexists with group responsibility, which, as we have seen, is associated with the payment of the *diya*.

In the event that the *diya* is applied, the amount stipulated to be delivered to the victim or their rightful claimants varies according to the nature of the person killed or injured. The *diya* is often the transaction agreed between the tribes involved in the crime, so there is, on the one hand, the *diya* for an established amount, that of the classical texts, and, on the other hand, the *diya* whose amount is agreed upon. The four principles which Fustel de Coulanges established in relation to the arrangement of monetary composition based on the context of ancient Roman and Greek societies[7] are valid in our object of study:

1. A *judicial authority* is present in the procedure;
2. Agreement on the amount of the compensation is not the sole objective of the procedure;
3. The oath, which—in our context of study—materializes in the repetition of fixed oral phrases, has a remarkable role;
4. Compliance with the arrangement is required by the ethics of *reconciliation* rather than by the effectiveness of the legal system.

In relation to Coulanges' second point, it is important to reiterate that the *diya* is not only a payment, it is also a reparation of the offended party's honour. Indeed, the *diya* is an arrangement comparable to that of Roman law or to the *wergeld* of Germanic law, as Tyan (1960) points out. In all these arrangements, the reconciliation between the parties is as important as the material compensation to the offended party, the amount of compensation depends on which person has been offended, every individual belongs to a group, which will participate in the collection.

[4]See Ben Hounet (2010).

[5]For details, see Chelhod (1980), p. 125 and Hakeem et al. (2012), p. 14.

[6]See Khan and Khan (2006), p. 132.

[7]For more details, see Terradas Saborit (2008), pp. 200–201.

To sum up, *diya* is a pre-Islamic composition adopted by the Koran. It is applied in cases of involuntary, and sometimes voluntary, manslaughter and acts as a mechanism that cancels the possibility of revenge. In *diya*, as in other expressions of composition,

1. Reconciliation between the parties is as important as the material compensation to the offended party;
2. The amount of compensation depends on which person has been offended, considering the total *diya* due to the death of a free man;
3. Every individual belongs to a group, and if he is a man considered responsible, that is, able to work, he is obliged to participate in an eventual collection of *diya*.

3 Forgiveness in the *Diya*

The current legal school in Mauritania, the Maliki, categorizes crimes as voluntary and involuntary. This differentiation is important to an understanding of the function of forgiveness.[8] In no case can forgiveness be considered in reference to the *ḥudūd*[9] crimes established in the Qur'an. On the other hand, when crimes are punishable by *qiṣāṣ* or *diya*, the victim or their rightful claimants can forego the application of the punishment to the guilty party (*qiṣāṣ*) in exchange for receiving a pecuniary composition (*diya*), or forgo everything, including the *diya*. In the latter case, it is understood that the waiver concerns the economic transaction, but not the pardon under any circumstances (Table 1).

Before proceeding with forgiveness, and based on the previous table, I think it is important to point out that, as Hassan Afchar,[10] recalls, it is the responsibility of the judge to deal with issues related to the two great areas of law: the divine, or *ḥaqq Allah*, and the human, or *ḥaqq adami*. That said, *fiqh* encourages believers to forgive. Moreover, the one who pardons will receive a divine reward. Indeed, in the texts, *fiqh* recommends the prevalence of the *diya* over the *qiṣāṣ*, even in the only case in which revenge is accepted, that is, death or injuries resulting from an intentional action.

It is of utmost importance to reiterate that, although the economic transaction included in the *diya* can be pardoned, the same does not happen with reconciliation, or *ṣulḥ,*[11] which is obligatory. Otherwise, the possibility of revenge would be left open.

---

[8]The Arabic word for forgiveness is ‘afū (عفو). Currently, the term is translated as "forgiveness" or "amnesty" (Corriente 2005).

[9]*Ḥudūd* is the plural of *ḥadd* (حد) "sanction statutory by the Koran". It comes from the verb "apply the Koranic penalty" (Corriente 2005, p. 214).

[10]Afchar (1977), p. 102.

[11]*Ṣulḥ*, (صلح) "peace, (re)conciliation; settlement, agreement" (Corriente 2005, p. 664).

Table 1 Compilation of offences, penalties and their variation

Right	Offences	Punishments	Responsibility	Modification
ḥaqq Allah[a]	• Adultery • Fornication • Slander • Theft • Apostasy • Banditry • Consumption of wine • Rebellion	*Hudūd*: • Stoning • Exile • Prison • Crucifixion • Flagellation	Individual	No
ḥaqq adami[b]	• Intentional homicide • Wounds voluntarily reported	*Qiṣāṣ*	Individual	The victim or the rightful claimants can substitute the penalty for the pardon and/or the *diya*.
	• Involuntary manslaughter • Wounds voluntarily reported	*Diya*	Group	No
	• Minor offences not foreseen in the Koran or Sunna	*Ta'zīr*[c]	Group	No

[a]*ḥaqq Allah* (حق الله), "the law of God" (Corriente 2005, pp. 27, 251)
[b]*ḥaqq adami* (آدميحق), "human law" (Corriente 2005, pp. 10, 251)
[c]*Ta'zīr* (تعزير)"discipline, corrective discretionary, penalty less than". It comes from the root *'azar*, "rebuke, censor, scold" (Corriente 2005, p. 766)

By way of synthesis in regard to forgiveness, in the case of intentional homicide, the rightful claimants have the option of requesting the penalty of retaliation or of forgiving the offender, giving way to the *diya*. In case of involuntary manslaughter, there is no place for rejecting the *diya*.

In the sources mentioned above, the importance which Islam gives to forgiveness is clear. It is interesting to note that in the case that the rightful claimants of a victim of an intentional act pardon the culprit and, therefore, the *diya* comes into play, the arrangement is no different from the *diya* due to accidental homicide. According to Terradas Saborit,[12] this lack of differentiation is due to the fact that vindicatory justice is based on the damage suffered, that is, the results of the act. The theory does establish a difference—depending on whether or not it was an accident—in the way of paying the *diya*, that is, in the amount of apportionments and in the characteristics of the animals if these are the object of transaction, making it easier to pay the *diya* for accidental homicide than for intentional homicide.

[12]Terradas Saborit (2008), pp. 397, 403.

4 The *Diya* in the Mauritanian Interwoven Legal System

Within the Mauritanian framework I analyze, there are two socio-legal models in place: one inherited from France, which acts as official law, and one based on custom. *Shari'a* is influential in both models, although it is reinterpreted. In Mauritanian law, three principles are affirmed which ratify the theses elaborated by the fathers of legal sociology which characterize legal pluralism: (1) the state does not hold a monopoly on law; (2) law is not originally a rational production in the sense that it is not elaborated on discursively in writing; (3) the foundation of law is social cohesion rather than individual freedom. If one expression of law is institutional, the other is social; one corresponds to the "received" law and the other to the "inherent" law, but, following the recommendations of Françoise Ki-Zerbo,[13] in my text I will try to escape from the dual law-custom, modern-traditional analysis to focus on the observation of law actually experienced, which I will particularly highlight when presenting the legal itinerary which follows a traffic accident with personal injuries.

Some countries, such as Sudan, Iran and Pakistan, have incorporated the *diya* into their official legal systems. Such is the case of Mauritania, whose current Penal Code was enacted in 1983. Upon the country's independence, in 1960, under the presidency of Mokhtar Ould Daddah, a dual system of official courts was adopted. On the one hand, there were the courts of the cadis, Muslim judges in charge of civil, judicial or religious matters, while on the other, a dual chamber established the dualism between Muslim law and the law inherited from France. Muslim law, however, took centre stage in the 1980s when Mohamed Khouna Ould Haidallah became head of state. A process of Islamisation of positive law took place, comparable to those undertaken in Algeria and Egypt at the same time. So, in 1983, the current Penal Code was enacted, which provides for *qiṣāṣ* for intentional homicides and *diya* for accidental homicides. In 1985, *fiqh* was officially established as the only source of law in the country.

Now, going back to the presence of the *diya* in the Mauritanian Penal Code: far from fulfilling the basic points of the Muslim concept which concerns us, the "official" version of *diya* is more like compensation, since reconciliation between the parties is not a factor. It is not made right from the point of view of the offended party, but a universal measure is applied, and it is not the group responsibility which is taken into account, but that of the individual. Be that as it may, the presence of the *diya* in official Mauritanian law, as well as other concepts of *shari'a*, is symbolically very relevant. In the 1990s, Mauritania made efforts to try to gain some international credibility by entering into an ambiguous game in which a legal apparatus with *shari'a* affinities was given shelter, but in which it was taken for granted but not made explicit that the *ḥudūd* penalties – which, as we recall, were the penalties established in the Koran and which, theoretically, no human being can modify— would not apply. This lack of clarity in the application of the laws facilitates the country's adherence to international treaties with which it fails to comply, as

[13]Ki-Zerbo (1997), pp. 5, 9–11.

demonstrated on 24th December 2014, when a man accused of apostasy, Mohamed Ould Mkheiter, was sentenced to death.

Islam is ubiquitous in Mauritania, and often represents the common denominator of all citizens. It is an Islam which claims to be related juridically to malikism and theologically to Acharism, and which leaves room for mysticism through the brotherhoods. As Baudouin Dupret maintains[14] countries with a Muslim majority have generally endowed *shari'a* with a special status within the legal framework. This is the case, as we have seen, in Mauritania.

Although the presence of *shari'a* concepts can be explained by didactic-pedagogical justifications, as declared by workers of the Ministry of Justice, or to facilitate the religious life of Muslims,[15] in the Mauritanian case I believe that it influences both the low credibility of non-Muslim laws, which are perceived as exogenous, and a political desire to provide the country with a Muslim legal context which links it with the fact that it is the first official Islamic Republic.

For many colonised countries, Islam represented the concept underlying their fight against the West, a value which unifies the people. Many of those countries abandoned the standard of Islam once they had acquired independence. This is not exactly the case in Mauritania, which has maintained some of the precepts of *shari'a* in its official legal system. Mauritania is one of the Islamic states whose criminal and private contractual arrangements have been consolidated, and, in parallel, vindicatory justice has been maintained and legitimised.[16] The Mauritanian legal system is an example of mixed justice in which positive law coexists with *fiqh* or Muslim law.

5 When the *Diya* Enters the Scene in Mauritania

Below we will look at the procedure which is mostly adopted to solve traffic accidents and, in general, involuntary homicides in which the guilty party and the affected party customarily negotiate. It is important to remember that the blood dispute is not concluded until a reconciliation or an act of revenge has taken place.[17] Although it can be inferred from reading the procedure that it is a long one, in contemporary Mauritania it is usually quite fast. According to the information collected during my fieldwork, the procedure can be completed in about 5 days if there are no complications in the negotiations between the parties. In this sense, Michael J. Kelly (2010), p. 21, points out that in Muslim contexts, and especially in Arab Muslim contexts, where quick rewards or punishments are usually preferred, criminal justice systems tend to act in shorter time frames than in the West. However, history shows that this has not always been the case. Among the Bedouins of Israel

[14]Dupret (1997), pp. 21, 27–28.

[15]For more details see Peters (2006), p. 144.

[16]Afchar (1977), p. 84.

[17]See Ginat (1997), p. 21.

analyzed by Joseph Ginat,[18] for example, the process may take several years. In his work, the author presents a hypothesis which seems plausible to me. When the Bedouins' living system was nomadic, the tribe of the offending party moved their camp to a safe distance from that of the offended tribe during the time of negotiations, to mitigate the possibility of revenge. This relocation does not make sense in current contexts in which the tribe is sedentary and the economy which dominates is one which revolves around wages, which forces at least some members of the group to go to their workplace on a regular basis, a routine which increases the risk of possible revenge. This would have led to the resolution of homicides with some speed.

On the African continent, making a broad generalization, the state apparatus is both omnipresent and almost absent. In general, Mauritanians perceive administration as an obstacle to be dispensed with. Anyone who has had to deal with African administration is aware of the many annoyances involved: slowness, corruption, incomprehension, etc. To this we must add the predilection of the *bīḍān* population towards acting with discretion, both in legal and, for example, in labor issues, so that there is a popular saying, 'Support your business with concealment'.[19] However, there are litigations which go beyond discretion and end up in court.

In Mauritania, if two parties start negotiations based on custom, they often reach an agreement sooner or later. The occasions in which the parties do not even begin the negotiation process are the ones which mainly result in the casuistry of resolutions in the courts.

According to the Mauritanian model, in which we can properly speak of overlap, the resolution of the offence is carried out according to custom but with official recognition. I would like to emphasize again that the legal procedure which I present, which is obviously the result of the data obtained during the fieldwork, reflects the double nature of the arrangement: being both a *reconciliatory* action and a *financial* donation at the same time.[20]

The police intervene in the first step of the conventional legal procedure following a traffic accident with personal injuries: going to the scene and arresting the culprit. If the collision has occurred between two vehicles and the occupants of one of them have died, the driver of the other vehicle is stopped. If the deaths have resulted from an accident involving a single vehicle, the driver of the car is stopped. The authorities make a finding and apply preventative detention to the guilty party. Sometimes this action is justified by the lack of insurance taken out, although it should not be forgotten that this measure is also a way to protect the alleged culprit against revenge.

If both parties agree, the police authorities release the defendant, who remains under the responsibility of the representative of their tribe. The representative, or someone authorized by them, signs a document according to which the culprit is

[18]Ginat (1997), pp. 22, 25–26, 48.

[19]Mohamed (n.d.).

[20]Terradas Saborit (2008), pp. 196–197.

under their responsibility and committing to hand over the subject should the police request it. To carry out this release, the offended tribe must also give its agreement. If, on the other hand, the parties choose to resort to official justice, they go to the insurance company—as long as the vehicle of the culprit is insured—and then to the official justice system.

The head of the detainee's tribe then contacts the head of the deceased's tribe. This is how relationships begin to put the arrangement into effect. They exhibit their willingness to carry out a visit to make their apologies and to conduct negotiations in order to establish the amount of the *diya*. Subsequently, a delegation from the culprit's tribe goes to the place where the group representing the victim's tribe is located and makes their apologies. In their statements, my informants told me of the existence of an animal sacrifice offered by the guilty party and eaten in communion between the two parties. However, they spoke of it as an ancient practice, now extinct in Mauritania.

Regarding the agreed price, the informants usually refer to *diya* amounts of between 100,000 and 300,000 MRU, that is, between £2200 and £6700. The cases that fall outside that range are exceptional. All the informants said that although Mauritanian customary law once distinguished between the *diya* agreed on the death of a man and that related to the death of a woman, nowadays the gender of the deceased does not affect the amount of the *diya*. The method of payment has a role in negotiations. If it is effective and made in a single delivery, the offender's tribe may try to convince the offended party to reduce the amount.

The collection of the *diya* is surprisingly fast. This is due to the need to calm tensions after a homicide, to reduce any possibility of revenge, to facilitate coexistence.[21] The information regarding the method and amount of the individual financial contribution goes from the attendees of the meeting to all the subjects of *mukallaf* status, that is, responsible persons. They give their contribution to the person who has represented them in the meeting, who in turn donates it to the head of the tribe. The transaction is usually made in cash. However, sometimes it is carried out by bank transfer.

Although the legal texts stipulate that the *diya* based on a voluntary homicide must be paid immediately while the one following an involuntary homicide must be paid in three annual instalments, that specificity has not emerged in the interviews.

As we have mentioned above, the delivery of the *diya* does not always take place, but the elimination of this point does not exempt the previous ones. That is to say, after a traffic accident with personal injuries, a report is written and the defendant is arrested. The offending party asks for forgiveness from the offended party and the negotiations begin. It is usually the case that the offending party collects the *diya*, and at the time of carrying out the delivery, the offended party rejects it, either because there is a pact between tribes, or because the statutory relationship between the two tribes is very disparate. In the first case, if two tribes maintain a matrimonial alliance, that is, if a member of one can marry a member of the other, the transaction

[21]Terradas Saborit (2008), p. 193.

of the *diya* does not take place. If the agreement were paid, it would be an offence. In these cases, if a subject of the tribe dies as a result of a homicide committed by someone from a tribe with whom the matrimonial alliance is maintained, the agreement has no meaning, and it is the deceased's tribe that collects money for the rightful claimants of the victim. Anyway, the tribe of the guilty party goes to give their condolences to the victim's tribe. Note that in this context, in which the *diya* is not present, there is no reason to speak of offence, neither offended party nor offender.

The following narration explains how the process of agreement begins in the first visit of the offender's tribe to the offended party. On the second visit, the stipulated price of the *diya* is delivered.

> You have to go to see people, you have to say hello, you have to apologise, give your condolences, say "this is something which unfortunately has happened. . .". Words like that. Smoothly. And you finish and you promise to go a second time. He is sure that this will happen. He knows it the same as you do. The day you return he will receive his money, but he doesn't know if the next day he will have to pay it back to you. These are things which must be done calmly, seriously.[22]

Once the forgiveness and the economic delivery of the *diya* are resolved, the parties appear before the notary, who confers a document which attests to the agreement and automatically removes the possibility of the parties resorting to official justice to solve the case in question.

It is usual that after a traffic accident the parties involved utter the phrase *haḏa riyādat mūlānā*, "this is the will of God". While this association of accident with religious fatalism can be read as a way of transferring the demand for justice to the supernatural,[23] in Mauritania we must also associate it, ultimately, with the forgiveness involved with the transaction of the *diya*.

> We must also say that it is very comment that people, because this is also allowed, excuse the *diya*. I go to see him, I say 'we agree, one of ours killed one of yours, we are willing to pay the *diya*'. And he says, 'thank you, we don't want to take anything for this, we think that we should not enrich ourselves at the expense of our dead, especially since it is an accidental death'.[24]

In yet another case, the victim is a minor from a *zawāyā* tribe. I find it interesting to quote the informant's explanation, since it gives rein to the habit of the *zawāyā* tribes by excusing the payment of the *diya*, as well as the influence of the profile of the dead person. If the deceased has people under their charge, as we have seen, the money given as *diya* can be equated to an aid to those individuals who have been left without financial support. On the contrary, if the subject is a minor, the economic repercussions of their death is practically nil.

The forgiveness of the economic part of the agreement must also be associated with the proximity of the parties involved in the accident. Thus, grosso modo, the

---

[22]Interview recorded in February 2015. My translation.

[23]See Terradas Saborit (2008), p. 20.

[24]Interview with Guigh Ould Deh. Recorded in February 2015. Own translation.

closer they are, the smaller the amount, and the farther apart they are, the greater. Be that as it may, with the repayment a *link* is established between the two parties. If the two parties are consanguineous, there is no transaction at all.[25] Such is the case in which the two parties belong to the same tribe, or two tribes between which there is a pact to forgive the *diya*:

> This is an old story. They say there are tribes which used to be the same. Before, there were tribes who gave the *diya* together. If you have a problem, we pay with you. Well, now I believe that each tribe deals with their problem. But there is something which remains. Maybe if there are problems in the two tribes, they solve it without *diya*, normally. Like Idawalhaj and Beñuk, they can fix it without *diya* because they are the same.[26]

> It depends on the person who has been killed, it depends on the family. There are people who have been killed and who have not received *diya* [referring to the rightful claimants] because there were agreements between the tribes so that if something like this happens, it gets forgotten.[27]

Another explanation exempted in the rejection of the diya is the supposed attraction of bad luck after having accepted a diya.

> They say that if it comes today [. . .] mavi al baraka. . . there is no *baraka* [divine blessing]. There is no baraka. It's going to go quickly, it's going to end quickly.[28]

Pierre Carlier[29] points out that it is plausible that before the gesture of the murderer to pay the agreement, the rightful claimants of the offended party refuse to accept it, in order to have the legitimacy to take revenge. This is also noticed by Joseph Chelhod,[30] among the Bedouins of Jordan who do not accept the agreement for the deliberate death of a minor, in order to be able to take revenge. This is not what I have observed happening in Mauritania. Certainly, the rightful claimants of certain tribes have the habit of *forgiving* the *diya*, which is not the same as *rejecting*. And since the representatives of the culprit have ritually requested forgiveness from the offended party right after the death, the revenge is cancelled out. In fact, and according to the generalisation of Joseph Chelhod (1980), p. 127, revenge is not a usual practice in the Mauritanian urban context.

The conventional legal itinerary which follows an accident with the dead in which the parties are *bīḍān* attests to the overlap of the customary and official ways. After the accident, the culprit is arrested. Later they are usually released under the responsibility of a member of their tribe. Once the agreement takes place, that is to say, once the apology of the guilty party to the offended party has been presented and accepted and the agreed money has been delivered, a notary must record the execution of the pact to eliminate the possibility of recourse to official justice.

---

[25] Terradas Saborit (2008), p. 187.

[26] Interview with Moulay. Recorded in February 2015. Own translation.

[27] Interview with Lemrabot. Recorded in May 2012. Own translation.

[28] Interview with Moulay. Recorded in February 2015. Own translation.

[29] Cited in Hivernel (2004), p. 149.

[30] See Chelhod (1980), p. 136.

Currently in Mauritania, if the parties agree between them, the itinerary begins and ends in the official scope.

There are cases in which the offended party does not accept the delivery of the money, although they take this decision after having received a representation from the tribe of the guilty party and having accepted their excuses. On these occasions the rightful claimants understand that the death, since it is involuntary, has occurred because of divine desire and, therefore, there is no place to profit from it. However, sometimes there is a subsequent economic transfer, even if the parties do not call it "*diya*".

6 By Way of a Conclusion

In Mauritania, in cases of involuntary homicide, individuals can appeal to the official justice system or opt for customary justice. In both cases the *diya* intervenes. The degree of distrust in the first case is high. Added to this is not only the preference to act discreetly and the fact that the *bīḍān* informants prefer to know at each moment what will happen instead of paying a judge, but also the absence of the request to the offended party for the pardon of the guilty party in the official way and, therefore, the non-reconciliation between the parties.

Cases of involuntary manslaughter that end up in the courts are usually those which could not be resolved customarily and those in which the guilty party does not have an economic support group, as is the case for foreigners. Another hypothesis brings us closer to the explanation of Antonio Pigliaru,[31] who has posited that in the pastoral context of Sardinia individuals find security, both natural and legal, in their home and in their village. In that sense, a crime committed outside the village does not constitute an offence. On the same theme, we can hypothesize that a blood crime in which one of the two parties does not have neighborhood ties is not an offence, and that is why its resolution is not carried out within the group but in the courts.

A strong cause of the preference among *bīḍān* for a customary pact between tribes to the detriment of official justice is that in this case, the *diya* is reduced to an economic transaction, leaving aside the forgiveness. This hypothesis has been ratified by the informants, who have also indicated the discretion and the knowledge of the various steps to be taken in the official way when appearing in public before the courts. They have also cited the fact of being dispossessed of power and remaining subject to the decision of an external authority. However, I maintain that the absence of the request for forgiveness between the parties in the official way implies that the informants do not believe that the case has been resolved, since the crisis between the two tribes has not expired. The *diya* is a practice of reconciliation between the offending party and the offended party. For the reconciliation understood in the agreement of the *diya* to take place, far from being imposed, the *diya* has

[31] Cited in Terradas Saborit (2008).

to be accepted by both parties involved in the offence. Stripped of its ritualistic side, in which, as we shall see, forgiveness is fundamental, the *diya* is not effective in achieving reconciliation in its parts but is reduced to a mere economic transaction.

References

Afchar H (1977) The Muslim concept of law. In: The international Encyclopedia of comparative law. J.C.B. Mohr, The Hague

Ben Hounet Y (2010) La Diya (Prix Du Sang): Gestion Sociale de La Violence et Logiques Sacrificielles En Algérie (Sud-Oranais). Annales de la Fondation Fyssen 24:196–215

Chelhod J (1980) Équilibre et Parité Dans La Vengeance Du Sang Chez Les Bedouins de Jordanie. In: Verdier R (ed) La Vengeance. Études d'ethnologie, d'histoire et de Philosophie, vol 1. Éditions Cujas, Paris, pp 124–143

Corriente F (2005) Diccionario Avanzado Árabe. Herder, Barcelona

Dupret B (1997) Política, Religión y Derecho En El Mundo Árabe. In: Borràs A, Mernissi S (ed) El Islam Jurídico y Europa. Institut Català de la Mediterrània d'Estudis i Cooperació, Barcelona, pp. 21–43

Ginat J (1997) Blood revenge. Family honor, mediation, and outcasting. Sussex Academic Press, Brighton

Hakeem FB, Haberfeld MR, Verma A (2012) Policing muslim communities. Comparative International Context. Springer, Berlin

Hivernel J (2004) La Vengeance de Sang Dans Un Quartier d'Alep: Entre Justice Privée et Justice d'Etat. Droit et cultures. Revue internationale interdisciplinaire 48:147–166

Kelly M (2010) Islam & international criminal law: a brief (In) compatibility study. Pace Int Law Rev Online Companion 8:2–31

Khan AA, Khan TM (2006) Criminal law in Islam. In: Encyclopaedia of Islamic law. Pentagon Press, New Delhi

Ki-Zerbo F (1997) Les sources du droit chez les Diola du Sénégal. Logiques de transmission des richesses et des status chez les Diola du Oulouf (Casamance, Sénégal). Karthala, Paris

Ould Mohamed AK (n.d.) La Tentación Canaria de Los Mauritanos. Avalaible via DIALOG. http://www.alwifaq.es/TENTACION.pdf. Accessed 15 May 2019

Peters R (2006) Crime and punishment in Islamic Law theory and practice from the sixteenth to the twenty-first century. Cambridge University Press, Cambridge

PNUD (2015) Rapport National Sur Le Développement Humain 2015. Nouakchott

Terradas Saborit I (2008) Justicia Vindicatoria:De La Ofensa e Indefensión a La Imprecación y El Oráculo, La Vindicta y El Talión, La Ordalía y El Juramento, La Composición y La Reconciliación. CSIC, Madrid

Tyan (1960) Histoire de l'organisation judiciaire en pays d'Islam. Brill, Leiden

The Vindicatory Roots of Civil Sanctions

From Roman Law to E.U. Intellectual Property Law Via U.S. Punitive Damages Model

Carlotta de Menech and Giorgio Remotti

Abstract This Chapter split into two parts. The first part raises the general question, from a historical perspective (and following this book's general theoretical premise), whether there exists an original function of 'vindicatory justice' in the Italian civil liability system. The Chapter will analyze this issue also studying the role of punitive damages, whose acknowledgment has been recently admitted in the Italian legal system. The second part examines some specific rules of the Italian civil liability system presenting peculiar profiles with respect to 'traditional' ones, to assess whether the legislative construction of these rules may have been affected by the ancient function of 'restorative' revenge.

1 Introduction

In the modern continental legal system, the function of tort law is the compensation of the injured person for the losses he had suffered. This function is accomplished by condemning the wrongdoer to pay a sum of money when reparation in kind is impossible. The assessment of monetary award shall comply with the principle of *restitutio in integrum*, which requires to restore the victim to the position it would have been in had the loss-causing event not happened. By this remedy, the full loss—no less but also nothing more—shall be compensated.[1]

Carlotta De Menech *wrote* §§ 1, 2, 3, 4. Giorgio Remotti *wrote* § 5 (and sub-sections).

[1] See Merkeuns (2012), p. 13 ff. The continuing validity of the compensatory principle is confirmed by some recent acts of the European Union: see Art. 3 Dir 2014/104/EU and Art. 31 Rec 2013/386/ EU.

C. de Menech (✉)
Department of Law, University of Pavia, Pavia, Italy
e-mail: carlotta.demenech@unipv.it

G. Remotti
Department of Law, University of Urbino "Carlo Bo", Urbino, Italy
e-mail: giorgio.remotti@uniurb.it

R. Márquez Porras et al. (eds.), *Vindicatory Justice*, Ius Gentium: Comparative Perspectives on Law and Justice 93, https://doi.org/10.1007/978-3-030-79595-5_12

Penal elements are instead unrelated to European tort law. Damages cannot serve the goals of satisfying the injured person's feelings or punishing and deterring unlawful acts.

Such tasks typically belong to the criminal law. The State and its organs have a monopoly on the punishment of wrongdoers by imposing sanctions that can take the form of imprisonment or monetary fines.[2]

In principle, the Continental legal systems divide private law and criminal law strictly. Therefore, they appear antithetical to the idea of vindicatory justice.[3]

However, in some European systems, it is possible to find civil remedies with penal characteristics and vindicatory echo.

For instance, German case law shows that sometimes the assessment of compensatory damages is based on the seriousness of the offense or the nature of the defendant's wrongdoing, and regardless of the actual harm.[4] Moreover, Italian courts often do the same.[5]

Or, to take another example, civil legislation of some European countries contains rules which state that the author of especially reprehensible conduct can be convicted to pay to the victim a sum which is over and above what would be necessary to compensate the losses occurred.[6] Provisions like these are very numerous in Italian civil law.[7]

Such remedies are criminal in their function because they are aimed at punishing the wrongdoer and at deterring others from behaving similarly. Nevertheless, they are civil in their structure: indeed, the process should be established and led by the victim against the tortfeasor, and the judge can impose a monetary award for wrong, which consists of a civil obligation whose creditor is the plaintiff. This mixture of criminal and civil elements within a judicial procedure seems to evoke the model of vindicatory justice.

These contemporary civil sanctions and their links with vindicatory justice will be analyzed in the second part of this essay. But, before then, it could be useful to trace out the roots of our civil sanctions, starting from the Roman Law and going through punitive damages law.

---

[2]See BGH 4 June 1992 in NJW, 1992, II, 3096; Corte cost. 25 October 1989, n. 487.

[3]As Terradas Saborit (2015) p. 129 explains, human societies can be divided into two categories: in the first category, there is a distinction between civil and criminal law; in the second one, this distinction is absent. Vindicatory systems belong to this second category.

[4]See, for instance, BGH 15 November 1994, BGHZ 128, 1 (Caroline of Monaco).

[5]See § 4.

[6]See, for instance, Art. 79 (1) of Polish Law on copyright and related rights (of 4 February 1994).

[7]See §§ 5 ff.

2 Private Criminal Law: Origin and Decline

Before the late Republican Age, Roman law did not conceive a distinction between tort and crime and did not provide a punishment-based public enforcement system. According to the reconstruction delineated by some authors,[8] during the most ancient times, the punishment of civil torts was based on a system of private vengeance. The victim was allowed to self-help remedy by using force against the offender: in particular, the injured party could impose a corporal punishment against the tortfeasor or enslave him. No rules were governing that reaction so that the victim could instinctively act according to his sense of justice.

The fundamental transition from a revenge system to one based on the vindicatory justice concept occurred in the mid-fifth-century BC when the Twelve Tables were composed. Because of the introduction of the Twelve Tables, the old system of private vengeance changed to a system in which the victim could impose regulated sanctions against the offender. Namely, the injured party could inflict the same form of damage he had suffered (*lex talionis*), or seize the wrongdoer (*manus iniectio*); and, alternatively, the victim could accept to receive a sum of money from the wrongdoer instead of taking vengeance. The Twelve Tables contained three provisions for personal injuries. About the *delictum* of *membrum ruptum*, XII Tab. 8.2 stated that the victim could inflict the same injury upon the wrongdoer, or reach a monetary settlement with him. Regarding the *delictum* of *os fractum*, XII Tab. 8.3 obliged the offender to pay a specific sum of money (fixed as 300 asses for a free man, 150 asses for a slave) to the injured party. Finally, Tab. 8.4 established for the *delictum* of *iniuria*, which means "affront of feelings" or "outrage", a penalty of 25 asses. Then there were some different rules about theft. In the case of *furtum manifestum*, XII Tab. 8.12-14 provided that the victim could lawfully kill the thief or, in other circumstances, the thief was first scourged and then assigned to the victim of the theft (*addiction*). For *furtum nec manifestum* XII Tab. 8.16 recognized only a pecuniary penalty for double the value of the stolen thing.

The pecuniary nature of the obligations arising from some *delicta* does not mean that they served as remedies to compensate for the harm resulting from the offense. The monetary award represented a *poena* for the wrongdoer and solace for hurt feelings in the eyes of the victim, serving to satisfy her desire for revenge and therefore avoid a violent reaction. Consistently, the monetary penalties were not commensurate with the actual extent of losses caused by the tort but were established by the lawgivers in fixed amounts likely determined in consideration of the seriousness of the offense.[9]

During the Roman Republic, there was a new stage in the process towards the separation between civil and criminal law. The victim's right to inflict corporal penalties (*talio*, *addictio*) against the wrongdoer disappeared, and victims were only

---

[8]See, in particular, Albanese (1970), p. 55 ff. It must be pointed out that written sources do not support this thesis.

[9]See, e.g., Cursi (2016), pp. 597–599.

allowed to recover a monetary award—still called *poena*—from the offenders as the result of their wrongful acts. This change occurred as a result of the introduction of the formulary procedure: indeed, in its typical structure, the *formula* necessarily ended with a *condemnatio pecuniaria.*

Although the possibility of corporal vengeance had disappeared, the monetary award retained his previous meaning of punishment of the offense and solace for hurt feelings, remaining a means by which to achieve a peaceful settlement of the dispute. Savigny explains that, in the course of Republican age, the so-called *actiones poenales* were aimed, not at awarding compensation for actual loss, but rather at preventing illegal acts of private revenge and at punishing civil offenses.[10] Consistently with these purposes, the author of *delicta* could be sued by the victim and convicted to pay her a sanction, which took the form of many fold reparation or of equitable sum: for example, the author of *furtum manifestum* should pay a sum of fourfold the value of the thing stolen; instead, the penalty for *iniuria* should be commensurate by a judge to whatever is *bonum et aequum*. It must also be pointed out that the *obligationes ex delicto* had several characteristics consistent with their punitive function.[11] First, they arose from torts individually regulated by *ius civile* or *ius pretorium* (namely typical torts). Second, the fundamental criterion of imputation was fraud. Third, the rules governing the *actiones poenales* relied on a criminal rationale. So, the *actio poenalis* could be cumulatively brought with *action reipersecutoria*; the victim was entitled to recover the full amount of *poena* from each joint tortfeasor; finally, the *action poenalis* was strictly personal and therefore could not be brought against wrongdoer's heirs.

Roman Law took a step away from the paradigm of vindicatory justice when *lex Aquilia* was enacted, probably in the third century BC. *Lex Aquilia* introduced the delict of *damnum iniuria datum*, namely the specific case in which somebody inflicts material harm to another, acting physically and wrongfully. For this delict, *lex Aquilia* provided that the wrongdoer should pay the victim the highest value that the damaged thing had had in the previous year (or, in certain conditions, in the nearest 30 days). This sanction was quite similar to the modern compensatory damages since it was related—not to a multiple but—to the single value of the thing. In this respect, the remedy introduced by *lex Aquilia* might seem to look like a civil remedy.

However, the *lex* prescribed to take into account (not the value that the thing had at the time of the wrongdoing) but the highest value that it had before then. According to this rule, the amount of Aquilian remedy could still be higher than the amount that would have resulted from strictly applying the principle of *restitutio in integrum.* Therefore, the Aquilian action retained a penalty value. For this reason, Gaius's Institutes classified it as a mixed action, meaning it was reipersecutory and penal at the same time.

---

[10] von Savigny (1915), pp. 277–279.

[11] Talamanca (2001), pp. 319–321.

The central development towards the modern law of civil remedies is linked to the development of the doctrine of *ius commune* and the principles of *natural law*.[12] In the context of the renewed study of Roman Law, after more than half a millennium of neglect, the nature of Aquilian action changed. It became a remedy suitable for prosecuting every damaging and guilty behavior and based on the principle of compensation of current losses. Because of its more comprehensive configuration, the Aquilian remedy replaced all the other delictual actions, which thereby disappeared. Moreover, the interpretative activity of intermediate age jurists leads to the disappearance of the penal features that had characterized the *actio ex lege Aquilia* (and the other *actiones poenales*) in the past.[13]

The doctrine of *ius commune* exercised widespread influence over the lawgivers who drafted contemporary civil codes. Indeed, most of them contain one provision that links compensatory damages to a general category of wrong and provides the compensation principle. To give some examples, article 1804 (new 1240) of French *code civil* states that "*tout fait de l'homme, qui cause à autrui un dommage, oblige celui par la faute duquel il est arrive à le réparer*"; article 1902 of Spanish *codigo civil* states that "*el que por acciòon u omission causa daño a otro, interviniendo culpa o negligencia, está obligado a reparar el daño causado*"; and article 2043 of Italian *codice civile* states that "*qualunque fatto doloso o colposo che cagiona ad altri danno ingiusto, obbliga colui che ha commesso il fatto a risarcire il danno*".

Such provisions show a clear division between civil liability and penal or vindicatory purposes. On the other hand, modern continental legislation qualifies the most serious offenses as crimes and provides for them a punishment-based public enforcement system, which is the result of a historical development begun during the late Roman age.[14]

3 Private Criminal Remedies in Contemporary Legislation: Punitive Damages

While civil-law systems seem to have left "hybrid" remedies, the most common-law countries still encompass a remedy whose rationales lie in both tort and crime. It is the remedy of exemplary damages (as they are called in England), or punitive damages (as they are called in the United States). Such damages could be described as sums awarded above and alongside the compensatory damages, and aimed at punishing the defendant for the severe misconduct. In England, exemplary damages are authorized only in the following circumstances: (i) oppressive, arbitrary, or unconstitutional action by the servants of the government; (ii) where the defendant's conduct has been aimed at making a profit which may well exceed the compensation

[12]See Rotondi (1916), pp. 248 ss.

[13]Ibid., pp. 250–251.

[14]Albanese (1970), pp. 65–69.

payable to the plaintiff; (iii) where exemplary damages are expressly authorized by a statute.[15] Instead, the United States has not taken such a confined and categorical approach to award punitive damages. Then punitive damages are usually awarded for acts committed with fraud, malice, gross negligence, or wanton disregard for the rights of another.[16]

The law of punitive damages has some features with the paradigm of vindicatory justice. First, the injured party plays a fundamental role in the legal proceeding: the victim plays the role of a private prosecutor, who starts and leads the action for punitive damages. Secondly, the offense suffered by the victim is strictly connected to an offense suffered by the community at large. Most conduct justifying punitive damages affect not only an individual interest but also public interest (for instance, environmental integrity, human health, consumers' safety). Third, the amount of sanction should reflect the seriousness of the offense, not the losses occurred and should be proportionate to the gravity of the tort.

The law of punitive damages, on the other hand, has some characteristics, which contrast with the vindicatory rationale. First, punitive damages can be awarded in cases of strict liability, which especially occurs in the context of product liability.[17] Secondly, some judgments allow vicarious liability for punitive damages and assess those damages against someone other than the person who committed the wrong-doing (for instance, the principal for the wrongful act committed by one of its agents within the scope of employment).[18] Finally, some courts have stated that it is not against the public policy to allow the liability insurer of a civil defendant to pay the punitive damages, assessed against that defendant, under the terms of the insurance policy, which protects him.[19]

Since the features of punitive damages do not clarify whether such damages deal with the paradigm of vindicatory justice, it is necessary to examine their cultural background.

It is highly likely that the origins of punitive damages are linked to the model of vindicatory justice. The first explicit articulation of the doctrine of exemplary damages appears in two English cases of the late eighteenth century: Wilkes v. Wood[20] and Huckle v. Money.[21] However, it is well established that the plaintiff could recover exemplary damages even before, in the context of the jury trial. From its classical form, the jury was a group of twelve local people who knew the facts of the case and came to the *veredicta*. Among the jury's tasks, was the assessment of

[15]Rookes v. Barnard, 1 All. ER 367 (Court of Appeal, 1993).

[16]See Kircher and Wiseman (2012), p. 212 ff.

[17]Owen (1974), p. 1291.

[18]Mendoza v. McDonald's Corp., 222 Ariz. 139, 213 P.3d 288 (Ct. App. Div. 1 2009); Flood ex rel. Oakley v. Holzwarth, 182 S.W.3d 673 (Mo. Ct. App. S.D. 2005).

[19]Lazenby v. Universal Underwriters Ins. Co., 214 Tenn. 639, 383 S.W.2d 1 (1964); Shelter Mut. Ins. Co. v. Dale, 914 So. 2d. 698, 699 (Miss. 2005).

[20]Wilkes v. Wood, 2 Wils KB 203, 95 Eng Rep 766 (1763).

[21]Huckle v. Money, 2 Wils KB 205, 95 Eng Rep 768 (1763).

damages. In doing that, jurors considered not only the actual harm suffered but also the nature of the tort itself and the contumelious disregard for another's rights. According to Paul Mitchell, this trend reveals that the Roman concept of *iniuria* was received into English common law.[22] Then, other scholars have traced out the historical lineage that might have led to this influence.[23] In summary, they have pointed out that all Thirteenth-Century Statutes provided multiple damages in some instances of wrongdoing; and have shown that those provisions were drafted following the example of Roman *actiones poenales.*

While exemplary damages formerly served (only) as solace for the injured feelings of the plaintiff and his sense of outrage over the conduct of the defendant, during the subsequent development of punitive damages, the rationale underlying them has become more complex. In particular, this occurred in the United States, where punitive damages arose as a result of the legal transplant[24] of the English model of exemplary damages. In the US, the punitive damages model has achieved great success because it has proved to be useful in pursuing many different functions, further than the original one. First of all, it is a common ground that punitive damages are aimed at deterring the defendant and others from engaging in wrongful conduct in the future. Moreover, punitive damages could serve to restore the losses that the plaintiff cannot prove and, therefore, the judge cannot take into account in assessing the compensatory damages. Finally, such damages are justified for providing the successful plaintiff with a means of offsetting litigation expenses which are not recoverable in civil litigation. The nuanced variety of functions now served by punitive damages explains why such damages also have non-revenge features: so, for example, the compensatory effects explain why insurance coverage for punitive damages is usually authorized.

4 Private Criminal Remedy in Contemporary Italian Case Law: Punitive Damages?

Although solace of hurt feelings is no longer the exclusive purpose of punitive damages, this model represents the vehicle through which the idea of vindicatory justice has returned into the Continental legal systems.[25]

After having adopted a purely compensatory approach to the tort law, civilian jurists have realized that, with the principle of *restitutio in integrum*, the amount of compensatory damages often results in inadequate with the seriousness of the infringement. Particularly, that occurs when the wrongdoer's conduct is highly reprehensible—e.g., wanton and willfull—but doesn't cause a significant harm; or

[22]Mitchell (2005), pp. 65–67.

[23]Taliadoros (2016), pp. 273 ff.

[24]Watson (1974), passim.

[25]See Wiegand (1991), p. 246.

when the defendant's act affects a personality right again without causing egregious losses; or, finally, when the profits wrongfully obtained by the injurer overcome the damages to be paid.

In such circumstances, some Italian judges award an amount to the victim, which is very similar to punitive damages, even if not expressly so called. For instance, a few years ago, Italian *Corte di Cassazione* condemned the Ministry of Transport and the Ministry of Defense to pay a very high sum to a victim of a severe infringement. The victim was a boy who had declared he was homosexual during the visit for military service and had been consequently convened by the motorization office for the revision of his driving license.[26] The court saw in the dissemination and the misuse of information relating to sexual orientation a grave infringement of the personality rights of privacy and dignity. The court further held that such conducts justify an award of damages more significant than the losses actually suffered and precisely proved by the victim.

It can be argued that some Italian judges introduce sanctions that equal punitive damages for the protection of personality rights. Behind this practice of the courts in assessing the damages, we can see a legal transplant of the U.S. model operated by our jurisprudence.

Can Italian courts legally do this? Indeed they cannot in reason of the principle of legality according to which conduct does not constitute a crime, and punishment is forbidden unless laid down before in the law (*nullum crimen, nulla poena sine previa lege*).[27] That is, there should be a legislative provision that states for a specific wrongdoing a particular punitive sanction. Which article 2043 and article 2059 of Italian civil code do not. Indeed, these norms describe the tort in general terms and establish the sanction of (pure) compensatory damages. Instead, in Italian private law, some provisions expressly state that the victim of particular infringement is allowed to recover a money sanction based on parameters (e.g., the gain the injurer ha made, the malice of the wrongdoer) which deviate from the ordinary principle of *restitution in integrum*: such provisions will be analyzed in the second part of this paper.

The limits mentioned above on the imposition of civil penalties have been set by a recent decision issued by the *Sezioni Unite* of *Corte di Cassazione*.[28] The court was called upon to decide whether a foreign judgment awarding punitive damages could be recognized and executed in Italy and therefore (according to article 64 of the l. n. 218/1995) if the punitive damages are in contrast with Italian public policy. In ruling on this issue, the court argued that punitive damages are not radically different from the Italian tort law. The main difference consists in the fact that while the American

[26]Corte di Cassazione, 22 January 2015, n. 1126. See also Corte di Cassazione, 25 October 2002, n. 15103.

[27]See Art. 23 and Art. 25 of Italian Constitution.

[28]Corte di Cassazione, sez. un., 5 July 2017, n. 16601. The same view seems to prevail in the legal doctrine: see, in this sense, Castronovo (2008), p. 331; Ponzanelli (2008), p. 28 ; Busnelli (2013), p. 246.

judges can create new figures of punitive damages, the Italian judges can only impose civil money sanctions if authorized by specific legislative provisions.

Although the *Sezioni Unite* expressed this authoritative opinion, some subsequent decisions again apply Art. 2043 or Art. 2059 assessing damages without a strict proportion to the caused loss and based on criteria suitable to reflect the seriousness of the unlawful behavior.[29]

The persistent jurisprudential trend shows that the border between civil and criminal law is not as well defined as we usually believe. Evidently, in the view of Italian judges, civil remedies are suitable for fulfilling the aims of punishment and satisfying the victim's desire for justice. Indeed, the payment of an amount higher than the losses occurred serves to make the offender poorer and, at the same time, the victim richer.

Behind this jurisprudential trend we could see a reminiscence of ancient *obligationes poenales ex delicto*.

However, this possible historical origin does not make legitimate the punitive damages awarded in the application of article 2043 or article 2059. By imposing such convictions, the judges claim the power to select the conduct worthy of punishment and to decide the amount of the sanction in total freedom. This discretionary power seems to collide with the principles of legality, certainty, and predictability of penalties that govern the modern Italian legal system.

5 Figures in the Italian Law Echoing a "Vindicatory Justice" Dimension

In the second part of this essay, it's useful to examine some legislative provisions of the Italian legal system, in which it seems possible to hear the "echo" of the dimension of a "vindicatory justice." Indeed, in the Italian legal system, no one figure falls certainly within the logic of vindicatory justice. Hence the choice to use the term "echo" is not dictated by stylistic reason, wants to recall the metaphor of an ancient sound that can still be heard amid other sounds. In other words, in the Italian civil liability system, it's possible to find some norms that set up a dispute settlement mechanism, for many profiles, similar to the notion of "vindicatory justice",[30] although this can never be considered the only purpose to which these norms are directed. If we look at the most modern civil remedies, we notice that most of them appear multi-functional. In fact, these modern remedies frequently could combine restorative, reparatory, retributive, and also punitive functions. This hybrid dimension determines uncertainty in the interpretation—and the application—of that

[29]See Corte di Cassazione, ord. 14 February 2019, n. 4316; Tribunale Milano 29 August 2018; Tribunale Bergamo, ord. 30 March 2018.

[30]See Terradas Saborit (2008), passim. And see also Id. (2015), pp. 131–133.

provisions by judges and stimulating doctrinal debates about their correct dogmatic classification.

However, among these figures, there are several examples that reveal traits that can somehow represent an echo of the primitive remedy of vindicatory justice. Finding these rules wasn't very difficult. This simplicity derives by this fact: the same clues that allow us to affirm a possible vindicatory origin of a civil liability rule are those that betray the "strictly compensatory dimension".[31] This is the reason why we can bring these figures out of the typical civil liability system, since they replace the compensatory model with the remuneration model, closer to the logic of reconciliation that characterizes the "Vindicatory Justice". It's impossible, here, to examine all the provisions present in the Italian legal system, where we can see profiles that seem to suggest a vindicatory genesis, in this work we decided to limit the area of investigation to the examination of three particularly perspicuous rules.

Specifically, we will analyze: firstly, the third paragraph of article 96 of the Code of Civil Procedure (after this abbreviated in c.p.c.), a norm which establishes a sanction for those who have undertaken or resisted in a jury-trial without a due reason. Secondly, the article 12 of the Law of the 8th of February 1948 (from now on called "Press Law"), a rule which establishes a sanction for those who have committed defamation in the press (libel cases). Thirdly and lastly, the third paragraph of article 125 of the Legislative Decree of the 10th of February 2005, n. 30 ("Italian Patent Code", after this abbreviated in c.p.i.), which provides the mandatory transfer of a sum of money to the victim of a counterfeit, other than compensation for damage.

5.1 *The Third Paragraph of Article 96 of the Italian Code of Civil Procedure*

The first figure on which it's necessary to fix our focus is one provided under the third paragraph of the art. 96 c.p.c. (added by art. 45, of the Law of 18th of June, 2009, n. 69), according to which, "in any case, when pronouncing on expenses according to art. 91, the judge, even ex officio, may also order the losing party to pay, in favor of the counterparty, a sum equitably determined".[32]

Article 96 c.p.c. belongs to the category of the so-called "provision without species facti". These norms don't contain statements that describe the specific situations in which they must be applied. Typically, the legislator adopts this standard drafting technique when it intends to assert a pre-eminent value. In these cases, the legislator does not take care of tracing the usual scheme for drawing up the rule of law. In fact, the usual structure of a rule is composed of the abstract and

[31] See the decision of Corte di Cassazione of the 19th of January 2007, n. 1183.

[32] See Granelli (2013), pp. 1762–1766.; Rizzo (2018), pp. 1823–1825; Navarretta (2019), pp. 21–22.

precise description of a given factual hypothesis, and the correlative forecast of its juridical treatment. In particular, in revising the art. 96 c.p.c., the legislator of the reform acted essentially driven by the scope to promote the proper functioning and efficiency of justice; and has entrusted to the generic debut engraved "in any case" the task of identifying the "species facti" to which the legal effect is linked, this provision limiting itself to the description of the remedial consequence. However, alongside the function of improving the efficiency of justice, another objective seems to be perceived: the norm tries to recompose the social quite, disturbed by the undue attempt of a subject of the community to curb damage to another subject of the same community through the jury trial (in other words an affront).[33]

Faced with the doubts left by the legal formula regarding the prerequisites of the innovative power of condemnation of the judge, literature and judges have tried to attribute a more limited meaning to those few words.[34] This activity finalized to completing the literal tenor of the last paragraph of the art. 96 c.p.c. has led to a vast majority, albeit not unanimous, solution: this solution is that among the constitutive facts of the case to which the remedy is referred to verbatim provided, there is an unlawful procedural attitude and, on the other hand, there is not necessarily damage.[35] Precisely—drawing inspiration from the first two paragraphs of the art. 96—it's believed that the sentence to the payment of an amount equitable determined in favor of the counterparty can be officially pronounced by the judge, where it results that the losing party has acted or resisted with bad faith or serious fault (argued by 1st paragraph of the Article 96); or if it is established that he has imprudently promoted the execution of a precautionary measure, transcribed a judicial request or registered a legal mortgage, or started or completed the forced execution (argued by 2nd paragraph of art. 96). In all these behaviors, we can see, something similar to an affront.[36]

Furthermore, also concerning art. 96, par. 3, c.p.c., that the sentence to the payment of an amount determined equitably can undoubtedly coexist with the sentence to pay damages, whenever a concrete and proven harm in the counterpart sphere has arisen from the unlawful procedural behavior of the losing party. The legislator expressly authorizes this accumulation, using the adverb "likewise" within the text of the provision. That's allows to affirm that through this additional sum recognized to the victim, the offense is repaired, and revenge is extinguished.

---

[33]On the notion of affront see Terradas Saborit (2015), pp. 133–135.

[34]See Dalla Massara (2011), pp. 55–56. Brenda (2013), pp. 1885–1892. And see also Fiengo (2016), p. 117.

[35]See Giordano (2010), p. 437.

[36]Giordano (2010), pp. 437–445; according to this thesis the case to which the power of judicial conviction is linked should instead be found outside of art. 96 c.p.c. and, precisely, would be identified with the intentional or even merely culpable violation of the duty to behave according to the loyalty and probity enshrined in art. 88 c.p.c., while it would prescind from the existence of a damage. In jurisprudence see: Tribunale Bari of the 28th of April 2011. In: Foro italiano (2011), I, 2171-2175; and Tribunale Torino, ord. Of the 16th of October 2010. In: Giurisprudenza di merito (2011), pp. 2701–2705.

Thus come to light those clues from which the echo of the model of vindicatory justice emerges. Precisely, as in the remedies that reduce revenge in a dispute resolution model, also for the art. 96 c.p.c., we can find: the offense suffered by the society at large, which consists both in the cost that undue jury trial determines for the community, and in the attempt to alter the quiet of the community with these unjustified jury trial; according to a remunerative and non-restorative perspective, the technique of commensuration of the sum is not related to the damage suffered, but proportionate to the offense; and at last, this sum must be paid in favor of the victim. Through art. 96 c.p.c., therefore, the injured party receives power and recognition by becoming the protagonist legitimized by the whole community and by this judicial procedure, which ends up translating into a legally recognized right.

5.2 *Article 12 of Italian Press Law*

A second figure that we can analyze is the article12 of the Italian Press Law, which gives rise to the victim's right to demand a sum commensurate with the gravity of the offense and the diffusion of the printed matter as a result of the crime consisting in defamation in the press; right that is entirely independent, therefore, from the ascertainment of a patrimonial or non-patrimonial damage suffered. If the detrimental consequences further result from the injurious behavior of the reputation, the same provision verbatim gives the injured party the power to request—in addition to the reparation—compensation for damages under article 185 of the Italian Penal Code.

That the damage does not become an integral element of the case on which the legal effect of the monetary reparation depends on the postponement made at the beginning of art. 12 to the criminally relevant fact of defamation in the press; it's, in particular, the crime of libel typed by art. 595 of the Penal Code aggravated by the fact that the offense of the reputation of others occurred by the press (argued by article 13 of Press Law). It's considered that among the constituent elements of the crime are: the conduct, the event, the causal link, the intent, but not the damage; as a result, strictly speaking, the financial reparation also disregards the existence of any prejudice.[37]

So, also in this figure, we can hear the echo of a model of "vindicatory justice". In this case, the affront, which provokes a feeling of revenge, finds a model of reconciliation. In fact, we can also see in this norm typical characteristics of the model of "vindicatory justice". First, the injured party plays a fundamental role in the legal proceeding. Second, the offense suffered by society at large. Third, the sum of punitive damages should reflect the seriousness of the offense and should be proportionate to the gravity of the tort.

[37]In this sense see (ex plurimis) the decision of the 7th of January of 2016 of Tribunale Salerno.

5.3 The Third Paragraph of Article 125 of the Italian Patent Code

Now, we can analyze a very general remedy that concerns the field of intellectual property, which has always represented an authentic testing ground. I refer to the general remedy of the reversal of profits provided for by paragraph 3 of article 125 c. p.i.

The dogmatic qualification of the provision in question raised a debate in doctrine, while jurisprudence was silent until recently, when the Court of Turin, in a case of violation of a trademark right, wondered about the possible return of the provision under art. 125 par. 3 c.p.i. within the civil liability system, and by this way, re-reading the theses of those who pointed out that the remedy was part of the compensation model.[38] If I see clearly, the thesis finds little support in doctrine today.[39] Indeed, before the introduction of the provision in question, no one voice emphasized that the Aquilian model has proved to be the most suitable vessel, in the instrument of civil protection to ensure the protection of new rights, and indeed the very possibility to affirm its juridical relevance, but this is not enough to frame the art. 125 par. 3 c.p.i. among the civil liability remedies.

The irreducibility of the remedy under art. 125 par. 3 c.p.i. the civil liability system can easily be demonstrated by analyzing the effects and functions of this provision. With regard to the effects, as mentioned above, the rule requires the return of an enrichment regardless of the damage. Echoing a form of retribution in which the traits of vengeful justice begin to be seen. The damage does not constitute an element subject to evaluation and thus not even that horizon, which is capable of marking the quantitative limit of the service—therefore not compensation, but precisely—restitution. The right holder has the right to obtain the reversion of the profits made by the infringer even when he is not using the right violated and not, even when—this is an important point—could not have used it. It is the offense that dominates the scene, not the damage.

According to an opinion of the doctrine, however, the reversal of profits could represent the compensable damage in its peculiar conformation of damage caused by a competitive illicit.[40] enrichment achieved by the person responsible for a competitive crime detects to realize the compensation protection that belongs to the injured party. This aspect of the norm reveals a function of standardization of the compensation under the heading of the lost profit that would bring into a discussion—also—the possible compensatory nature of the remedy provided by art. 125 par. 3 c.p.-i. However, the thesis is here inapplicable, given that the reversion referred to in paragraph 3 of the art. 125 operates regardless of the demonstration of damage, that is both when the damage is inferior or non-existent, and when the loss suffered

[38] For this thesis see Galli (2012), p. 109.

[39] See Pardolesi (2015), pp. 145-148.

[40] See Floridia (2012), pp. 5-6.

exceeds the profit realized by the offender, as among other things, he correctly pointed out the Court of Turin in the sentence of the 21st of June 2018.[41]

In literature observes that calculating the loss of earnings means basing the compensation on a hypothetical judgment on the amount of sales that the right holder could not make or could not make with profit margins that would have been legitimately expected without the infringement while calculating the profits to be returned is a transaction firmly anchored to the historical reality and the capacity of management of the own company by the author of the violation.[42] In other words, compensation—even when a presumption of damage exists, as happens, for example, under art. 2600 par. 3 of the Italian Civil Code [43]—always looks at the sphere of the injured, while the reversal always aims at the sphere of the injurer, thus disregarding the limit of the compensation that, however, informs the system of civil responsibility. This structural difference between the remedy in question and the compensatory one prevents the subsumption of the former in the latter. But there is more.

Refers to the function, it must be pointed out that the most authentic aim of civil responsibility is to restore the loss caused in terms of perfect equivalence. In other words, the damage is the horizon of the compensation, because the measure of the effect of the liability depends exclusively by the entity of the fact that determines it. This means that the most authentic function of civil liability is to restore a lost unjustly realized in the victim's legal sphere. And, as is known, "unjustly" means that the injury has passed a double judgment, namely: that the injured interest is worthy of protection and therefore the damaging fact "contra ius"; and that this harmful act is not "skimmed" by a deserving interest of the injuring party, namely that the damaging fact is—also—not legal.

About the reversion of profits, no double judgment is required. The only element request by art. 125 par. 3 c.p.i. it's a historical fact of the violation of an intellectual property right, to nothing detecting any exemptions. The structural diversity reveals the different function. Doctrine observed that the restitution is directed to guarantee to the owner of an injured right the peaceful enjoyment of the competitive advantage deriving from the exclusive right.[44]

These are—the main—reasons that demonstrate a structural and functional diversity that prevents adhering to the thesis for which the reversal of profits can be reduced to the discipline of compensation. As highlighted by the Court of Turin, the provision of art. 125 par. 3 c.p.i., cannot, therefore, qualify as a compensation penalty.

---

[41]See the decision of Tribunale di Torino of the 21st of June 2018. In: Il diritto industrial (2019) 406-417.

[42]See Sirena (2005), pp. 256-258; and see also Beuthien and Wasmann (1997), p. 255.

[43]See third paragraph of art. 2600 of the Italian civil code, under which "Having ascertained the competitive acts, guilt is presumed".

[44]See Ricolfi (2004), pp. 41-42; and see also Frassi (2000), pp. 93-95.

Also, in this figure, therefore, as in the first one examined in art. 12 of the Press Law, we hear the echoes of the vindictive paradigm: first, the injured party plays a fundamental role in the legal proceeding; secondly, the offense suffered by the society at large; thirdly, the sum of punitive damages should reflect the seriousness of the offense, and should be proportionate to the gravity of the tort.

List of Cases

(a) Italy

Corte costituzionale, 25 October 1989, n. 487
Corte di Cassazione, 25 October 2002, n. 15103
Corte di Cassazione, 9 January 2007, n. 1183
Corte di Cassazione, 22 January 2015, n. 1126
Corte di Cassazione, sez. un., 5 July 2017, n. 16601
Corte di Cassazione, ord. 14 February 2019, n. 4316
Tribunale di Salerno 7 January 2016
Tribunale di Bari 28 April 2011
Tribunale di Torino, ord. 16 October 2010
Tribunale di Bergamo, ord. 30 March 2018
Tribunale di Milano 29 August 2018
Tribunale di Torino 21 June 2018

(b) Germany

BGH 4 June 1992 in NJW, 1992, II, 3096
BGH 15 November 1994, BGHZ 128, 1

(c) England

Wilkes v. Wood, 2 Wils KB 203, 95 Eng Rep 766 (1763)
Huckle v. Money, 2 Wils KB 205, 95 Eng Rep 768 (1763)
Rookes v. Barnard, 1 All. ER 367 (Court of Appeal, 1993)

(d) United States

Lazenby v. Universal Underwriters Ins. Co., 214 Tenn. 639, 383 S.W.2d 1 (1964)
Flood ex rel. Oakley v. Holzwarth, 182 S.W.3d 673 (Mo. Ct. App. S.D. 2005)
Shelter Mut. Ins. Co. v. Dale, 914 So. 2d. 698, 699 (Miss. 2005)
Mendoza v. McDonald's Corp., 222 Ariz. 139, 213 P.3d 288 (Ct. App. Div. 1 2009)

References

Albanese B (1970) Illecito civile (storia). In: Enciclopedia del diritto, vol XX. Giuffrè, Milano, pp 50–90

Beuthien V, Wasmann D (1997) Zur Herausgabe des Verletzergewinns bei Verstößen gegen das Markengesetz. GRUR:255–280

Brenda R (2013) L'art. 96, comma 3, c.p.c. ed i punitive damages. Considerazioni in margine ad un caso giudiziario. Giurisprudenza italiana 8–9:1885–1893

Busnelli FD (2013) Deterrenza, responsabilità civile, fatto illecito, danni punitivi. In: Busnelli FD e Patti S (eds) Danno e responsabilità civile, 3rd edn. Giappichelli, Torino, pp 27–46

Castronovo C (2008) Del non risarcibile aquiliano: danno meramente patrimoniale, c.d. perdita di chance, danni punitivi, danno c.d. esistenziale. Europa e diritto privato 2:310–330

Cursi MF (2016) The scope and function of civil wrongs in roman society. In: Du Plessis PJ, Ando C, Tuori K (eds) The Oxford handbook of roman law and society. OUP, Oxford, pp 596–605

Dalla Massara T (2011) Terzo comma dell'art. 96 cod. proc. civ.: quando, quanto e perché? Nuova giurisprudenza civile commentata 2:55–72

Fiengo G (2016) La responsabilità processuale aggravata ai sensi dell'art. 96, comma 3, c.p.-c. Corriere giuridico 1:115–123

Floridia G (2012) Risarcimento del danno e riversione degli utili nella disciplina della proprietà industriale. Il diritto industriale 1:5–11

Frassi P (2000) I danni patrimoniali. Dal lucro cessante al danno emergente. In: Ubertazzi LC (ed) Annali Italiani del Diritto d'Autore. Giuffrè, Milano, pp 93–125

Galli C (2012) Risarcimento del danno e retroversione degli utili: le diverse voci di danno. Il diritto industriale 1:109–120

Giordano R (2010), Brevi note sulla nuova responsabilità processuale c.d. aggravata. Giurisprudenza di merito:437–445

Granelli C (2013) In tema di «danni punitivi». Responsabilità civile e previdenza 6:1762–1773

Kircher J, Wiseman C (2012) Punitive damages: law and practice. WEST, Eagan

Merkeuns L (2012) The punitive damages debate in continental Europe: food for though. In: Merkeuns L (ed) The power of punitive damages. Is missing Europe? Intersentia, Cambridge, pp 13–30

Mitchell P (2005) The making of the modern law of defamation. Hart, Oxford

Navarretta E (2019) Il risarcimento in forma specifica e il dibattito sui danni punitivi tra effettività, prevenzione e deterrenza. Responsabilità civile e previdenza 1:5–26

Owen D (1974) Punitive damages in products liability litigation. Mich Law Rev 74:1258–1371

Pardolesi P (2015) An Italian way to disgorgement on profits? In: Hondius E, Janssen A (eds) Disgorgement of profits: gain-based remedies through the world. Springer, Dordrecht, pp 139–170

Ponzanelli G (2008) I danni punitivi. Nuova giurisprudenza civile commenata 2:20–40

Ricolfi M (2004) Dal diritto interno al diritto europeo: la parabola del risarcimento del danno da contraffazione del marchio. In: Sena G et al (eds) Il risarcimento del danno da illecito concorrenziale e da lesione della proprietà intellettuale. Giuffrè, Milano, pp 39–78

Rizzo N (2018) Le funzioni della responsabilità civile tra concettualizzazioni e regole operative. Responsabilità civile e previdenza 6:1811–1825

Rotondi G (1916) Dalla "Lex Aquilia" all'art. 1151 cod. civ. (Ricerche storico-dogmatiche). Rivista di diritto commerciale 1:236–295

Sirena P (2005) La restituzione del profitto ingiustificato (nel diritto industriale italiano). In: Auteri P, Mangini V, Ubertazzi L (eds) Studi in onore di Gerhard Schricker. Giuffrè, Milano, pp 256–274

Talamanca M (2001) Elementi di diritto privato romano. Giuffrè, Milano

Taliadoros J (2016) The roots of punitive damages at common law: a longer history. Cleveland State Law Rev 64:251–302

Terradas Saborit I (2008) Justicia vindicatoria: De la ofensa e indefensión a la imprecación y el oráculo, la vindicta y el talión, la ordalía y el juramento, la composición y la reconciliación. Consejo Superior de Investigaciones Cientificas, Madrid

Terradas Saborit I (2015) La vendetta nell'ordinamento vendicatorio. In: Di Lucia P, Mancini L (eds) La giustizia vendicatoria. Edizioni Ets, Pisa, pp 129–143

von Savigny FC (1915) Le obbligazioni, vol. II, Italian translation by Pacchioni G, Utet, Torino

Watson A (1974) Legal transplants: an approach to comparative law. Scottish Academic Press, Edinburgh

Wiegand W (1991) The reception of American law in Europe. Am J Comp Law 39:229–248

From the Duty to Redeem the Spilled Blood to the Duty to Redeem Themselves (Repentance)

The Tension Between Customs, Institution and Ideals in the Jewish Normative Experience

Cosimo Nicolini Coen

Abstract In this paper we shall argue the thesis according to which the Jewish normative experience shows a certain degree of friction between at least three levels of obligations. First, the ancient customary obligation to avenge the murdered kin's blood; we will label this level as customary. Second, the Jewish law's prescriptions aiming to project into an institutional framework this kind of duty, as well as to reframe it accordingly to the necessity of a fair trial; we will label this level as institutional. Third, the Jewish law's interdiction to a private vengeance as well as the obligation to repentance for one owns past actions; we will label this level as metaphysical. In that way, we shall outline some main theoretical points, starting from the proximity of the second level of obligation—institutional one—to some aspects of Terradas Saborit's paradigm. We shall then focus on the etherogeneity of the Jewish normative world, namely on the tension between its different levels: the opposite poles of customary and metaphysical obligations and the intermediate region of the institutional obligations. Albeit these differences we shall recognize the centrality of the concept of 'duty' as key feature of the Jewish normative experience. On this ground, and with particular attention to the obligation on repentance, we shall draw a theoretical consideration, through Levinas, about the concept of obligation: its conditions of possibility and its relevance beyond the Jewish experience.

God saw what they did, how they were turning back from their evil ways.

I'm thankful to doctor Riccardo Mazzola for inviting me to write about this topic and to investigate it in more depth at Oñati Seminar (2019), and to professor Paolo Di Lucia, whose teaching was essential to me. Over the space of a year I discussed the topic of the paper with professor Anna Callow, who kindly agreed to present part of it at Oñati Seminar, taking the critical remarks into account. For the references to Terradas which follow I am therefore grateful to her.

C. Nicolini Coen (✉)
Department of Jewish Philosophy, Bar Ilan University, Ramat Gan, Tel Aviv, Israel

R. Márquez Porras et al. (eds.), *Vindicatory Justice*, Ius Gentium: Comparative Perspectives on Law and Justice 93, https://doi.org/10.1007/978-3-030-79595-5_13

> And God renounced the punishment He had planned to bring upon them, and did not carry it out.—*Jonah 3: 10,* Ritual Reading of Yom Kippur, The Day of Atonement

> Et d'abord, tout le monde a des devoirs, moi compris, moi surtout, puisque le devoir, exprimant l'inachèvement infini de l'être moral, est avant tout appel et vocation.—Vladimir Jankélévitch, *Le paradoxe de la morale*, 1989

1 The Jewish Experience of Duty: The Passing into Law of a Practice (Blood Revenge) or the Codification of a Metaphysical Ideal (Repentance of Criminals)?

In this article, developing the model of vindicatory justice formulated by Terradas, we will attempt to argue that the experience of the law in Judaism (where in juridical and religious dimensions intersect) gives such preeminence to obligation or duty that it is possible to detect a transition between two prescriptive poles. From one extreme, where the body of legislation acknowledges the customary practice of the local population (blood revenge), to another, where the body of legislation, in the name of certain ideals, imposes increasingly demanding duties, concerning repentance and forgiveness, framed in accordance with written and oral principles formulated by the Torah.[1] In between these two extremes we find an institution—blood revenge exacted by the victim's next of kin on the basis of a court verdict—which appears to correspond to the criteria of the model of vindicatory justice (Terradas Saborit, 2008), as we will set out in the following paragraphs. Here are the phases of the transition between these two extremes: (1) the passing into law of the customary duty to avenge the blood of a murdered kinsman; (2) reformulation of this duty within an institutional framework, (3) (negative) duty not to bear a grudge and not to exact revenge; (4) duty to show repentance and to accept (given a set of conditions) the repentance of others, including that of the criminal. These latter two duties lead to phenomena such as exhortation or prayer for the criminal's repentance, dealt with in the conclusion of this contribution, which provides a final theoretical account (citing Levinas) of the concept of duty in its broader meaning (Table 1).

1. *Goel ha-dam*: Spontaneous practice, rooted in the customs of the population, shared in terms of the latter's collective intentionality, aimed at controlling intersubjective relationships.
2. *Neqamah*: Constitution of an institutional practice which, on one hand, re-elaborates elements of the pre-existing spontaneous practice and, on the other, binds it to an institutional context—correlated precept of establishing courts (*Deuteronomy; 16, 18*)
3. *Lo tiqqom*: Ban on exacting revenge and bearing grudges (*Levitico; 19, 18*) combined with duty to "love thy neighbour" (*Leviticus; 19, 18*).

[1]This second case would seem to be close to the *Grundnorm* model of a static-material nature delineated by Kelsen (1934), Italian edition (2000).

Table 1 Jewish revenge: names and concepts

Name	Phenomenon	Deontic statute	Principles and values
1. Goel ha-dam (blood avenger)	Social custom acknowledged by the law	Duty, falling to the victim's next of kin, to avenge blood	Sanctity of blood (*Genesis*; 1, 6)
2. Neqamah (justice) Nb, the Hebrew word could mean also "revenge", cf. § 4. 1	Legal reformulation of the social custom	Said duty is only exercised within a judiciary framework (presence of a third party, judge, *Targum Onkelos Genesis; 9, 6*)	Sanctity of blood reinterpreted on the basis of the principle which states that every man is made in God's image (*Genesis*; 1, 27)
3. Lo tiqqom (you shall not exact revenge, you shall not bear a grudge)	Intersecting juridical and religious spheres	(Negative) duty to not exact private revenge	Piety and mercy *raḥamim, ḥesed,* (*Psalms;* 103, 4)
4. Teshuvà (repentance)	Legal sphere of religions (or moral) experience	(Positive) duty to show repentance and accept others' repentance; correlated exhortation (prayer) for the repentance of the criminals	*Ibidem*

4. *Teshuvà*: Duty to show repentance (conversion), correlated duty to acknowledge—dependent on certain conditions—the repentance of others; exhortation to criminals to repent (*Talmud Bavli, Berakot 10a*). Here we come across a value dimension antithetical to spontaneous practice.

Therefore, if, in point 1., we find traces of a spontaneous practice, according to W. R. Smith Lectures on the Religion of the Semites (London, 1889), then, in point 2., we find some salient features of the model of vindicatory justice. Specifically, there is the idea of justice as fitting recognition of a wrong suffered and the collocation of the instinctive move to retaliate within an institutionalised system, having at its centre the figure of a judge, where the injured parties—the victim's next of kin—play an active role in implementing the verdict. However, we should question ourselves as to what phenomenon lies intrinsic to the duties introduced in points 3. and 4. A dimension of duty which, articulated on the basis of the principles stated in the Torah, demands an out-and-out reconversion—high significance of the word Teshuvà—of the individual, in terms of his actions as well as his intentionality. This aspect, clearly identifiable in Maimonide's comment on banning one's neighbour from bearing a grudge, leads (not chronologically) both to an understanding of the exhortation, contained in the Talmud, to redeem criminals, and, specularly, to a return to that transition mentioned above: from a body of legislation as a regulator of pre-existing practice, to a body of legislation enacted to shape not merely new actions but, in addition, a new and different subjectivity.

2 The Handling of Blood Shedding: Between Custom and Law

2.1 *Custom: The Blood Avenger*

Following in the footsteps of anthropologist W.R. Smith it can be noted how the so-called "law of blood revenge", named in the bible as "blood avenging", was widespread practice not just amongst Middle Eastern populations.[2] The practice of blood avenging would appear to respond to a physiological need to right a wrong, to an instinct for reparation.[3] It would, therefore, seem correct to detect in it a spontaneous form of social organisation which predates the establishment, in oral and written form, of any institutional reality.[4] This paragraph investigates the transition from the spontaneous practice of "blood avenging" to the institutional practice—sanctioned by the sources and therefore by Jewish law—of the handling of blood shedding as an act which comes under the jurisdiction of a given and recognised (transcendent or immanent) authority.[5] How does this shift come about? To answer these questions we need, first and foremost, to identify some of those moments in biblical-rabbinical literature[6] where we find both the shift from a description of the spontaneous practice of "blood avenging" to one of the institutional practice of the handling of blood shedding and an explanation of those precepts which establish that new social reality[7] within which the spontaneous practice of "blood avenging" becomes illicit while, on the contrary, a precise method of handling blood shedding (*neqamah)* is established. The descriptive and prescriptive linguistic levels, although discernible to a later analytical study are, when they first appear in the sources, often intertwined. A salient element of the language of Jewish sources is indeed, the hendiadys of rule and narration, of *halakah* and *aggadah.*[8] While this hendiadys,

---

[2]"The law of blood-revenge [. . .] is the basis of the tribal system", e "the law of Israel is the law of every well-ordered ancient community", Smith (1889–1894), pp. 72 and 55.

[3]Nussbaum identifies in such a desire for retaliation a "profoundly human [. . .] instinct", Nussbaum (2016), Italian edition (2017), pp. 62–63.

[4]"But can there be a law without juridical propositions? The answer to the question must be yes because society is older than juridical propositions (. . .). In the period of the so-called prehistory of law there were no courts as yet; disputes were either resolved in a friendly fashion, by means of compromises, or ended with blood vendettas", Ehrlich in: Conte et al. (1913 [2013]), pp. 51–55.

[5]This distinction between spontaneous social phenomenon and legally constituted social phenomena may be analysed, as we will see, in the light of Kelsen's notions regarding subjective meaning (or self-interpretation) and objective meaning of the social act, Kelsen (1934), Italian edition (2000), pp. 49–50.

[6]From the point of view of Tradition the two teachings – written biblical and oral rabbinical – cannot be distinguished on the basis of chronological criteria and indeed written teachings are joined by a common thread to oral teachings, Banon (1987).

[7]On this theme, and for relative bibliographical references related to the theme of performatives within the sphere of the law, see Amselek (2012–2013), p. 273.

[8]See Bialik (1917).

according to Robert Cover, is a constant in the universe of law, it is, nevertheless, true that a prominent aspect of Jewish narration is its central reference to the transcendent, God.[9] The shift from spontaneous to institutional practice is enabled by the emergence of a third, authoritative, figure in addition to the parties (the next of kin of the murder victim and the murderer). This third figure is modelled on God and subsequently seen in authoritative figures (Moses, the judges), whose role is ultimately given legitimacy by God. We can isolate some phases in this transition:

1. The attribution to a God—self-attribution according to biblical narration—of the authority to handle blood shedding. This attribution can be seen in the episode of the murder of Cain at the hand of his brother Abel;
2. The attribution, on the part of God, of the authority to handle the blood shedding (*neqamah*) to Moses, and therefore to the judges, or rather to the courts. This attribution can be found in the biblical verses, as well as in Onkelos's Aramaic translation-comment of the verse of *Genesis* 9, 6 (Onkelos, 110; 1911), that announce the shift of jurisdictional power from God to Moses and from them to chosen men. As we have stated we can trace in this shift various points of convergence with the model of vindicatory justice: first of all, the formulation within an institutional framework of the practice of blood avenging.

2.2 *The Shift from Custom to Law: God and the Judges as Institutional Framework*

In *Genesis 4*, 8–15 we read:

> And Cain said unto the Lord: "My punishment is greater than I can bear. [...] and I shall be a fugitive and a vagabond in the earth; and it shall come to pass, that every one that findeth me shall slay me".
>
> And the Lord said unto him, Therefore whosoever slayeth Cain, vengeance shall be taken on him sevenfold. And the Lord set a mark upon Cain, lest any finding him should kill him.

From a reading of this passage we can deduce the existence of the social phenomenon of blood avenging as a spontaneous practice or a custom, whose *ratio* is acknowledged in the biblical text. Yet God, in claiming as his any power over Cain, refuses to allow anyone who might approach him, recognising him as the murderer, the chance to independently avenge blood. An authoritative source, or rather (leaving aside the narrative figures it is expressed in) a prescriptive sphere emerges that positions itself on a higher plane than spontaneous need. It is within this sphere that the decision is taken how to handle the blood shedding and if, as happens in the Cain episode, this operation should be handled magnanimously.[10] The proposition being "And the Lord set a mark upon Cain, lest any finding him should

[9] See Cover (1983).

[10] On the concept of grace and goodness [*ḥesed*], see the final paragraph of the paper.

kill him". The distinctive mark seems to play a genuine performative role, allowing the sphere of Ought, represented by God, to be impressed on the spontaneity of custom. This mark, by virtue of the authoritative power of the Lord, of whom it is a tangible trace, indeed neutralises the practice of blood avenging on the part of private individuals. The exile inflicted by the God-judge is represented as *neqamah* (a practice established on an authoritative basis).[11]

In *Exodus 18*, 13–22 we read:

> Next day, Moses sat as magistrate among the people, while the people stood about Moses from morning until evening. But when Moses' father-in-law saw how much he had to do for the people, he said, "What is this thing that you are doing to the people? Why do you act alone, while all the people stand about you from morning until evening?" Moses replied to his father-in-law, "It is because the people come to me to inquire of God. When they have a dispute, it comes before me, and I decide between one person and another, and I make known the laws and teachings of God." But Moses' father-in-law said to him, "The thing you are doing is not right; you will surely wear yourself out, and these people as well. For the task is too heavy for you; you cannot do it alone.
>
> Now listen to me. I will give you counsel, and God be with you! You represent the people before God: you bring the disputes before God, and enjoin upon them the laws and the teachings, and make known to them the way they are to go and the practices they are to follow. You shall also seek out from among all the people capable men who fear God, trustworthy men who spurn ill-gotten gain. Set these over them as chiefs of thousands, hundreds, fifties, and tens, and let them judge the people at all times. Have them bring every major dispute to you, but let them decide every minor dispute themselves. Make it easier for yourself by letting them share the burden with you.

In this passage we encounter a system of delegating power—promulgated by the Transcendent, bequeathed by Moses and ending with the judges. Within this system, if the prime and sole legislator is God, jurisdictional power is awarded the task, by interpretation and deliberation, of applying the received laws and of producing laws that are in compliance with the principles contained in the precedents.[12] These aspects merit further study. Here we are interested in understanding how the bible excerpt attests to the creation of that particular sphere of social behaviour constituted by the juridical universe. It is within this specific sphere of power and action that the spontaneous practice of blood avenging is substituted with the institutional practice of the handling of blood shedding, or rather with the practice of "rendering justice" (*neqamah*).[13]

---

[11]And he who wished to shed the blood of Cain autonomously, in agreement with spontaneous practice would in turn be subject to *neqamah*, or punishment according to justice on the part of God-judge. Likewise, God asserts his exclusive authority by taking it upon himself to avenge blood in *Deuteronomy 32*, 43.

[12]See Ferrari (2012), pp. 174 and 184–187. The theme of the relation between divine and human authority in Jewish law is complex, see Bali et al. (2010) and Fisch (2016).

[13]An analogous process can be found in classical Greece, drawing on the myth of Erinyes, Nussbaum (2016), Italian edition (2017), pp. 15 and 204 ff.

2.3 Law: Blood Avenging as Institutional Practice

> Who so sheddeth mans blood, by man – on the basis of witnesses and according to the judges' sentence – shall his blood be shed: for in the image of God made he man.[14]

In Onkelos's propositions we can detect the shift, to use the language of Hans Kelsen, between self-interpretation of the social act and its objective interpretation. If the practice of blood avenging on the part of the private individual is, in terms of both the deed and intentionality of those who carry it out, identical to that of the handling of blood shedding on the part of an authority, the difference is, as we can see, the institutional setting.[15] Or, rather, the presence of a law (the Torah) that attributes power to an institution (Tribunal) and validates its acts.[16] In the spontaneous practice of blood avenging it is the murder victim's next of kin who seeks to strike the culprit, while in the institutional practice established by Jewish law the identification of the culprit takes place within the context of a court and through witnesses. As in Kelsen's famous example—which counterposed the execution of a tyrant by a secret organisation and the execution of a condemned man following sentencing by a competent authority—here too the act, that which Kelsen calls "the external aspect" is, in and of itself, the same but its meaning changes. Now, in the wake of the establishment of a system of legislation, there is a hiatus between the meaning of an act carried out by private individuals—which has become unlawful—and the act legitimised within the context of the court.[17] However, there is still a trace of the former spontaneous practice in that those who are given the task of carrying out the sentence are still kinsmen of the murder victim.[18]

3 Blood Avenging and the Cities of Refuge

A further example of the establishment of a new institutional framework for handling blood shedding—or, if one prefers, reparative justice—is seemingly represented by the cities of refuge. On one hand, these are designed to protect those guilty of manslaughter from the fury of the "blood avenger" or the victim's next of kin while,

[14]See *Targum Onkelos Genesis* 9, 6.

[15]See Anscombe (1958).

[16]See Kelsen (1934), Italian edition (2000), pp. 49–52.

[17]We might also ask ourselves, to echo J. R. Searle, if we can distinguish here between social act and institutional act. The case seems to resemble that of the case of "war" treated by Searle (1995), Italian edition (2006), pp. 103–104, in so far as the act of shedding the murderers' blood is, as we have widely seen, an act that has its roots in pre-institutional collective practice and intentionality and yet, as in the case of armed conflict, once this act is disciplined by institutional power, thus creating a division between what is unlawful (blood avenging) and lawful (justice), we are dealing with something that resembles an institutional act, since here too it is perspicuous that "x equals y in z"—the act of killing is equal to justice within the context of a verdict delivered by a presiding court.

[18]See Levi Della Torre (2003); Nussbaum (2016), Italian edition (2017), pp. 249 ff.

on the other, they contribute towards the reformulation within an institutional framework—that is, one which foresees judges and a court—of the practice of blood avenging. In *Exodus 21*, 12–14 we find:

> He that smiteth a man, so that he die, shall be surely put to death. And if a man lie not in wait, but God deliver him into his hand; then I will appoint thee a place whither he shall flee.

We are, perhaps, in the presence of a situation of compromise between a former custom and an institutionalised form of justice. Consistent with the shift from spontaneous practice to institutional and juridical practice, noted thanks to Onkelos's translation, here too the power of *go'el ha-dam* is eroded, or anyway limited, starting with the juridical act intended to establish whether it be a question of wilful murder or manslaughter. Between the murderer and the *go'el ha-dam* other figures are therefore interposed: the elders, the "assembly", presumably those "judges and officers" cited in *Deuteronomy* 16:18. They discipline the activity of the *go'el* preventing him from acting on his own initiative and delegating to him the task of executing their verdict.

4 From the Duty to Redeem Blood to the Duty to Repent

4.1 One Word, Two Meanings

Once the figure of the judge has been established, those taking the law into their own hands "take revenge" (*naqam*), in the modern sense of the term, therefore committing a violation. The archetypal biblical figure embodying the perils of justice being dispensed by the injured party is Lemech, one of the patriarchs named in the genealogies of *Genesis.*[19] We have seen how the shift, ushered in by repeated decrees in biblical and rabbinical sources, from spontaneous practice or "blood avenging" to institutional practice or the handling of blood shedding by means of justice [*neqamah*] leads to a divergence, in terms of meaning, between what is sanctioned as unlawful i.e. the private individual's avenging of blood and what is sanctioned as lawful i.e. justice [*neqamah*] served in an institutional context. This latter meting out of justice, as we were saying, resembles the model of vindicatory justice. From our point of view, as hinted, this divergence is revealed in Kelsen's distinction between a self-interpretation and the objective meaning of the social act.[20] We can see this hiatus in the ban on vendettas and grudges:

[19]*Genesis 4*, 23–24.

[20]Indeed, those who, following the birth of the institutional sphere of the courts and hence of administrative justice [*neqamah*], were to persist in the private practice of blood avenging, might conceive of their own act as being equivalent to what would have happened after sentencing. From this perspective one could point out that an analogous principle is in force in both the private and the institutional act: retaliation in the first case and retribution in the second, the difference between the two being merely one of appearance. See Nussbaum (2016), Italian edition (2017), pp. 33–37, 42–47; p. 250 ss; pp. 260–262; p. 271.

> Thou shalt not avenge, nor bear any grudge against the children of thy people, but thou shalt love thy neighbour as thyself: I am the Lord.[21]

What is particularly interesting is that the same word *naqam* which, within the framework of the sources here analysed, designates the handling of blood shedding in a context in which there is an authoritative third party (God or the judges), simultaneously designates, in the way the ban is worded, the private and individual act of exacting justice. This semantic proximity is no coincidence since, as we have observed, the distinction rests on the level of attribution of sense, or meaning, and not on the level of the externality of the act—which remains identical. This linguistic phenomenon which, in time, is progressively radicalised to the point of breaking down the root *nun, qof, mem* into the single semantic field of 'vendetta', enables us to better understand the distinction between the externality of the act (its merely factual aspect), its self-interpretation (or intention of the agent) and its objective interpretation (derived from a law that acts as a "qualification scheme").[22] The ban on vendettas and grudges confirms the hiatus between self-interpretation and objective interpretation in so far as it signals how the act that is not recognised as justice (*neqamah*) (to the extent that it is committed outside the institutional framework) is now, in terms of the law, unlawful and morally reprehensible.

4.2 The Ban on Vendettas and Grudges: The Norm as an Ethopoetic Device

In the decree of *Leviticus* 19, 18 the ban on a man taking the law into his own hands is followed by the ban on bearing grudges. Correlated to this is the obligation to "love thy neighbour".[23] Here we witness a major phenomenon of the universe of Jewish laws and philosophy—although it belongs exclusively to neither—which is the intrusion, so to speak, of the law in the perception, in the sentiments and in the inner life of the individual himself. This leads to the acknowledgment of the centrality of the emotional dimension of the inner life, and the desire to incorporate it within the prescriptive sphere while, simultaneously, envisaging a dimension wherein emotivity, impulses and outbursts are gradually replaced by duty.[24] It should be noted how, by means of the subordination of the emotive dimension to the prescriptive dimension, Jewish law aims not only to manage social dynamics, or rather intersubjective relationships, but also to build and fashion an inner life centred on the plane of Ought, thereby delineating something we might define as

---

[21] *Leviticus*; 19, 18.

[22] See Kelsen (1934), Italian edition (2000), p. 50.

[23] For an analysis of the meaning of the command—precept—to 'love', Giuliani (2013), pp. 10–19. On how to understand the noun, and relative concept, of "neighbour", Cohen (1919), Italian edition (1994), pp. 252 and 557.

[24] See Nussbaum (2016), Italian edition (2000), pp. 104–106.

ethopoetic.[25] Here acting conditionally on, and in compliance with, a law will also entail educating one's own perception, orientating one's own sentiments and not just one's own behaviours, on the basis of the correlated ethical ideal.[26] This latter aspect clearly emerges in the explanation provided by Maimonides of the passage from *Leviticus* cited below:

> He who takes vengeance of his fellow transgresses the negative commandment: 'Thou shalt not avenge' (*Leviticus*; 19, 18), and although whipping is not applied, it is considered a very great evil. It is comely for man to overlook things in worldly affairs because to those who are wise everything is vain and foolish and not worthy of vengeance.[27]

Thus in banning an individual from taking justice into his own hands we may detect both a general aim to preserve the unity of the community to which one belongs and a specific ethopoetic aim to form individuals free of emotions such as grudges which are damaging to their relations with others.[28] However, in our view, this ethopoetic aim extends beyond the pragmatic purpose of community unity to embrace an ideal—*eidos*—of justice and magnanimity. An ideal which, in the lexis of Jewish philosophy, is defined as *qedušah*, or distinction or sanctity, and *raḥamim*, or clemency or love. The fact that Maimonides explains the ban on vendettas and grudges by deliberately drawing not on a case of murder but on a minor breach, linked to ordinary everyday life, heads in this direction. It is not simply a question of managing the criminal exception but of regulating, disciplining and "sanctifying" (elevating) the apparently marginal detail, act.[29]

4.3 Decrees, Exhortations, Ideals: The Duty of Forgiveness and the Ideal of Magnanimity

The sources of Jewish law—written *Torah* and Talamudic literature—comprise a complex web of texts where decrees in the strict sense are accompanied by controversies, minority opinions, exhortations, prayers and decisions of an ethical-moral

[25] See Foucault (1984).

[26] Amedeo Giovanni Conte proposes the term *nomotropismo* to signify "acting on the basis of rules", a case in point being the acting on the basis of and in compliance with a deontic rule Conte (2000).

[27] See Maimonide (1170–1180), English edition (1990), p. 7, 7.

[28] See Nussbaum (2016), Italian edition (2017), pp. 62–63.

[29] Not due to an idealised anthropological notion but due to the awareness that the *conatus essendi*, lacking legal restraints, threatens an individualistic drift. The idea that the Torah subverts the *conatus essendi* – the pure causal logic of being—is a recurring idea in Levinas. However, from Levinas's point of view the sphere of Ought introduced by the Torah meets a need that rises in man starting with the intersubjective dimension—where the heteronomy of moral sentiment is formed by the trauma of the encounter with *autrui* rather than by any law. In this sense the Torah in particular and, more structurally, the law, limits the "hostage" condition in which the subject finds himself when faced with the *autrui*; Levinas (1974), pp. 192–205.

nature.[30] The prescriptive aspect (duty, permission, prohibition) is accompanied by a heuristic aspect—the formulation, using the language of exhortation, of prayer or narration, of ethical ideals. It follows how the language of the sources reveals a veritable "life form" or a plurality of use patterns and linguistic levels.[31] However, within such heterogeneity duty and prescription come first and foremost, as well as, stemming from this, the ideal of magnanimity.[32] Thus, the aforementioned ban on vendettas and grudges, becoming a part of this web, connects both with other prescriptions, such as that relating to forgiveness in the wake of repentance [*tešuvah*],[33] and with elements of a heuristic nature, for instance the controversies surrounding the theme of individual justice,[34] as well as with eidetic aspects, ethical ideals and metaphysical perspectives relating to themes of the unity of community,[35] justice [*ṣedeq*], magnanimity [*ḥesed*], sanctity [*qedušah*] and repentance [*tešuvah*], where the categories of prescription and exhortation are blurred. If, on one hand, banning vendettas and grudges satisfies a need to keep the community united, on the other, it satisfies an ideal need for justice and repentance. It therefore follows how the principle of retributive justice does not comprehend the entirety of the *forma mentis* and of the *modus operandi* of Jewish culture.[36] Indeed, we can recognise the existence of a sense of justice understood not as the righting of a wrong but rather as an opportunity—and obligation—for the guilty party to repent of their acts, so as to redeem themselves. It is this capacity that leads to the emergence of exhortation, *prima facie,* and, after meeting a set of conditions, the emergence of the duty to forgive on the part of the injured party. The duty to repent [*tešuvah*], and corresponding duty to forgive, is a declination within the sphere of intersubjective relationships of the relation between the act and the idea of *tešuvah* of the single individual/entire population and the Lord's faculty for forgiveness and quality of magnanimity [*ḥesed*]. The subordination of the body of legislation pertaining to intersubjective relationships to that pertaining to the relationship between Israel and the Lord is not incidental. In truth it allows us to understand how every law—including that of the handling of blood shedding, the ban on vendettas and grudges—attempts to elevate Israel to a model, to an ideal.[37] Not without

[30]The heterogeneity of the sources of Jewish law brings to the fore a phenomenon that variously cuts through the entire body of legislation—as Lombardi Vallauri highlights in reference to, for instance, Italian law in Medieval communes; Lombardi Vallauri (1967), pp. 188–192. See also Bobbio (1961), p. 5.

[31]See Wittgenstein (1953), Italian edition (1967–2009), §19, p. 17.

[32]On the centrality of duty and prescription in Jewish law, see Cover (1987).

[33]For an analysis of the verb "to forgive" as a "performative", "factive" and "*anairetico*" (producing a disintegration of a state of things) verb, Conte (1992).

[34]*Bava qamma, 27b.*

[35]*Talmud bavli, Yoma 9b; Giṭṭin 55b,* identify in discord and gratuitous hatred the cause of the destruction of the Second Temple (70 e. v).

[36]Principle of retribution acknowledged to underlie pecuniary compensation that is proportional to the wrong suffered as well as the handling of blood shedding.

[37]See Hansel (1998).

compromises and incongruities, which are inevitable when the ideal seeks contact with reality. What we have witnessed concerning the transformation of the spontaneous practice of blood avenging into institutional practice is found within this framework. On one hand, there is the implementation of a practice predating the Torah while, on the other, this practice is bound to procedural justice and related to the moral principles of [*ḥesed*] and repentance [*tešuvah*].[38] However, the subordination of the laws inherent to intersubjective relations to the rules pertaining to Israel and the Lord always guarantees that the ideal has the final say, so to speak. This is what emerges from the instance of keeping «the doors of *tešuvah*» or repentance "ever open".[39] It is not so much by virtue of the duty of man to forgive those who come to him begging to be forgiven but by virtue of the duty of the Lord to guarantee men—even criminals—the chance to redeem themselves. The subordination of the practice to the ideal is highlighted by the above-mentioned text, drawn from the sources, according to which decrees are accompanied by prayers, exhortations or, in other words, hopes and ideals. It is from this perspective that Beruryah's invocation—an invitation to the violator to do his duty and repent—can be read:

> The criminals in the Me'ir neighbourhood were tormenting him to the point that he implored their death. His wife Beruryah said to him: "Why are you doing this? Indeed, it is written: *the sins shall end*.[40] Does it perchance say 'sinners'? It says 'sins' (...) You should instead beg for mercy for them so that they repent".[41]

From this appeal to pray for the redemption of others (namely criminals) we can grasp not just an essential feature of Jewish law but also a broader theoretical aspect. The philosopher Emmanuel Levinas, in his analysis (1982) of the institution of the Cities of Refuge (which we have examined above), proposes an heuristic reading, according to which we should discern in all our cities—the metropolises of the Western world—a kind of "ville refuge", a city of refuge. From this point of view, we should regard ourselves as though we were (potentially) guilty of manslaughter, that is guilty of causing harm inadvertently and through negligence. At the same time, we should regard the people who express their anger in the streets of our cities as though they were relatives of those people we have in some way harmed. A perspective of this kind seems quite relevant nowadays, in an age of global economy and mass migration, where it would appear not to be so easy to claim one's innocence. In any case, the nature of the core of the issue is, ultimately, rooted in a moral and (critical) phenomenological, rather than political, view. What emerges is the primacy of obligation. We may have a right to live in safety, meaning the right to affirm our *conatus essendi*, nevertheless we are—beyond our individual lifestyle choices—summoned to perform a duty, rooted in our encounter with the Other

[38] With the aforesaid notion of legal frame, we mean the primary duty to set up courts, from the perspective of the Torah for all peoples; *Talmud Bavli, Sanhedrin 56*; on the concept of Noahide duties, Benamozegh (1914).

[39] See Maimonide (1170–1180), Italian edition 1983.

[40] *Psalms*, 104.

[41] *Talmud Bavli, Berakhot, 10a.*

(*autrui*), which makes our safety and wellbeing feel somehow uncomfortable to us. Here we can see how the moral and phenomenological dimensions are intertwined. Indeed, from Levinas's perspective, we are compelled to perform this duty endlessly, starting from our condition of passivity in the face of the—weak, vulnerable—Other, as pointed out by philosopher Chalier (1998). It is not a moral road paved by reason, but one rooted in our perception, albeit *autrui* is thought to be beyond all intentionality, according to Levinas' criticism of phenomenology (1961): to see his face is to hear the commandment: you shall not murder. From this perspective, the law only subsequently comes into play in order to delimit this duty which is, in itself, infinite. The prayer for the redemption of criminals, for the sake of their teshuvà, can therefore be read as a prayer for us too, an appeal to acknowledge our duties, starting from the duty to redeem ourselves. From Levinas's perspective, this is not something that only has value in a Jewish cultural context. We may add and affirm that if in the Jewish experience of the Law there is something like the appeal and the duty to repent—the end consequence of which will be reconciliation with the other—it is because this is an intrinsic feature of humankind. We are all capable of perceiving some sort of sense of duty when faced with the spilled blood of our relatives, as the habits and laws of Semitic populations have shown us. At the same time, some of the obligations enshrined in Jewish laws reveal to us a mirror aspect: we all have the capacity to imagine, and feel, something resembling the duty to repent—to redeem ourselves—as well as the duty to forgive someone who has acted in order to atone for his past faults. Seemingly this latter duty is only afforded to those who have had harm done to them. Perhaps there will be no reconciliation after the blood has been shed. There will, however, be a convergence of intentions and actions, namely the recognition of the primacy of duty: the obligation to atone for one's acts, which corresponds to a duty not to hinder such redemption. This leads to a prayer not for the death of criminals, but for their redemption.

References

Amselek P (2012–2013) Cheminements philosophiques dans le monde du droit et des règles en générale. Armand Colin, Paris

Anscombe GEM (1958) On Brute facts. In: Conte AG, Di Lucia P, Ferrajoli L, Jori M (eds) (2013) Filosofia del diritto. Cortina, Milano, pp 295–302

Bali J, Franzinetti V, Levi Della Torre S (2010) Il forno di Akhnai: una discussione talmudica sulla catastrofe. Giuntina, Firenze

Banon D (1987) La lecture infinie Les voies de l'interprétation midrachique. Seuil, Paris

Benamozegh E (1914) Israël et l'humanité. Étude sur le problème de la religion universelle et sa solution. Leroux, Paris

Bialik HN (1917, Italian edition 2006) Halachah e Aggadah: sulla legge ebraica. Bollati Boringhieri, Torino

Bobbio N (1961) Comandi e consigli. Rivista trimestrale di diritto e procedura civile XV:369–390

Chalier C (1998) Pour une morale au-delà du savoir Kant et Levinas. Albin Michel, Paris

Cohen H (1919, Italian edition 1994) Religione della ragione Dalle fonti dell'ebraismo. San Paolo, Cinisello Balsamo
Conte ME (1992) Semantica del predicato 'perdonare'. In: Galli G (ed) Interpretazione e perdono: atti del dodicesimo Colloquio sulla interpretazione, Macerata, 15–19 marzo 1991. Marietti, Genova, pp 13–21
Conte AG (2000) Nomotropismo: agire in funzione di regole. Sociologia del diritto 27(1):7–32
Cover RM (1983) Foreword: Nomos and Narrative Supreme Court 1982 Term. Harv Law Rev 97:4–68
Cover RM (1987) Obligation: a jewish jurisprudence of the social order. J Law Religion 5(1):65–74
Ehrlich E (1913) La sociologia del diritto. In: Conte AG, Di Lucia P, Ferrajoli L, Jori M (eds) Filosofia del diritto. Cortina, Milano, pp 51–60
Ferrari S (2012) Introduzione al diritto comparato delle religioni: Ebraismo, Islam e Induismo. Il Mulino, Bologna
Fisch M (2016) The rationality of religious dispute. Brill, Leiden
Foucault M (1984) Le Souci de soi. Gallimard, Paris
Giuliani M (2013) Si può comandare l'amore? Osservazioni sullo Shema' Israel. Humanitas 6:10–19
Hansel G (1998) Explorations talmudiques. Odile Jacob, Paris
Kelsen H (1934, Italian edition, 2000) Lineamenti di dottrina pura del diritto. Einaudi, Torino
Levi Della Torre S (2003) Zone di turbolenza Intrecci, somiglianze, conflitti. Feltrinelli, Milano
Levinas E (1961) Totalité et infini. Essai sur l'extériorité. Livre de poche, Paris
Levinas E (1974) Autrement qu'etre ou au-delà de l'essence. Livre de poche, Paris
Levinas E (1982) L'Au-delà du verset Lectures et discours talmudiques. Les Éditions de Minuit, Paris
Lombardi Vallauri L (1967) Saggio sul diritto giurisprudenziale. Giuffrè, Milano
Maimonide M (1170–1180, Italian edition 1983) Mišneh Torah Norme sul pentimento. DAC, Roma
Maimonide M (1170–1180, English edition 1990) Mišneh Torah, a Rav Touger E (edit.). Moznaim, Jerusalem York
Nussbaum M (2016, Italian edition 2017) Rabbia e perdono La generosità come giustizia. Il Mulino, Bologna
Onkelos (110, edition of 1911) Sefer Mikhtav Elohi Torah ve-Targum Onkelos, perush Rash Pentateuco con commento di Onkelos e Rashi. Belforte, Livorno
Searle JR (1995, Italian edition 2006), La costruzione della realtà sociale. Einaudi, Torino
Smith WR (1889–1894, 2005) Lectures on the Religion of the Semites. Fundamental Institutions. Adamant Media Corporation
Terradas Saborit I (2008) Justicia vindicatoria: de la ofensa e indefension a la imprecacion y el oraculo, la vindicta y el talion, la ordalia y el juramento, la composicion y la reconciliacion. Consejo superior de investigaciones científicas, Madrid
Wittgenstein L (1953, Italian edition 1967) Ricerche Filosofiche. Einaudi, Torino

History and Memory Before the Court

A Re-enactment of Justice for WWII in Crete

Elena Mamoulaki

Abstract With the outbreak of the so-called economic 'crisis' (2009–), there have appeared discourses and reactions concerning the past military occupation and the relationship between Greece and Germany. These practices renegotiate social memory bringing to the fore traumatic experiences of occupation, in the climate of a new precarity. In 2015, a German historian, was accused that in his book he willfully denied recognized war crimes committed in Crete by the German military between 1941 and 1945 and that in that same book he insulted the people of Crete, on the grounds of their race and ethnic origin. Based on ethnographic research, and on interviews, this chapter explores local perceptions of the memory of the Second World War, as a current in negotiating the present economic 'crisis', as a vindication of a right, as a part of local identity and as a claim for the future.

1 Introduction

In 2015, in reference to his book, *Operation Mercury: The Occupation of the Island of Crete,* Dr. Heinz Richter, a German historian and Professor at the University of Mannheim, was accused of willfully denying recognized war crimes committed in Crete by the German military between 1941 and 1945 and, in that same book, of insulting the people of Crete on the grounds of their race, genealogical and ethnic origin.[1] A few months before the official accusation and the beginning of the trial, the University of Crete had awarded Richter an honorary doctorate on the basis of his work and his contribution to the study of Modern Greek history.[2] This award

[1]In November 2015, the public prosecutor of Rethymno after ordering a preliminary inquiry indicted Richter under Article 2 of the recently effective law 4285/2014 known as "anti-racist" or "hate speech" law, for "denying Nazi crimes against the people of Crete". This was the first case that was brought to court under this law.

[2]His research mainly focuses on the Balkans and on the contemporary history of Greece and Cyprus and is published in numerous books and articles in both German and Greek.

E. Mamoulaki (✉)
Department of Philosophy and Social Sciences, University of Crete, Rethymno, Greece

R. Márquez Porras et al. (eds.), *Vindicatory Justice*, Ius Gentium: Comparative Perspectives on Law and Justice 93, https://doi.org/10.1007/978-3-030-79595-5_14

infuriated a considerable number of the local Cretan population and provoked noisy reactions in the local mass media for months.[3] As a result, the trial attracted attention not only on a local but also on a national level, driving journalists and scholars—mainly historians—to express their opinions on the subject.

On the one hand, journalists and academics wrote articles to defend the freedom of speech and the independency of academic research noting that it is unacceptable for a modern state to bring a book, result of the academic research before the court. On the other hand, politicians, representatives of local associations and a handful of academics denounced Richter's honorary awarding and his allegations regarding the Cretan people as an insult to the memory of the dead and the dignity of the living victims of war. Between these two diametrically opposed views, prevalent in the public discourse, this chapter aims to shed light on the perspectives and ideas of the ordinary people who attended the trial and formed a kind of a vindicatory community. As we shall see later, contrary to their representation in the press as provincial fanatics or unwitting victims who are led by politicking, these ordinary people hold critical, sensitive and abundant perspectives on the issue. Their views were not given attention and thus they remained voiceless.

Although important studies deal with the denial/minimization of war crimes in the fields of history, jurisprudence and political science, little has been written from an anthropological point of view.[4] The ethnographic and anthropological approach can contribute to the understanding of the ways 'ordinary' people (especially those morally or materially affected by the juridical processes and decisions) experience, comprehend and correlate with law, justice, history and memory in the context of their lives.

Richter's case raises a number of issues that are complex and multifaceted: the relationship between history and law, academia and society, local identity and memory, international politics and economic relations, nationalism and orientalism, institutional power and grassroots claims, traumatic memories of WWII and the subsequent civil war, convenient silences and painful acknowledgements.

This chapter is based on ethnographic research undertaken at Richter's trial in 2016 inside and outside the first instance criminal court in the town of Rethymnon, Crete, and on interviews with people involved but mainly with trial audience. However, in the limited space of this chapter we will primarily focus on the local

[3]Numerous articles in the local press. E.g. *Richter earthquake in Crete* (*Ethnos*, 21 November 2014).

[4]Memory laws, the denial of crimes against humanity and other legal issues of great importance and relevance to this trial have been elaborated on by various legal scholars. The discussion over the boundaries between freedom of speech and hate speech and the related damage to persons, groups and the society that the constraint of the first and the immunity of the latter might cause, reveals the multifaceted and often contradictory character of memory laws. Although these discussions are very interesting in contextualizing and understanding some legal aspects of our case, these will not further elaborated on the issue given the limited space in this chapter. For more on the subject see: Belavusau and Gliszczyńska-Grabias (2017), Heinze (2018), Koposov (2017), Nuzov (2019), Fronza (2018). Κουσουρής (2014), Κούρτης (2019).

perceptions of the memory of WWII, as a factor in negotiating the recent economic 'crisis', as a vindication of a right, as a part of local identity and as a claim for the future. This chapter seeks to reveal the way in which historical memory is locally produced and elaborated. It also sheds light on the complexity of a dispute which when contemplated from a certain—geographical and/or sociocultural—distance (e.g. from the perspective of academic and intellectual circles in Athens and elsewhere) might seem simpler if not obvious. This probably happens, as I will argue, because in the micro-level and from the point of view of certain groups and individuals, the perception of history becomes a much more complex and multifaceted issue.

2 The "Battle of Crete" and "Operation Mercury"[5]

In the context of WWII and in the final stage of the Axis powers conquest of Greece, the German army embarked on an airborne invasion of Crete on May 20, 1941. While the occupation of the island was eventually successful, the German army received very heavy casualties. The determined resistance, comprised not only from the few troops of the Greek army and the Allied forces but also from an extensive number of civilians, was crucial. The triumphant German military officers were outraged that some civilians used sticks, knives, stones and even bare hands to attack the troops and they made extensive use of reprisal measures that included mass shootings and the burning down of entire villages.[6] After the Battle of Crete and during the occupation (1941–1945) several groups of locals formed resistance groups that supported the island population and organized a number of sabotage operations against the occupying forces. At the same time, the German troops continued the reprisals and by the end of the occupation, between 2000 and 3000 Greek civilians were executed in Crete alone by the German army, and about 1600 out of 6500 villages and towns were destroyed (Nessou 2009, p. 204).[7]

It is important to emphasise that, in the narrations of my informants, the Battle of Crete which lasted for about 10 days is fused with the occupation/resistance period which lasted 4 years and is represented as a unifying and heroic period. Furthermore,

[5]The distinct titles of the German and the Greek version of the book reflect the different perceptions and representations of the same historical event. In the German version the significance is related to the innovative character of the military mission to occupy Crete only with air forces. In the Greek version, the title is related to the remarkable resistance from the part of the locals and the ally forces against the Nazi invasion.

[6]Another similar reprisals operation in the village of Kontomari, more than 30 men were shot because close to the village, a few German soldiers' corpses were found during the Battle of Crete. The day after the Kontomari massacre, the town of Kandanos was razed to the ground by the German troops as reprisal to the local resistance.

[7]For more on the subject see: Αρχοντάκη (1995). The population of Crete in 1940 numbered about 4,30,000 people.

although local resistance was not at any given moment homogenous, the heroic aspect of resistance is prevalent in this memory while antagonisms over power are quietly forgotten.[8] The social memory of resistance is highly interrelated with the process of its official recognition by the Greek state and its characterization as national, which in turn, is related to the prevalent social and political forces and the international context.[9] Thus, this has been a long process often involving contradictory stances towards resistance. However, the recognition of the National Resistance in 1982 was linked to the idea of national reconciliation after the Civil War (1946–1949) and the dictatorship (1967–1974) and served as a means of integrating large groups of the population (which were previously excluded as left-wing "enemies of the Nation") into the political system.[10]

In the process of the construction of a unified and heroic resistance the oblivion of the conflicts and clashes needed to be forgotten. Recent studies have questioned the character of the 'unanimous' Resistance investigating controversial issues such as

[8]During and after the Occupation period, antagonisms and clashes among different local resistance groups were also part of the situation since different leaders and members of the partisan groups often held opposing political and ideological views and conflicting plans and interests for the future

[9]Although resistance was recognized soon after the war and occupation were over, in the anti-communist, cold war political situation, this recognition only included the rightists. Left-wing resistance was not only silenced but also criminalized and persecuted as related to the civil war that took place after the end of WWII, 1946–1949. What PASOK (Panhellenic Socialist Movement) legislated on the recognition of the National Resistance in 1982, during metapolitefsi, included the leftists and communists (members of the EAM—National Liberation Movement mainly) and provided all recognized members of the National Resistance with a defined pension. That is, apart from the social and moral recognition, there was a material compensation to the people who suffered during the occupation and the civil war due to multiple discriminations. The law and the related pension were part of the project called "National Reconciliation" which aimed at "lifting the consequences of civil war 1944–1949" and the division of the Greek society caused by the exclusion from the political body of a large part of the population. A dramatic moment of this project was the public burning of secret police files that contained information about the so called "dangerous citizens". However, it is important to note that gradually from the early '90s, and especially after 2000 until today, the memory of the 1940s is a topic of constant negotiation and reinterpretation as regards its meanings and facts not only among the academic circles of historians and other social scientists and public intellectuals but also in the public sphere. Although 1982 represents a crucial turn regarding the memory of WWII and the civil war there is still a constant renegotiation of the issue. According to recent studies, the last 20 years the memory of the 1940s has been cultivated as a cultural trauma (Αντωνίου et al. 2013). That is traumatic memory is conceived as a cultural construction with different functions. During the recent crisis, this memory has been also used as a way of understanding the current condition using meanings and terms from the distant past. Cf. Avgeridis (2017), Στριφτόμπολα (2015); Βόγλης (2015); Φλάισερ (2009); Χανδρινός (2015); Ανδρέου et al. (2015).

[10]The recognition of the National Resistance was an official law-backed action by the Greek government that shook Greek society. Although it was common knowledge that, due to the result of the civil war and the persecutions of the Communists and democrats, a considerable portion of the Resistance suffered all types of discriminations, deportation, incarceration and even execution, there was up to that point, an "internal" awareness which no one dared to publicly acknowledge and restore the victims. Official recognition of the National Resistance moved it decisively from "cultural intimacy" (Herzfeld 2016) to social integration and justice.

that of collaborationism.[11] Furthermore, studies that reveal the divided and contested nature of the memory of Resistance in many communities have also triggered discussions.[12] While some scholars include Richter's work in this trend of historical research that deconstructs the vital myths of the nation,[13] his book was criticized as belonging to a revisionist trend, which seeks to justify and legitimize Nazi war crimes, thus laundering Germany's image and role in the war.[14] Furthermore, his argumentation was received as an attempt to confute the very essence of the act of resisting and confronting the invader, characterizing it as illegal, brutal and 'primitive' and thus turning victims into abusers.

In Crete, the memory of the resistance against the German invasion and occupation has been an important part of local identity. Many villages have centrally placed monuments referring to that period, usually a marble memorial plaque on which the names and ages of those lost are inscribed; the social memory of the victims is told in stories of their heroism.[15] They are remembered for their bravery, leaving behind orphans and devastated families as they defended their land and values. Local identity is largely built on this memory of brave heroes who resisted the Nazi invaders. Every year on National Remembrance Day, as well as in local anniversaries related to the attacks, students march in parades and local officials place wreaths on monuments. Popular songs and tales refer to the period, while several objects of that time can be found in locals' houses.[16] In both rural and urban Crete, extended family networks and people of different generations are closely connected to the remembrance, as younger generations are heirs of this traumatic legacy mostly from their grandparents' recounting of events. The Battle of Crete (with important celebrations throughout the island every year) holds an especially important place in the genealogy of resistance in the long history of the island's occupation, which includes Venetian, Arab, Ottoman, and of course, German occupation.[17]

The constructed memory of an undivided massive resistance against the Nazis constitutes a necessary, vital, national narrative, largely circulated not only in Greece but, in similar ways albeit for different reasons, in many other countries involved in WWII including France, Netherlands, Belgium and, along with the emphasis on the idea of victimization by the Allies, even Italy and Germany themselves (Mazower

---

[11] See Κουσουρής (2014), Μιχαηλίδης et al. (2008), Χανδρινός (2012), Χαραλαμπίδης (2012) and others.

[12] Δρουμπούκη (2014).

[13] https://www.kathimerini.gr/841044/article/epikairothta/ellada/h-istorikh-episthmh-sto-edwlio.

[14] See, Benz 2015 and also http://www.haniotika-nea.gr/voles-kata-ch-richter/.

[15] For more on the WWII memorials on the island of Crete, see Kagiadaki (2015).

[16] The local musical tradition includes types of songs such as kritika, rizitika, and mantinades. In the Historical Museum of Crete there is a permanent exhibition dedicated to WWII in Crete where "special reference is made to the reuse of military equipment remaining on the island after the end of the war" see https://www.historical-museum.gr/eng/collections/view/b-pagkosmios-polemos.

[17] "For the Cretans, the Battle of Crete and the Resistance constitute integral parts of their local history that seem to testify to their free, persistent, brave and rebellious nature and to shape their collective memory" (Kagiadaki 2015).

2001, p. 17). In the case of Greece, an idealized representation of a compact and united memory of Resistance was important for the building of the post-civil war society where former collaborators of the Nazi's, exiled partisans and orphans of the civil war fighters had to live together in the context of *metapolitefsi* (polity change) after the fall of the military junta (1967–1974).

In Crete's case, this vivid memory of a massive resistance obscures the violent incidents against the leftist partisans, and the role of some National Resistance groups in the "cleaning" of the communist threat. However, to certain extent, the spontaneous and widespread reaction of large parts of the local population is reported in different sources, both local and international, and has been also testified to by various historians (Δετοράκης 1990, Beevor 2004 and others). Indeed, material and immaterial traces, stories and narrations of the period that are found and are circulated in family and other local social contexts attest to the extended degree of involvement in the resistance by large parts of the local population. The impact of this involvement on the younger generation is still significant and is manifested in different ways and circumstances. For example, the dramatic rise of Golden Dawn and other extreme right/Neonazi political parties, in the context of the recent crisis, was not supported by the Cretans who proudly boasted that on the island, those parties secured the lowest percentage in the national elections.

That is, both intergenerational memory and its cultural representations completely clash with, Richter's claims about the Cretan's primitive and savage way of fighting, in contrast to the civilized of the German army.

3 The Outrageous Contentions: Victims into Abusers

In 2011 Heinz Richter's book, titled *Operation Mercur: Die Reoberung de Isle Kreta im Mai 1941 (Operation Mercury: The conquest of the island of Crete in May 1941)* was published in Germany. A few months later the book was translated and published in Greek[18] and presented at the Historical Museum of Crete in June 2011.[19]

In his book Richter attempts a day-by-day description of the Battle of Crete, mainly from the perspective of military operations, emphasizing the role of the British and the Allied forces on the evolution of the battle. He also tries to examine why the German army decided to attack and conquer Crete, as well as the island's geostrategic importance to Hitler. The writer assesess each side's intentions and decisions, while extensively elaborating on the issue of local resistance warfare and the retaliations to it.

[18]In Greek it was published with the title "The Battle of Crete", which is the most common term for this battle with reference to the celebrated resistance of the Cretans.

[19]During the presentation there were several reactions against Richter's allegations.

In the first weeks after the book release, critical reviews appeared in the Greek press, drawing attention to several of its controversial points.[20]

It is important to consider that Richter's book can be situated in a larger historiographic, no less social or political, trend that marks a turn in the writing of history of WWII towards relativization of the war crimes and the victimization of the German people. In some countries it appears this revisionist historiography was, if not celebrated at least, accepted, while in others, such as Poland or Greece it incited disputes and public confrontations between historians, political scientists and other scholars and public personas. It is not a coincidence that this turn began in the early 1990s after the fall of the Berlin Wall and the new political and ideological hegemony in the post Cold-war era.[21] While addressing German society with the aim of overcoming the guilt and facing history without qualm, it also represents Allies (especially Soviet) violence as similarly destructive and condemnable as the Nazi crimes. At the same time, the introduction and institutionalization of the two poles (Nazism-Communism/Stalinism) scheme further fed the idea that Nazism was not an absolute evil and that it can be considered, and, in a way normalized when viewed from a comparative perspective while at the same time it demonizes Communism as an equally atrocious regime. While the book does not directly refer to the two-poles scheme (although in Greece, and elsewhere, the main Resistance group was directly related to the Communist Party)[22] Richter insists on the legalistic analysis and evaluation of war crimes that interrelates the offensive and the defensive violence.

Richter stresses that the civilians committed atrocities against the wounded German soldiers. This, in his view, violated the Law of the War and, in a way, drove the German army to retaliate. According to Richter, the battle of Crete was the "final 'fair' military enterprise of WWII and the beginning of a 'dirty war', which included 'illegal' attacks by partisan groups and reprisals by the German army".[23] His allegations were criticized by other historians who denounced his one-sidedness in his use of sources from the Nazis reports and archives, thus fully adopting their

[20] "[S]ome of the writer's views will provoke reactions. It is obvious e.g. that sympathy expressed towards Kurt Student, who after the conquest of the island took on its military administration" Βιστωνίτης (2011).

[21] Rondholz (2015), Βόγλης (2015), Χατζηιωσήφ (2015), and Γαρδίκα et al. (2015).

[22] In Crete the issue of the memory of the Battle of Crete and the Resistance during the Occupation is rather complicated. The majority of the leading figures who immediately after the war and to this day were associated and honoured as the leaders of the local resistance were not related to EAM, and they were protagonists in the elimination of the communist "threat" on the island during and right after the liberation. While they have been identified as part of the resistance, in the context of the trial, it appears that people talk about it in terms adopted by the official discourse on the National Resistance silencing the internal clashes and antagonisms.

[23] Richter (2011), p. 440. This issue of legal vs illegal acts in the context of WWII has been discussed by other writers and has provoked public disputes and confrontations. The attempt to present the "good German soldiers" who fell victims to the "bad guerrillas" has been made and denounced in the case of Herman Frank Meyer and his book "Red Edelweiss" published in Greek in 2009.

views and disgraceful propaganda. It is important to note that Richter also argues that because the defending population were civilians who fought illegally they cannot be included in the protection of victims under the Hague Treaty.[24]

The book provoked intense reactions because it was considered an attempt to shift the blame onto the resisting Greeks and Allies themselves, while trying to restore the reputation of the German army and the paratroopers. His explanations were considered as almost appearing to represent the victims as the abusers.[25] The Cretans, according to Richter, in savage and 'primitive' ways[26] based on their ancient/ancestral customs, tortured and amputated the injured or dead bodies of the German soldiers, causing reasonable indignation on the part of the Germans, which resulted in the reprisals. According to Richter, the crimes committed by the Cretan partisans to the German soldiers, and vice versa, were thus interrelated in cause and effect.[27] In sum, Richter argues that the Cretan resistance was brutal and illegal[28] and thus the reprisals which were for Richter accepted (even legitimate) by the International Law of that period[29] were caused[30] by the partisans' savage and illegal actions. According to the attorney, this argument could be used to weaken the pleas for war reparations for the victims. Richter's argument could be used to support the idea that the victims of the Battle of Crete should not be recognized as protected by the Law and so should not be compensated.

[24]More specifically, Richter argues that the British knew about the German air attack on the island (Richter 2011, pp. 396–409) and they took time to orchestrate the Cretan resistance, deliberately not providing the locals with army markings, which would protect them under the Hague Treaty and the Law of War of the period (Richter 2011, pp. 403–404). However, taking into account the fact that Crete was disarmed due to the local movement against dictator Metaxas in 1938 together with the fact that there was lack of the Greek army troops to defend Crete because the majority of forces was at that time at the country's northern borders invalidates the allegation that the resistance was carefully orchestrated by the British. In a few days after the information that Germany would invade Crete only limited number of troops from the northern front could arrive to Crete and the conscription of the local population could not be successful in only a few days.

[25]Richter repeatedly underlines that the partisans' resistance, was illegal—not protected by the Law of War—and thus, the Cretans cannot be considered victims of war as in other military conflicts. Richter also argues that the 'primitive' and savage Cretan way of fighting had its roots in the period before the Hague Convention and breached the Law of War of the period. He states that those were the first partisan attacks in WWII (Richter 2011, p. 404), which introduced the unequal war with tremendous consequences for both parties.

[26]Richter (2011), p. 409.

[27]Richter (2011), pp. 413, 442.

[28]Richter (2011), p. 404.

[29]Richter (2011), p. 421.

[30]"Without the violation of the rules of International Law from the part of the Cretan partisans The reprisals would not have happened" (Richter 2011, p. 414).

4 Savage Primitives Against Idealist Knights

Richter describes the Cretans' resistance by stating, "This was a war in its most savage and primitive form";[31] and continues, "injured soldiers were murdered and the dead bodies were maltreated. What prevailed was an ancient Cretan tradition, the contempt of death. The maltreatment of the dead bodies was not in this sense an act of punishment but a gesture which revealed the disdain of death. The result was hate, resentment, and the desire to revenge [...] From the part of the Cretan partisan groups what prevailed was a primordial disposal to annihilate the enemy. They would not show any mercy and they would not forgive the enemy even if he would want to surrender".[32] Furthermore, Richter provides no sources to support his allegations regarding the Cretan custom of a contempt for death. The representation of the Cretans as 'primitive' can also be related to a colonialist-orientalist gaze from the part of the writer. Of course, the Nazi propaganda that represented the resisting Cretans as savage is related to the then prevalent attitudes in Western Europe and, in particular the racist Nazi ideology which categorized people as inferior and superior, those who belonged to the Aryan race and those who were considered inhuman.

It is interesting to consider the way Richter uses notions of tradition and the culture in interpreting the alleged savageness of the Cretans, as reported by the Nazi propaganda. Richter represents Cretans as bearers of ancient traditions while the Germans are, in his view, youngsters of their epoch who idealize their role and participation in the war. In this sense, we can trace a typical "allochronism"[33] situating the Cretans from another epoch in relation to German paratroopers.

Richter praises the "knightly" paratroopers and argues for their "idealism," which should be recognized in that final "fair" and "clean" battle of the war. In the book's final paragraph, Richter states that "it should not be missed that those young paratroopers were the victims of a culture which aimed at obedience and blocked the development of critical thinking. They were enthusiastic youngsters, who knew that they belonged to an elite. Their idealism was received in the worst way. They gave the best they could and risked their lives without being aware of the incentives. It is time to recognize this about them" (Richter 2011, p. 450). Richter insists that the paratroopers' mission had no ideological incentives (Richter 2011, p. 442) and that the war on the part of the Germans was "ιπποτικός", characteristic of knights (Richter 2011, p. 439).

[31] Richter (2011), p. 409.

[32] Richter (2011), p. 410.

[33] Fabian (1983).

5 The 'Moderate' Response to the Local's 'Dirty' War

Richter supports the view that the German army leadership was rather hesitant and moderate in imposing of reprisals[34] or the commitment of other atrocities, triggered by the 'savage' fighting of the local population. In emphasizing that the reprisals were limited, he was accused of denying the seriousness and extent of the crimes and of diminishing the degree and the cruelty of the German atrocities. He further supported that the numbers of German casualties and victims were far greater than the number of Cretans'.[35] He bases this reasoning on German army archives and considers all other estimates (Greeks and Allies) to be "excessive". Following these distinctions, Richter seems to use the German oral and written testimonies as trustworthy, while believing those of the Cretans and of allies that do not agree with his argumentation as 'exaggerations'.[36] He also argues that the reprisals could have been much worse, and that so few Cretans were murdered because the German Commander, Kurt Student, imposed moderate reprisals.[37] He states that the condemnation of Student by the court was unfair and that the trial of Brauer and Muller which concluded with their sentence of death, had many dark sides.[38]

6 The Time of the 'Richter Case'

In February 2014, the Department of Political Sciences at the University of Crete decided that the German historian Heinz Richter would be awarded an honorary doctorate. The ceremony, which was open to the public, was scheduled to take place in a central theatre in Rethymno. However, due to dozens of citizens protesting against the nomination, the ceremony could not be held. The protests were partly incited by published objections[39] claiming that the university should not proceed, given the writer's position on WWII, and, in particular his bias against Cretan resistance to the German invasion. They claimed that his bias was in opposition to well-known historical facts and could be detrimental to justified national claims regarding war reparations from Germany. In the end, the ceremony took place the

[34] Richter (2011), pp. 413–414, 418, 430, 439, 437, 442, 450.

[35] "The number of executions carried out by the Germans was much lower than the number of the Germans killed by the Cretan guerrillas". (Richter 2011, p. 420).

[36] Richter (2011), pp. 415, 420.

[37] Richter (2011), p. 409. According to the German archives, only 200 people were killed in the first days of the war (Richter 2011, p. 415), this number was much lower than the number of German soldiers killed.

[38] Richter (2011), pp. 447–448.

[39] Among others the National Council for the Claim of War Reparations and several academics.

day after the original date in an auditorium on the university campus (which at that time was squatted by students), without any prior announcement and in the presence of only a few members of academic staff.

At the end of 2014, the Regional Council of Crete and the World Council of Cretans called upon the University to withdraw the award. In this climate, the Prosecutor of the Court of Rethymnon ordered, on an ex-officio basis, a preliminary examination of whether a formal procedure for the prosecution could be followed, as well as the substance of the complaints by individuals and entities.

According to the indictment in his book, 'The Battle of Crete', there were references of "denial of crimes of Nazism against the Cretan people with derogatory content". Thus, Heinz Richter was prosecuted under the Law 4285/2015 for "publicly approving, denying or minimizing crimes of genocide, crimes against humanity and war crimes, the holocaust and the Nazi crimes that have been recognized by decisions of international courts or the Greek parliament when the behavior turns against a group of people or a person which can be defined in reference to race, color, religion, genealogical origins, ethnic or national origins, sexual orientation, gender identity or disability when this behavior is demonstrated in a way that can incite violence or hatred or is of a threatening or insulting character against a group or a member of such a group", Id. Article 2, amending Law 927/1979 article 1 § 1.[40] This trial lasted for 14 sessions.[41] The decision did not enter into substantive issues. On the contrary, it was based on the unconstitutionality of Article 2 of Law 4285/1414 because, according to the judge, it violated the clauses that protect freedom of expression and academic freedom. However, during this lengthy hearing—in the absence of Heinz Richter, who was represented in absentia by lawyers acting for him—the contents of the book and its aims were thoroughly examined. The Court of Justice did actually enter into substantive issues related to (a) the methodological constitution of the research and the judgments made by the author, in order to examine whether this book was compatible with the rules and methodology of scientific research and writing in the art of historical science; and (b) its insulting content and whether it fell into the category of hate speech.

7 Social and Political Context of the Trial

In order to understand the context of the book's reception, three important parameters related to the setting and circumstances surrounding the trial must be taken into consideration: the economic crisis and the leading role of Germany in decision-making regarding austerity measures, the issue of WWII reparations which was very much debated at that time, and the legacy of WWII Resistance in Greece, which is

[40]For more on the legal aspect of the trial see Tourkochoriti (2017), p. 161.

[41]Starting from 25-11-2015 and ending on 10-2-2016.

highly divisive and controversial due to the civil war and its impact during the post-war era.

Firstly, we need to understand the context of the so-called "economic crisis" and the role Germany played in Greek politics.[42] In 2015 Greece was already counting almost 6 years of savage austerity that dramatically impacted the middle and lower classes. Compounding this, Greek people were being subjected to an unprecedented derogatory stereotype. According to the international media, they were forced to suffer impoverishment and unemployment because their lazy and unreliable national character had led the Greek economy to a dead-end.[43]

Quite apart from the economic and material devastation, the Greek people also suffered moral and psychological abuse.[44] In his research on the historical relevance of the crisis stereotypes, Dordanas (Δορδανάς and Παπαναστασίου 2019) points out that "it is interesting that the Germans during the Occupation accuse the Greeks by means of stereotypical characterizations that we have encountered in recent years in German media. Reading German military reports shortly after the Occupation began there are the same qualifications: "lazy Greeks who do not do well with order and goodwill, which we must teach them to comply with and obey." Thus, along with the economic 'crisis' with Germany playing a critical role in this power game, a political-ideological crisis revolving around nationalism was also taking place.[45]

The representations of Greece as a subordinate, corrupted, unreliable, weak and devastated country facing the omnipotent, rational, efficient and bossy Germany was the symbolic framework through which Richter published his work in German and Greek and was honoured with one of the highest intellectual awards. It is important to stress this background because, as discussed later in this paper, in this case economic and political power are symbolically executed in the context of the trial and the discourse around it.

[42]In Greece, as in many European and global South countries, the 2008 economic crisis was followed by neoliberal 'austerity' (Powers and Rakopoulos 2019; Knight and Stewarts 2016) measures taken by the governments, which led to an abrupt forfeiture of social services and rights (work, housing, education, healthcare) together with an increase in unemployment, affecting the middle and lower classes as well as low morale (43% increase in suicides) for a great number of people of the countries that suffered the so-called 'structural adjustment' and 'fiscal reforms'. At the same time, following the TINA doctrine of the imposition of brutal neoliberal policies, the governments have either denied or justified as "necessary sacrifices" the damage that their policies have caused to the suffering populations. Instead of providing compensation of any kind, the ruling class tried to blame the 'lazy' and 'immature' peoples/countries for not controling their economies. Racist stereotypes accompanied the 'immature' and 'irresponsible' South, which has to make sacrifices in order to achieve the 'right' path of growth has largely been used in German media, concealing the political and economic causes related to the global capitalism crisis.

[43]These statements undermined the role of hypercapitalism (Piketty 2020) in the global crisis, which was stressed by many economic analysists. As a result, the image propagated by the international media of a "lazy nation" in turn, fed, a previously defunct nationalism in Greece.

[44]The mouthpiece of this were German and other mass media but the actual agent of this propaganda was not clearly defined and often identified with international funds and interests.

[45]For more on the aspects of German nationalism in relation to the process of the European integration see Χατζηιωσήφ (2017).

The leading role played by the German state and policy in the structural programmes of Greece, and the perceived strict, judgmental and ruthless stance of the government representatives, inflamed the Greek people's old traumas related to the German occupation.[46] This troubled past was expressed in a number of different ways: Books, films, documentaries, TV broadcasts, public talks, round tables and other events related the time of the 'crisis' to the period of the occupation. During anti-austerity demonstrations, Angela Merkel and Wolfgang Schauble were depicted on placards in Nazi uniforms and people declared the new occupation of the "Fourth Reich." In German press, Greeks were presented as lazy cheaters who should consider selling their islands or even the Acropolis so as to repay their debt. On the front page of Focus, of a German popular magazine, the Venus of Mylos, was depicted wearing a deformed and filthy Greek flag and making an inappropriate gesture with the title "Betruger in der Euro-familie" (Crooks in the Euro-family).[47] At the same time, there was a video on the magazine's official website showing a pair of Germans expressing concern about whether the fraudsters in the south would grab the money of honest German taxpayers. Seven Greeks pressed charges against 13 of the magazine journalists. The charges that journalists faced following the lawsuit were vilification, contempt of Greek state symbols and defamation. The tribunal found them not guilty.[48]

In this specific context, the fact that a recognized German historian wrote a book in which he argued that the Greek people illegally resisted the Nazi invasion and occupation and that due to their 'savage' customs the whole of WWII was turned from a 'clean' military enterprise into a 'dirty war' was perceived as another example of, as several informants said, 'hubris'[49]

Much of the criticism towards German policy in Greece after 2010 used references to the German occupation during World War II and employed Nazi-era symbols to protest the way Greece was being treated. Mentions of war crimes and unpaid German reparations became more frequent in the press. One could wonder why the Greek people did not insist on reparations for the victims of the German occupation. There are reports and studies on the weak attempts and long-term passivity on the part of the government and the political establishment in Greece regarding this subject. The dependency of the political elite on American and European lobbies and the corruption of the politicians, often appear as possible explanations for this passive attitude. However, it is important to notice that during the recent economic crisis, a large number of people in Greece, from different generations and social groups, called personally and collectively for war reparations

[46]For more on the subject see A nation under attack: perceptions of enmity and victimhood in the context of the Greek crisis Bithymitris G, Lialiouti Z, (2013).

[47]https://www.focus.de/magazin/archiv/jahrgang_2010/ausgabe_8.

[48]Source: iefimerida.gr.

[49]Several informants used the term this same term "hybris" to express their outrage.

more loudly and strongly than ever before.[50] Why now and not then? I will venture a hypothesis based on the idea of vindicatory justice and its usefulness regarding reparations of homicides, as introduced by Terradas Saborit earlier in this volume, that nothing can produce life in exchange of death; the group of people who claim the loss of a human life cannot be properly compensated for through monetary terms. The grieving post-WWII widows and orphans were not, at the time, concerned about getting specific economic compensation for their lost loved ones. "In Vindicatory societies, homicide stands as an offence for which only gifts can serve to recognize its real unattainable reparation." While it seems paradoxical that only 10 or 15 years after the war, people from martyred villages went to Germany as Gastarbeiters (guest workers), or a few years later found themselves receiving German currency from the developing touristic industry, a relevant hypothesis is that, apart from necessity and poverty, those phenomena—even if mutually beneficial as freely agreed-upon economic exchanges—could be morally (even though silently) accepted in the context of a symbolic act of recognition and reparation.

In the social arena, this contact with the German people, along with positive representation and the impact of investments of German corporations, was probably a way of coming to terms and making peace with the past.

The fact that all this emerged with the crisis again, attests to the view that they had covered up the trauma, especially the traumatic memory of the civil war. A typical example is the burning of the police files, led by both the Right and the Left, in 1989—a date that marks the end of the Cold War.[51] And a trauma that is silenced and covered up is following some "underground paths" that arose with the crisis, which was, among others, a crisis of values.

But the so-called Greek crisis, and the patronizing and dismissive discourse of the ruling German politicians and the press, which was also adopted by a significant portion of the population and was expressed with pejorative and degrading characterizations of the Greeks by the German press and politicians triggered traumatic memories of past suffering by the Occupation during the 1940s. The many examples of this type of attitude, along with the actual experience of the dictated political doctrine of austerity, which led to the impoverishment represented in the dominant German press in terms of 'cleansing' of the population, drove many people to protest against those politics. Furthermore, this humiliating, sometimes racist discourse (the "lazy Greeks"), stood diametrically opposed to the process of even passively restoring the trauma, even if the fairness and honesty of this process was very contestable. This past trauma, the mass shootings, the burning down of houses and villages, the bombing of the cities, and the famine[52] were re-awakened, especially in the face of the concurrent impoverishment, the marked rise in unemployment, and the dramatic

[50]Publication of monographs and edited volumes related to the German atrocities during the war and the issue of the war reparations should be noted. Noticeably an increasing number of public events and conferences related to the subject were organized after the 2008 crisis.

[51] Καραμανωλάκης (2019).

[52] Argenti (2019) and Knight (2015).

change of everyday life in the cities. Thus, more than 70 years after the occupation, the 'crisis', experienced as a brutal economic and moral attack, was the trigger point for a dramatic turn in the social memory of the war, along with dozens of publications, public presentations, conferences, films, documentaries, press reports, and academic surveys and articles.

8 The Legacy of the Resistance and the Left in Greece

Last but not least, it is important to note that resistance remembrance was not celebrated in post-war Greece in the way it was in many Eastern and Western European countries due to the subsequent civil war from 1946 to 1949.[53] Seen through the lens of the civil war, resistance against the Nazi invasion and occupation and the German atrocities is still divisive within communities whose past was marked by the events of WWII. Since the memory of the period was written by the winners of the civil war, that is the Right, the Left-wing partisans were depicted as responsible for the atrocities of the German troops against the local population and their forced suffering throughout the 1940s. The agitation of this past has always been related to the political legacy and to current circumstances. And the period of the 'crisis', as was the case in 2015 and 2016, was highly polarized politically speaking, with the rise of the Left as well as the dramatic rise of the extreme Right and the Neo-Nazi political entities. Thus, within the courtroom, the ghosts of the past together with political passions and interests of the present were apparent in legal arguments as well as among the audience.

However, as in many other parts of Greece, the crisis and the role of the German government has ignited the discourse over past traumas. During the intervals in the trial, I heard conversations revolving around the fate of the Left in Greece and the ongoing anti-communism, which appears every so often and under different circumstances. The context and the content of the trial awakened social and political divisions rooted in the prewar period and which lasted during the postwar civil war.

In Greece, unlike other European countries such as France or Italy, once the war was over and the Nazis were defeated, the great majority of people and collectivities that actively resisted and fought the invaders were not recognized but demonized and persecuted. This happened because the resistance was largely organized by the communist party and by the end of the war, anti-communism in Greece was prevalent. The new enemy became the progressive and the Left who craved a new democratic and socialistic society. For this reason, with few exceptions, some of the collaborators and other defenders of the Nazis retained their privileges and even occupied political and administrative offices. The state propaganda depicted the Left

[53]Just as the Nazi troops were leaving the country, a savage civil war broke between Greek government army and the Democratic Army of Greece (DSE)—the military branch of the Communist Party of Greece (KKE). The Greek civil war was one of the first conflicts of the Cold War.

as 'dangerous citizens'[54] who needed to be expelled from the political body of the healthy homeland, and they were thus detained or deported to remote islands.[55] The Resistance on the part of the Left was, according to the propagand, a responsible for the German atrocities and the reprisal.

Antonis, a 55-year-old man who attended the trial, said:

> The problem is what is considered unfair. Let's look at the Cretans taking their weapons and organizing themselves - like Maquis in France, who were originally autonomous and then went with the De Gaulle Army. Like the Cretans did with the British, the allies, they too had 'a consciousness' of resistance and co-operation with an allied army. But what happened in France is that after the war, Maquis entered the government, being a Communist was not a crime in France while in Greece it was. The Communist Party was lawful and powerful, had MPs and monuments in the honour of the Nazi fighters. In Greece, there was a war against the Communists, and in a sense this war is continued by Richter and the various revisionists. While in France it is clear what Nazism did, there is no attempt to diminish their crimes nor confuse them with the fight against Nazism. In France, Richter would probably be condemned legally, not only politically, ethically and socially for saying that the resistance was savage and that they were fighting the "civilized Nazis".

Here Antonis seems to question the institutional context and the hegemonic discourse of the trial by comparing it to a country that is considered a leader in human rights issues. He thus responds to the concerns that, due to this trial, the Greek legal world might be characterized as obsolete, reactionary, and provincial. He also stresses that the civil war works as the lens through which the memory of WWII and Occupation is still viewed.

Since the major pillar of Ritcher's lawyers' defense revolved around "freedom of speech", people attending the trial often tried to reflect on the subject and clarify their views. Practically none of the trial audience was against "freedom of speech," but they tried to understand how and why what for them was considered clearly an insult and that propaganda was tolerated and even celebrated by a large part of the media as well as the political and academic establishment.

9 The Trial: The Facts of History and the Masks of Ideology

During the trial the judge seemed to examine the substance of the indictment. He persistently asked, inquired, disputed, and gave time to many witnesses to develop their thoughts as to whether the work was offensive and/or propagandistic. A few local representatives, including mayors and deputies, as well as many university professors, were examined as witnesses. While the former were considering whether Richter's claims were true in the direct experience/knowledge of their villages (the number of victims, house disasters, infrastructure, etc.), whether there were morals and customs that were identical to Richter's descriptions, the latter were called upon

[54] Panourgia (2009).

[55] Kenna (2001), Voglis (2002), Mamoulaki (2015a, b), and Pantzou (2011, 2015).

to argue whether the book was scientific or propagandistic regarding its methodology and content. Few scholars carefully stated their skepticism regarding Richter's work. However, the majority of the scholars (university professors, public intellectuals, writers, etc.) both inside and outside the court (that is, in the press) defended Richter's right to express his ideas whether right or wrong. Some argued that there is no historical truth, only a range of different nuances, and that it is unacceptable to legally advocate a single historical truth, especially in the context of a court. Most of Richter's supporters claimed they either hadn't read his work or having read it, they thought the book mediocre and did not constitute any penal offense and, thus, that he should not be persecuted. Instead of a trial, many of them stated, Richter's argumentation could be discussed in the context of a scientific conference. However, to date, no initiative has been taken to discus the issue at any kind of academic event.

It is interesting to note that the majority of academics and the general audience said that they had not read the book, or they had just skimmed the excerpts that were discussed in the court. That is, the symbolic meanings and stakes were what drove them to participate in the process. On the one hand, some were there to defend the freedom of speech, without having a clear idea of the content of that speech, and the others were there to resist the offence to the memory of the dead, without having a thorough knowledge of the book.

The audience consisted mainly of older people, residents of Rethymnon or nearby villages who had been informed and were interested in attending and presenting evidence at the trial. Some came from martyred villages whose families had suffered during the German Occupation. Soon these people met each other and exchanged views, commented on the participants and the attendants at the trial, exchanged information about the course of the trial, and gradually formed a type of community—a vindicatory community. This rather open and non-homogenous group of people recognizes historical memory as an immaterial common good that is shared under certain unwritten rules. Observing their related discussions, we can trace the moral and the prescriptive enclosure of this common good. The respect to the memory of the dead and the recognition of the righteous cause of Resistance seem to be the two main boundaries which were considered as being encroached by Richter's claims. This encroachment was crucial in the formation of a vindicatory community which often referred to the actions that would have to take at the outcome of the trial (especially if the decision was exculpatory). Most of them were pensioners, something they themselves repeatedly commented on, since the court meetings coincided with work and school hours. "Those who should listen to what is waiting for them are absent!" During the intervals, I participated in their discussions to get to know their life stories more, and I asked open questions that would encourage them to express the opinions, views, motives and intentions of those people who did not have an official voice in the trial. I had explained the theme and questions of my research and they often came up with suggestions for people whom I should meet and talk to, or places/villages/sites that would be worthwhile, in their opinion, for me to visit to know more in relation to my questions.

Considering the findings of the fieldwork and the interviews with the majority of the people from the trial audience, I will venture to argue that what people wanted was the social recognition and acknowledgement that the offence should be repaired morally. At most, they wanted it publicly acknowledged that Richter's statements were false. They didn't ask, at least not in that particular circumstance, for a real economic reparation, at least not from Richter. But they wanted to retain the right of asking reparation by the culprit, the German State, then led by the elected government of the Nazis.

Inside the court, two types of justice systems were operating: On the one hand, the juridical context and the official setting of a tribunal referred to the Penal Law; on the other hand, the cultural context of the trial and its audience pertained to an ethos linked to social memory and ideas of justice related to morals, kinship, politics and local identity. The ethnographic analysis of this court case forms a meaningful example of the convergence of the Vindicatory and Penal systems of law and their limitations and inconsistencies. Compounding the mistreatment of the German Occupation victims, the insult to the suffering of the locals by the German author and his subsequent honorary doctorate from the local university, led to the reaction of a large part of the local population. While in Crete the Vindicatory justice system has a long tradition[56] and in this case the honour of the dead heroes from every local village was publicly offended, justice was pursued, only partially through the Penal system. Elements of Vindicatory justice were expressly evident throughout the trial. It would be expected that there be at least respect for the suffering inflicted in the past and in the present. Otherwise, a sense of Vindicatory justice emerges, claiming to pay for the excessive outrage.[57]

According to Terradas, "[t]he beginning of the vindicatory justice process is recognition. It is the social ("social" in the widest sense of the term) acknowledgement of offences. The offence can be primarily a subjective feeling, but its juridical relevance is given by the fact that simultaneously a group of people also acknowledges the offence. It is also an intersubjective phenomenon inserted into the general principle of reciprocity."[58] At the other end of this spectrum are Richter's assertions. Not only does he not stand in solidarity with the victims, but he also claims that the anti-Nazi Cretans' resistance was illegal and even savage, while the Wehrmacht's parachutists were idealists and paladins who *knew* that they belonged to an elite and did not have any political and/or ideological motive.[59] While a stereotype exists of Cretans holding guns, praising their manhood related to an agonistic—even militant—character, the people with whom I talked were not offended for not being recognized as the brave fighters and partisans, nor for not having received the proper economic reparation for the loss of their parents and relatives, or for the loss of their

[56]Τσαντηρόπουλος (2004), Herzfeld (2012), and Αστρινάκη (2013).

[57]https://tvxs.gr/news/egrapsan-eipan/brontero-oxi-sto-nazismo-i-germaniki-ybris-kai-i-eperxomeni-nemesis.

[58]Terradas Saborit (2019), pp. 14.

[59]Richter (2011), p. 450. The German retaliations were based on the concept of "collective responsibility" of the population. If the guerrillas killed German soldiers, they could in turn kill Greek citizens.

opportunities in life. They were there to defend the honour of the dead as victims who died for a cause and not as justified casualties provoked by the local resistance, to attest their own truth, their own right to memory. "If this book or other of the kind are later taught in our schools, if our children find and read these 'awarded' writer what should they think of their ancestors? That they were brutal barbarians who illegally defended their land, who preyed on the bodies of the young idealists because they were told to act like this by the British! If our own university honours this writer, if President of our Democracy has already honoured him with one of the highest awards,[60] where and how are we going to defend our deceased, their brutal death of execution, torture and famine while those young idealists were 'civilizing' the occupied Crete?" Richter questioned the very fact of the offences, the deaths, and the homicides, claiming they were *caused* by the 'illegal' fight of the Cretans. This assault on the only act of reparation, which was the recognition of the unjust deaths of those resisting the wholly illegal and brutal invasion of Crete had a tremendous impact on the morale of the people I talked to, especially the older generations. While they were often represented as fanatics, as quaint, identifying them with some local agents who took the chance for politicking, all my informants were in favour of the freedom of speech, claiming that the book should not be banned but that the university should repeal the award given to the writer, and since the case came into court, they expected a verdict that would somehow redress the offence. "Richter is an old man, probably a paid intellectual/writer like so many others out there, daily writing articles in the newspapers, on the internet etc. He should not go to jail, there are millions of people claiming their ideas and ideologies and unfortunately many of them are fascists, racists, Nazis. But if an official institution like the Greek University and more ironically of Crete,[61] and now a Greek court vindicates and honours him we are obliged to stand up against these practices which represent the whole society and the accepted truth" (Marinos, a 68-year-old from Rethymno).

10 Which Community?

During the penultimate court hearing, the entire prosecution was suspended by the judge. The reason was that, according to the judge, the complainants had not been subject to violence or hate as a result of the book excerpts. Neither do those passages have threatening or insulting content that turns directly to the complainants and their specific characteristics which would have threatened their peaceful social cohabitation. Furthermore, "the complainants coming from Crete, might have a specific

[60] In 2000 Kostis Stefanopoulos, at that time President of the Greek Democracy, awarded Heinz Richter with the Gold Cross of the Order of the Phoenix for his "exceptional acts, which raised the international prestige of Greece".

[61] In the local press there appear often articles characterizing the University of Crete as the ornament and pride of the island. The local political/administrative authorities closely cooperate and give grants and funding to university-led research and projects.

identity related to the island of origin and residency, its history and local customs, however, they form part of the greater Greek population and in no case they form a distinct group of persons identified in relation to the general population based on their race, colour, religion genealogy, national or ethnic origin, sexual orientation or sex identity or disability." The court did not recognize the insult nor the community itself as a distinct entity.

The vindicatory community was spontaneously formed on the basis of the common type of vindication. While in the prosecutor's accusation the notion of community was mentioned, recognizing the existence of such a community of Cretans, a community with the right to mourn or to be insulted by Richter's assertions was questioned by the defense attorneys. However, such a community was scarcely represented by mayors of martyr villages whose testimonies were only briefly examined compared to those of the 'experts'. There was often dissatisfaction that the majority of witnesses were experts of 'special knowledge': "Why do experts who have no idea what happened in our villages can talk and not us?"[62]

Mr. Vassilis, who survived a shooting in his village close to Rethymno told me his story: "The three women, my mother, my grandmother and my aunt died. Me, my brother and my father managed to survive. After we were knocked down [by gunfire, people were dying one by one. And I remember my aunt saying, 'Katerina is alive,' 'Maria has expired,' etc. There was a strong south wind and our bodies were covered with sand, like floured fish, one next to the other. If my father did not cover us with his jacket, we would have been stabbed. A six-month-old baby was crying inexorably – his mother, a fat woman with huge arms, had received three bullets and was bleeding to death. Someone said we should take the baby to the sea and drown it because its loud cry would give us away. It was taken by his aunt in her arms to calm down and others said, "We will all die together, or none of us". Indeed, the baby calmed down and after 12 hours hidden under the corpses, we cleaned the sand from our faces, quickly buried our dead and left. And they have the boldness to tell us today that we were the barbarians and I do not know what else. There is no truth, our professors said. Not black or white, only nuances, right? And what are our dead people?"

Katina, a 90-year-old survivor of the occupation said: "I remember seeing the airplanes for the first time in my life and thought they were giant birds. That was such a strange spectacle to watch parachutists falling from those big flying birds. I do not know what will happen. I am an illiterate, I never went to school and I cannot talk to those who have degrees, they do not understand me." During the trial, I observed that on several occasions Vassilis, Katina and other members of the audience were crying. When there were ironic comments or even laughter against the resistance, they could not bear to see and they would run out of the room. Several people teared

[62]It is also important to consider that archives, on which historians based their investigations, are created and stored only by institutions or by individuals/groups who have some type of authority. 'Ordinary' people do not keep records and this creates a gap between historical research and what actually happened. In this way, important social categories are excluded from the historical foreground.

up, cried, shouted, grumbled, and abruptly left the courtroom, unable to contain their intense feelings of anger and pain.

It is interesting to consider that in the 1940s German invaders clearly recognized the subject/entity of the local resistance the community; therefore, the reprisals were against certain villages—in their view supporting or otherwise related to partisans—and not against specific individuals or other kinds of social groups. German sociologists such as Ferdinand Tönnies[63] and others with important works on community and society attest to the well-rooted tradition of communal life in their homeland. Cretans were familiar with the concept and practice of collective responsibility/guilt and retributive justice due to the long-lasting tradition of vendetta. However, the custom of vendetta was more concerned with solving conflicts and much more moderate in terms of the loss of human lives.[64] Although the law and the court did not recognize the community as an entity, the audience identified as Cretans and thus felt insulted by Richter's allegations.

11 Richter in Crete: Legal Norms and Ethical Values

> But this was a moral question, and the answer to it may not have been legally relevant.—Hannah Arendt, *Eichmann in Jerusalem: A Report on the Banality of Evil*

Richter repeatedly points to his understanding of the Law of War, but he seems to forget that Germans and Cretans did not get involved in a concerted and regulated duel: the Germans invaded Crete, killing people and sacking the country. The Cretans reacted, defending their lives with less powerful weapons. They maintained their right to oppose the offense, which the Germans inflicted without any provocation from the Cretans. It was the German imperial drive and the Nazi ideology that was responsible for the war, not an irrational attack begun by Cretans against Germany.

The majority of scholars and public intellectuals took pains to defend the freedom of speech and academic freedom against, in their view, an emerging local nationalism whose myths were deconstructed, and whose fame was traumatized. Cretans, according to this argument, did not agree with the representation of their local identity, and therefore they took on Richter with the desire to censor him. However, this argument underestimates the more effective power of stronger states against weaker ones. One can argue that some parts of the book advocate for a specific kind of German nationalism, probably the most extreme one. Not pointing to and not criticizing the connection of such argumentation to German nationalism is like taking sides in terms of power and deep-seated prejudice.[65]

---

[63] Tönnies (2017).

[64] Τσαντηρόπουλος (2004).

[65] It is important to note that some historians and political scientists took sides and slated Richter's book such as Margaritis, Xenakis, Skalidakis, Kotrogiannos, Veremis, and others, some of whom

The Richter case can be seen as one in which freedom of expression and right of historical research defeat factual truth and consequent local indignation: the verdict defended the legal good of academic freedom. However, it is important to note that the resolution from people's reaction to Richter's claims came from where it actually started: the university. The Department of Political Science decided to ask for Richter's nomination as an Honorary Doctor of the University of Crete to be repealed.[66]

As far as the trial is concerned and the specific accusations towards Richter, the verdict of the court of Rethymno was 'not guilty' because, according to the judge, the specific article[67] under which Richter was prosecuted was contrary to the principles of the Greek Constitution related to (a) freedom of speech and the academic freedom, (b) the recognition of historical facts and crimes by the Greek Parliament (and not by International Courts) and (c) against the European Law under which this specific article was introduced to Greek law.[68] While Richter was acquitted on that charge based on the wording of an article of the Law, it seems that in the territory of the university, Richter was declared guilty. This can be seen as a moral condemnation of the accused, despite the verdict of not guilty because of the legalistic inapplicability of the specific article of the Law. In parallel, at the University of Crete, it took some difficulty and time from different parts and agents to proceed to the revocation of the honorary title. The Rectorate of the University of Crete accepted the unanimous decision made by the Department of Political Science to revoke the title. On the 29th of January 2019, the Rector of the University of Crete, in a formal letter, requested the return of the honorary degree as well as any

---

participated as witnesses against Richter. But they were clearly a minority compared to the much larger number of academics and public intellectuals who wrote against the indict, leaving aside the content of the book and the impact to certain people and communities. Skalidakis, a Greek historian, in his article "It's not the case, even if you think so Mr. Richter" addresses the Greek academic historians wondering: "Why this tolerance? Has relativism become so prevalent that the only red line is the denial of Soa and everything else is debatable? Has the fear of identifying a reasonable critique with, generally and indefinitely, nationalism, localism, anti-Europeanism, led to self-censorship? The result is that poorly understood political correctness and restless academicism seem to ignore that the central issue is how history will be written and rewritten in the future. Here again the period of World War II is a crucial one, as we see in the comparisons of "totalitarianism" by the European Parliament and the revival of Nazism in Eastern Europe. Let us not exclude the domestic version of revisionism that methodically rewrites the history of the 1940s in our country in a manner analogous to works like Richter's". See: http://rednotebook.gr/2016/02/den-ine-etsi-ki-etsi-nomizete-k-richter-tou-gianni-skalidaki/.

[66]The procedures and the discussion took almost 3 years, but finally the Rector of the University sent a formal letter to Heinz Richter to inform him about the Senate of the University's decision 385/29.3.2018 asking for the return of the title and anything related to it. The reasoning was (a) due to his publicly declared disrespectful positions towards the institution and its reputation, and (b) because the Senate adopted the twice unanimous decision of the Department of Political Science regarding the repeal of the Honorary title.

[67]Article 2 of the Law 4285/14 the so called "antiracist Law".

[68]In the European Law this article clearly states that only crimes recognized by final decision or judgements by Member State National or International Courts.

related document or emblem.[69] Although institutional justice did not, according to the vindicatory community, respond to its demand to protect their right to memory, the wider local society, including the University, finally justified their plea. In this, the attitude and specific public statements of Richter were probably catalysts. Richter claimed (in interviews in TV programmes and newspapers) that the Greek state owes about 83 million euros to the German state and that the issue of war reparations from Germany to Greece is fictional. He talked about Cretans as fanatics who belong to another race and he argued that his Greek colleagues are in danger of losing their jobs at Greek universities if they dared support an unpopular truth, thus insulting both the institution of the university and his colleagues. After this, the local society along with the university had many more reasons to recall the award.

In Social Anthropology it has been argued that several types of corporate groups like lineages, clans or communities that appear in one way or another in a corporate fashion do not 'really' exist as such, that they have been invented by the classificatory perspective of the anthropologist. But in the field of Legal Anthropology they appear as clear-cut groups both demanding and being liable for responsibility.[70] In this case, it is a demand for responsibility made by a concrete community of offended people. It is precisely the nature and extent of the offence that defines the community.

In this case the community is asking for the acknowledgment of war crimes in a context of re-victimization: the justification of war crimes means a fresh outrage, given the condition of the Cretan (and other Greek people) when their democratic will (via referendum) has been trampled on by the German led financial European interests that have humiliated both the Greek government and people. What they are asking for is the most urgent and elementary form of justice: acknowledgement of wrong-doing and the willingness to reconcile with them as the victims and to repair the damage done, rather than adding fresh outrage to the past crime. It is not revenge that is requested, as the existing Penal law cannot fulfill such a claim. Even the trial kept an uneven struggle between the two parts: an underrepresented community of the offended and an over represented community of scholars (and it seems like only to them the right of corporate solidarity was acknowledged).

The whole process of events and interpretations remains on a long-term vindicatory ethos in an interplay between those who write (compose/craft) history and those who remember, who (re)construct and perform memory as a political gesture. It stands for the History of Justice, waiting for a final reconciliation or for a fatal oblivion.

Acknowledgments This research is implemented through IKY scholarships program and co-financed by the European Union (European Social Fund-ESF) and Greek national funds through the action entitled "Reinforcement of Postdoctoral Researchers", in the framework of the Operational Program "Human Resources Development Program, Education and Lifelong Learning" of the National Strategic Reference Framework (NSRF) 2014–2020.

[69]In the website: http://agonaskritis.gr/.

[70]Cf. Terradas (2008:433, 2019:92–125).

References

English References

Argenti N (2019) Remembering absence: the sense of life in Island Greece. Indiana University Press, Indiana

Avgeridis M (2017) Debating the Greek 1940s: histories and memories of a conflicting past since the end of the Second World War. Historein 16(1-2):8

Bithymitris G, Lialiouti Z (2013) The nazis strike again: the concept of the German enemy. Party strategies, and mass perceptions through the prism of the Greek economic crisis. In: Karner C (ed) The use and abuse of memory. Routledge, London

Belavusau U, Gliszczyńska-Grabias A (2017) Law and memory: towards legal governance of history. CUP, Cambridge

Fabian J (1983) Time and the other, how anthropology makes its object. Columbia University Press, New York

Fronza E (2018) Memory and punishment, historical denialism, free speech and the limits of criminal law. TMC Asser Press

Heinze E (2018) Theorising law and historical memory: denialism and the pre-conditions of human rights. Queen Mary School of Law Legal Studies Research Paper No. 290

Kagiadaki M (2015) Crete visual memories of war. In: Carr G, Reives K (eds) Heritage and memory of war: responses from small islands. Routledge, London, pp 274–291

Kenna M (2001) The social organization of exile: Greek political detainees in the 1930s. Harwood Academic Publishers, Amsterdam

Knight D (2015) History, time, and economic crisis in Central Greece. Palgrave Macmillan, London

Knight D, Stewarts C (2016) Ethnographies of Austerity: temporality, crisis and affect in Southern Europe. History and Anthropoly 27:1–18

Koposov N (2017) Memory laws, memory wars: the politics of the past in Europe and Russia. CUP, Cambridge

Mamoulaki E (2015a) Pictures of exile, memories of cohabitation: photography, space and social interaction in the Island of Ikaria. In: Carabott P, Hamilakis Y, Papargyriou E (eds) Camera Graeca: photographs, narratives, materialities. Ashgate, London, pp 295–312

Mamoulaki E (2015b) From poetic anamnesis to political commemoration: grassroots and institutional memories of the Greek Civil War on an Aegean Island. In: Carr G, Reeves K (eds) Heritage and memory of war. Responses from small islands. Routledge, London, pp 55–74

Nessou A (2009) Deutsche Besatzungspolitik und Verbrechen gegen die Zivilbevölkerung. Eine Beurteilung nach dem Volkerrecht. Vandenhoeck & Ruprecht, Gottingen

Nuzov I (2019) Freedom of symbolic speech in the context of memory wars in Eastern Europe. Hum Rights Law Rev 19:231–253

Panourgia N (2009) Dangerous citizens. The Greek Left and the terror of the state. Fordham University Press, New York

Pantzou N (2011) Materialities and traumatic memories of a 20th century Greek exile island. In: Mayers A, Moschenska G (eds) Archaeologies of internment. Springer, Dordrecht, pp 191–205

Pantzou N (2015) War remnants of the Greek archipelago: persistent memories of a fragile heritage? In: Carr G, Reeves K (eds) Heritage and memory of war: responses from small islands. Routledge, New York, pp 234–254

Piketty T (2020) Capital and ideology. Harvard University Press, Cambridge

Powers T, Rakopoulos T (2019) The anthropology of austerity. Focaal J Glob Hist Anthropol 83:1–12

Terradas I (2008) Justicia vindicatoria. CSIC, Madrid

Terradas Saborit I (2019) La justicia más antigua. CSIC, Madrid
Tönnies F (2017) Community and culture. Routledge, New York
Tourkochoriti I (2017) Challenging historical facts and national truths: an analysis of cases from France and Greece. In: Belavusau U, Gliszczyńska-Grabias A (eds) Law and memory: addressing historical injustice. CUP, Cambridge, pp 151–174
Voglis P (2002) Becoming a subject: political prisoners during the Greek Civil War. Berghan Books, New York

Greek References

Beevor A (2004) Κρήτη. Η Μάχη και η Αντίσταση. Γκοβοστης, Αθήνα
Benz W (2015) Από την αμνησία στην κουλτούρα της μνήμης: Διαχείριση του παρελθόντος στη Γερμανία. Στο: Γαρδίκα Κ, Δρουμπούκη ΑΜ, Καραμανωλάκης Β (επιμ) Η μαρκά σκιά της δεκαετίας του '40. Αλεξάνδρεια, Αθήνα, σσ 26–32
Herzfeld M (2012) Η ποιητική του ανδρισμού. Αλεξάνδρεια, Αθήνα
Herzfeld M (2016) Πολιτισμική Οικειότητα: Κοινωνική Ποιητική στο Έθνος Κράτος. Αλεξάνδρεια, Αθήνα
Κούρτης Δ (2019) Η συλλογική μνήμη της γενοκτονίας του ελληνισμού του Πόντου ως κανονιστικό ζήτημα. Στο: http://clioturbata.com/kourtis_genocide/
Mazower M (2001) Σκοτεινή ήπειρος: Ο ευρωπαϊκός εικοστός αιώνας. Αλεξάνδρεια, Αθήνα
Richter H (2011) Η Μάχη της Κρήτης Εκδ. Γκοβόστη, Αθήνα
Rondholz E (2015) Η επιλεκτική μνήμη των ηττημένων. Στο: Γαρδίκα Κ, Δρουμπούκη ΑΜ, Καραμανωλάκης Β, (επιμ) Η μαρκά σκιά της δεκαετίας του '40. Αλεξάνδρεια, Αθήνα, σσ 81–98
Ανδρέου Α, Κακουριώτης Σ, Κόκκινος Γ, Λεμονίδου Έ, Παπανδρέου Ζ, Πασχαλούδη Ε (επιμ., 2015) Η δημόσια ιστορία στην Ελλάδα. Χρήσεις και καταχρήσεις της ιστορίας. Επίκεντρο, Θεσσαλονίκη
Αντωνίου Γ, Δεμερτζής Ν, Μαραντζίδης Ν, Παναγιωτόπουλος Π, Πασχαλούδη Ε, Σιδέρης Ν, Τσέκου Κ, Χιονίδου Β. (επιμ., 2013) Εμφύλιος: Πολιτισμικό τραύμα. Αλεξάνδρεια, Αθήνα
Αρχοντάκη Σ (1995) Ο θάνατος στον πόλεμο του '40 και στην Κατοχή: Κοινωνικές επιπτώσεις των απωλειών στην κοινωνία της δυτικής Κρήτης. Πεπραγμένα του Ζ΄ Διεθνούς Κρητολογικού Συνεδρίου, τόμος, Γ1:37–52
Αστρινάκη Ρ (2013) Παράδοση βίας και ιδιώματα κρατικότητας στις ορεινές κοινότητες της δυτικής Κρήτης. Στο: Παπαταξιάρχης Ε, Πλεξουσάκη Ε, Ροζάκου Κ (επιμ) Αναθεωρήσεις του πολιτικού. Αλεξάνδρεια, Αθήνα
Βιστωνίτης Α (2011) Η πύρρειος νίκη του Γκέρινγκ, https://www.tovima.gr/2011/06/19/books-ideas/i-pyrreios-niki-toy-gkeringk/yrreios-niki-toy-gkeringk/
Βόγλης Π (2015) Διαμάχες για το παρελθόν; Η δεκαετία του 1949 ανάμεσα στη δημόσια ιστορία και την ιστοριογραφία. Στο: Γαρδίκα Κ, Δρουμπούκη ΑΜ, Καραμανωλάκης Β (επιμ) Η μαρκά σκιά της δεκαετίας του '40. Αλεξάνδρεια, Αθήνα, σσ 351–368
Δετοράκης Θ (1990) Ιστορία της Κρήτης. Ιδιωτική έκδοση, Ηράκλειο
Δορδανάς Σ, Παπαναστασίου Ν (2019) Ο Μακρύς ελληνογερμανικός εικοστός αιώνας. Οι μαύρες σκιές στην ιστορία των διμερών σχέσεων. Επίκεντρο, Αθήνα
Δρουμπούκη ΑΜ (2014) Μνημεία της λήθης. Πόλις, Αθήνα
Δρουμπούκη ΑΜ (2015) Οι πόλεμοι της μνήμης συνεχίζονται. Στο: Γαρδίκα Κ, Δρουμπούκη ΑΜ, Καραμανωλάκης Β (επιμ) Η μαρκά σκιά της δεκαετίας του '40, Αλεξάνδρεια, Αθήνα, σσ 395–420
Καραμανωλάκης Β (2019) Ανεπιθύμητο Παρελθόν: Οι φάκελοι κοινωνικών φρονημάτων στον 20° αιώνα και η καταστροφή τους. Θεμέλιο, Αθήνα
Κουσουρής Δ (2014) Δίκες των Δοσιλόγων 1944-1949 Δικαιοσύνη, συνέχεια του κράτους και εθνική μνήμη. Πόλις, Αθήνα

Μιχαηλίδης ΔΙ, Νικολακόπουλος Η, Φλάισερ Χ (2008) Εχθρός εντός των τειχών: Όψεις δοσιλογισμού στην Ελλάδα της Κατοχής. Ελληνικά Γράμματα, Αθήνα

Στριφτόμπολα Ε (2015) Μαθήματα δημόσιας ιστορίας από το ελληνικό κοινοβούλιο. Η περίπτωση του νόμου 1285/1982 «Για την αναγνώριση της Εθνικής Αντίστασης του Ελληνικού Λαού εναντίνο των στρατευμάτων κατοχής 1941-1944». Στο: Ανδρέου Α, Κακουριώτης Σ, Κόκκινος Γ, Λεμονίδου Έ, Παπανδρέου Ζ, Πασχαλούδη Ε (επιμ., 2015) Η δημόσια ιστορία στην Ελλάδα. Χρήσεις και καταχρήσεις της ιστορίας. Επίκεντρο, Θεσσαλονίκη, σσ 239–249

Τσαντηρόπουλος Α (2004) Η βεντέτα στη σύγχρονη ορεινή Κεντρική Κρήτη. Πλέθρον, Αθήνα

Φλάισερ Χ (2009) Οι πόλεμοι της μνήμης. In: Ο Β΄ Παγκόσμιος Πόλεμος στη δημόσια ιστορία. Αθήνα, Νεφέλη

Χανδρινός Ι (2012) Το τιμωρό χέρι του λαού. Η δράση του ΕΛΑΣ και της ΟΠΛΑ στην κατεχόμενη πρωτεύουσα 1942–1944. Θεμέλιο, Αθήνα

Χανδρινός Ι (2015) Εθνική Αντίσταση. Ιστορικές, πολιτικές και θεσμικές εννοιολογήσεις από το 1941 στο σήμερα. Στο: Γαρδίκα Κ, Δρουμπούκη ΑΜ, Καραμανωλάκης Κ. (επιμ.), Η μακρά σκιά της δεκαετίας του ’40. Πόλεμος-Κατοχή-Αντίσταση-Εμφύλιος. Αλεξάνδρεια, Αθήνα, σσ 191–213

Χαραλαμπίδης Μ (2012) Η εμπειρία της Κατοχής και της Αντίστασης στην Αθήνα. Αλεξάνδρεια, Αθήνα

Χατζηιωσήφ Χ (2015) Ένα Ευρωπαϊκό φαινόμενο και η ελληνική του εκδοχή: Ο αναθεωρητισμός στην ιστοριογραφία της Αντίστασης και του Εμφυλίου. Στο: Γαρδίκα Κ, Δρουμπούκη ΑΜ, Καραμανωλάκης Β (επιμ) Η μαρκά σκιά της δεκαετίας του ’40. Αλεξάνδρεια, Αθήνα, σσ 369–394

Χατζηιωσήφ Χ (2017) Η ευρωπαϊκή ενοποίηση, η Γερμανία και η επιστροφή των εθνικισμών. Βιβλιόραμα, Αθήνα

Γαρδίκα Κ, Δρουμπούκη ΑΜ, Καραμανωλάκης Κ (2015) Η μακρά σκιά της δεκαετίας του ’40. Πόλεμος-Κατοχή-Αντίσταση-Εμφύλιος, Αλεξάνδρεια, Αθήνα

Defenselessness, Offense and Counter-Offense in Legal Disputes Between Employers and Female Domestic Workers

Raúl Márquez Porras and Sílvia Bofill-Poch

Abstract Domestic workers in Spain occupy a vulnerable position in the labor market and in society in general, due to economic, legal and cultural factors. This vulnerability manifests itself in the defenselessness of workers in front of state justice. This chapter deals with the logic of some judicial conflicts between domestic workers and employers—conflicts in which the former is sued by the latter for alleged theft—in the light of the vindicatory theory. The chapter reconstructs in detail three cases particularly emphasizing the lived experience of the worker, in which notions of offense and underservingness, as well as of helplessness and a cry of justice stand out. It also addresses the specific logic of plaintiffs (employers), in which a sense of offense and a search for a disproportionate retaliation maintains a prominent role.

1 Introduction

Certain disputes concerning female domestic workers and their employers, settled in the criminal justice system, appear to corroborate Terradas Saborit's statement regarding the family-related character of these conflicts and the persistence of a vindicatory element "in the background and within the limits of our own system of law".[1] They can be considered *extreme* or exceptional cases insofar as, among other aspects, they begin as more or less ordinary labor disputes but later develop into criminal accusations (of theft, robbery or fraud). The employers' response is disproportionate, and they seem to be acting without any compositional intent. But, on the other hand, these cases do appear to be imbued with some vindicatory elements: appeals to honor and betrayal, offense and counter-offense, defenselessness and outcries about the injustice they (the workers) have suffered.

[1]See Terradas Saborit (2021), p. 3.

R. Márquez Porras (✉) · S. Bofill-Poch
Department of Social Anthropology, University of Barcelona, Barcelona, Spain
e-mail: raulmarquez@ub.edu; bofill@ub.edu

R. Márquez Porras et al. (eds.), *Vindicatory Justice*, Ius Gentium: Comparative Perspectives on Law and Justice 93, https://doi.org/10.1007/978-3-030-79595-5_15

These vindicatory elements are not only present in both parties' actions, but also in those of the judicial staff (judges, public prosecution and, especially, lawyers) in different stages of the dispute. At the beginning, we find an offense felt by the employer and committed by the worker (as a result of her demanding payment of overdue wages or resigning from the job), to which the employer responds with a criminal complaint as part of a reaction charged with personal and emotional considerations. It seems more like a form of retribution or retaliation (payback for the offense) than like a strictly labor-related/legal dispute. But a retaliation which is intended more as a form of punishment than as a quest for reparation, which, added to its lack of proportion, contravenes the usual principles of vindicatory justice systems.[2]

In spite of these peculiarities, and of the very fact that what we are analyzing here are disconnected aspects of a vindicatory background present in some criminal cases, we believe that this type of case is relevant for illustrating the intertwining of logics (vindicatory and civil-criminal), and the limitations and inconsistencies of a state justice. In this regard, it proves the value of the vindicatory theory as a heuristic device, "a standpoint from which to look at other systems", in Terradas' words, and from which to better understand "problems dealing with the social conception of justice".[3] Here the aim is to shed light on the (partially) vindicatory logic of some civil-criminal cases, in which we can observe the (disproportionate) retaliation for an offense or the cry for justice based on defenselessness, in a context marked by inequality and lack of reciprocity between the parties.

In order to explore this matter, we will consider three paradigmatic cases: those of Manuela, Aurora, and Lucía. From a methodological standpoint, the three cases have been reconstructed in different ways: Aurora's case has been solely based on the case file; the other two—Manuela and Lucía's cases—are based on the defense lawyer's account and the direct testimony of the worker herself. This implies that the missing information in each case differs for the purpose of our interpretation, and that, added to the fact that the circumstances in the three cases are somewhat different, each one is particularly useful for shedding light on one of the specific aspects concerning disputes between women workers and their employers. However, the context around the three cases is similar: circumstances marked by the precariousness and vulnerability—as well as the defenselessness and lack of access to justice—of female domestic workers. This vulnerability persists despite the legislative progress made in Spain (Law 27/2011, Royal Decree 1620/2011 and 29/2012), and can be associated with a long-standing cultural undercurrent that undervalues domestic work and those who perform it—all the more so if they are migrants and women.[4]

[2]See in this volume, for instance, Alonso Cabré, Ortuño, Rosés Tubau, and Terradas Saborit.

[3]See Terradas Saborit (2021), pp. 12–13.

[4]Following Mackenzie (2014), we view *vulnerability* as a higher probability of suffering harm and a difficulty in defending one's own interests. The legislation passed in Spain in the last decade is supposedly aimed at regulating and dignifying the domestic work sector: promoting the inclusion of its workers in the Social Security system, their formal hiring by employers, etc. However, it has

2 Cases Brought to Court

We will give a brief account of the three cases, for reference and before proceeding with an analysis. Manuela, who was born in Bolivia and later became a Spanish citizen, began working in 2014 in the home of a well-to-do family, signing a contract to care for a 97-year-old woman during the daytime (the family had other hired help as well). One year later, she decided to leave, presenting her voluntary resignation. The main reason was the workload, far heavier than what was stated in the initial agreement (she worked about 77 h a week, when the contract stated a 40-h week, and in addition to caring for the elderly woman, she cooked, cleaned, greeted guests, etc.). According to Manuela, she "never had a moment's rest." Five months before she resigned, she had managed to get paid for those extra hours, after negotiating with the family and threatening to call the Labor Inspectorate; the elderly woman's son—a businessman and attorney—began depositing the overdue amounts into her bank account. However, several days after she had resigned, he demanded that she return several amounts which he claimed to have deposited by mistake. Manuela refused to do so, saying that the employers still owed her the last month's wages, and again threatened to report them to the Labor Inspectorate. Shortly thereafter, she received a claim of fraud from her former employer, concerning an allegedly duplicated deposit of three monthly-wages due to a trick planned by Manuela (she had supposedly convinced the elderly woman to ask her son to deposit those amounts). Advised by a court-appointed lawyer, Manuela in turn filed a claim for the amounts owed (slightly over €10,000). At the pre-trial investigation, the employer denied all the employment irregularities and emphasized the trust his mother had placed in Manuela, whom he then proceeded to accuse of not only taking the unduly deposited money, but also of stealing €3000 in cash from his mother's closet. This was never proven. The private prosecution requested a 3-year prison sentence for Manuela, plus €5000 in damages. At the trial, held in the Provincial Court of Barcelona in 2017, Manuela was acquitted of the crime of fraud. The acquittal was based on the implausibility of an uneducated worker deceiving an attorney and businessman.[5] Months after the labor lawsuit—with no previous attempt at conciliation and on hold until the criminal trial was resolved—an agreement was reached for Manuela to receive €2000. However, the case had a devastating effect on her. She fell into a depression, went back to Bolivia for a year, and returned to Spain after deciding never to work in a private household again.

Aurora, an Argentine-Italian dual citizen, began caring for a woman who lived in her building after being put in touch with her by the doorman, who in turn was the woman's partner. Aurora did not live in her employers' apartment. Ten months after she was hired, upon returning from a vacation which her employers had not

evident limitations, one of the most glaring of which is that female domestic workers are considered as agents in a "special labor relationship", contributing to a "Special System" of social protection.

[5]There was also a reference to all citizens' duty of care (concerning their property, etc.) to avoid being swindled or deceived.

authorized, she was fired. One month later she was reported to the police for theft and robbery: specifically, for having withdrawn money from her employer's accounts on several occasions, amounting to a total of €24,000, and having taken €30,000 worth of jewelry from the safes. During the investigation, the private prosecutor repeatedly requested a new preparatory inquiry, which was refused, and in his prosecution report he emphasized the employer's situation of helplessness along with Aurora's "coldness" and "turpitude" in taking advantage of her trust. Aurora's defense lawyer attempted to redirect the dispute towards the area of labor, with an accusation related to the breach of Social Security requirements and the intention of avoiding compensation payment for unfair dismissal. At the trial, the private prosecution requested 9 years and 9 months in prison for fraud, aggravated theft, and falsification of documents; the public prosecution requested 4 years and a half. According to the judgment of the Provincial Court of Barcelona, in February 2015, Aurora was sentenced to exactly 2 years for the continuing crime of fraud with aggravating breach of trust and for the theft of money (despite the jewelry theft not having been proven). The judgment stated that Aurora had followed "a premeditated plan" taking advantage of her easy access to the employer's bank accounts, and, in general, of the "special trust" involved in the relationship between the employer and her caretaker, despite also shedding some doubt on the private prosecution's testimony. Both the private and the public prosecution appealed the judgment before the Supreme Court, on the grounds that the sentence imposed did not correspond to the proven offense. The Supreme Court raised the sentence to 2 years, 4 months, and 15 days. After the sentence, Aurora requested to have the prison sentence replaced by deportation from Spain, which the private prosecution opposed; she subsequently requested pardon from the Ministry of Justice, which was refused. Aurora went to prison, serving the last part of her sentence in open detention.

Lucía began working for a well-to-do family, headed by a former military officer in the Franco regime, shortly after she arrived in Spain from Venezuela. She worked as a live-in domestic worker, charged with the task, among others, of caring for a woman with Alzheimer's who attended an adult day care center until 5:30 p.m. on weekdays. The woman passed away, and 6 months later Lucía presented her resignation, claiming several overdue payments. The night that she presented her resignation to her late employer's children, they kicked her out of the house suddenly and without justification. She was also accused of having stolen jewels, a handbag, and a dress—totaling €20,000 in value—although she only found out about the accusation months later and by chance, when she went to the police to renew her residence permit. The accusation (submitted by the late employer's children) was based solely on circumstantial evidence: it would have been easy for Lucía to steal the jewels because she worked in the home and had "freedom of movement"; she "had the opportunity" of stealing (although nobody saw her do it); she left the house "quickly and unexpectedly" and had a visit from a friend who left carrying heavy bags. In addition, according to the claim, she contradicted herself in court about whether she knew that friend, the late employer's family found bags from a jewelry resale shop in the room she had been living in, and she gave an implausible version of her employer's request to have Aurora sell some of her jewelry (considered "illogical" because the employer was an antique dealer and the family was financially comfortable). Lucía was sentenced for theft, aggravated by breach of trust, to one year and one day in prison. She served the entire term because her defense lawyer (a court-appointed attorney) made no appeal and because at no moment after being imprisoned was she granted any right to parole or prison privileges. The main arguments for proceeding this way were her delays in paying compensation to her former employers—which, according to the judge responsible for sentence enforcement, showed "[the lack of] a true will clearly aimed at repairing the damage caused, [...] and resistance to compensation." In addition, her presenting a job offer for domestic work as the reason for being granted Grade 3 imprisonment (with day release) was valued negatively due to her supposed risk of recidivism.

In the following section we further examine certain contextual elements that allow us to better understand the cases of Manuela, Aurora and Lucía, and specifically the defenselessness experienced by female domestic workers. Next, in Sects. 4 and 5 we will take a detailed look at the vindicatory aspects that arise in the conflicts with their employers.

3 Elements of Objective Defenselessness

To understand the origin and the outcome of the cases presented here, we must take into account certain elements which, in our opinion, configure a situation of severe precariousness and vulnerability experienced by female domestic workers. These elements are the following:

1. The legal context in which they perform their work, specifically in the form of what we could describe as *dependent adult care contracts*.[6] As we pointed out in the Introduction, the increased use of contracts in the domestic work sector does not appear to be warranting the empowerment and dignification of women workers. Since most of them are migrant women who need an employment contract in order to achieve legal status (being able to keep their residence permit), acceptance of the employment agreement occurs under duress. Even more than in other cases, the contract appears as a fiction that overlooks the severe de facto inequalities between the employer and the employee.[7] These inequalities are only aggravated by the fact that the work is performed in the private sphere, where neither the Government nor any other third parties are capable of

[6]See Supiot (2000), pp. 342–343.

[7]See Terradas Saborit (2008), pp. 32–25.

guaranteeing compliance of the agreement,[8] and where the employers can exercise absolute authority over the employees: their home is their *kingdom*.[9]

2. In the context of these relationships, the false charges of theft, robbery or fraud—often involving theft of jewels and other personal belongings—are used by the employers as a form of blackmail aimed at steering the conflict away from the labor-related area where they tend to be *in the wrong*. They either have not registered the employee in the Social Security system or have not done so for the full number of working hours; they owe her backed-up wages or have forced her to work more hours than those agreed upon; they have assaulted her or have seriously violated her rights in other ways. But it is also interesting to note that the employers' claims tend to be accepted by the court despite their vagueness and lack of evidence. The charges and the sentence are based on circumstantial evidence, logical assumptions in which prejudices against female domestic workers play a key role, as we will see further on. In addition, once again, a fundamental element is the fact that the conflict arises in the private sphere, in relationships which are both employment-related and personal, thus leading to the aggravating aspect of breach of trust being raised in many cases and also being accepted in court. Furthermore, another key factor in the employees' vulnerability is the weak defense they receive, usually carried out by court-appointed lawyers.
3. In both the labor-related and the judiciary areas, we find the underlying phenomenon of negative stereotyping, as we mentioned earlier: the portrayal of migrant woman workers as ungrateful, lazy, and thieving. These portrayals play a role in the configuration of the prosecution and its credibility, as well as in the outcome of the case in court, activating prejudices that are shared by employers, police officers, and the judicial staff in general.[10] In our cases, we encountered the recurrent notion of a foreign worker who takes advantage of the help offered to her, is lazy, and only works under pressure; or that she is not to be trusted and willing to harm the employer if given the chance, taking advantage of the helplessness of the people in her care. These prejudices, among others, make the private prosecution's weekly-supported accounts seem plausible and reasonable, as we will see shortly.

An interesting point—one that aims to be the main contribution of this article—is that the legal proceedings in which the worker is accused of theft or robbery appear to be part of a retaliatory action taken by the employers, whose development contains elements that follow a vindicatory logic. As we mentioned, this logic is present not only in the employers' actions, but also in those of their representatives, the police officers, and the judicial staff. We will now analyze these vindicatory logics in detail, alternating between the perspectives of the employers, the employees, and the other agents involved.

---

[8] See Supiot (2000), pp. 334–336.

[9] Or, as Lucía's employer would tell her, 'what happens at home, stays at home'.

[10] See Eilbaum (2011).

4 The Employer's Sense of Offense and Disproportion

To a large extent, the conflicts we examined arose from an offense perceived by the employer in reaction to the employee's claim for certain rights. Manuela, for example, quit her job rebelling against her employers' breaches of contract and against the exploitation to which she was being subjected; afterwards, she demanded payment of her overdue wages.[11] Aurora took a break without permission and went on vacation partly defying her employers. Lucía resigned from her job in an attempt to escape from the oppressive environment to which she was subjected by her employers, also asking them for the money they owed her upon her departure.

The offense perceived by the employer is also caused by the employee's quitting her job. The employee's departure has a deeper meaning; it is viewed as a form of abandonment, of breaking away from certain obligations and loyalties: the worker appears to be betraying the expected reciprocity, owed by those who have been *helped* and treated as "one of the family."[12] In fact, the entire conflict is presented as a family affair: the family home has been abandoned, and the employment-related claim affects the family as a whole. In all three cases, coincidentally, the employer's legal representative is a son or someone close to the family: a friend of the businessman son in Manuela's case, a friend and neighbor of the employers in Aurora's case, and one of the sons in the family in Lucía's case. This *family logic* is also present in the way the stolen goods are valued, being described as *special* objects, with jewels portrayed specifically as family heirlooms.[13]

However, the employer's offense and indignation also arise from the perception of the worker's claims and quitting the job as acts of insubordination, as challenges to the employer's position. These must be met with a response that will put things back in their place, maintaining an unequal system of order and privileges as part of what could be described as a class logic. The employer demands *reparation*—an unusual type of reparation, different from that offered by vindicatory justice, as it is not based on the principle of reciprocity, there is no recognition of the harm caused nor of the legitimacy of the other party—and does so through a criminal accusation. The answer is clearly disproportionate, as we mentioned earlier, disproportionate (in terms of the vindicatory paradigm): as there is no equivalence between the offense and the counter-offense (the discussion of working conditions is replicated with a criminal complaint), nor is the principle of prudence followed (of causing with the retaliation "the least possible harm").[14]

[11]Certain workers like Manuela had never been submissive. She demanded that the woman under her care pay the overdue wages, and when the woman gave her evasive answers claiming that her son would pay Manuela in cash, Manuela insisted that she wanted the payments to be deposited to her bank account.

[12]See Pérez and Canevaro (2016), and Canevaro (2015).

[13]For example, Lucía's sentence states that the alleged theft of jewelry "has left the couple's five children without any family memories".

[14]See Terradas Saborit (2012), Terradas Saborit (2021).

The employers' criminal prosecution is marked by a form of anger that seems to be beyond a vindicatory logic, that resembles more to *brute* vengeance or non-regulated retaliation. Others approaches and disciplines would help to understand its logic. From a more psychological perspective, it could be associated with an urge to reinstate a certain control and hierarchy. In Nussbaum's terms, it is the type of anger resulting from down-ranking or status injury.[15] This type of anger attempts to regain control over the other—the offender (the worker)—and stems from the lack of gentleness and empathy towards that person: the ability to understand her experience would eliminate the desire for revenge, according to Nussbaum.[16] The action that seeks to reinstate a previous (and uneven) balance of status also attempts, more immediately, to return the humiliation and make the offender suffer for the affront committed.[17] Incidentally, the offended party need not act upon it directly: "I may want someone else, or the *law*, or life itself, to do it for me"[18] [the italics are ours].[19]

In any case, the employers' criminal lawsuits (their testimonies, the tone of their written statements, etc.) are imbued with a morality that ventures beyond the legal realm. The employers and those representing them seem to be seeking punishment, hoping to give the worker *what she deserves*. This is particularly evident in Aurora's case. The narrative offered by the employers' lawyer has that personal, visceral tone; for example, his prosecution report states:

> Abusing the trust my client had placed in her [...] [Aurora] acted with extreme turpitude, stealing everything she could without caring in the least about the repeated injury she was causing, and, with absolute coldness, proceeded to steal the money, subsequently manipulating the savings account records and stealing the jewels while she continued to deal with my client as if nothing whatsoever had happened.

---

[15]Nussbaum (2016), p. 20. We do not share Nussbaum's view of the desire for payback, because we consider it individualizing and somewhat contradictory. She describes the desire for revenge as a *childish* mistake—the belief that returning the pain will fix something, what she refers to as the "payback fantasy" (2016), p. 39; "a type of magical thinking" (2016), p. 25. However, Nussbaum also points out that the motivation is status injury, which places the matter at a more complex, social level, given that status is a relational category.

[16]Nussbaum (2016), pp. 21–53.

[17]Nussbaum (2016), pp. 21–25.

[18]Nussbaum (2016), p. 22.

[19]Certain forms of hatred mentioned by Nussbaum (2016, p. 50) that are based on the negative judgment of the *other* and everything she does, and on the urge to eliminate her—including feelings and reactions related to racism and xenophobia—apply to the cases examined here. On the other hand, and despite the differences, retaliation aimed at re-establishing a given status is usually found in highly hierarchical societies such as Brazil, where certain actions performed by subordinates are judged as offenses or challenges and met with culturally established responses (formulas such as "você sabe com quem está falando?") that remind of and reinstate the difference in positions—Da Matta (1997). Also in the Brazilian context, Coelho describes how exchanging gifts among female domestic workers and their employers is a way of playing out (and reinforcing) the power relationships between them, even though, in certain cases, a gift that is an *excessive* reminder of the hierarchy can offend the worker—Coelho (2006), pp. 65–79.

This charged tone is also present in the statement of objection to Aurora's request for travelling abroad in order to visit her ill aunt:

> It is obvious that [Aurora] intends to escape [...] We are under the obligation to unmask the defendant's intention to deceive the court with tear-jerking arguments [...]. The defendant is lying, she is lying shamelessly, abusing her constitutional right to lie in her defense, extending it maliciously to avoid justice [...] Does she truly intend to delude us all? Is it not quite a coincidence that this allegedly dying aunt has asked that the defendant be the one to help her in her last days? This is not a matter of being heartless or not, of being cruel or tough; it is a matter of outright deception [...]. This party does not know whether it is true that a member of the defendant's family is dying, and nothing would please us more than to see her show the human sympathy she clearly lacked when she stole from a poor elderly woman. [...] She offers nothing. She only demands, demands with lies, trying to fool us all.

This makes it apparent that—above and beyond professional diligence—the matter seems to have another dimension for the employer's legal representative: he feels equally deceived and offended. His diligence seems out of proportion. And we find further proof that the matter ventures beyond the strictly legal realm in, among other things, his extremely hard-line position in demanding a sentence. Initially, he requested a term of 9 years and 9 months; later on, he appealed the judgment (when the defendant was sentenced, but to only 2 years of prison) and thus managed to have Aurora actually go to prison. Finally, he opposed the request to have the prison sentence replaced by deportation.

An *extralegal* tone and the moral stance of an offended party are also present in the police officers' narrative—despite their not being directly affected by the workers' actions in any of the cases. Furthermore, in Aurora's case, the report submitted by the Mossos d'Esquadra [the Catalan police force] is full of prejudices and assumptions about her and her ill will, and about the employers and their disadvantage. In a revealing paragraph, we read the following (note the heated tone):

> Ms. Aurora took advantage of the trust these people had placed in her, acting maliciously for over six months. She even had a set of keys to the house, so that she could come and go as she pleased. Ms. Aurora used trickery with the aim of becoming the caretaker and helping Ms. M. because she suffers from a chronic disease and has reduced mobility. She used her employer's disability to take advantage of her and steal items such as money from her bank accounts (which could be savings for old age) and jewelry, which were kept in the home (without any consideration for the sentimental value they may have).[20]

[20]It makes no sense to be surprised about the domestic worker having a set of keys to the employer's home when her work requires that she have full access. It is also noteworthy that the prosecuting attorney repeated the same argument, along with the same prejudices about the helplessness of the woman in Aurora's care, the latter's maliciousness, etc.: "[Aurora] acted with particular turpitude against a poor woman suffering from Parkinson's who was helpless, elderly, and disabled, taking advantage of these special circumstances while she was 'caring for her' in her home" [the quotation marks are theirs].

5 The Feeling of Offense Among Female Domestic Workers and Their Imprecation of Justice

As regards the other party, the domestic workers accused of robbery and fraud, they also feel offended. They feel that the truth is not being told, and, more specifically, that their reputation is under attack. And they express these feelings using thoroughly vindicatory language—the kind of language that appeals to honor, to (not) deserving the treatment received and to injustice. They build a response, a defense, based on their "good work" and "honest name". After their experience in court, when their expectations of justice are dashed, and faced with a sentence they consider extremely unjust, they voice what can be viewed as imprecations of justice or, more precisely, cries for justice: cries for help that stem from the defenselessness and injustice suffered, and from the null expectation that someone or something will listen and repair the situation.[21]

The domestic workers are offended, first and foremost, by the image that the judicial staff portrays of them and their work. In Lucía's case, the prejudice about adult care being a form of *nonwork* is apparent. To quote the judgment, "during many hours, she did not have to care for the woman in her charge, who was in an adult day care center." According to the worker, those were precisely the worst hours, because she was constantly at the beck and call of the woman's husband, and worked "twenty-four hours, seven days a week". In Lucia's case, as in the other two, there are also mentions of the assumptions about the *objective* risk involved for employers by the presence of these workers in the private sphere, where they can "take advantage of the circumstances" to commit an offense. And these views are conveyed specifically in the court case—and, in turn, in the jurisprudence: the accusations include *breach of trust* as an aggravating factor, given the "social duty of loyalty" that the workers ought to show towards the employers by virtue of living with them, and which supposedly had been violated.

In general, the workers feel offended—and expresses itself in vindicatory terms too—by the contents of these prosecution reports, orders, and judgments that violate their honour, because they "tell a reality" that differs entirely from their own experience (which routinely include abuse, humiliation and exploitation). Lucía was bothered by the mention of "absolute freedom of movement" at her employers' home when she was a live-in domestic employee working in almost slave-like conditions. For example, the employers would time her to see how long it took her to throw out the trash and did not allow her to receive any visitors or to have a cell phone. She was not given enough to eat (she ate the same thing—boiled vegetables—7 days a week) and was insulted on a daily basis (being called "filthy" and told that she "talked like an Indian"). Comparing her time working in that household with her prison sentence—and adding on the time she had to wait between the initial

[21]See Terradas Saborit (2019), pp. 96–97; Terradas Saborit (2008), p. 15

claim and her imprisonment—Lucía said, "I didn't spend 361 days in prison, I spent nine years!". She also felt that she had more freedom in jail:

> Here [in jail] I can come and go from my room [cell] whenever I want; there are gardens outside. There [at her employers' home] I didn't see any gardens. Here I can talk with the other women; there I had no one to talk to. Here I have a phone, so I can be in touch with my daughter; there I couldn't. Here I have someone who can give me a hug; where I was before, I didn't.[22]

Recalling the dispute, Manuela also listed the many humiliations she had to endure. She specifically remembered that the woman in her care "never got used to calling me by my name" even though she told her time and time again that she wanted Manuela to take care of her until the end of her life. Manuela would confront her and answer, "I don't think so, Madam, because your son is not paying me what he's supposed to". However, as an example of the ambiguity and complexity of this type of relationship, after the trial and the acquittal, Manuela wept because she would never see the woman again. And this is not an exception. Lucía, for example, also claimed to have become attached to the woman in her care, despite how poorly she was treated.

These women workers are also offended by the lawyers in charge of their defense. Lucía's court-appointed lawyer sexually harassed her and showed obvious negligence: he arrived late for the trial and did not appeal the conviction or make any other possible allegations. Lucia literally said, "I had no defense"—emphatically expressing awareness of her defenselessness. In her case, she was also dismayed by the way the judges repeatedly refused to grant her a sentence suspension and open detention, using false facts such as claiming that she was residing in the country illegally or had not served half of her sentence. Lucía could not understand these mistakes or inaccuracies, which she found enormously frustrating and made her feel defenseless before the authorities. She felt that "there is no justice" ("don't you come and tell me that he's an impartial judge. He isn't!"), that she "has no rights at all" and that "everything's rigged". with the judges and other civil servants "lying the whole time". Lucía was treated in a way she feels to be highly unfair and discriminatory, which she associates with her being foreign: "I'm foreign, and I never forget that fact, because I've been told so many, many times".

Manuela felt that discrimination as well. Her attorney described how the judge did not seem to believe her during the trial, assuming she was "another South American woman who had been stealing [...]." However, he changed his view

---

[22]Lucía was subjected to constant humiliations and assaults, from the beginning to the end of the working relationship. For example, she recounted her attempts to obtain the documents for renewing her residence permit (a census certificate): "I had to beg [the employer], it was humiliating. I told him: 'You can't do that, I have a family!' I'm not a piece of shit, which is what they've been making me feel all this time. He'd say, 'If you're good to me, you'll have [the papers]". And in reference to being subjected to recurrent sexual assaults by the employer, she explained, "If I hadn't let him touch me, I would have been fired". She was also offended at the end, when they accused her of having "abandoned" the woman she was caring for, when Lucía claimed they had kicked her out mercilessly: "They stuck all my things in garbage bags and put me out on the street at 11 at night".

when he was faced with the employer's arrogant tone and carelessness ("Are you trying to tell me that a person without an elementary education has swindled a respected businessman like you? [. . .]", the judge blurted out at him). But Manuela feels offended by the very fact of being reported, which—again in terms of vindication—she views as a blemish to her honor: "Never in my life had I been called in by the police. I have no criminal record, I'm from an honest family. We've never been reported. It was so hard to take!".[23]

All these offenses, the blemish to their honor, led them to want to clear up their reputation and seek compensation. Lucía expressed it as follows: "All I want is to have these three years go by and be able to get rid of the criminal record and prove to Spanish society that I'm not the monster the judge says I am". She feels offended by a judgment that states, again, that she abandoned the woman in her care—"I would never abandon anyone [. . .], I never stopped caring for her"—and by the fact that she was described in writing as "a thief". Significantly, the fact is that she, like Manuela, never admitted her guilt, thus not being granted any prison privileges, among other things.

It is difficult for these women to make sense of what they have experienced. On the whole, they feel that it was enormously unjust because of the gratuitousness and disproportion of the attack (criminal prosecution) and its consequences—having to go to prison (in Aurora and Lucía's cases), having to pay a large amount of compensation, health issues, etc. And all of this leads to their voicing imprecations or cries for justice; calls for something or someone to intervene and redress the harm suffered. In a last effort reminiscent of the logic of vindication.

6 Concluding Remarks

The disputes between domestic workers and employers described here show a certain vindicatory substratum. The employers' legal complaints are—from their point of view—the response to what is perceived as an offense; but it is far from the paradigmatic form of retaliation: it seeks to punish and not to compose the (labour) conflict, it is far away from a framework of reciprocity and mutual recognition. Instead, it should be understood in relation to a context marked by an extreme inequality between the parties and the desire to restore a position of dominance and privilege. In addition, retaliation is carried out through the criminal system of justice, a justice that does not precisely level the position of the parties and, furthermore, which is traversed by many cultural and extralegal biases, being an

[23]The consequences, however, did not only concern *honor*. The health impact was devastating. Aurora and Lucía still suffer from severe depression, among other ailments resulting from the experience. As Lucía explained, "I collapsed. It's as if the earth had sunken under my feet and I couldn't get back up [...] I'm afraid to be outdoors, in open spaces. I feel I'm being followed, like I'm in danger. I'm afraid of everything". As for Manuela, she claims to have decided never to work in a private home again. "I've been left with this trauma. What they've done to me is inhuman".

accomplice in the subjugation of the workers—because of the very logic of the procedural functioning, which individualises the conflict and focuses on the criminal complaint, or the prejudices against domestic workers (due to their condition of women, poor and foreigners) shared by legal operators.

We find in the reaction of the women workers, on the other hand, an attempt to *read* the aggression they have suffered, and a reaction in terms of vindicatory justice (in a stricter sense): the need of restitution for the damage and the outraged honour, the search for justice and reparation. But this takes place in a situation of almost total defenselessness and lack of empowerment. For this reason, the only thing that seems to remain for them is the imprecation or cry for justice. The use of which, in vindicatory systems, is a last resort among those who find barred their access to the justice of men. In the cases we have examined here, women in situations of extreme defenselessness appeal to society, to a vague subject or authority in their quest to seek justice and repair to the damage they have suffered. But—unlike what happens in societies ruled by vindicatory justice systems—their call does not seem to get any echo.

References

Canevaro S (2015) Juicios, acusaciones y traiciones. Moralidades en disputa en el servicio doméstico en Buenos Aires. Século XXI–Rev de Ciências Sociais 5(1):26–52

Coelho MCP (2006) Valor Das Intenções, O-Dádiva, Emoção E Identidade. FGV Editora, Rio de Janeiro

Da Matta R (1997) Sabe com quem está falando? Um ensaio sobre a distinção entre indivíduo e pessoa no Brasil. In: Da Matta R (ed) Carnavais. Malandros e Heróis. Para uma sociologia do dilema brasileiro. Rocco, Rio de Janeiro, pp 179–248

Eilbaum L (2011) Familia, justicia y moralidades en el conurbano bonaerense. Rev Anthropológicas 22(1):7–35

Ley 27/2011 de 1 de agosto sobre actualización, adecuación y modernización del sistema de Seguridad Social

Mackenzie C (2014) The importance of relational autonomy and capabilities for an ethics of vulnerability. In: Mackenzie C, Rogers W, Dodds S (eds) Vulnerability. New essays in ethics and feminist philosophy. Oxford University Press, New York, pp 33–59

Nussbaum M (2016) Anger and forgiveness. Resentment, generosity, justice. Oxford University Press, New York

Pérez I, Canevaro S (2016) Entre lo público y lo privado: empleadores y trabajadoras domésticas frente al tribunal del trabajo doméstico de la ciudad de Buenos Aires. Política y Sociedad 53 (1):169–186

Real Decreto 1620/2011 de 14 de noviembre por el que se regula la relación laboral de carácter especial del servicio del hogar familiar

Real Decreto-ley 29/2012 de 28 de diciembre, de mejora de gestión y protección social en el Sistema Especial para Empleados de Hogar

Supiot A (2000) The Dogmatic Foundations of the Market (comments illustrated by some examples from labour law and social security law). Industrial Law J 29(4):321–346

Terradas Saborit I (2008) Justicia vindicatoria. CSIC, Madrid
Terradas Saborit I (2012) Què és la justícia vindicatòria? (Definició i característiques fonamentals). Recerques 64:13–30
Terradas Saborit I (2019) La justicia más antigua. Teoría y cultura del ordenamiento vindicatorio. CSIC, Madrid
Terradas Saborit I (2021) Introduction. Understanding vindicatory systems. In: Márquez Porras R, Mazzola R, Terradas I (eds) Vindicatory justice. Beyond law and revenge. Springer, Heidelberg, pp 10–39

A Vindication of the Rights of Women. Equal Participation in Rituals in a Festival Context

Lidia Montesinos and Margaret Bullen

Abstract Although women's participation in intangible cultural heritage has long been challenged by feminist groups in Spain, it is only in the past two decades that their claims have been taken up by government. In this article, we reflect on the application of the principle of equality to rituals in the festival context and argue that women's demands to take part may be considered a vindication, a call for retribution of a historical offence: the exclusion of women from public and symbolic spaces of their community. We contend the symbolic efficacy of their actions, a transformative power that entails reparation both in the symbolic arena and in the social, political and legislative order. Rituals in festivals emerge as contexts where women might obtain compensation and reparation for the historical discrimination not amended in the judicial or legislative arena.

1 Introduction

Two reports recently published with funding from the Institute for Spanish Cultural Heritage bear witness to the growing interest in women's participation in intangible cultural heritage.[1] The creation of the Observatory for Gender Equality in Culture by the Spanish Ministry for Culture and Sport, in March 2019, brought official recognition for a field of study and intervention previously overlooked. Although UNESCO had begun to address the part played by women in the transmission of heritage in 1999, and incorporated a decidedly more gendered perspective after

[1] Cagide et al. (2019) and Montesinos (2019). The latter presents the results of a project led by Gabeiras Foundation and in which the authors took part, see Gabeiras Foundation (2019).

L. Montesinos (✉)
Doctorate School, University of the Basque Country UPV/EHU, Donostia-San Sebastián, Spain

M. Bullen
Faculty of Education, Philosophy and Anthropology, University of the Basque Country UPV/EHU, Donostia-San Sebastián, Spain
e-mail: maggie.bullen@ehu.eus

R. Márquez Porras et al. (eds.), *Vindicatory Justice*, Ius Gentium: Comparative Perspectives on Law and Justice 93, https://doi.org/10.1007/978-3-030-79595-5_16

2003, it was not until 2015 that it published a more exhaustive report on the need for more research into the subject.[2] In the Spanish context, although generic mention is made of gender equality in the Law to Safeguard Immaterial Cultural Heritage (Law 10/2015 of 26 May), this aspect is barely developed in the National Plan to Safeguard Intangible Cultural Heritage.[3]

However, from the nineties onwards, there have been a number of anthropological studies, mostly from a feminist perspective, which have revealed the persistence of a gender system that discriminates against women and is deeply rooted in expressions of popular and festival culture in Spain.[4] The rituals analysed in these studies and the cases included in the aforementioned reports—especially where the presence of women is the cause of conflict—have highlighted the need for a gendered approach to such manifestations of intangible cultural heritage. These studies have often emerged as a response to "ethnographic emergences", events that bring to the surface something that had been hidden or bring into view something that had previously gone unnoticed.[5] In this case, we refer to processes instigated by women based on their demand to participate in public rituals in the festival context,[6] in roles traditionally reserved for men and in positions of responsibility in the organisational structures.

The ritual nature of the activities discussed here is critical to our arguments. We understand the performances, parades and processions in which women seek to take part mediate between the symbolic order of the festival and the social order of the wider community, where gender relations and roles are systematized. The criteria for qualifying as ritual the activities described are that they follow a standardized and repetitive, culturally or religiously prescribed order for carrying out a series of rites

---

[2]UNESCO (2015), Rostagnol (2015), Bullen and Pérez (2019) and Cagide et al. (2019).

[3]Title II of the Law, article 3b states: "The principle of equality and non-discrimination. The traditional character of intangible manifestations of culture will in no way serve as a cover for actions which may constitute an infringement of the principle of gender equality". The Plan only mentions the gender variable in order to emphasise the diversity of symbolic appropriations of heritage, and of women, in order to recommend that the media's treatment of intangible culture should bear in mind "the representative nature of all social groups implicated in all social practices (the role of men and women, above all when they develop their activity behind the scenes...)". Nevertheless, it should be noted that the Constitutional Law (3/2007 of 22 March for the effective equality of women and men) and especially some autonomous laws of equality refer to equality in the cultural and festive realm, references that have to a large extent been incorporated as a result of the conflicts we address in this article.

[4]Bullen (1997, 2000), Heuzé (1999), Bullen and Egido (2003), Farapi (2009), Gisbert (2010), Lafita (2013) and Moral (2014).

[5]Díez and Bullen (2012).

[6]It is difficult to translate the culturally specific term *fiesta*. The English "festival" barely renders the social sense of the *fiestas* celebrated once a year in every town, village and neighbourhood of Spain. Within each *fiesta* there are one of more emblematic events or activities, parades or performances, which assume a ritual nature. We will refer to these as "festival rituals" or "rituals in the festival context", but we will also use the Spanish term *fiesta*.

or solemn acts. In our case, these rituals are central to the celebrations of local fiestas.[7]

In this chapter, we highlight the persistence of gender inequality in the ritual-festival realm and the resistance to the incorporation of women in many municipalities of Spain, triggering local disputes and social divides. We will show how the analysis of festival rituals from a gender perspective allows us to reflect on the practical application of the principle of equality and, especially on methods of social transformation advocated by different activists in the struggle for gender equality and from different strands of feminism. We contend that these collectives' demand for equality in the ritual-festive space takes on the nature of a vindication in response to the historical offence implied by the exclusion of women from these spaces of symbolic community representation.[8] We maintain that their gestures and actions are replete with symbolic efficacy,[9] with a transformative power that entails reparation within the ritual and symbolic space, but whose vindicatory force is also demonstrated in the social, political and legislative order, intervening moreover in modifying the customs, imaginaries, educational practices and social relations that reproduce discriminatory practices. In addition to this transformative potential, we stress that the anthropological analysis of rituals in the festival space reveals them to be arenas of local representation and political dispute where women might obtain compensation and reparation for the historical discrimination not amended in the judicial or legislative arena.[10] It must be taken into account, moreover, that the Interamerican Court of Human rights has recognised the importance of symbolic reparation on many occasions—most recently in relation to femicides in Mexico—as a constitutive element of juridical reparation that should not be underestimated in comparison with other measures proper to the civil-penal justice system.[11] As we shall argue, the symbolic efficacy of this reparation in the ritual context influences and modifies the social order in ways that are often more effective than a judicial sentence or recognition in law.

---

[7]Bullen (2003), pp. 226–230.

[8]Gisbert (2011).

[9]Lévi-Strauss (1958), Sperber (1978) and Bourdieu (1998).

[10]In order to understand the variety of forms that these rituals of reparation and composition might adopt, see the chapter of this volume by Ignasi Terradas, "Introduction: Understanding Vindicatory Systems" and also Terradas (2008, 2019).

[11]International jurisprudence has repeatedly established that a sentence that declares a violation of human rights constitutes a form of reparation *per se,* a question that directly refers to the symbolic nature and effect of judicial resolutions. cf. Case of Las Dos Erres Massacre v. Guatemala, Sentence of 24 November 2009; the Gonzalez, Monreal and Monarrez (or the "Cotton Field") v. Mexico Case, Sentence of 16 November 2009; the Dacosta Cadogan v. Barbados Case, Sentence of 24 September 2009; the Anzualdo Castro v. Peru Case, Sentence of 22 September 2009; and the Neira Alegría and others v. Peru Case, Sentence 19 September 1996.

2 Gender Roles in Rituals in the Festival Context

Numerous ethnographic studies have shown how different kinds of rituals, performed in ceremonies and festivals dramatize power relations—both internal and external—in the community or municipality that organizes or represents them.[12] The rituals in the *fiestas* analysed over the past two decades in Spain and revised in Gabeiras[13] are no exception: public and religious (Catholic) authorities play a prominent role and the leading figures, whether in the public eye (parades, cavalcades, processions, dramatisations…) or behind the scenes of the event's organisation, are mostly males who personify hierarchical structures of prestige, seniority and status.[14] The centrality of these male figures is defined by an oppositional relationship with female figures who either line the streets or watch from windows as spectators or cheerleaders of the event, or take charge of domestic chores, looking after the family and seeing to administrative tasks that underpin the festive ritual, as female-carers or mother-figures.[15]

In some cases, as a result of historical change, women might also accompany male figures or make an appearance in spaces reserved especially for them, as a decorative appendage that reaffirms the prestige of the festival and the symbolic power of masculinity. These female figures epitomize the values of youth and beauty and in some cases are elected by the men and parade alongside their fathers, uncles and brothers. Their exhibitionist role as fetish/object correlates with that of a symbolic possession available for the matrimonial market. Many of these female roles are embodied by young women, of between approximately 18 and 25 years of age, single and who have not had children. In some cases studied, girls are excluded from an early age because the festival is considered to constitute a space of male socialisation; in other cases, young women are separated out during puberty, when their bodies begin to develop. From that moment on, they are obliged to adopt the clearly defined roles assigned to their gender: woman as object or fetish. The rituals analysed thus reproduce patterns of sexual differentiation that magnify male power and virility, and produce a delightful and colourful show of women at a marriageable age.[16]

As Pierre Bourdieu[17] describes in *Masculine Domination*—following Gayle Rubin[18]—the incorporation of a gender perspective in the comparative analysis of rituals in the festival context shows how they reproduce gender practices and stereotypes which are generally not perceived to be discriminatory by the people

[12]For example, Hocart (1927), Gluckman (1954) or Gramsci (2011).

[13]Gabeiras Foundation (2019).

[14]Ortner and Whitehead (1981) and Gisbert (2010).

[15]Bullen (1997) and Gisbert (2010, 2015).

[16]Rubin (1975), Bullen (1997), Bourdieu (1998), Bullen and Egido (2003), Gisbert (2010, 2015) and Antuña (2017).

[17]Bourdieu (1998).

[18]Rubin (1975).

who participate in them. This is because gender differentiation and subsequent subordination is assumed something "natural" and interiorised through formal and embodied learning, communication, beliefs and feelings. This naturalisation is tantamount to *symbolic violence*[19] or *moral* violence:[20] a type of invisible, unconscious violence that is not perceived as such because, to some extent, using Fernández's expression *it transforms relations of domination and submission into affective relations,*[21] or in Segato's words, into routine microscopic images of everyday life.[22]

Nevertheless, from a historical perspective we can observe modulations in the gender system, together with a growing awareness of the naturalisation of inequalities. In Spain, during periods of greater freedom that brought the recognition of women's rights—under liberal or progressive governments—it was easier to introduce change into the festival arena. In the late nineteenth century, some women, for example, attained prestigious positions in the bourgeoisie or aristocracy and in the 1920s and 1930s, during the political and revolutionary fervour of the Republican years, women appear in the public space of the *fiesta.* However, over the following 40 years of Franco's dictatorship and National Catholicism, when cultural and gender policies reinforced sexual differentiation and female subordination, women were once more relegated to the domestic sphere and their reproductive functions.[23]

As the political situation eased, women gradually began to denounce this discrimination from the 1960s onwards and then more forcefully in the 1970s and 1980s, following Franco's death and the promulgation of the Spanish Constitution in 1978. New legal codes were drawn up to address the historical and political construction of sexual division, together with the formal recognition of individual rights in questions of gender equality. The 1978 Constitution, which included the principle of equality and non-discrimination as a fundamental pillar of the Spanish legal system, was vital for the demands of women in general, and in the case which concerns us, provided support for their requests to participate in rituals in the festival context.[24]

[19]Bourdieu (1998).

[20]Segato (2003).

[21]Fernández (2005), p. 9.

[22]Segato (2003), p. 119.

[23]Sánchez (2003), Moreno and Kerexeta (2006), Moral (2014), Martínez (2015) and Antuña (2017). The Spanish Republic's 1931 Constitution laid out the principle of equality of the sexes, allowed the development of the divorce law and introduced wide-reaching legislative advances in matters of equality between men and women. The Franco dictatorship (1939–1975) represented an enormous setback for the rights of women, relegated to the home, procreation and family care.

[24] Gisbert (2010),Alcaraz (2014), Martínez (2015) and Domene (2015). In 1987, in Villena (Alicante), women who wanted to participate in the festival of Moors and Christians denounced as unconstitutional the festival's statutes for stipulating the participation of "all male individuals". Fearing a resolution favourable to women, the men decided to modify the statute and regulate the incorporation of women, with restrictions (Domene 2004, 2015) and the court effectively ruled the modification of the statute. Legal action subsequently taken in Alcoi (Alicante) and in the Bidasoa area (Basque Country) was additionally protected by article 14 of the Constitution: *Spaniards are*

From the 1980s onwards, many such rituals were reinvented or reinforced by the newly constituted governments of the democratically defined state of autonomies and *fiestas* in general were opened up to a greater participation increasingly linked to leisure and amusement rather than exhibition and commemoration.[25] In this context, many women took part in the organisation of new festival events or were incorporated into rituals in which their participation became necessary or desirable for financial reasons or for lack of participants, as in the case of the Easter processions or of some troupes of Moors and Christians.[26] However, where festivals were thriving—usually the oldest and most prestigious—the mostly male organisational committees resisted innovation and the festival structure slowed down a process of transformation in keeping with social change and impeded the achievement of equality.

As mentioned above, the indispensable role of women as carers and assistants in rituals in the festive context—an invisible labour force rarely acknowledged in the maintenance of intangible heritage—has gone hand in hand with a limited participation, restricted to decorative, passive and secondary roles accompanying men. Although these roles may exclude them from the most important acts and representative activities of the ritual (for example, playing an instrument, carrying a weapon, singing or marching) they at least allow women to appear in the public space for the first time. Our report shows that this was, to a large degree, the result of their repeated demands and insistent campaigning. Sectors opposing the incorporation of women—and some of those in agreement—are of the opinion that rather than marching as soldiers, combatants or in any other role associated with masculinity, women should accept parts seen to be in keeping with their gender. For those who think this way, festival dress, uniforms or outfits should befit what is referred to as the "sexual nature" of each body,[27] otherwise, they would cease to be appropriate ritual garments and become fancy dress costumes. Such cross-dressing is seen to be transvestism or transgression and such reactionary arguments are often tinged with homophobic or transphobic attitudes.[28]

Towards the end of the twentieth century, then, women's demands shifted towards achieving more active leading roles in the *fiesta*. When they met with resistance, one strategy adopted was to create new female figures, in keeping with the aesthetic, historical and mythological meanings of the festival. A paradigmatic case is that of the *aguadora* or Water-Carrier in the Tamborrada of Donostia/San Sebastián, created *ex proffeso* to facilitate the acceptance of women's participation in

equal before the law, without discrimination on account of birth, race, sex, religion, opinion or any other personal or social condition or circumstance.

[25]Boissevain (1992), Ariño and García (2006) and Alcaraz (2014).

[26]Sánchez (2003) and Domene (2004).

[27]The statute of the festival of Moors and Christians of Alcoi states that the participant should "represent the nature of the character" (Gisbert 2010).

[28]Farapi (2009), Lafita (2013) and Montesinos (2019).

the festival[29] or the *patgessa* (page) Nazira in the King's Cavalcade of Igualada.[30] In a number of towns in Alicante, specific female garments have been created for women to participate in the Moors and Christians parades, but this initiative was taken by the sectors initially opposed to women's participation: a strategy to admit them—in the face of social pressure—but in a segregated way and without practically any rights.[31]

These female figures assume gender differentiated, sexually segregated roles intended to facilitate their progressive entrance into the festival and make it easier for reactionaries to assimilate their presence. In some cases, this strategy has allowed women relatively fast access to the festival, before going on to assume other typically male roles.[32] However, these new female figures may suffer the same problem as their previous ornamental counterparts: that is, that women may be pigeonholed in these roles, with special costumes just for them, preventing them from achieving equality in all ritual acts and actions. Although such participation may satisfy the demands of some women, it raises other problems, since the sexually differentiated outfits reproduce gender stereotypes that ultimately prevent egalitarian participation.[33]

Another aspect worthy of mention is the debate over mixed spaces and the intermingling of men's and women's bodies in the ritual space. From the perspective of the hegemonic construction of gender, this intermingling is deemed dangerous and undesirable, and in some cases it is a taboo, since the festival reproduces the separation and differentiation of the sexes laid down by social norms linked to sexuality, marriage and reproduction. In this sense, in the cases studied in Montesinos[34] there is a refusal to mix men and women, since shared spaces may blur gender hierarchies, corporal differences and the traditional understanding of the sexes. This generates resistance, defended in terms of aesthetics but responding to binary, puritan and religious moral customs that consider contact between male and female bodies problematic. These attitudes are, moreover, intensely heteronormative: there is no questioning of contact between people of the same sex who may have a different sexual orientation.

However as Moral[35] has emphasised with regard to the Tamborrada, mixed spaces are not necessarily egalitarian or equal: there are usually far fewer women than men and the former may not have access to all parts and positions. What is open

[29]Farapi (2009) and Moral (2014).

[30]Lafita (2013).

[31]Domene (2004) and Gisbert (2010).

[32]Moral (2014).

[33]Tulles and ornaments hinder the ability to shoot in the battles of Moors and Christians; skirts and sashes can be uncomfortable when it comes to urinating during the long hours that the Tamborrada lasts; female garments offer less protection from the cold in the winter Caldereros festival; and complements like the boots and fans of the serving girls in the Alardes of the Bidasoa cause blisters and sores, affirming a popularly accepted relationship between the values of beauty and sacrifice.

[34]Montesinos (2019).

[35]Moral (2014).

to debate, in a performative, practical and material sense, is the meaning of equality and how it may be achieved. The most radically egalitarian positions demand that men and women have the same opportunities to perform any role in spaces that allow undifferentiated access; only free choice can guarantee real equality. Nevertheless, the sectors opposed to this idea raise infinite objections and devise numerous strategies that combine segregation and discrimination. They mock demands for women to wear male dress or for men to don women's clothing; this cross-dressing is associated with homosexuality and in conservative homophobic sectors, condemned as absurd or an aberration.

In this sense, the reversal of gender roles in festivals underscores the leading role of men and their symbolic power, since they have had the prerogative to perform specifically female roles.[36] This transvestism is considered an acceptable transgression, specific to the ritual and, therefore, representing order and tradition. In contrast, it is not acceptable for women to dress up as men, perform male roles, or for men to perform non-prestigious female roles. The danger of such transgressions—their opponents contend—is that they "carnivalize" the festival, causing it to lose its serious, sacred and formal character, defended by those who seek to perpetuate a tradition—in many cases military and religious—based on male domination.[37]

As stated at the outset, the analysis of conflict arising from disputed gender roles in festivals, functions as an allegory of the debates within feminism about what equality between men and women means or how it may be achieved. Feminisms of difference would argue for differentiated roles, while feminisms of equality postulate equivalent or equal parts; others propose to deconstruct gender roles, in recognition of the performance of gender and the possibility of exchangeability, along queer and transfeminist lines.[38] The analysis of the symbolic meanings of rituals in the festival context, the singularities and nuances of their signifiers, channels into political and feminist reflection, while at the same time revealing the social construction of gender and sexuality.

[36]For example, that of the Virgin Mary in the Mystery of Elx (Montesinos 2019), or the queen and her ladies-in-waiting in the Caldereros of Donostia/San Sebastián (Farapi 2009).

[37]Bourdieu (1998).

[38]In the cases analysed, this possibility is ridiculed, seen to be outrageous or treated as taboo: for example, the idea of a male *cantinera* in the Alardes or a boy Beautiful Easo in the children's *Tamborrada*.

3 Laws Against Customs and the Symbolic Efficacy of Demands

As previously mentioned, the promulgation of the Spanish Constitution in 1978 was pivotal for the advancement of women's claims for equal participation in festival rituals.[39] To some extent, the Law demonstrated both its symbolic and instrumental efficacy,[40] permitting restorative social—and legal—processes that responded to women's demands. However, that efficacy was limited and in some municipalities, insufficient to overcome opposition to the incorporation of women into the festivals where traditionalists refuted the existence of any gender discrimination in their *fiesta*. Some refused to acknowledge the legitimacy of the women's requests or the applicability of the principle of equality consigned by the legislation to cultural manifestations seen to be subject to tradition alone.[41] We should point out that men have not been the only opponents to the incorporation of women; female voices, organised in collectives and associations, have also expressed their rejection of the vindication, defending and reclaiming traditional roles instead. At the same time, they convey their offence at the underestimation of their role in festive rituals and refute the idea that the tradition was unfair or discriminatory.

We propose that Spanish legislation—as an ideal code and declaration of intent—has failed to deliver its entire equality mandate because it meets with emotional attachment and ritualized customs, nostalgia and respect for ancestral traditions, channelled through intergenerational family and community relations and the defence of certain values and beliefs including differentiated gender roles. We are witnesses to what Segato refers to as "automatic sexism",[42] a structural violence founded on and reproduced through deeply rooted customs and traditions, gestures and routines that articulate relations of power and subordination. In the face of the intricate functioning of this gender systems, the law reveals itself to be limited in the transformation of discriminatory customs, habits, practices and hierarchical relations based on male superiority.[43]

Terradas has underscored the existing contradiction between on the one hand, the legislative will to abolish machismo as a social scourge and the reminiscence of a past that has been surpassed by an egalitarian morality, and on the other, the recognition of the persistence of deeply socially rooted sexist practices and attitudes

---

[39] Alcaraz (2014).

[40] García-Villegas (1993) and Segato (2003).

[41] Bullen and Egido (2003), Farapi (2009) and Gisbert (2010).

[42] Segato (2003) p. 121.

[43] The tension linked to the birth of the State and the system of civil/penal positive Law is well known: the opposition or complementarity between Law and custom. As the polysemy of the concept of custom is beyond the reach of this chapter, see Terradas (2010), Gluckman (1956) or Malinowski (1926) for a definition of custom in the legal sense, and Assier-Andrieu (2001) for a critical update.

constituting what the Law terms "sociocultural conditioners".[44] Following the reflections of Terradas, Segato and our own research[45] there is a clear need to address this tension in the implementation of more efficacious processes and policies aimed at combating sexism and achieving greater levels of equality.[46] We understand that the demands of women to take part in rituals in the festival context function effectively to transform a reality of everyday discrimination, reinforced through the cyclical repetition of local festivals and their rituals, in spite of the Law. The action of these women and assertion of their rights acquires greater symbolic power when it erupts into the ritual and festive space or what González—Requena calls "the matrix of the meaning of the myth",[47] in this case, that of male domination and the subordination of women.

In this regard, the arguments of those who oppose women's participation in festival rituals are illuminating. They maintain it to be a question of tradition, that it has always been done this way or that it is a commemoration of historical events in which women did not take part. Others argue that the "people" or the "majority" want the festival to remain as it has always been; it belongs to the "people", they say, it represents "our" identity. It follows that whoever wants to change the ritual does not identify with it nor understand it, does not "feel" it: they are outsiders. A whole series of justifications that appeal to tradition and a collective identity based on moral sentiments, is raised to combat the criticism of being unfair and discriminatory. The most conflictive cases studied demonstrate that there is no consensus on the meaning and form in which to apply the principle of equality, especially in relation to these naturalised and essentialised traditions, where subtle, invisible violence is much more difficult to reveal than physical violence.[48]

According to Anderson and Gellner arguments revolving around emotion, feelings and territorial identifications are more befitting of conservative and nationalist forces who seek to protect their privileges, in the case in hand by converting the ritual or festival into intangible heritage and presenting it as representative of the whole community.[49] The ritual practices transmitted from generation to generation, are packaged as symbolising "the people", but in fact reproduce relations of status

[44]Terradas (2018) analyses the jurisprudence in questions of gender violence in Spain and the Constitutional Law 1/2004 of 28 December, on the Measures for Comprehensive Protection against Gender Violence.

[45]Terradas (2018), Segato (2003) and Gabeiras Foundation (2019).

[46]The *Convention on the Elimination of All Forms of Discrimination against Women* (United Nations General Assembly Resolution 34/180, New York, 18 December 1979, ratified by Spain in 1983) also emphasises this question: *State Parties shall take all appropriate measures to modify the social and cultural patterns of conduct of men and women, with a view to achieving the elimination of prejudices and customary and all other practices which are based on the idea of the inferiority or the superiority of either of the sexes or on stereotyped roles for men and women* (article 5).

[47]González-Requena (2009) p 30.

[48]Bourdieu (1998) and Segato (2003).

[49]Anderson (1983) and Gellner (1983).

and subordination that are able to resist the principle of equality "because of tradition". In denying the legitimacy of women's demands and the offence they denounce, it becomes apparent that to concede these claims would require a transformation at the core of their own community's power structure and this of course enters into conflict with certain interests and privileges.

The expression of women's claims calls into question the differential status of men that pivots on an asymmetric power relationship with regard to women and informs a local and collective identity. Values such as virility, bravery or the ability to wage war, having a voice to lead worship or call people into battle, being invested with the authority to manage the symbolic capital of ritual or orchestrate power relations as active political subjects, have historically been the prerogative of males, the metonymic image of the "people" or the nation.[50] If women take part equally alongside men, that is, if they march as soldiers, as warriors in the battle between Moors and Christians, if they sing "flirtatious" songs in the festival of the (male) Caldereros, or join them in a procession in honour of the Virgin Mary, this challenges the symbolic gender order represented by the ritual and by extension, reproduced in the social order. As we saw earlier, many who reject the incorporation of women think that if they take part as "men" then the festival is devalued, loses prestige and becomes a carnival; as roles are blurred, masculinity loses its symbolic hegemony.[51]

This is why the demands of women are often received as an offence, as an attack on tradition and its values. Defenders of tradition may adopt intolerant and occasionally aggressive attitudes, defending prestigious male positions and mobilising forces of resistance in the face of the changes implied by the incorporation of women.[52] While the transformation of the gender system may result in some form of violence, since it implies not only the modification of deeply rooted customs but also wider structural change, we cannot forget that this transformation responds to the need to correct a historical injustice against women which, once vindicated, can no longer be overlooked. The tension produced by the demands for justice or the alleged brusqueness of the movements that call for the rights laid down by the law, is not comparable to the violence exercised by the reactionary sectors. Moreover, the defence of privileges and status finds no arguments that can be legally justified; there is no right or law which protects the unfair or discriminatory customs that have been brought into question, rather legislation has been drawn up to eradicate them.[53] As

---

[50]González-Abrisketa (2013).

[51]Rubin (1975) and Gisbert (2010).

[52]Asensio and Iraola (2018).

[53]In this sense, both K. Marx (Bensaïd 2007) and Thompson (1980) pointed out that legal customs were those that emerged among the popular classes, based on necessity and equity in order to survive; their legitimacy stemmed from communitarian consensus of their importance for peaceful coexistence, and for that reason they should not provoke any opposition. Customs established by force, by the imposition of a law or favouring certain privileged groups were considered "bad customs" or "unfair customs", not established spontaneously through communitarian social life but through the abuse of power and protection of specific interests (González 1981). F. K. Savigny,

Segato emphasises, legislation should mediate and administer the coexistence of different customs and moralities, as long as they do not go against the fundamental principles of the law or avoid abiding by it using arguments based on social majorities or local, national or patriotic identifications.[54]

We propose that actions based on the demands for change from women's collectives are effective in making visible the implicit symbolic violence of rituals in the festival context. These rituals are laden with a symbolic efficacy that, as suggested by Lévi-Strauss[55] and developed by Sperber[56] and Bourdieu,[57] is capable of spanning multiple learning mechanisms and spheres of meaning. Insofar that festive rituals are *total social events,*[58] embedded in social, family, political or economic life,[59] the visible presence of women or the vociferous condemnation of their absence are significant gestures with meaningful effects. They contribute to the modification of relations, feelings and imaginaries, everyday bodily practices that make up the consuetudinary law linked to the *fiestas* in specific municipalities. We maintain that such demands are charged with symbolic efficacy because their actions, gestures and words intervene in the symbolic order, dialogue with it, question and interrupt it, provoking reactions and transformations on the social plane and in the corporal order, in practices and emotions, in the *habitus* and in customs otherwise difficult to modify. As participation in ritual connects spaces and meanings that have repercussions beyond the gesture itself, these women's demands acquire the status of a magical, transforming force that traverses and deconstructs the symbolic order. In doing so, they reclaim justice and reparation for the historical discrimination that women have suffered and contribute to the modification of consuetudinary aspects that the Law alone is insufficient to eradicate. It is an ethical and political wager that, moreover, affects political, legal and legislative debates and resonates in a variety of ways in the social order.[60]

however, argued that the customs of the governing upper classes should also be considered, and this had consequences in the thought of the historical school of the German Right, which emphasised the fundamental character of custom ("the spirit of the people") in constructing the Law, and the recognition of the consuetudinary law of "peoples" in its ethnicist and romantic version (González 1981; Rodríguez 2011). Savigny's thought and that of the German school influenced legal and anthropological thought in the Spanish state before and after the Franco dictatorship, and especially in the study of folklore and popular culture divested of its class component (Costa et al. 1902; Velasco 1990). Following Segato (2003) we stress that there is no continuity between "unfair" customs and the law, between the discriminatory moral and religious system and the legal system, between the status and privilege system and the contract system based in the principle of equality.

[54]Segato (2003).

[55]Lévi-Strauss (1958).

[56]Sperber (1978).

[57]Bourdieu (1998).

[58]Mauss (1924).

[59]Polanyi (1977).

[60]The incorporation of women into the public and organisational part of rituals in the festival context suggests similarities with the arguments put forward by *The Politics of Presence* (Philips 1995) in regard to political or powerful positions. Here, too, women's demands go beyond mere

4 Discrimination Against Women as Legal Exceptionalism

Just as a gendered analysis of rituals in the festival context mirrors a broader struggle for equality, so the study of the resistance to the incorporation of women reveals the obstacles met in the struggle to achieve gender equality in other areas too. The examination of conflicts in the festive and ritual environment reveals—again in accordance with Bourdieu, Segato and Ortner and Whitehead[61]—that the hierarchical festival structures which underpin relationships of status and prestige linked to the Church and/or conservative sectors (in Spain historically connected to Francoism) are not surprisingly found to be the most resistant to change. As we have seen, arguments based on emotion and feelings, faith and belief, the family, nation and identity, mobilise populist and intolerant passions which distain the principles of diversity and inclusion.

Furthermore, the pronounced androcentric nature of the Law and jurisprudence is evidenced in the legal exceptions that permit the perpetuation of discrimination against women, generally constructed from a positivist point of view, intrinsic to legal dogmatism and linked to the concept of freedom under private law.[62] When women's demands find no response from those in charge of the festival and their local councils take no pro-equality measures—whether by omission or complicity—the next step is to take legal action. First, as in many of the cases studied, they might resort to an ombudsperson, centre for women's affairs or authority for equal rights.[63] These bodies have always taken a stance against discrimination, in favour of equality and the right of women to take part in rituals, but their resolutions are not binding and compliance with their recommendations depends on the good faith of those involved in the conflict.[64] Where they find themselves without defence, they might resort to legal action, appealing to article 14 of the Constitution and the principle of non-discrimination.[65]

In the case of the Alardes of Irun and Hondarribia, the most conflictive examples in Spain, the first legal sentences recognised the right of women to participate in these parades on an equal footing with men, given that they were public events subsidised by local councils, which also took part in the organisational structures and

participation to achieve more ambitious goals in the modification of certain values and meanings of the festival. Nevertheless, the transformative potential of incorporating women into the festival is often reduced to the struggle over admission, forcing other wider-reaching objectives to be put on hold or sidelined (Lafita 2013).

[61]Bourdieu (1998), Segato (2003) and Ortner and Whitehead (1981).

[62]Marín (2000) and Saborido (2011).

[63]Gisbert (2010) and Moreno and Kerexeta (2006).

[64]In spite of the official nature of these institutions, the ombudsperson's recommendations have been ignored in Alcoi and also in Irun and Hondarribia. This situation of exceptionality led the Valencian Síndic de Greuges to declare the Town Council of Alcoi "hostile" for turning a deaf ear to its recommendations (Gisbert 2010) and encouraged some collectives to resort to the legal route, often relying on legal arguments developed by ombudspersons.

[65]For the summaries and analyses of jurisprudence concerning such conflicts—most surrounding the case of the Alardes—see Montesinos (2019).

in certain acts of protocol.[66] The courts considered that these festivals were not an exact recreation of the events being commemorated and, as such, the exclusion of women was not justified on the basis of the argument that they were not present during those historical events (wars, battles, rituals). Yet even if they were exact recreations, as the courts observed, a custom could not go against the principle of equality. As a result, the court ruling recognised, the existence of discrimination and urged the councils to take every measure possible to support and guarantee the presence of women in the festival.[67]

However, these sentences and the precautionary measures they recommended in order to guarantee the safety of women who wanted to take part, did not put an end to the continued boycott against their incorporation: the resolutions were not carried out and the conflict resulted in a problem of public order managed by the Basque Ministry of the Interior and the Ertzaintza (the Basque police force). This led to a situation of defencelessness for women facing sustained aggression during the festivals and continued harassment on a day-to-day basis. The atmosphere in these two municipalities became increasingly tense and men and women opposed to the incorporation of women in the ritual were free to express their opposition fiercely in the streets and devise a legal strategy to avoid abiding by the sentences. These "traditionalist" nuclei at the centre of the organisational structures of the Alardes set themselves up as private bodies, creating a foundation in Hondarribia and an association of societies in the case of Irun. In this way, the organisation of festival rituals was disassociated from the town councils and the public sphere of intervention, rendering the sentences favourable to the women's claims null and void, since they could not be applied to some "new" private events.[68]

In response to this manoeuvre, considered by some analysts as legal fraud, the women again made a formal complaint, this time against the decision by the town councils to hand over the organisation of the Alardes to private organisations which excluded women from taking part as soldiers and orchestrated a discriminatory event in the public sphere with the councils' permission.[69] However, somewhat ambiguously, the courts declared that the "traditional" private Alardes did not discriminate against women, because a private body was free to organise acts according to its own rules and criteria. This is possible because in the private sphere the principle of equality is weaker than in its public counterpart, since the notion of the "autonomy of free will" takes precedence and protects the freedom of each body to establish its method of functioning and its objectives. Although the Law of Public Events

[66]Moreno and Kerexeta (2006).

[67]Article 9.2 of the Constitution states: *It is the responsibility of the public authorities to promote conditions ensuring that freedom and equality of individuals and of the groups to which they belong are real and effective, to remove the obstacles preventing or hindering their full enjoyment, and to facilitate the participation of all citizens in political, economic, cultural and social life.*

[68]The Alardes were then carried out by first asking for permission to march (according to the right to congregate) and then through municipal permission to hold an event in public (according to the Law of Public Events). See Burzaco (2006) and Montesinos (2019).

[69]Lekuona (2006) and Asensio and Iraola (2018).

prohibits organising discriminatory acts, these sentences exempted the town councils from subsidising these events and deemed an act of free choice the option of reserving for women the exclusive role of *cantineras* or serving girls. They claimed that women could organise their own march if they wanted to (an issue that had in fact already taken place in Irun), and therefore the festival was not being monopolised by men to the exclusion of women.

There was, therefore, an impasse in the situation of legal exceptionality with regard to the application of the principle of equality, which we find again in the Easter processions (subject to canonical law), where for a long time the decision on the incorporation of women had fallen to the assemblies and councils of the *cofradías* (significantly, brotherhoods) or guilds. Although some Church dioceses have encouraged women's participation in the guilds, forcing the adaptation of the brotherhoods' statutes to frameworks dictated by the Church, in practice many guilds function at will, defending their sovereignty, accepting women or not and allowing them varying degrees of access to positions therein. This is in practice indirect discrimination, based on "private" spheres and so eluding the dictates of legislation. We hold that this is a question of exceptionalities because it hides discrimination behind the concept of the "autonomy of free will", but as we have seen in the aforementioned sentence of Villena, as well as in the case of Alcoi, according to the Law of Associations, women cannot be excluded explicitly from an association if joining it is the only means of participating in a popular festival, nor can they be excluded from an association merely on account of being a woman—without any logical or justifiable argument—even if there is a majority vote against their incorporation.[70]

The only "exceptional" justification that has been accepted by the courts is the right of private bodies to organise the Alardes, on the grounds that their goal is to organise the parade in the traditional manner, without women (except as *cantinera*). This justification resorts to the legal fiction that it is a festival organised by a private body, when in fact it is the central and most emblematic event of the main local festivals in both Irun and Hondarribia. The legal discussion over such exceptionalities in applying the principle of equality is a matter open to legal debate, because it is not at all clear what those exceptionalities would be in the private sphere. Above all, it is open to debate whether a festival ritual, the identifying symbol of a town's identity, can be considered a private matter, and even more so when the very process of privatisation is under question.

It is important to draw attention once more to how the principle of equality and non-discrimination, and issues concerned with the protection of rights and the physical integrity of women, stretch the limits of their application and recognition on the basis of fairly ambiguous legal exceptionalities located in the private sphere. The Law shows its limitations when it comes to understanding social conflicts beyond judicial dogmatics and without recourse to fiction or fraud. It becomes apparent that there is a need for a broader conception of rights, which attends to

[70]Montesinos (2019).

the complexity of social phenomena; for mediation directed at the restoration of minimal conditions for coexistence; and a response to the demands for justice and reparation for women without recourse to historicist or "traditionalist" excuses.[71] It is in this sense that we wish to stress the potential anthropological function of ritual as a space for the reparation of social conflicts, the public recognition of damage caused and composition.[72]

5 Conclusions

We have shown that the comparative study of conflicts surrounding women's participation in rituals in the festival context is a fascinating field of analysis and reflection on the wider problem of discrimination against women and gender inequalities. Each case allows us to explore the motivations, desires and strategies of specific women and a variety of collectives who organise in opposition to the situation of subordination in and exclusion from certain festive and ritual spaces. The identification of a broad range of strategies, employed by specific individuals and entities in Spain, allows us to signal common elements to place in dialogue with feminist theories on how to achieve substantive equality.

At the same time, these case studies reveal the conservative forces that resist change and oppose the incorporation of women in the public space of *fiestas* as subjects with full rights. As in other spheres, in order to impede processes based on such demands by women, social and legal mechanisms and strategies are put in motion which allow for, tolerate and even reinforce the ideological denial and practical avoidance of the principle of equality. Here the division between Public Law and Private Law stands out, a central question in the history of feminist demands which continues to present a decisive challenge: to deconstruct the private and domestic space, "domesticating" politics and Law.[73]

The analysis of such conflicts, moreover, highlights the importance and the vitality of the arguments and demands of the different feminisms that appear in the cases studied. In this way, it implies a field of political work that is demonstrating a significant impact in institutional policy, a resonance in the media and even in legislative efforts, a question that reinforces the restorative symbolic efficacy of such demands, since they have direct consequences in the social and political order. The performative and corporal dimension of these demands implies, further, a microphysical, emotional and almost subconscious transformation, the importance of which becomes crucial for the transformation of the symbolic order which resists transformations in the social order. In some way, the cases analysed demonstrate the

---

[71] Segato (2003) and Montesinos (2015).

[72] This has been demonstrated among others by Malinowski (1926), Gluckman (1954, 1956), Di Martino (1959, 1961) and Terradas (2008, 2019).

[73] Segato (2016).

force of festive rituals as spaces of political confrontation in which to dispute the hegemony of those who reproduce symbolic violence and in which to address social problems as important as that of gender discrimination, as well as those of racism, colonial inheritance, capitalist commercialisation and the mistreatment of animals.

In the face of the limitations of the civil/penal system to address and resolve the social conflicts analysed—due to its limitations when it comes to modifying deeply rooted practices and customs—it would appear possible to convert these ritual spaces into sites of collective reflection and social cohesion, enjoyable and creative debate aimed at achieving fairer and more equitable societies.[74] In contrast to the violence and exceptionalities of positive Law, justice and reparation can be found in other places, in the ritual practices of the community, its beliefs and customs, all capable of repairing the offence committed towards women. On the basis of the concrete materiality of seemingly banal demands, such as taking part in a march, the festive ritual reclaims or takes on a restorative character in social conflicts. That is where we locate the symbolic efficacy of women who want to participate in the festivals, who want to be recognised as members of their communities with full rights, where their words and declarations, their corporality and their actions mobilise a universe of meanings which activate the reparation of a secular injustice in the social and symbolic order. Through the restitution of their rights recognised by the law, these collectives call out for an exonerative act of justice, inextricably tied to gender equality.

References

Alcaraz M (2014) Constitución, tradición y fiestas: la igualdad de las mujeres en el espacio público festivo. Corts Anuario de derecho parlamentario 28:137–160

Anderson B (1983) Imagined Communities: Reflections on the Origin and Spread of Nationalism. Verso, New York

Antuña E (2017) De reinas a majorettes: representaciones de la mujer en el ritual festivo de la España contemporánea. Actas del VI Encuentro Internacional de Jóvenes Investigadores en Historia Contemporánea, pp:1–22

Ariño A, García P (2006) Apuntes para el estudio social de la fiesta en España. Anduli Revista Andaluza de Ciencias Sociales 6:13–28

Asensio M, Iraola A (2018) Alardeak. Ukatutako Plazara. Berria / Elkar Argitaletxea / Jakin

Assier-Andrieu L (2001) Penser le temps culturel du droit. Le destin anthropologique du concept de coutume. L'Homme 160:67–90

Bensaïd D (2007) Les dépossédés. Karl Marx, les voleurs de bois et le droit des pauvres. La fabrique, Paris

Boissevain J (1992) Revitalizing European Rituals. Routledge, London

Bourdieu P (1998) La domination masculine. Le Seuil, Paris

Bullen M (1997) Las mujeres y los Alardes de Hondarribia e Irún. Arenal 4:123–145

[74] Along the lines of the proposals of restorative justice analysed by Riccardo Mazzola in the chapter of this volume "'To Restore' vs. 'To Vindicate': A Comparative Analysis".

Bullen M (2000) Hombres, mujeres, ritos y mitos: Los alardes de Irún y Hondarribia. In: del Valle T (ed) Perspectivas feministas desde la antropología social. Ariel, Barcelona, pp 45–78
Bullen M (2003) Basque Gender Studies. University of Nevada Press, Reno
Bullen M, Egido JA (2003) Tristes espectáculos: Las mujeres y los alardes de Irún y Hondarribia. UPV/EHU - EMAKUNDE
Bullen M, Pérez B (2019) Desde la reivindicación de la participación a la incorporación del género en el patrimonio cultural festivo en el Estado español. In: Gabeiras Foundation (ed) Patrimonio inmaterial y desigualdades de género. La Cultivada, Madrid, pp 12–57
Burzaco M (2006) Recorrido por la jurisprudencia sobre los denominados “Alardes”: una fiesta plagada de conflictos. Estudios de Deusto 54(2):201–230
Cagide C et al (2019) Análisis de la participación de las mujeres en el patrimonio cultural inmaterial: situación actual, experiencias y perspectivas de futuro. Ministerio de Cultura y Deporte - Instituto del Patrimonio Cultural de España
Costa J et al (1902) Derecho consuetudinario y economía popular de España. Manuel Soler, Barcelona
Di Martino E (1959) Sud e magia. Feltrinelli, Milan
Di Martino E (1961) La terra del rimorso. Contributo a una storia religiosa del Sud. Il Saggiatore, Milan
Díez C, Bullen M (2012) Fiestas, tradiciones e igualdad. Kobie Antropología Cultural 16:13–33
Domene JF (2004) La integración de la mujer en las Fiestas de Moros y Cristianos de Villena. Conferencia en la I Jornada La Dona en la Festa, organizada por la Asociación Fonèvol, 27 de marzo, Centro Cultural de Alcoi
Domene JF (2015) Las fiestas de Moros y Cristianos. Publicacions Universitat d’Alacant, Alicante
Farapi (2009) Análisis de las fiestas del territorio histórico de Gipuzkoa desde una perspectiva de género. Diputación foral de Gipuzkoa - Diputación foral de Nafarroa
Fernández JM (2005) La noción de violencia simbólica en la obra de Pierre Bourdieu: una aproximación crítica. Cuadernos de trabajo social 18:7–31
Gabeiras Foundation (2019) Patrimonio inmaterial y desigualdades de género. La Cultivada, Madrid
García-Villegas G (1993) La eficacia simbólica del derecho: examen de situaciones colombianas. Ediciones uniandes, Colombia
Gellner E (1983) Nations and Nationalism. Cornell University Press, Ithaca
Gisbert V (2010) Ni moras ni cristianas: género y poder en las fiestas de Moros y Cristianos de Alcoi. Tesis de máster, GEMMA Master’s Degree in Women’s and Gender Studies, Universidad de Granada - Universidad de Utrecht
Gisbert V (2011) Feminidades y masculinidades en la Fiesta de Moros y Cristianos de Alcoi. In: Rosado MJ, Rodríguez A (eds) Feminidades y Masculinidades. Prisma Social, 7:92-119
Gisbert V (2015) En nombre de la tradición: conflictos socio-festivos por razón de género. Anuari del Conflicte Social 5:385–401
Gluckman M (1954) Rituals of rebellion in South-East Africa. MUP, Manchester
Gluckman M (1956) Custom and Conflict in Africa. Basil Blackwell, Oxford
González F (1981) La crítica de Marx a la escuela histórica. Sistema Revista de ciencias sociales 43-44:3–24
González-Abrisketa O (2013) Cuerpos desplazados. Género, deporte, y protagonismo cultural en la plaza vasca. AIBR. Revista de Antropología Iberoamericana 8(1):83–110
González-Requena J (2009) La eficacia simbólica. Trama y fondo: revista de cultura 26:7–30
Gramsci A (2011) ¿Qué es la cultura popular? PUV, Valencia
Heuzé L (1999) Des femmes ensauvagées: les “Negras” de la fête de Moros y Cristianos à Petrer. Clio Histoire, femmes et societés 10:175–184
Hocart AM (1927) Kingship. OUP, Oxford
Lafita S (2013) Las patgesses en la fiesta de Reyes de Igualada. Puesta en escena de un conflicto sobre los modelos de género. TFM inédito, máster en Estudios feministas y de género EHU/UPV, curso académico 2011–2012

Lekuona G (2006) El derecho a participar en el Alarde, sea público o privado. In: Moreno G, Kerexeta X (eds) Los Alardes del Bidasoa: Pueblo versus Ciudadanía. Ereta bilduma, Irun, pp 149–177

Lévi-Strauss C (1958) Anthropologie Structurale. Librairie Plon, Paris

Malinowski B (1926) Crime and Custom in Savage Society. Kegan Paul, London

Marín JJ (ed) (2000) Los alardes: una perspectiva jurídica: libertad e igualdad en las relaciones entre particulares. Casino de Irún, Irun

Martínez MA (2015) La mujer en las fiestas de moros y cristianos. Revista de Antropología Experimental 15:79–87

Mauss M (1924) Essai sur le don Forme et raison de l'échange dans les sociétés archaïques. Année sociologique 1:30–186

Montesinos L (2015) La antropología y el derecho ante los fenómenos posesorios: entre la comunidad y la propiedad. Revista de Antropología Social 24:53–81

Montesinos L (2019) Patrimonio inmaterial y desigualdades de género. Análisis y propuestas desde una perspectiva antropológica y jurídica. In: Gabeiras Foundation (ed) Patrimonio inmaterial y desigualdades de género. La Cultivada, Madrid, pp 58–330

Moral B (ed) (2014) Paso a paso hacia una tamborrada en igualdad. Negociado de Igualdad - Ayuntamiento de Donostia/San Sebastián

Moreno G, Kerexeta X (eds) (2006) Los Alardes del Bidasoa: Pueblo versus Ciudadanía. Ereta bilduma, Irun

Ortner SB, Whitehead H (eds) (1981) Sexual Meanings: The Cultural Construction of Gender and Sexuality. CUP, Cambridge

Philips A (1995) The Politics of Presence. OUP, Oxford

Polanyi K (1977) Livelihood of Man. Academic Press, Cambridge

Rodríguez GD (2011) Marx revisitado: apuntes sobre el Derecho y el Estado en la obra temprana de Karl Marx. Via Juris 11:91–106

Rostagnol S (2015) ¿El patrimonio tiene género? Una mirada al patrimonio cultural Inmaterial desde la perspectiva de género. Primer encuentro nacional de patrimonio vivo. Diversidad cultural y Estado. Escenarios y desafíos de hoy. Buenos Aires, 12–13 August 2015

Rubin G (1975) The traffic in women: notes on the "political economy" of sex. In: Reiter RR (ed) Toward an Anthropology of Women. Monthly Review Press, New York, pp 157–210

Saborido P (2011) La ficticia igualdad entre mujeres y hombres en su participación en cofradías y hermandades. La necesaria protección del derecho privado. In: El levantamiento del velo: las mujeres en el derecho privado. Tirant lo blanch, Valencia, pp 1255–1280

Sánchez P (2003) Mujeres y cofradías en Málaga. Editorial Arguval, Málaga

Segato R (2003) Las estructuras elementales de la violencia. Universidad Nacional de Quilmes, Quilmes

Segato R (2016) La guerra contra las mujeres. Traficantes de Sueños, Madrid

Sperber D (1978) Le symbolisme en général. Hermann, Paris

Terradas I (2008) Justicia Vindicatoria. De la ofensa e indefensión a la imprecación y el oráculo, la vindicta y el talión, la ordalía y el juramento, la composición y la reconciliación. CSIC, Madrid

Terradas I (2010) Antropología jurídica: costumbres y conflictos. In: Marco J, Rodríguez S, Luque E (eds) Nos-otros Miradas antropológicas sobre la diversidad. Asamblea de Extremadura, Mérida, pp 609–623

Terradas I (2018) Legitimidad en la jurisprudencia. A propósito del machismo. In: Bilbeny N (ed) Legitimidad y acción política. Edicions Universitat de Barcelona, Barcelona

Terradas I (2019) La justicia más Antigua. CSIC, Madrid

Thompson EP (1980) Customs in Common. The New Press, New York

UNESCO (2015) Igualdad de género. Patrimonio y creatividad

Velasco H (1990) El folklore y sus paradojas. Reis Revista española de investigaciones sociológicas 49:123–144

Index

R. Márquez Porras et al. (eds.), *Vindicatory Justice*, Ius Gentium: Comparative Perspectives on Law and Justice 93, https://doi.org/10.1007/978-3-030-79595-5

CPSIA information can be obtained
at www.ICGtesting.com
Printed in the USA
BVHW040728191121
622027BV00025B/5